The
Anglo-Russian Convention
of 1907

The
Anglo-Russian Convention
of 1907

By
ROGERS PLATT CHURCHILL

BOOKS FOR LIBRARIES PRESS
FREEPORT, NEW YORK

First Published 1939
Reprinted 1972

Library of Congress Cataloging in Publication Data

Churchill, Rogers Platt, 1902-
    The Anglo-Russian convention of 1907.

    ([BCL/select bibliographies reprint series])
    Reprint of the 1939 ed.
    Bibliography: p.
    1. Eastern question (Central Asia) 2. Gt. Brit.
--Foreign relations--Russia. 3. Russia--Foreign
relations--Gt. Brit. I. Title.
D378.C57 1972   341'0266'42047   72-000073
ISBN 0-8369-9956-8

PRINTED IN THE UNITED STATES OF AMERICA
BY
NEW WORLD BOOK MANUFACTURING CO., INC.
HALLANDALE, FLORIDA 33009

TABLE OF CONTENTS

CHAPTER   PAGE

I. FORSAKING RIVALRY: THE ANGLO-RUSSIAN
   AGREEMENT OF 1899   I

II. TOWARDS A BETTER UNDERSTANDING, 1900-
   1905   33

III. THE NEGOTIATION OF THE CONVENTION, 1905-
   1907   107

IV. THE ARRANGEMENT RESPECTING TIBET   .   177

V. THE ARRANGEMENT RESPECTING PERSIA   .   212

VI. THE CONVENTION RESPECTING AFGHANISTAN   269

VII. THE RECEPTION OF THE CONVENTION .   .   309

   BIBLIOGRAPHY   351

   INDEX   357

PREFACE

THE Anglo-Russian convention took such an unconscionable time to mature that Sir Sidney Lee thought it was an excellent illustration of the proverb "Tout vient à point à qui sait attendre." Its progress was accompanied and often delayed by several extraneous events, which none the less exercised a decisive influence. The first two chapters of this volume sketch the course of the Anglo-Russian reconciliation through the years between the first overture in 1898 until after the close of the Russo-Japanese war, during which period the idea of arriving at a general understanding barely managed to survive. The chronological course of the final, successful negotiations, and the contemporaneous attitude towards them of the most interested outsiders, are recounted in the third chapter. Then follow three other chapters devoted to the positions occupied, and to the settlements reached, by Great Britain and Russia in the three Asiatic countries specifically concerned in the treaty, which were so utterly helpless to command any consideration of their own desires. In the last chapter the reception accorded the convention in its own day is recalled, while a fresh interpretation of its worth concludes this study.

In quoting from documents and books (among which there is not much material available in Russian) I have regularized the spelling of proper names, and I have generally followed the style used by the *Journal of Modern History* for capitalization and arrangement of footnotes. I have received much helpful assistance in writing this account. I am greatly indebted to Professors Samuel N. Harper and Bernadotte E. Schmitt, of the University of Chicago, who saw me through the whole of this work. For their criticisms and suggestions, which saved me many mistakes, and for the kindness with which these were given, I am heartily thankful.

CHICAGO, ILLINOIS,
21 JANUARY 1939.

CHAPTER ONE

FORSAKING RIVALRY: THE AGREEMENT OF 1899

ONE April day in 1899, in the quiet of his office in the Wilhelmstrasse, the crabbed Friedrich von Holstein put into writing some thoughts on German foreign policy over which he had earnestly brooded. It seemed probable, to start with, that the incessant rivalry between France and Great Britain in colonial questions could not be settled. The concessions that could be offered by Great Britain would not be sufficient to pry France loose from its alliance with Russia, and the French position in Morocco would be unwelcome to Great Britain, because it lay athwart the British control of the shortest sea route to Egypt and India. It would be still more difficult for Russia and Great Britain to compose their sharp quarrels, because the concessions that the latter could offer were even less than could be given to France. Anyhow, the leaders of Russian policy were surely convinced that a strong Germany was essential to their country, and there were no interests between the two nations which collided. What Germany might have to fear in the future was not Russian state policy, but only an occasional outburst of national feeling. The antagonism between Russia and Great Britain, however, appeared to be an unalterable fact, which could be counted upon in the determination of a proper German foreign policy.[a] The time was close at hand when no political opponent of Germany would dare attempt anything without being previously sure of the German attitude. They would soon be approaching Germany seeking its friendship on such terms and conditions as it should choose to exact. The only danger that the German ambassador in London, Count Hatzfeldt, could think of was

[a] Johannes Lepsius, Albrecht Mendelssohn Bartholdy, and Friedrich Thimme, editors, *Die Grosse Politik der europäischen Kabinette 1871-1914. Sammlung der diplomatischen Akten des Auswärtigen Amtes*, (Berlin, 1922-1927), XIV, part II, no. 4016, p. 536. (This collection is subsequently designated by the initials *G. P.*) See also Otto Hammann, *Deutsche Weltpolitik 1890-1912*, (Berlin, 1925), p. 97.

that Great Britain might succeed in making a firm, political understanding with Russia.[b]

No important German diplomat believed, in 1899, that there was any likelihood of such an understanding. After 1898, when Great Britain first desired to escape from isolation as the skies of the future began to cloud over, an early proposal was made to Germany for an agreement. The German reaction was cool, because that government saw no need for limiting its freedom of action, but preferred to make its choice of sides when the occasion should arise, and then on its own terms.[c] Allusions to some new direction that would be given to British policy, such as courting a peaceful settlement with Russia, cost what it would, if Germany stood off too haughtily, never won much credence.[d] While the kaiser was visiting at Windsor, in November 1899, Mr. Balfour, by then Lord Salisbury's heir-apparent, mentioned that Asia was big enough to hold both Russia and Great Britain, so that there need be no unbridgable gulf between them, but the German foreign minister, Bernhard von Bülow, remained unruffled.[e] Similar Russian statements were treated with even less interest. The Russian minister for foreign affairs, Count Muravyev, told Prince Radolin, German ambassador in St. Petersburg, on 29 June 1899, that Russia and Great Britain were not irreconcilable rivals, and that an understanding between them in Asia was quite possible, as the Chinese agreement of the previous April testified. Muravyev was such a voluble sycophant that he was seldom taken seriously, so Radolin never quivered an eyelash at his "bombastic phrases." They were only manufactured threats: Great Britain would never be duped for long by Russia, nor would Russia resign from all its pretensions in Asia for the sake of peace with an old enemy.[f]

[b] *G. P.*, XIV, part II, no. 4019, p. 544.
[c] J. L. Garvin, *The Life of Joseph Chamberlain*, vol. III, *Empire and World Policy, 1895-1900*, (London, 1934), pp. 254-277. Eugen Fischer, *Holsteins grosses Nein. Die deutsch-englischen Bündnisverhandlungen von 1898-1901*, (Berlin, 1925), p. ix. Morrison B. Giffen, *Fashoda: the Incident and Its Diplomatic Setting*, (Chicago, 1930), p. 194.
[d] Garvin, III, 275.
[e] Fischer, pp. 201, 202. *G. P.*, XV, no. 4398, p. 415.
[f] *Ibid.*, XIV, part II, no. 4022, pp. 551-552. In Berlin, on 5 May 1899, the Russian ambassador, Count Osten-Sacken, had informed Bülow that it was

Holstein's thoughts on unalterable antagonisms and impossible combinations did not become dogmas in German foreign policy all at once, but the foreign office increasingly counted upon the permanence of the clash of interests between France and Russia on the one hand, and Great Britain on the other. It was not long, however, before this political phenomenon was believed "with the assurance with which astronomers await an eclipse of the sun." [g] When a second attempt for an Anglo-German agreement was being pushed in 1901 by Lord Lansdowne, the British foreign secretary, the German government was interested, but stood out for better terms, which it did not obtain.[h] The mockery and scorn which greeted every suggestion that Great Britain, rebuffed by Germany, would turn to Russia, were unrestrained. Holstein distrusted "the friendship storms of Chamberlain and Company," while every threat of seeking an accommodation with France or Russia was nothing less than an "absolute swindle," or "nonsense and swindle." Bülow considered the warning to be merely a "bugbear." [i]

Indeed it did seem at the turn of the century sound doctrine to hold that such strange creatures as personified by the whale and the bear were certain to remain implacable and constant enemies for a still further, and undisclosed length of time. The animosity which was characteristic of the relations of Russia and Great Britain was a development of the nineteenth century. Before that century began, the intercourse between these two countries had not been particularly abnormal, and the first quarter of the century had not produced any specific scene of conflict. From that time onwards, however, for well over fifty years, with only temporary interludes, the policies and objectives of each nation crossed, and created such distrust that each commonly considered and referred to its antagonist

possible that Muravyev might make a more inclusive arrangement with Great Britain than the recent Chinese agreement had been. Both of the Russian empresses cherished Anglophil sentiments, while Witte, because of financial reasons, might use his influence for closer Anglo-Russian relations. *Ibid.*, no. 4020, p. 547.
[g] Fischer, pp. ix-x.
[h] Sir Sidney Lee, *King Edward VII. A Biography*, (London and New York, 1925, 1927), I, footnote 1, p. 798; II, 572. *G. P.*, XVII, no. 4982, p. 19.
[i] *Ibid.*, no. 4984, p. 22; no. 4985, p. 22. Bernhard, Fürst von Bülow, *Deutsche Politik*, (Berlin, Volksausgabe, 1916), p. 25.

as the chief enemy. When actual events did not serve to maintain the mutual aversion, the accumulating suspicion of each other's aims did. In consequence, each power endeavored to thwart or curtail the achievements of the other in the affairs of Europe and of Asia, often needlessly or excessively, with the British generally being the more successful. This antagonism reached its culmination only a few years before the end of the century, when it first allowed some outsider to take advantage of the situation and become a greater menace to the special interests of both Russia and Great Britain than either was to the other. In the closing years of the nineteenth century, then, a few leading statesmen in Russia and Great Britain first cautiously tried to discover a method whereby to allay this deep-seated hostility.

In general, there were two main areas where Russian and British policies conflicted during the nineteenth century. First in point of time, and of longer duration, were the persistent efforts made by Russia to obtain a warm water outlet to the west through control of the straits of the Bosphorus and the Dardanelles. These efforts involved several wars of aggression against the Ottoman empire, which possessed these coveted places, and the objective of Russian policy was, for the most part, to undermine the existence of that empire in the hope of becoming its actual, even if undesignated heir. To this purpose there was added the religious desire to replace the Mohammedan crescent by the Orthodox cross on the ancient Christian church of Saint Sophia, while increasingly during the century the "historic mission" of the Russians to free their weaker, Balkan Slavonic brothers from the Turkish yoke, regularly declared to be oppressing them, became more impelling and served as an humanitarian cloak for more selfish Russian aims. Whatever the form it might assume, this forward movement long met with stubborn British resistance. British interests seemed to require that an independent Turkey be preserved in the eastern Mediterranean, although how weak or how corrupt that state might be was of less importance. A strong Russia in this part of the world would be, in all probability, too great a danger along the best route to India, where British power was not yet fully secure in a land already become the brightest jewel of the British crown, which would be even richer in the future when a more perfect control should be established.[j] The other scene of rivalry between the two powers developed in the regions of central Asia with the territorial expansion of Russia into the Turkestan steppes and the Mohammedan khanates, and the infiltration of Russian influence into Persia and Afghanistan. The British again perceived in these advances a serious future military threat to their supremacy in India, despite the protection of towering mountains guarding the northwest frontier and the difficult, arid distances a Russian army would have to traverse before it could become a real menace. Russian motives were the increase of the economic exploitation of Persia, the quest for a warm water port on the Persian Gulf, besides a possibly sincere desire to keep in check the spasmodic forays of the nomadic tribes of central Asia into Russian territory.[k] For the first half of the nineteenth century British rivalry with Russia in Asia had been a secondary affair; in fact, in Persia both countries went along "hand in hand." [l] The check to Russian ambitions in the Near East administered by the defeat in the Crimean war caused a marked acceleration of Russian expansion in Persia and central

[j] Communist writers seldom let slip the opportunity to point this out, and assert that India has been one of the most thoroughly exploited countries of modern times. See A. Popov, "Anglo-russkoye soglasheniye o razdelye Kitaya (1899 g.)," [The Anglo-Russian Agreement for the Partition of China in 1899], *Krasny Arkhiv*, [Red Archive], XXV (1927), 112; and the same author's "Angliyskaya politika v Indii i russko-indiyskiye otnosheniya v 1897-1905 g. g.," [British Policy in India and Russo-Indian Relations in 1897-1905], *Krasny Arkhiv*, XIX (1926), 53-63.

[k] Calchas, "The Anglo-Russian Agreement," *Fortnightly Review*, LXXXVIII (1907), 539. Sufficient details of this Russian expansion can be read in F. A. Skrine, *The Expansion of Russia 1801-1899*, (Cambridge, 1905) ; Alexis Krausse, *Russia in Asia*, (New York, 1899).

[l] Theodor Schiemann, "Russisch-englische Beziehungen unter Kaiser Nikolaus I," *Zeitschrift für osteuropäische Geschichte*, III (1913), 490-492. On 26 May 1844 the *Journal des Debats* expressed the French official belief that Russia was building "a great central Asiatic state to menace British India," and this the London *Times* denied in "two succeeding articles." (*Ibid.*, p. 493.) Sketches of the early penetration of Russia and Great Britain are given by Mary M. McCarthy, *Anglo-Russian Rivalry in Persia*, (Buffalo, 1925), pp. 27-44, and by William Habberton, *Anglo-Russian Relations concerning Afghanistan, 1837-1907*, (Urbana, Illinois, 1937), pp. 9-22.

Asia. While the Russians consolidated their advantage in northern Persia, the British strove to block them off from an outlet on the Persian Gulf and from approaching the Indian frontier through southeastern Persia. Nevertheless, as the Russian conquests in central Asia continually brought troops closer to the Indian border, the British became ever more alarmed, until this rivalry began to usurp first place among the causes which poisoned Anglo-Russian relations.[m] In opposition to the Russian movement the British policy was a hostile, annoying one of "alternate threat and scuttle," which succeeded only in further straining relations.[n] Russian pronouncements, on the other hand, already disclaimed any intention to injure Great Britain along the route to India, and insisted that Russia sought only to obtain the necessary means of defence against what was felt to be British hostility. There is trace of a Russian proposal to Great Britain, evidently early in 1877, to determine together "Persian affairs in the interest of our reciprocal tranquillity," but the British government seems not to have replied to this friendly suggestion.[o]

The embitterment of Anglo-Russian relations reached its highest intensity in the years immediately following the Congress of Berlin. Once again Russia had been effectively blocked in the Near East, and this time no longer sought to maintain the rivalry with Great Britain in this region. The years following the congress until the peaceful settlement of the Afghan border incident which occurred at Penjdeh in 1885, were certainly among the most trying that ever existed between the two governments. In the early 'eighties the Russians advanced rapidly and completed their occupation of the Turkestan steppes and the half-barbaric khanates, culminating with the seizure in 1884 of the oasis of Merv, always described as beautiful.[p] Russian policy had been steadily trying to acquire

---

[m] From an article said to be "inspired": "The Marquis of Salisbury," *Quarterly Review*, CXCVI (1902), 659. Habberton, p. 23.

[n] Calchas, *Fortnightly Review*, LXXXVIII, 539.

[o] Gorchakov to Shuvalov, 18/30 May 1877, "Unprinted Documents. Russo-British Relations during the Eastern Crisis: VI. The Russo-Turkish War," *Slavonic Review*, V (1927), 424.

[p] See Skrine, *op. cit.*, for details. Habberton, pp. 40-43. A. L. P. Dennis, *The Anglo-Japanese Alliance*, (Berkeley, California, 1923), p. 15. S. A. Korff,

preponderant influence in northern Persia, and especially over the shah at his capital of Teheran. This policy was meeting with considerable success, while the British position was becoming weaker each year, until it was a distinct burden to retain influence in southern Persia and around the Persian Gulf. Russian commerce with Persia began to flourish, especially when favored with preferential tariffs and subsidized by government bounties. As a further aid in maintaining and strengthening the Russian hold in central Asia and in Persia, the government constructed the Transcaspian railroad between 1885 and 1888.[q] It had already become apparent to one British minister at Teheran that Persia was safely in Russian hands.[r]

The rapid Russian advance in central Asia caused British statesmen to feel considerable alarm for the security of India, and to seek ways to check any further approach. The British government had for some time been strengthening its influence with the Amir of Afghanistan, while the Russian government had voluntarily declared, in arrangements given in 1872 and 1873, that it "recognized that Afghanistan is entirely outside its sphere of action," and had renewed this assurance on numerous subsequent occasions.[s] The British government in the time of Lord Beaconsfield inaugurated the effort to establish a protectorate over Afghanistan, in order to use it as a buffer state between Russia and India.[t] When the Afghans resisted this interference and sought to retain their full independence by the war of 1879-1882, Russia sincerely perceived in the British action a threat of aggression against its own po-

Russia's Foreign Relations during the Last Half Century, (New York, 1922), p. 33.
[q] Lord Onslow, "Lord Carnock," *Slavonic Review*, VII (1929), 543.
[r] Sir Arthur Nicolson wrote to Lord Dufferin in 1886: "Unless we are prepared to offer some kind of guarantee to Persia we should not waste our energies in endeavoring to counteract Russian influence on the central government at Teheran. This part of the world is lost to us and we should devote the modicum of attention which we seemed disposed to give to Persia to the south alone." Harold Nicolson, *Sir Arthur Nicolson, Bart. A Study in the Old Diplomacy*, (London, 2nd edition, 1930), p. 65.
[s] G. P. Gooch and Harold Temperley, editors, *British Documents on the Origins of the War 1898-1914*, (London, 1927-), I, no. 376, p. 306; no. 377, enclosure, p. 310. (This collection will hereafter be cited by the initials *B. D.*) Habberton, pp. 41, 87-89.
[t] Korff, pp. 32-33. Dennis, p. 15. Habberton, pp. 37-46.

sition in Asia, and public opinion vigorously urged the government to take counterbalancing regions.[u] Constant friction and misunderstandings persisted between Russia and Great Britain in consequence of these forward policies. When Baron de Staal came to London in 1884 to begin his long term as Russian ambassador to the court of St. James, the pacifically inclined Russian foreign minister Giers had prepared detailed instructions explaining what Russian policy in the affairs of central Asia aimed to be. The Russian movements had been dictated by the desire to protect legitimate interests, and by the necessity of securing a defensive position against the hostility shown by Great Britain during the Crimean and the more recent Turkish wars. Now, however, in consequence of large sacrifices, Russia could consider the control of its holdings as fully protected, and desired nothing further than peace in order to consolidate them. The Russian government was prepared to go along with Great Britain in either a pacific or a hostile manner as the latter should choose. Giers realized that the British domination of India was founded essentially upon prestige, and he hoped to be able to assist the Gladstone ministry of the time in its policy of peace and moderation. The Russian foreign minister closed his statement with this conviction:

We believe that this purpose can be attained if he [Gladstone] wishes to persuade himself that the position taken by us in central Asia is a purely defensive one, which does not have in view at all to do damage to the Indian interests of Great Britain, but on the contrary to induce it to live with us in peace, good understanding, and friendship.[v]

It was neither possible, nor sometimes seemingly desirable, to maintain good relations in central Asia. Oftentimes the actions of the local representatives of both countries could not be regulated by their distant superiors. The imperfections in the boundaries for Afghanistan, which had been arranged jointly by Russia and Great Britain in 1872 and 1873, left

---

[u] Irene Grüning, *Die russische öffentliche Meinung und ihre Stellung zu den Grossmächte 1878-1894*, (Berlin, 1928), pp. 62-63.
[v] Baron Alexander Meyendorff, editor, *Correspondance diplomatique de M. de Staal (1884-1900)*, (Paris, 1929), I, no. 7, p. 41.

much still uncertain, and the matter became ever more disquieting to the British government as the progress of Russian conquests approached nearer to the western Afghan provinces.[w]
Equally uncertain was the point where the Persian and Afghan
frontier should be considered as meeting, and the British consistently strove to push this point as far as possible to the
north for the purpose of increasing the distance which would
separate the Russians from the important Afghan city of
Herat.[x] In 1884 another joint boundary commission was set
up to revise and improve upon the former traces for Afghanistan. It was while this commission was awaiting the arrival
of the chief Russian delegate that the Penjdeh incident occurred which threatened, for a brief period, to lead to war,
and which did mark the climax of the bitter Anglo-Russian
relations in those rancorous 'eighties.

The incident arose out of a dispute whether or not the fer-
tile Penjdeh district on the northern Afghan border belonged
to that country. At the same time the Russians asserted a
claim to the Zulfikar pass, which the Indian military authorities were determined to retain for Afghanistan.[y] A special
Russian committee had met in St. Petersburg in December
1884 to consider

the danger of an extension of Afghan pretensions, encouraged by Great
Britain, especially with regard to Penjdeh, already occupied by the
Afghans, but inhabited by a Turkoman tribe, the Sarouks. In sacrificing
them the prestige of Russia can be injured among the Turkoman population of the Transcaspian region.[z]

It was finally decided to proceed at once with military measures
to forestall "a probable advance of Afghan forces" by the
occupation of two points to insure the Russian position. Russian troops marched into the disputed territory, occupying as

---

[w] *Ibid.*, no. 8, pp. 44-45.

[x] *Ibid.*, p. 47. It will be interesting to note that the British worked for this
same objective in describing the course of the line for the Russian northern
zone in the Persian arrangement of 1907.

[y] A. W. Ward and G. P. Gooch, *The Cambridge History of British Foreign
Policy*, (Baltimore, 1923), III, 189. This work is subsequently indicated by the
initials *C. H. B. F. P.*

[z] Meyendorff, I, 136, the *procès-verbal* of the Special Committee. This committee was convoked on 24 December 1884, and its conclusions were approved
by Tsar Alexander III on 31 December.

much of it as possible, and on 30 March 1885 defeated Afghan forces with a loss of 500 lives, driving them entirely out of Penjdeh.[a] This Russian attack and victory greatly excited the British, and the secretary of state for India did not conceal from Staal his alarm at the strained situation, nor its possible grave consequences. War seemed near, but was prevented when the Amir of Afghanistan took an indifferent attitude, while by 10 September the substance of a settlement had been agreed upon by which Russia retained its spoils in Penjdeh, but the Zulfikar pass was assigned to Afghanistan.[b] Then the boundary commission went peacefully about its work and, in the course of a few years, a series of boundary agreements were signed, so that the Penjdeh incident remained merely illustrative of the dangers inherent in Anglo-Russian relations in Asia.[c]

The difficulty of avoiding trouble over so small a matter seemed to show to a few individuals how dangerous the continuance of such distrustful Anglo-Russian rivalry might become, and to suggest that possibly the points of friction could be settled by peaceful means. The conservative part of the Russian press still demanded no abandonment of the strong forward policy in middle Asia, but the less numerous liberal organs urged that an end should be put to this quarrel and a return made to the real Russian tasks in the Balkans and at the Straits.[d] In England, a few persons in high places who

[a] *Ibid.*, I, 137. *C. H. B. F. P.*, III, 189. Nicolson, p. 62. Habberton, pp. 53-54.
[b] Meyendorff, I, no. 24, p. 164. *C. H. B. F. P.*, III, 191. Nicolson, p. 62. Habberton, pp. 54-55. At the time of the incident the Amir Abdurrahman was visiting the viceroy, Lord Dufferin, in India at Rawalpindi. Two contradictory versions relate the Amir's attitude and his part in the solution of the crisis. According to one the Amir "was persuaded not to take the episode tragically, and, on Lord Dufferin's suggestion, he agreed to abandon Penjdeh, on condition that Zulfikar pass remained to Afghanistan." (*C. H. B. F. P.*, III, 189.) In the other account the credit is given entirely to the Amir "who did not wish for war, [and] generously released us from our difficulty by stating that he did not care about the Penjdeh valley in the least." Nicolson, pp. 62-63.
[c] These are the most important of the several Afghan boundary arrangements: Protocol signed at London on 10 September 1885, completed by a Protocol signed at St. Petersburg, 10/22 July 1887. Others of lesser importance came in 1888 and 1893, and the Pamirs boundary delimitation of 11 March 1895. See Meyendorff, I, note, p. 260. Korff, p. 36. Habberton, pp. 56-57, 60-67, 89-92. William L. Langer, *The Diplomacy of Imperialism, 1890-1902*, (New York, 1935), I, 145-146.
[d] The *Vestnik Evropy* during April and May 1885 expressed this point of view. "A combination with India, of which perhaps a few of our patriots

strove for an improvement in Anglo-Russian relations thought it would be wise to consider the possibility of an agreement over the causes of estrangement in Asia. One of the earliest, but meteoric upholders of this new conception was "ce batailleur politique" Lord Randolph Churchill, who undertook a journey to Russia in November 1887, and remained well into the following year, to the consternation both of the Russian and British foreign offices.[e] Lord Randolph had been given a letter to the tsaritsa by the Prince of Wales, who also was becoming more convinced of the desirability of better relations with Russia, but the traveller had been warned to keep away from Giers, and not to discuss international relations with other Russian authorities, since this might lend an official color to his visit. Once inside Russia Lord Randolph characteristically broke all bounds and, "according to his communications to the Prince, proclaimed in all Russian quarters — official and social — a complete identity of interest between England and Russia," and declared that Alexander III had expressed his desire for an agreement.[f]

Sir Henry Drummond Wolff, at this time British minister at Teheran, was also a convinced, but more rational proponent of improved Anglo-Russian relations. He influenced the Prince of Wales, particularly by his proposal of an economic partition of Persia into two spheres, the British to predominate in the south and the Russians in the north where each had their greatest interest. Sir Henry was well acquainted with Staal and expressed these opinions to him on many occasions, which the Russian ambassador reported home, while assuring Drummond Wolff of his own agreement.[g] Again

dream, would shift the center of gravity of Russia towards Asia and rob us for a long time of the legitimate share of influence in Europe. The Balkan peninsula would then finally fall to the control of Austria. One should not forget that our paramount interests[o] lie not in Asia, but in Europe; our political future is bound up with the fate of the Dardanelles and the Bosphorus, these two natural keys of our house, which have for us an immeasurably greater significance than all the keys to India." Grüning, p. 88.

[e] Meyendorff, I, 376. It is said that British ambassadors in other nearby capitals sent in a flood of protests to the foreign office. Lee, I, 683.

[f] Ibid., pp. 682-683. Queen Victoria was angry about this activity and demanded that the prince, who was himself not greatly displeased, should endeavor to restrain the man.

[g] Staal wrote to Giers on 7/19 February 1888: "I have believed it to be my

without consulting the foreign office, the Prince of Wales
furnished Sir Henry with a letter to the tsar, and urged him
to lay his ideas before the Russian ruler in Berlin where, in
the autumn of 1888, Alexander was visiting the German court.
At the meeting the tsar expressed his readiness to come to an
understanding with Great Britain in Persia. "We have no
interêsts in common in Europe. Our common interests lie in
Asia. There I desire to live in friendship with her, and to
establish an understanding which will enable us to be friends." [h]
When Salisbury first learned of this direct appeal he resented
it, and did not place much hope in the kind phrases of the
tsar, nor in those that Giers had used.[i] For a while he acted
with noticeable reticence, but by the summer of 1888 he was
surprizing Staal with his sympathetic language in regard to
Russia, and by the end of the year the British ambassador in
St. Petersburg was repeating Drummond Wolff's idea of two
commerical spheres in Persia to a still hesitant Giers.[j]

The opponents of this trend found new vigor under the
leadership of that congenital Russophobe, George N. Curzon,
whose ponderous volumes summing up his library researches
on Persian archaeology combined with his recent travel ex-
periences and political opinions, were hailed in 1892 as authoritative works.[k] British policy in Persia, according to that
writer, was incomparably nobler than Russian, which he traced
as "avowedly hostile." He was "surprized to find British

duty to report to your excellency Sir H. D.-Wolff's profession of faith. It
seemed to me to be too explicit not to derive from instructions of the principal
secretary of state for foreign affairs." Meyendorff, I, no. 16, pp. 392-393; II,
no. 18, pp. 136-137.

[h] Lee, I, 687.

[i] Lord Salisbury "was not averse from Drummond Wolff's general principles,
though he deprecated precipitate action and judged Wolff's Persian dream unlikely to come true for at least a generation." *Ibid.* See also Meyendorff, I,
no. 24, p. 403.

[j] Staal reported some remarks by Salisbury in August, and added: "It has
been a long time since similar words have been pronounced by a British minister
in an official meeting." (*Ibid.*, I, no. 62, p. 439; no. 68, p. 444.) These flattering
comments, spoken at a Mansion House dinner, caused a conservative party
member (Mr. Alfred Austin) to inquire "what he was to understand from such
civility to the traditional enemy." Lady Gwendolen Cecil, *Life of Robert,
Marquis of Salisbury*, (London, 1932), IV, 83.

[k] George Nathaniel Curzon [later Baron, Earl and Marquess Curzon of
Kedleston], *Persia and the Persian Question*, (London, two volumes, 1892). Of
most interest here is the last chapter of the second volume, "British and Russian
Policy in Persia."

influence so powerful at Teheran as I take it to be," even if
he did need to admit the fact of much Russian control in
Persian affairs.[1] He expounded his belief that Great Britain
should demand that a line be drawn which would protect
British commercial and political ascendancy not only in southern Persia, but also in the center, where Curzon almost alone
claimed that it existed. Thereupon Persia should warn an
invader from the north "thus far and no further." In these
regions the British would then no longer need to ask for any
exclusive privileges, nor to exercise any dictation, nor to em-
ploy any threats, soldiers or guns, since all future triumphs
would be the result of peaceful penetration of "common interests," "industrial development" and "domestic reform." [m]
Despite his announced hope of being absolved "from the
charge of Russophobia," the Russians never ceased to distrust
Curzon; were pleased when his travels in the Pamirs region
were impeded,[n] and apprehensive upon his appointment to a
subordinate post in the foreign office, but still more alarmed
when he was designated viceroy of India.[o]

It did not seem impossible for Great Britain to reach an
understanding with Russia in Asia. It would be easier to
recognize the acquisitions and special interests of each other
which were securely possessed, where the other nation would
have small chance of successful competition, than for Great
Britain to come to similar solutions with France or Germany

[1] Of this regeneration of British influence since 1885 which so surprised the
author, and doubtless others, Curzon wrote: "It is not now, nor at any time
in this century has it been, one of territorial cupidity. England does not covet
one square foot of Persian soil. The eighth and tenth commandments stand
in no danger of being violated by us." (Ibid., II, 619-621.) Compare this with
nearby passages where he mentions some important places that it would be
well for Britain to have (pp. 588, 620-621). For a unique account of Russian
policy and its steady growth since 1813, see pp. 589-603; and for British policy,
pp. 621-627.
[m] Ibid., II, 588, 620-621.
[n] On 4 September 1894 Staal wrote to Giers: "Your excellency will notice, I
think, with satisfaction the decision which the viceroy of India took in hinder-
ing the trip of Mr. George Curzon. It is hard not to see an attention to our
consideration on the part of the new viceroy; Lord Elgin avoids the least
incident of a nature disagreeable to us. Lord Kimberley has made known this
decision to the embassy by an official note." Meyendorff, II, 249.
[o] "Mr. G. Curzon makes his appearance at the foreign office and he seems,
like Chamberlain for the colonies, a bad augury." (Ibid., II, 256.) When he
became viceroy he was known to be a proponent of a "forward policy," and a
"bitter and irascible person." Popov, Krasny Arkhiv, XIX, 56.

over colonial expansion in parts of Africa and Asia where the
rivalry was fresher, and where positions were less secure, or
not yet sufficiently consolidated. Furthermore, British statesmen craftily noted that it was less necessary for them to draw
Russian animosity upon themselves at a time when Russia was
encountering sufficient opposition from Germany and Austria
to progress in the Balkan peninsula and the Ottoman empire.[p]
Britishers began to take less stock in the scares of a Russian
onslaught upon India, about which in the more hostile 'seven-
ties and 'eighties two shilling pamphleteers had so frantically
written.[q] More credit was given to provident Nature for the
marvellous mountain barriers protecting India; to the handicap of the huge distances any Russian army must first traverse,
and then, at last, if war should ever threaten, to the possible
ability of the British and Indian army to defend the Indian
empire. It was also more frequently suspected that in reality
the Russian government had not so often harbored the hideous
intentions as had been imputed to it, but had, no doubt with
grim humor, only threatened in order to obtain some British
concession in another matter.[r] What the actual truth might
have been was of far less weight than the fact that the mass
of the British people habitually suspected the Russian intentions. Very few understood that Russia, in turn, feared British
aggression against its central Asian properties and against its

[p] Meyendorff, II, 333. Nicolson, p. 34. "The Marquis of Salisbury," *Quarterly Review*, CXCVI, 659-660.

[q] See, for example, H. E. H. Jerningham, *Russia's Warnings*, (London, 2nd
edition, 1885), and a later work in the same fire-frothing vein by Archibald
Ross Colquhoun, *Russia against India; the Struggle for Asia*, (New York,
1901).

[r] "If the tsar's government ever hints at dark plans concerning India, it can
only be to amuse itself with the owner." (A. Rustem Bey de Bilinski, "Great
Britain and Russia," *Nineteenth Century and After*, L [1901], 727-728.) "The
only possible excuse for the British conservatives of Disraeli's camp who trem-
bled for their Asiatic possessions, was their absolute lack of knowledge about
Russia and the Russians." (Korff, pp. 29-30.) Salisbury had come to consider
that Russian threats against India were not earnestly intended. (*C. H. B. F. P.*,
III, 79.) On 19 February 1875 he had written to Lord Northbrook, then viceroy
of India: "I agree with you in thinking that a Russian advance upon India is
a chimera. But I am by no means sure that an attempt to throw the Afghans
upon us is so improbable." (Lady Gwendolen Cecil, II, 72.) In retrospect Sir
Edward Grey could remark to the Committee of Imperial Defence on 26 May
1911: "I do not really think that Russia ever had designs on the Indian frontier
for the invasion of India." *B. D.*, VI, Appendix V, p. 783.

growing influence in Persia.[s] The difficulties in the way of an Anglo-Russian agreement were more the result of febrile imagination than of material obstacles, which required willingness and confidence more than anything else in order to reach a settlement.

British statesmen were becoming more desirous of better Anglo-Russian relations because the policy of "splendid isolation" was beginning to appear inadequate. It was more difficult to maintain the former close association and friendship with the powers of the Triple Alliance, especially after the accession of the Emperor William II and the start of the restless German quest for a place in the sun.[t] When the colonial expansion of other European powers "began to invade the vast solitary preserves of British enterprise," most of all in the scramble for Africa, and to set "a killing pace throughout the eighties and nineties," the weakness of splendid isolation without any allies was forcibly brought home.[u] Great Britain was embroiled in a state of constant friction over colonial questions with most of the great European nations, in which the least unpleasant incident promptly excited the public and the press; and, although war never came, the rumors of war were frequent. This rivalry without friendships became too nerve-wracking in the face of seriously growing antagonism with Germany, and isolation began to appear as a positive danger. Slowly, with great caution, the Conservative government of Lord Salisbury from 1896 onwards made efforts to improve the British international position.[v]

There had already been talk of settling the outstanding difficulties in Anglo-Russian Asiatic rivalry in conformity with the special interests of each power as they had come to exist. This preparation had taken place with no other nation, and

[s] *Slavonic Review,* V, 424. Meyendorff, I, no. 7, p. 41, and p. 136.
[t] Grey attributed the expression "splendid isolation" to Mr. Goschen, chancellor of the exchequer in Salisbury's cabinet of 1892. (Viscount Grey of Fallodon, *Twenty-Five Years, 1892-1916,* [New York, 1925], I, 4.) Curzon, critical of the policy, feared that it was likely to become one of "masterly inactivity." (Earl of Ronaldshay, *The Life of Lord Curzon,* [London and New York, 1928], I, 276.) See also Giffen, pp. 124-125.
[u] *Ibid.,* pp. 120-121.
[v] *B. D.,* VI, Appendix V, p. 782. Garvin, III, 241-253. Meyendorff, II, no. 30, p. 323. Fischer, p. 201.

it may therefore have been simpler for British statesmen to
continue their efforts to persuade Russia that the hostility of
the Crimean war and Berlin congress days was past, so that
the time had come to reach an understanding on some, at least,
of their quarrels. The problem would be to convince the Russians that this new attitude existed, and to cause them to take
more tangible steps than merely to agree that something ought
to be done. What once had been Drummond Wolff's "dream"
now became Joseph Chamberlain's "favorite thesis," and the
more the latter reflected the more he succeeded in persuading
himself, and others, that Great Britain and Russia were not
separated by any irreconcilable interests.[w] Chamberlain frequently expressed this conviction to the patient Russian ambassador, who assured him that Russia would not fail to
reciprocate his sentiments for an agreement. A few days after
one of these conversations Balfour spoke to Staal in the same
tone "if not with the same abandon."[x] This possibility was
further discussed during the tsar's visit to England in the
summer of 1896, when he confessed his willingness to go along
in harmony with the British. He declared that there would
be no trouble in regard to India and "admitted only a single
theme of friction between the two countries — the opening of
the Dardanelles to Russian ships, which he deemed a matter
of primary importance."[y]

Salisbury continued his favorable attitude towards Russia
and, at the Lord Mayor's banquet near the end of the year,
he took occasion to reply openly to some assertions by Prince

[w] Meyendorff, II, no. 27, p. 358.

[x] Ibid., no. 6, p. 309. Chamberlain professed to believe: "Russia was vast
enough not to be inclined to colonial expansion, so that consequently no serious
rivalry was able to spring up between it and Great Britain, and that the
[proposed] entente between the two countries was a valuable pledge to bring
forward to the cause of peace and civilization." See also Langer, I, 251-253.

[y] Ibid., p. 330. Lee, I, 696. The tsar then went to France where he was
received with marked attention. This inspired a sagacious correspondent to
write Salisbury shortly afterwards of the "great gain" it would be "to the
world, and to England not least, if England could come to a friendly understanding" not only with Russia but with France as well. (Ibid., p. 697.) British
relations with France, however, were particularly strained at this time. Consequently Chamberlain thought it wise to try to reach an entente first with
Russia, and then "par ricochet" with France. (Meyendorff, II, no. 27, p. 358.)
The reverse of this actually happened by the agreements of 1904 with France,
and the convention of 1907 with Russia.

Bismarck, who had declared that the antagonism between Russia and Great Britain was a fundamental element in the existing political situation. Salisbury countered with the declaration that Anglo-Russian relations would permit a most perfect entente, and that possibly at the present moment Great Britain had less contradictory interests to discuss with Russia than with any other power.[z] Early in the next year the British prime minister, criticising the British policy of the Crimean and Berlin epochs, made his famous remark that Great Britain "had put her money on the wrong horse," although important figures as Lord Cromer and Curzon still insisted otherwise.[a] Chamberlain also persisted in expounding his favorite thesis to Staal "with as much conviction as talent" that it would be a sane policy for Great Britain to emerge from complete isolation by arranging ententes with Russia, and France the ally of Russia.[b]

Despite the fine phrases in speeches and conversations, the old antagonism between Russia and Great Britain was still virulent in 1898, and Russian policy remained hostile to Great Britain in the Near East and throughout Asia. The viewpoint of the Russian foreign minister Muravyev was not friendly, and he let it be known in Berlin that Great Britain remained the chief enemy of Russia.[c] The Russian press was as spiteful as ever when concerned with British policy, while Nicholas II expressed the ungratified wish that he might live to see England turned out of Egypt. Rivalry in China, for political influence and commercial concessions, although comparatively new, was becoming unpleasantly intense.[d] This conflict in interests centered particularly in the grant of foreign loans to China to be used in payment of the indemnity due Japan, arising out of

[z] *Ibid.*, no. 34, p. 327. Bismarck had been making his comments in the *Hamburger Nachrichten*, a paper under his influence.

[a] *Ibid.*, p. 335. Sir J. A. R. Marriott, *The Eastern Question: an Historical Study in European Diplomacy*, (Oxford, 1918), pp. 249, 265. Staal reported in March 1898 that there was no likelihood of a Crimean combination being resuscitated since this was now "actually condemned" by most eminent British statesmen. Meyendorff, II, 378.

[b] *Ibid.*, no. 27, p. 358.

[c] Giffen, pp. 165-166. Popov, *Krasny Arkhiv*, XXV, 112. *G. P.*, XIII, no. 3451, p. 89.

[d] Grüning, p. 79. Giffen, p. 166. *G. P.*, XIII, no. 3444, p. 82. *B. D.*, I, no. 1, pp. 1-2. Langer, I, 400.

the defeat in war and the provision in the treaty of Shimonoseki of 1895; and, in the second place, from other loans for
new railroad construction contemplated by China. Some of
these lines would eventually connect with the Russian-owned
Chinese Eastern railway in Manchuria, thereby further exposing that province to the penetration of Russian influence.
British banking interests desired to share with Russia the
opportunities, which were certain to come in the future, for
underwriting additional loans. Russian policy at Peking ex-
erted pressure upon the Tsung-li-Yâmen, the Board for Foreign Affairs of China, to keep other powers out of Manchuria,
while British policy tended to leave to Japan the task of restraining Russia in Korea, and sought to maintain British
imperialistic interests unimpaired in the Yangtse valley.[e]

These dissensions were made more acute by the seizure of
Kiaochow by a German naval squadron (14 November 1897),
which was followed after a short interval by the despatch of
some Russian warships to Port Arthur (4 December) to winter there, so Muravyev first declared.[f] Right at this juncture,
for reasons not precisely known, Salisbury suddenly took up
the idea of obtaining an understanding with Russia which
Chamberlain had been voicing, and prepared to act upon it.[g]
In a pithy telegram to the British ambassador in St. Petersburg, Sir Nicholas O'Conor, Salisbury desired, if it were practicable, that Witte, as the strongest man in the Russian government, should be sounded whether it would be possible for
England and Russia to work together in China, for their ob-

[e] Popov, *Krasny Arkhiv*, XXV, 111-114. *B. D.*, I, no. 1, pp. 1-2. Langer, I, 396-399.

[f] The murder of two German missionaries, Fathers Neis and Henle, killed by Chinese at Kia-chwang on 1 November 1897, furnished the pretext for the German occupation of Kiaochow, which had already been determined upon. (A. M. Pooley, *Japan's Foreign Policies*, [London, 1920], p. 143. *B. D.*, I, Editors' Note, p. 1; no. 2, p. 3; no. 53, p. 34. *C. H. B. F. P.*, III, 232. Langer, I, 450-451. Garvin, III, 250-253.) The British soon foresaw that the Russians might remain definitely at Port Arthur. (*B. D.*, I, no. 4, p. 5.) Some unfriendly comments by English newspapers are summarized in Meyendorff, II, no. 26, p. 354.

[g] *Ibid.*, p. 362. Popov, *Krasny Arkhiv*, XXV, 114. Langer, I, 465. In the debate on the Anglo-Russian convention of 1907 in the house of lords on 10 February 1908, Viscount Midleton (formerly Mr. Brodrick) declared that he well remembered that "in 1898 the mind of the late Lord Salisbury was much set on coming to some arrangement with the Russian government with regard to Asia." *Parliamentary Debates*, 4th series, CLXXXIII, 1312.

jects "are not antagonistic in any serious degree." Salisbury wrote also: "We would go far to further Russian commercial objects in the north, if we could regard her as willing to work with us." [h] In his interview with Muravyev the British ambassador expressed his own opinion that a really effective understanding ought not to be confined to some troublesome questions in the Far East alone, but that it "ought to extend to the general area of our respective interests." Although evidently hesitant himself to make definite proposals, beyond discussing in some detail the Russian sphere of influence wanted from Peking northwards into Manchuria, the Russian foreign minister expressed his agreement with the idea for a "closer understanding," as well as his readiness to consider immediately any proposal Lord Salisbury might formulate, and "to put his cards on the table, if your Lordship would do the same." [i]

With remarkable decision and brevity Salisbury clarified his general meaning in a telegram to O'Conor of 25 January 1898:

Our idea was this. The two empires of China and Turkey are so weak that in all important matters they are constantly guided by the advice of foreign powers. In giving this advice Russia and England are constantly opposed, neutralizing each other's efforts much more frequently than the real antagonism of their interests would justify; and this condition of things is not likely to diminish, but to increase. It is to remove or lessen this evil that we have thought an understanding might benefit both nations.[j]

He hastened to add that "we aim at no partition of territory, but only a partition of preponderance," and hoped that the power less interested in such regions would give way, or even assist the other where it possessed an interest.[k] Both Mura-

[h] *Ibid.*, no. 5, p. 5. Lord Newton, *Lord Lansdowne. A Biography*, (London, 1929), p. 214. Popov, *Krasny Arkhiv*, XXV, 114-115; and see pp. 113-114 for an indication of the importance with which Russian diplomacy looked upon northern China.

[i] *B. D.*, I, no. 6, p. 6. Popov, *Krasny Arkhiv*, XXV, 114-115. Langer, I, 467-470.

[j] *B. D.*, I, no. 9, p. 8.

[k] "We contemplate no infraction of existing rights. We would not admit the violation of any existing treaties, or impair the integrity of the present empires of either China or Turkey. These two conditions are vital." *Ibid.*

vyev and the influential Witte seem to have taken kindly to the British proposition, especially because it would allay an insecure feeling which bothered Russia in its existing position in the Far East. The Russian government had been seriously displeased with the German seizure of Kiaochow, because no official in it had known at the moment that the tsar had previously agreed to the importunities of the kaiser not to obstruct such action by Germany.[1] Witte told O'Conor on 23 January 1898 that Russia might be forced to stay on at Port Arthur, and he hazarded the question: "What would England say if Russia's occupation of Port Arthur became permanent?" The animosity between Russia and Japan was already developing, and the tsar's ministers were most anxious that the British should make no alliance with Japan which might include a promise of support against Russia. Witte's nervousness was evident to O'Conor, who did not think it advisable to exclude this possibility from the former's political vision.[m] The British ambassador also sensed the Russian apprehensiveness of complications in the Far East before the Transsiberian railroad should be completed, and that this fact made the proposal for an Anglo-Russian agreement over interests in China welcome to the Russians under the existing circumstances.[n]

Muravyev told the tsar that the British proposal was valuable, and he recommended the acceptance of Salisbury's proffer

[1] There are several versions which vary in details but agree that the kaiser sprung this request for Kiaochow upon the unsuspecting tsar during a visit at Peterhof in August 1897. The tsar was displeased, but consented. It was only after Muravyev and Witte had protested against the German seizure that Nicholas owned up how he had given his consent. For details see *G. P.*, XIV, part I, pp. 3-75; no. 3733, p. 121. *B. D.*, I, Editors' Note, p. 1; no. 4, p. 5; no. 53, p. 34; no. 59, p. 38; III, no. 435, minutes, pp. 381-382. Meyendorff, II, 354, 365. Count S. Yu. Witte, *Vospominaniya*, [Memoirs] (Berlin, 1922), I, 112, 123; (see English translation by Abraham Yarmolinsky, *The Memoirs of Count Witte*, [Garden City, N. Y., 1921], pp. 123, 410-411. This is not an acceptable selection of the original Russian work). *C. H. B. F. P.*, III, 232. Otto Hammann, *Der neue Kurs*, (Berlin, 1918), pp. 115-117. E. J. Dillon, *The Eclipse of Russia*, (New York, 1918), pp. 247-248. A. M. Pooley, *Japan's Foreign Policies*, pp. 143-147; also his *Secret Memoirs of Count Tadasu Hayashi*, (London, 1915), p. 98. The last book is later cited as Pooley, *Hayashi*.

[m] *B. D.*, I, no. 8, p. 7. Popov, *Krasny Arkhiv*, XXV, 125.

[n] *B. D.*, I, no. 6, p. 6. At the same time O'Conor warned his government "to take care that any understanding we may come to gives no such headway that it cannot be set aside when it may seem to Russia to have served its temporary purpose."

of a division of China into spheres of influence, so that Russian interests would predominate in the region north of the Yellow river, with British interests supreme in the Yangtse basin. Such an agreement would accomplish the double purpose of according Russia "full liberty of action around the Gulf of Pechili" at the same time that it would furnish the possibility of restraining "the British from every interference in the affairs of northern China." If the tsar would consent, Muravyev was ready to enter into an exhaustive interchange of ideas with the British ambassador on the basis of the proposal made by Salisbury, provided that the discussions were limited to what concerned China. Nicholas II did give his approval to the inauguration of discussions within this scope; and, at a court ball on the evening of 1 February, he encouraged O'Conor when he declared such an arrangement to be "most desirable and he believed the negotiations would succeed." [o] On the following day O'Conor called upon Muravyev, who explained his readiness to enter upon conversations for reaching an agreement, the scope of which should at first be limited to Chinese affairs which were then most pressing. Possibly later this could be extended to the question of spheres of influence in Turkey, and to the removal of any uneasiness arising from suspected Russian designs upon the British position in India. The ambassador desired that Muravyev would consider Salisbury's original suggestion for a broader understanding, but he was unable to persuade him to go any further at once. The tsar refused to permit such an extension, so the negotiations had to be confined from the outset exclusively to Chinese affairs.[p]

[o] *Ibid.*, no. 10, p. 9. Popov, *Krasny Arkhiv*, XXV, 115-116. In a marginal note dated 27 January the tsar expressed his doubt of reaching an agreement: "Unfortunately, I am not convinced of the favorable outcome of such an arrangement with England, that [by it] all our interests in the Far East will be taken into account." *Ibid.*, footnote 3, p. 114.

[p] *B. D.*, I, no. 11, p. 9; no. 12, p. 10. Popov, *Krasny Arkhiv*, XXV, 116, 118. O'Conor persisted in believing that "now is the time . . . to make it clearly understood that the arrangement between the two countries shall extend not only to China but to all other regions where we have conflicting interests." (*B. D.*, I, no. 13, p. 10.) Salisbury, however, was less certain: "The difficulty about extending the arrangement to Persia is that the northern part of Persia which would be the natural sphere of Russian preponderance includes Teheran." *Ibid.*, no. 14, p. 11.

The Russian foreign minister showed great interest in trying to find out the details of the exact sphere of influence in
northern China over which the British government would
recognize Russian predominance, and precisely what extent of
the Yangtse valley the British intended to demand for their
compensation. The prospect of an agreement over the spheres
each power should possess in China was obviously the outcome
of the negotiations desired by the Russians. Muravyev gave
O'Conor to understand that if the Russian sphere should comprise the part of China north of the Yellow river, Russia
would be prepared to recognize British influence in the southern part of the Chinese empire.[q] Before Salisbury got around
to defining the British sphere, two other questions arose to
cause trouble, which took up most of the negotiations; while
Muravyev became ill and Count Lamsdorff carried on temporarily in his place.[r]

The first difference arose over a possible new British loan
to China, which poisoned the atmosphere of these negotiations
from the start. The Chinese had obtained two loans in 1896,
one from Russia and the other from an Anglo-German syndicate, but these were not sufficient. In 1897 negotiations were
renewed with the latter syndicate for a further advance of
£16,000,000, against which the Russian government protested
at Peking, and threatened action.[s] This rivalry between Russia and Great Britain was still undecided when Salisbury turned
to Russia with his proposal for an understanding, and the
British ambassador attempted to persuade the Russian foreign
office to withdraw its objections so that the negotiations for a
Chinese agreement would not commence with "any angry
question between us." Soon afterwards Muravyev informed
O'Conor that he had heard that China had broken off the

[q] *Ibid.*, no. 12, p. 10; no. 13, p. 10. Popov, *Krasny Arkhiv*, XXV, 117.
[r] *B. D.*, I, no. 13, p. 10; no. 17, p. 18. Meyendorff, II, 364.
[s] *B. D.*, I, no. 1, p. 2. The technical terms of this loan which Great Britain
was trying to make to China are always omitted from the *British Documents*,
as they were really of little importance. A slight explanation of the British and
Russian attitudes is given by Popov, *Krasny Arkhiv*, XXV, 116-118, and some
observations are in *G. P.*, XIV, part I, pp. 174-189. In the British estimation
this loan was primarily a commercial and bankers' transaction; the Russians always asserted that the terms had political implications and alienated Chinese
rights to the disadvantage of Russia.

loan negotiations.[t] While he did not know the exact conditions
Great Britain had proposed, they were nevertheless regarded
as unfavorable to Russian interests in China, and he objected
to the conclusion of such a loan. He thought that the subject
could be discussed between the governments during their
efforts to compose their conflicting purposes in China.[u]

O'Conor then inquired whether Salisbury would consider
making a joint loan with Russia, or preferred to keep it entirely in British control, while discussing the conditions for it
with Russia. Salisbury saw no advantage in attempting to
agree upon a joint loan, to which both sides appeared indifferent. The British were especially disinclined because, although
presumably engaged in conversations with Russia for a settlement of their discords in China, circumstances had changed:

Certain concessions were almost at once obtained by Her Majesty's
government from China in compensation, though not ostensibly so, for
this refusal to accept a British loan. . . . These concessions having been
secured, both the loan and the understanding with Russia became matters of comparative indifference to Her Majesty's government and the
negotiations dropped.[v]

Nevertheless, on 12 February 1898, O'Conor did give Lamsdorff a note summarizing the course of the negotiations with
Russia as far as they had gone, because this had been enough
to warrant some more serious discussion of details. Lamsdorff then assumed full control in place of the ailing Muravyev. He obtained the tsar's consent to consider the conditions
for a British loan to China, and to present the Russian counter-
demands for this possible concession to Great Britain.[w]

These Russian counter-demands introduced the second, but
less serious obstacle to the conversations. During an interview
on 16 February Lamsdorff revealed the Russian intention to
lease Port Arthur and the nearby Talianwan for a period of

[t] *B. D.*, I, no. 1, p. 2; no. 11, p. 9; no. 14, p. 11.
[u] Popov, *Krasny Arkhiv*, XXV, 117-118. Meyendorff, II, 364; no. 4, p. 369.
[v] *B. D.*, I, no. 1, p. 2; no. 13, p. 10; no. 14, p. 11; no. 15, p. 11; Editors' Note,
p. 11. Salisbury could still inform Sir Claude MacDonald, the British minister
at Peking, that "we have had some interchange of friendly language at St.
Petersburg, but they are insincere and their language is ambiguous." *Ibid.*, no.
15, p. 11.
[w] *Ibid.*, no. 16, and enclosure, pp. 11-13; no. 17, p. 14; no. 20, p. 15.

time, possibly twenty years, or else some other port in northern
China which might later appear more desirable, as a future
railroad terminal, as an ice-free commercial outlet, and as a
safe harbor where Russian ships in the Far East could dock
and coal. He hastened to add that such a lease would not
destroy Chinese sovereignty.[x] O'Conor promptly labelled the
Russian demands "disproportionate and of a totally different
nature" to the objects desired by the British government. On
22 February he neatly summed up the position into which the
negotiations had come when he ventured to think:

The question now resolves itself to the point of considering whether it
is best not to oppose Russian demands and to go on with the negotiations
for a good understanding; or to risk Russia getting what she wants
without our acquiescence and to see the negotiations break down leaving
inevitably behind them much sore feeling.[y]

Most probably the British government was no longer so
anxious to reach an understanding with Russia. After the first
Chinese refusal, on 2 February, to contract a loan with the
Anglo-German syndicate, the British had secretly continued
their efforts to induce China to conclude the loan. Suddenly,
on 1 March, the announcement was received in London that
a definite agreement for an Anglo-German advance had just
been signed; and Staal relayed this information to the Russian foreign office on the following day.[z] When O'Conor
called on Lamsdorff the next time he was plainly told of the
Russian displeasure on the conclusion of this loan, and that the
tsar was deeply offended by what he considered to be double-
dealing.[a] The loan increased the irritation in Russia which
the recent British political and commercial concessions obtained
from China had called forth, and the clauses guaranteeing the
repayment of the loan were considered in St. Petersburg as

[x] Meyendorff, II, footnote 3, p. 362; footnote 2, p. 372. B. D., I, no. 18, p. 14.
Popov, *Krasny Arkhiv*, XXV, 114.
[y] B. D., I, no. 19, p. 15.
[z] *Ibid.*, no. 21, p. 15. Meyendorff, II, no. 10, p. 372.
[a] It is clear that the tsar was incensed at the British methods. "The loan
concluded in accord with Germany, to the exclusion of Russia, indisposed the
Emperor Nicholas II so strongly that he repulsed the overtures for an arrangement respecting the affairs of China and Turkey which Lord Salisbury had
sketched." Meyendorff, II, footnote 1, p. 359; also pp. 362, 364, footnote 2,
p. 372. B. D., I, no. 24, p. 17.

constituting an alienation of rights on the part of China, detrimental to Russian interests and to the service of prior loans.[b] The British ambassador was able to gather that the Russian government "did not seem inclined to pursue, for the moment, at all events, the discussion of the broader question," and that the negotiations "have certainly had a severe check" with little chance of being resumed before the annoyed tsar had first been put in good humor.[c]

When the conversations for the understanding with Great Britain appeared blocked, Muravyev no longer dallied with British objections, but proceeded rapidly to the ultimate solution of the Russian position about Port Arthur.[d] He was prolific with his justifications for the contemplated Russian action. He explained the desire for a lease of Port Arthur and Talianwan as simply following the precedents established by Germany and Japan, and as proper, although belated reward for Russian assistance rendered China in making peace with Japan at Shimonoseki. No Chinese sovereignty would be impaired or destroyed by the lease, which also would not infringe "rights and privileges guaranteed by existing treaties between China and foreign countries."[e] Muravyev took sounder ground when he claimed that the occupation of Port Arthur was "a vital necessity" because of its strategic value to Russia in its location as "the Bosphorus of the Far East."[f] The port would serve as an ice-free naval harbor for the Russian fleet in the Pacific, to dock and to coal safely. It would make the

[b] *Ibid.*, no. 22, p. 16. Popov, *Krasny Arkhiv*, XXV, 125, 130.

[c] *B. D.*, I, no. 22, p. 16. Popov, *Krasny Arkhiv*, XXV, 118. Meyendorff, II, 362: "The negotiations closed on 3 March." The editors of the *British Documents* remark that "the British overture to Russia between January and March 1898 . . . was terminated by Russia's seizure of Port Arthur." (*B. D.*, I, p. xi.) This is not correct. The Russians, not the British, suspended the negotiations as a result of the conclusion of the Chinese loan. Port Arthur was only occupied by force permanently on 16 March. Russia obtained the agreement for the lease from China on 27 March. Yet the negotiations were dropped on the 3rd. *Ibid.*, no. 1, p. 2; Note, p. 22.

[d] *Ibid.*, no. 36, p. 23; no. 38, p. 24; no. 41, p. 28. Calchas, "Why Not a Treaty with Russia?" *Fortnightly Review*, LXXIV (1900), 678. The article is a criticism of British policy in regard to the seizures of Kiaochow and Port Arthur.

[e] *B. D.*, I, no. 18, p. 14; no. 22, p. 16; no. 36, p. 23; no. 37, p. 24. Meyendorff, II, no. 14, pp. 375-377.

[f] *B. D.*, I, no. 37, p. 24. Meyendorff, II, 336. Witte, *Vospominaniya*, I, 120; see English translation, pp. 99-100.

Russian position adequate for the defence of its interests in northern China and the Gulf of Pechili, although Port Arthur would still be of little value against Japan, unlike some fine haven in Korea such as Masampo, because of the distance away from Japan, as well as the vulnerable separation of eleven hundred miles from Vladivostok.[g] The Chinese government was powerless to withstand the Russian demands for the lease of Port Arthur, Talianwan, and the territory surrounding them on the Liaotung peninsula, although it did object.[h] On 15/27 March 1898 the Chinese government granted this region to Russia on a lease for twenty-five years, along with permission to construct a branch line to connect with the Transsiberian railroad.[i] That seemed time enough in which to make sure of Russian predominance in Manchuria.

The British government had not originally intended to obtain compensation for the German seizure of Kiaochow, but after Russia had extorted the lease of Port Arthur from China, it quickly decided to demand some "makeweight" as an "equivalent compensation within the British sphere."[j] Some consideration had already been devoted to the availability of Weihaiwei, for which Curzon had pleaded in the last days of 1897, but the place was not attractive because it "would require too large a military force for its defence, and except for appearances would be worth little to us if fortified and still less if unfortified."[k] Before Weihaiwei could be obtained from China, negotiations were first carried on with Japan, which was in temporary possession of the place, to secure the promise of its transfer into British control upon its

[g] "Die zaristische Diplomatie über Russlands Aufgaben im Orient im Jahre 1900," *Kriegsschuldfrage*, VI (1928), 653-654, 659-660. This is a translation of Russian documents printed in *Krasny Arkhiv*, XVIII (1926). See also *B. D.*, I, no. 18, p. 14. Meyendorff, II, no. 14, p. 376.

[h] To overcome these objections and to secure the lease before other powers could aid China, Witte resorted to the bribery of two Chinese ministers, whose political careers were soon ruined. Witte, *Vospominaniya*, I, 125-128, 131.

[i] *B. D.*, I, no. 41, p. 27. Witte, *Vospominaniya*, I, 127.

[j] *B. D.*, I, no. 3, p. 4; no. 32, pp. 21-22; no. 41, pp. 28-29. Meyendorff, II, no. 15, p. 378. Newton, p. 214. The Russians were not surprized by this action, and Lamsdorff seems to have offered no objections when it was hinted to him that something might be taken by Great Britain. *B. D.*, I, no. 18, p. 14.

[k] *Ibid.*, no. 32, p. 22; no. 53, p. 35. Ronaldshay, I, 285. Meyendorff, II, no. 16, p. 379.

evacuation. Japan could do little else than agree to the British request, and if Weihaiwei had to go to some other nation, Japan preferred that it should fall into the hands of one presumably more "disposed to assist in maintaining the independence of China."[1] The demand for the lease of Weihaiwei was pressed upon the Chinese government "at an interview lasting three hours." As the Chinese objected and delayed an answer, the British minister presented what was virtually an ultimatum, threatening in the event of anything other than an affirmative reply within a short time to place the matter "in [the] Admiral's hands," who was on his way with the British fleet from Hongkong to the Gulf of Pechili.[m] China was utterly incapable of resisting such pressure, so the Tsung-li-Yâmen agreed, on 2 April 1898, to lease the harbor of Weihaiwei to Great Britain upon the same conditions as Russia had obtained Port Arthur. The actual possession was to be taken at the time that Japan should withdraw, and was to be retained as long as Russia remained as the occupant of the Liaotung peninsula. By another arrangement an extension of territory was granted Great Britain on the Kowloon promontory of the mainland opposite Hongkong.[n] All that China could do was to ask to retain certain privileges in the harbor of Weihaiwei, and to receive support in resisting claims for territorial concessions by other powers which were expected to arise out of this surrender to Great Britain.[o] British influence at Peking, and the balance of power in the Gulf of Pechili, upset by the German and Russian seizures, were deemed to be restored.[p]

[1] B. D., I, no. 30, p. 21; no. 45, p. 30; no. 46, p. 30. At the time of this negotiation both nations were conscious of a friendliness which was the initial step on the way towards the Anglo-Japanese alliance of 1902. Ibid., no. 48, p. 32; no. 50, p. 33. Pooley, Hayashi, p. 83.
[m] B. D., I, no. 39, p. 25; no. 42, p. 29; no. 43, p. 29. Meyendorff, II, no. 16, p. 379.
[n] B. D., I, no. 44, pp. 29-30. The texts of these agreements are in British and Foreign State Papers, XC, 16-18.
[o] France eventually sustained "her claims to consideration in the provinces contiguous to Tongking." In 1899 Italy put in a bid for some spoils, and inquired about the British attitude towards the venture. Salisbury replied that "it would always be a matter of great satisfaction to us to have the Italians for neighbors." The Chinese successfully stood off the Italians. B. D., I, no. 33, p. 22; no. 60, p. 40.
[p] Ibid., no. 47, p. 31; no. 53, p. 35. Meyendorff, II, no. 16, p. 380.

Such negotiations as still went on between Russia and Great Britain had the character of "bargaining over trifles," but they led in the end to a resumption of the original attempt for a local understanding in China.[q] From July 1898, when Sir Charles Scott replaced Sir Nicholas O'Conor as the British ambassador at St. Petersburg, the Russian foreign office was "bombarded" with notes and despatches to obtain an agreement upon railroad concessions in China, and over the terms of loans by which China could finance actual construction. Even the tsar thought it would be possible to reach an understanding of this nature with the British.[r] The Russians still objected to making any broad settlement, and asked for a precise definition of what the British intended to include in their sphere. This was eventually delimited to comprise "the provinces adjoining the Yangtse river, and in addition the provinces of Honan and Chekiang." It was left to the Russians to particularize the limits of their sphere in northern China.[s] Some of the bitterness in Anglo-Russian relations was disappearing, and the French minister for foreign affairs, Delcassé, who had recently assumed office, expressed his approval. This early he revealed an objective of his own foreign policy when he declared:

He . . . had not failed to let it be known in St. Petersburg that the government of the Republic feel great anxiety that there should be no misunderstanding between Great Britain and Russia, believing as they do that there is no insuperable obstacle to the maintenance of harmony between them.[t]

The first draft of an agreement to regulate railroad concessions was prepared by the British foreign office, and handed to the Russians on 16 September 1898. According to this the British sphere comprised the Yangtse basin, and the Russian sphere was located indefinitely in Manchuria. The one power promised not to seek any railroad concessions, either on its own behalf or for its subjects, in the region designated for the

[q] Popov, *Krasny Arkhiv*, XXV, 119. The *British Documents* do not show how these negotiations were resumed.
[r] Popov, *Krasny Arkhiv*, XXV, 121.
[s] *Ibid.*, p. 122. *B. D.*, I, no. 61, note 3, p. 41.
[t] *Ibid.*, no. 58, p. 37. Popov, *Krasny Arkhiv*, XXV, 121.

other, nor there to oppose the acquisition of concessions by
that power for itself, or for its subjects whom it supported.[u]
When this solution to that Anglo-Russian rivalry appeared to
be on the threshhold of success, unanticipated objections postponed its acceptance, and a lapse of nearly two months held
up the conversations. Witte was dissatisfied with the arrangement primarily because it prevented the participation of his
creation, the Russian Chinese bank, from affairs in the south
of China.[v] By 2 November he had changed his viewpoint sufficiently so that he assured Scott that "there was nothing he
had more at heart than the establishment of a thoroughly sincere and satisfactory understanding, and of frank and friendly
relations between Russia and Great Britain on this and on all
other questions." [w] He then explained to the ambassador, as
he was often later to repeat, that he was himself no diplomat.
In his opinion "he did not regard paper agreements on such
concrete questions as the best way" to secure a satisfactory
understanding because "a far more solid basis for our future
relations would be established by a general agreement concluded between the two governments and ratified by their
respective sovereigns." [x]

British statesmen were also becoming favorably inclined
again to the idea of an agreement with Russia, now that proposals for one with Germany had failed.[y] After the conversations were resumed Salisbury brought out other proposals
which, upon examination, were entirely unacceptable to the
Russians, who felt that they were required to make all the
concessions with no equivalent gains. If it were to prove im-

[u] *Ibid.*, p. 122.
[v] *Ibid.*, p. 123.
[w] *B. D.*, I, no. 59, p. 38.
[x] *Ibid.*, no. 59, p. 39. Salisbury, who was a diplomat, feared "that if we concluded an agreement in M. de Witte's language it would be a good deal laughed
at," while Balfour believed that Witte's suggestion was "derisory." *Ibid.*, no.
59, minute, p. 40.
[y] After the negotiations with Russia had fallen down on 3 March 1898,
Chamberlain and Balfour quickly turned to Germany with proposals for a
purely defensive alliance as the next move away from isolation. After a brief
course these negotiations failed, largely because the German foreign office was
indifferent and set too high a price. For details see *G. P.*, XIV, part I, pp.
193-256. On the British side these negotiations were privately conducted by
Chamberlain and Balfour, so that few references appear in the British collection. *B. D.*, II, p. xii. See also Garvin, III, 254-277. Langer, II, 485-535.

possible to obtain separate spheres for concessions, they preferred to make no agreement at all.[z] Yet an understanding with Great Britain was desirable both for its own real value, and to forestall any possible British support of Japan in the existing troubled relations with that country. The natural solution for Russian diplomacy was, therefore, to reject the subsequent British proposals and to return to the original idea of two distinct spheres in China wherein to acquire railroad concessions as set forth in the first British draft of 16 September 1898.[a] Some definite Russian move was necessary in the face of a growing British impatience and tendency to try for railroad privileges in districts which Russia desired to retain for its own exploitation. The Russian government admitted its readiness to arrive at an agreement with Great Britain in order to avoid conflicts which might arise at any time in the future out of their interests in the affairs of China. It was worth while to reach peaceful solutions of "all questions in the realm of the development of their industrial and commercial interests," especially because the Peking government had decided to expedite the construction of railroads throughout its extensive territories. A Russian note therefore revived the negotiations with the virtual repetition of the British proposals of the previous 16 September, offering not to oppose any British railroad enterprize in the region of the Yangtse basin, in return for a similar British attitude toward Russia in the area now defined as lying to the north of the Great Chinese Wall.[b]

Muravyev thought that it would be easy to reach such an agreement, as it was completely in harmony with the propositions which Great Britain had first submitted to Russia. The British government did, indeed, quickly take up the Russian offer, all the more so as it faced the prospect of war in South Africa, and doubtless desired to terminate the Chinese negotiations in the good position of an agreement with Russia, which would do much to remove friction between them in the

[z] Popov, *Krasny Arkhiv*, XXV, 124.
[a] *Ibid.*, p. 125.
[b] *Ibid.*, pp. 126-127.

Far East. A note of 3 March 1899, handed to Scott by Mura-vyev, contained all the material necessary for the conclusion of this partial agreement between the two rivals, and a final draft was at last signed at St. Petersburg on 28 April 1899. By this understanding the spheres for railroad concessions for the two powers were left unaltered from their previous defini-tion. Both piously agreed that they had no intention of in-fringing the sovereign rights of China or of impairing any existing treaty provisions. The Chinese government was to be informed of this arrangement, and consoled with the ex-planation that the interests of China itself would really be better served, because the agreement averted "all cause of complications" between Russia and Great Britain. In addi-tion, in supplementary notes, a few British rights to certain railroad lines outside its delimited sphere, which had already been obtained, were recognized and defined.[c] After more than a year of negotiation from the time of Lord Salisbury's first suggestion, a partial Anglo-Russian agreement had been at-tained.

The Chinese government did not placidly accept the terms of this agreement when informed of it by the two contracting parties. The Tsung-li-Yâmen announced in reply that it could not recognize the treaty as binding upon China, because the fact that information of its conclusion had been received did not constitute an acceptance of its terms, nor an obligation to respect it at a later time.[d] Although the Russian minister did not send a written rejection of this Chinese attitude, he did recommend to his government that the first favorable oppor-tunity should be seized to impress upon the Chinese that parts of their empire had entered indubitably into the sphere of Russian influence. After sustained pressure the Tsung-li-Yâmen was compelled to accede to the Russian demand for a promise not to alienate to any power except Russia "the right of railroad construction from Peking in a northerly or north-

[c] The full texts of the agreement and the supplementary notes are printed in *British and Foreign State Papers*, XCI, 91-94. Partially complete texts, or summaries are in Popov, *Krasny Arkhiv*, XXV, 122, 127-128. *B. D.*, I, no. 61, p. 41. Langer, II, 682-683.
[d] Popov, *Krasny Arkhiv*, XXV, 128.

easterly direction."[e] Russian opinion rapidly attached great value to this security for their concessions in the northern sphere of China, because it matched the gains British diplomacy had obtained for its interests in the previous year, and because the Russians quickly believed that no real profit had come to them from this first step towards an understanding with Great Britain.[f]

[e] *Ibid.*, pp. 128-129. The Chinese ministry communicated this concession in notes of 20 May and 9 June 1899.

[f] *Ibid.*, p. 130.

CHAPTER TWO

TOWARDS A BETTER UNDERSTANDING, 1900-1905

THE conclusion of the Anglo-Russian agreement of 28 April 1899 in regard to railway enterprises in China was a cautious step in the new British policy away from isolation, as well as an attempt to reach some peaceful settlement of all the clashing interests with Russia. This first treaty, obtained after much difficulty, removed from the list only one of many causes of friction, and British diplomacy was not satisfied with the partial achievement. From the outset a broad and frank understanding had been the British goal. The ultimate realization of this had not been abandoned, although it had to be dropped for the moment when the tsar refused to permit the discussion of more than a specific problem. Late in the year 1898, however, the British ambassador had had a long and cordial conversation with the influential Witte who, with little restraint, expressed his belief in the advantage of reaching an agreement with Great Britain on the Chinese and "all other questions." [a] Throughout 1899 there seems to have been considerable optimism in England that it would be possible to come to an agreement over Persian interests with Russia, as the latter did not then appear to be in a rapacious mood.[b] Salisbury had already noted as an objection that any arrangement made must concede to Russia northern Persia, with the seat of the government at Teheran. That would lay the British government open to the charge of having deserted the feeble shah in order to bargain with Russia.[c] If, as some well-informed persons believed, no agreement could be reached in Persia with Russia, whose position there was too strong and whose policy too selfish, there remained other possibilities by

[a] *B. D.,* I, no. 59, p. 38; see also no. 6, p. 6, for an earlier expression of the British viewpoint.
[b] Stephen Gwynn, editor, *The Letters and Friendships of Sir Cecil Spring Rice. A Record,* (Boston and New York, 1929), I, 285.
[c] *B. D.,* I, no. 14, p. 11.

which Great Britain could break away from its isolation.[d] Chamberlain, who had previously advocated a general understanding with Russia, and then, in 1898, an alliance with Germany, now a year later was espousing his latest project of an alliance between Great Britain, the United States and Germany, but had succeeded only in arousing the distrust of the Kaiser and the scorn of the Russians.[e]

The new French minister of foreign affairs, Théophile Delcassé, endeavored to foster good relations between his Russian ally and the British government. On 29 August 1898 he took occasion to explain his hopes to Sir Edmund Monson, the British ambassador in Paris:

He could see no reason why all the supposed divergent interests [between Great Britain and Russia] should not be reconciled, just as he thought it possible that every difficulty between England and France could by patience, and by a conciliatory spirit, be peaceably solved. He had always . . . regarded as eminently desirable a cordial understanding between England, France, and Russia; and begged me to assure your Lordship [Salisbury] that he is most anxious to co-operate "as far as his feeble means could enable him" in smoothing the way both at St. Petersburg and Paris for the attainment of this object.[f]

Despite the evident willingness of Great Britain for a more general agreement with Russia, and the beginnings of a French policy looking towards improved relations among Great Britain, Russia, and France, Russia was still conscious of its power, unhumbled by any recent military defeats, and showed

[d] Gwynn, I, 278, 285. Grey, I, 148. Korff, p. 37. In 1900 Muravyev summarized Russian policy as having made northern Persia "completely inaccessible to foreigners," and as opposed to any official recognition of British interests in southern Persia, which were by no means as yet thoroughly secure. *Kriegsschuldfrage*, VI (1928), 651-652.

[e] Meyendorff, II, no. 17, p. 434. *B. D.*, I, no. 53, pp. 34-35. William II lectured the British Lieutenant-Colonel J. M. Grierson, sent to attend him on his approaching visit to Windsor: "Your government in England appears to have two heads, Lord Salisbury and Mr. Chamberlain, and the one will not do what the other wants." (*Ibid.*, no. 154, p. 129.) Baron de Staal came to the conclusion that "Mr. Chamberlain would do better, in his own interest, not to touch upon subjects which entirely escape his competence." Meyendorff, II, no. 17, p. 434.

[f] *B. D.*, I, no. 262, p. 216. Using his "feeble means" at St. Petersburg, Delcassé informed the Russians of the "great anxiety" felt by the French government "that there should be no serious misunderstanding between Great Britain and Russia, believing as they do that there is no insuperable obstacle to the maintenance of harmony between them." *Ibid.*, no. 58, p. 37. Maurice Bompard, *Mon ambassade en Russie (1903-1908)*, (Paris, 1937), pp. iii-vi.

no readiness to take any further step in agreement with the British.[g] No sooner was Great Britain well involved in the struggle with the Boers in South Africa than Muravyev's unfriendliness became evident. In one respect was his attempt to embarrass Great Britain by courting the association of other governments in making offers of mediation. Another way, little known at the time, was his consideration of what profits could be obtained for Russia in many regions of the world while effective British objections were impossible.

Even before the actual outbreak of the Boer war Muravyev began his efforts to create a group of continental powers which should institute "common action against the ever-increasing aggressions and expansion of England." [h] While temporarily stopping at Biarritz, on 4 October 1899 he paid a hasty visit to the Queen-Regent of Spain in San Sebastian, which at once gave rise to suspicions. While nothing definite was suggested to the Spanish government, Muravyev was supposed to have been optimistic that an understanding between Russia, Germany, and France could be arranged and directed against Great Britain, from which Spain should not remain aloof.[i] The next call Muravyev made was in Paris, and British diplomats displayed considerable curiosity about the details of his proposals to Delcassé, as well as the degree of acceptance which they may have received. The information picked up, even if not official, was at least reassuring, for Delcassé was soon reported as having told Muravyev that the best policy for France was "to keep on a friendly footing with England," while the Russian minister returned home disappointed that no other European power had hastened to join him in taking advantage of British preoccupation.[j] Nothing happened during the remainder of 1899 because the German government,

[g] Langer, II, 789-790.
[h] B. D., I, no. 286, p. 233; no. 287, p. 234.
[i] G. P., XV, no. 4212, p. 132; no. 4399, p. 420; no. 4496, p. 540. B. D., I, no. 287, pp. 234-235
[j] Ibid., no. 286, pp. 233-234; no. 287, pp. 234-235; no. 290, p. 237; no. 294, p. 239. Count Goluchowski, the Austro-Hungarian minister of foreign affairs, whom the British ambassador at Vienna characterized as "seldom loth [sic] to pass criticism on his St. Petersburg colleague," believed that while Muravyev had stayed in Paris his time had been "chiefly taken up with the amusements and seductions of that city." Ibid., no. 291, p. 237.

by order of the kaiser, was not disposed to participate in any joint intervention. It also professed to believe that the Russian intentions were unduly magnified from French sources.[k] Count Benckendorff, stopping at Copenhagen on his return to his post in London, remarked on New Year's day 1900 that the tsar was striving to keep down Russian public feeling against Great Britain, and that there would be no Russian interference with the course of the Boer war.[l]

Muravyev nursed his bitterness towards Great Britain and persevered in his desire to form some association of European powers for joint activity against it. On 12 January 1900 Count Osten-Sacken, the Russian ambassador at Berlin, inquired "for the third time" whether the German government would be prepared to take up a common position against Great Britain should that power actually attempt to close the harbor at Delagoa Bay to traffic in arms going to the aid of the Boers, but Bülow declared that Germany was not willing to do so.[m] On the following day the kaiser called on the ambassador to offer felicitations at the beginning of the Russian New Year whereupon, according to the German account of the visit, the ambassador renewed his suggestion of joint representations to Great Britain. He asked in plain words if, in the existing circumstances, "a coalition against England were not thinkable," but the kaiser refused to join any or to "give up his hitherto neutral attitude, so long as he was not compelled to do so as a result of British inconsiderateness which went too far."[n]

---

[k] G. P., XV, no. 4459, p. 501, and Anlage, p. 502; no. 4460, p. 503. B. D., I, no. 302, p. 244; no. 307, p. 247.

[l] Ibid., no. 303, p. 244. Benckendorff also made the surprizing remark that "Count Muravyev is loyally seconding the determination of His Imperial Majesty." The "pacific bent" of the tsar was already reported. Ibid., no. 290, p. 237.

[m] G. P., XV, no. 4463, pp. 506-507; no. 4464, pp. 508-509.

[n] Ibid., no. 4465, pp. 509-510. Something should be said of the version offered by Sir Sidney Lee (I, 761-773). The account is given by paraphrases of letters written by Osten-Sacken to Muravyev, copies of which were preserved in the Russian embassy in London, where they were consulted by Lee. He speaks of the kaiser's visit to Osten-Sacken as taking place on 1 January 1900, whereas it was on Russian New Year's, the 13th. The kaiser is portrayed as cherishing the "nefarious plan . . . to persuade Russia to initiate a coalition of the powers which should take advantage of England's difficulties in South Africa by making war upon her during her time of stress." (Ibid., pp. 761-763.) This is far too strong to agree with any of the rare translations of Osten-Sacken's letters, and no other documents substantiate the charge. In March, when Muravyev sought

Osten-Sacken then asked whether Germany would attack Russia in Europe, if it became involved in "serious complications in Asia" and had to intervene there "in the interests of peace and quiet." The kaiser answered this question by remarking that he "stood guard just as little for Great Britain in India as for the [Franco-Russian] Dual Alliance in East Africa." [o]

Muravyev, however, finally succeeded in persuading Delcassé to join with Russia in sounding out Germany concerning a future joint action to be made in London, in which Germany should take the initiative.[p] In consequence Muravyev's only known definite proposal was sent from St. Petersburg on 15/27 February, and was received in Berlin on the following day. It declared that the time had come when, as a result of the first important British victories in the South African war, it was desirable for the governments of Europe to join in friendly pressure upon Great Britain to put a stop to the bloody destruction, which could only end in the complete suppression of the Boer republics. In the event that the governments of Germany and France sympathized with this idea, the Russian government would be pleased to coöperate with them in an action in keeping with the humanitarian principles professed by the powers at the recent Hague conference.[q] The French reply to this overture is not known, and is of slight importance; for it depended primarily on the attitude of Germany whether this proposition for common representation was to

---

to convey the impression that the kaiser had suggested through Osten-Sacken that the Russian minister should take the initiative in proposing joint action against Great Britain, the denials by the kaiser and the German government were prompt, angry, and scathing. (See below, p. 38.) Lee never mentions these, although he must have known that they existed; and Muravyev needed no promptings from anyone to take the initiative in planning for representations to Great Britain, which he had actually begun in the previous October. This matter was still being disputed in the British foreign office early in 1907. *B. D.*, III, no. 445, Appendix B, pp. 426-433.

[o] *G. P.*, XV, no. 4465, p. 510. Some rumors sprang up in European capitals that secret negotiations were in progress between France, Germany, and Russia. Sir Charles Scott reported from St. Petersburg that the kaiser had told an unnamed diplomat: "The moment had now come for the powers to fall upon Great Britain, and he only marvelled that this did not happen." The German government denied this assertion. *B. D.*, I, no. 308, p. 247. *G. P.*, XV, no. 4469, p. 513; no. 4470, p. 514; no. 4471, p 515.

[p] *Ibid.*, no. 4474, and footnote *, p. 518.

[q] *Ibid.*, no. 4472, p. 516, where the French text of Muravyev's proposal is reproduced; see also footnote on p. 541. Lee, I, 766.

become a reality. All hope of this vanished because any German association with the other powers would only have taken place after their acceptance of almost impossible conditions.[r] The German government declined in any event to take the initiative in approaching Great Britain, and returned the compliment by pointing out how much more appropriate it would be for Russia to do this.[s]

The Russian minister considered the German attitude to be an "unequivocal rejection" of all participation, which bitterly disappointed him. Yet he made a last attempt to win German adherence by representing that it had been the kaiser who had first broached the subject to him through Osten-Sacken.[t] The kaiser indignantly labelled this assertion as "a brazen lie," declared that the ambassador "must correct his own minister," and expressed his unbounded contempt for Muravyev by calling him "ein kaltschnäuziger Lügnerischer Hallunke ohne Gleichen!"[u] Not only did the kaiser vigorously deny putting the idea up to the Russians, but he quickly revealed the nature of the proposal for joint mediation to the British.[v] However much the incurably loquacious kaiser attributed to his own efforts the forestalling of unfriendly continental combinations against Great Britain, the Russian foreign secretary's plan for embarrassing the British forthwith sickened and died. By the end of March 1900 British victories in South Africa made hopeless further prospects for interference. There were too many European preoccupations for other great powers to be free for the venture, while for political and financial reasons Russia was both unwilling and unable to accomplish anything

[r] G. P., XV, no. 4472, p. 517; no. 4476, p. 520; no. 4486, p. 528; no. 4496, pp. 541-542.

[s] Ibid., no. 4472, pp. 516-517; no. 4473, p. 517; no. 4476, p. 520, and the kaiser's marginal note 5.

[t] Ibid., no. 4476, p. 519; no. 4486, pp. 528-529.

[u] Ibid., no. 4486, kaiser's marginal notes 2 and 3, p. 530; and another pungently expressed denial: "Faule Fische, ich habe nie was ähnliches verlautbaren lassen," no. 4476, kaiser's marginal note 2, p. 520. For complete repudiations by the German government see no. 4496, p. 542; no. 4497, pp. 542-543; also no. 4394, footnote **, pp. 406-407; no. 4493, footnote *, p. 534.

[v] B. D., I, no. 313, p. 254. Lee, I, 769. G. P., XV, no. 4478, p. 521. For the British acknowledgments of the kaiser's communications, which pleased him, see Lee, I, 770, and G. P., XV, no. 4478, p. 521; no. 4480, pp. 523-524; kaiser's notes to no. 4475, p. 519.

alone.[w] Very likely Muravyev's own hatred of Great Britain
was the chief motivation, and therefore Goluchowski could
well express his conviction that, everything considered, Great
Britain "could not have entered on the contest in South Africa
with a freer hand." [x]

In January and February 1900 several of the Russian ministers did join Muravyev in composing memoranda revealing
what political advantages it seemed possible to pick up for
Russia in several parts of the world.[y] Muravyev was so fanciful that he suggested that Russia might purchase Ceuta from
Spain. Ceuta, which lay opposite Gibraltar, could be the answer to the British seizure of Weihaiwei in 1898, besides having an excellent strategic importance in the event of a war with
Great Britain.[z] Turning his restless thoughts next in the direction of the Near East, Muravyev continued with the idea that
Germany could not be permitted "to play the leading part at
the Bosphorus." The Russian ambassador in Berlin should
undertake to secure an agreement whereby Germany, as in the
time of William I, would recognize the exclusive right of

[w] B. D., I, no. 290, p. 237; no. 292, p. 238; no. 321, p. 258. Lee, I, footnote 1,
p. 771. G. P., XV, no. 4374, p. 388; no. 4464, footnote *, p. 508; no. 4486, pp.
529-530. See the kaiser's concluding note to no. 4458, p. 497, and his remark
to Sir Frank Lascelles: "I have kept those two tigers [France and Russia]
quiet." (B. D., I, no. 313, p. 254.) The editors of the Grosse Politik recognized
that the kaiser spoke too colorfully. It suits Lee's humorless point of view to
take seriously all that the kaiser claimed. (Lee, I, 769-773.) What the kaiser's
real attitude was to this entire question is best disclosed in two words minuted
on a report submitted by Bülow on 2 June 1900: "Count Alvensleben reports . . .
that Dr. Leyds also still holds on to the hope of an intervention of Russia and
France in case the governments of both these states had the certainty that Your
Majesty's government would associate itself with them [here the kaiser noted:
"No!"], or would at least let the action quietly occur [here the kaiser noted:
"yes," with no exclamation point]." G. P., XV, no. 4500, p. 546. Langer, II,
652-653.

[x] B. D., I, no. 290, p. 237. G. P., XV, no. 4491, p. 533; no. 4492, p. 533.

[y] Kriegsschuldfrage, VI, 645. The original Russian documents are printed in
Krasny Arkhiv, XVIII (1926), 3-29. A German commentary by V. A. Wro-
blewski, "Murajews Denkschrift aus dem Jahre 1900 und die englisch-russische
Konvention von 1907," is in Kriegsschuldfrage, V (1927), 1221-1228. Langer,
II, 665-667.

[z] Kriegsschuldfrage, VI, 646. Muravyev's opinion was opposed by the acting minister of the marine, Tyrtov, who pointed out how worthless Ceuta
would be to Russia, and by Witte as being too costly a possession. (Ibid., pp.
657, 661-664.) Something was known about Muravyev's activity since Goluchowski characterized it as "some absurd scheme." (B. D., I, no. 291, p. 237.) At San
Sebastian, on 5 October 1899, Muravyev, lying brazenly, told the Spanish
prime minister Silvela: "Russia did not have the slightest desire for" Ceuta.
G. P., XV, no. 4212, p. 131.

Russia "to the protection and in case of need to the actual occupation of the Bosphorus."[a] Russian diplomacy should try to win the assurance from Turkey that the Bosphorus would not be fortified. If the sultan could be made to promise that no railroad concessions would be granted to any foreign power, except Russia, within a definite region along the southern shore of the Black Sea, that would be adequate compensation for the concessions accorded Germany for the construction of the Bagdad railway.[b] There had been some suspicion in Europe during recent years that Russian policy was becoming more active in Balkan affairs, but the absorption of Russian attention all over Asia inclined foreign diplomats not to worry seriously about Russia and the régime of the straits.[c]

When Muravyev and his colleagues considered what advantages could be won for Russia in Asia, their proposals became more realistic. Further strengthening of the Russian dominating position in Persia seemed possible in several ways. The suggestion to seize a port on the Persian Gulf was laid aside as being too costly an undertaking, nor was anything done with the idea that a friendly understanding for the delimitation of spheres of influence should be reached with Great Britain. In 1900 Russia was too haughty and too successful to bargain and share.[d] Russian influence was so high that it seemed only necessary to give the weak shah of Persia a formal warning that Russia would not stand idly by if Persia should concede a port on the Gulf, or any nearby territory, in response to British demands, but that equivalent measures would be taken to reëstablish the Russian position.[e] Indeed Russia had just made another loan to the shah, which would probably result in the further ascendancy of Russian influence in Persia.[f]

[a] *Kriegsschuldfrage*, VI, 648-649; see also Kuropatkin's view as minister of war, p. 661.
[b] *Ibid.*, p. 648.
[c] *B. D.*, I, no. 367, and enclosure, pp. 296-297; no. 369, p. 298; no. 372, p. 301.
[d] *Kriegsschuldfrage*, VI, 650-651. Still later, on 26 August 1901, the Austro-Hungarian finance minister declared succinctly: "Every year that passed made Russia more powerful and more independent." (*B. D.*, I, no. 372, p. 301.) France was described as being disappointed "at the egotism and indifference of Russia." *Ibid.*, no. 351, p. 283.
[e] *Kriegsschuldfrage*, VI, 650-651. Langer, II, 752-759.
[f] *B. D.*, I, no. 310, p. 249. At the time this loan was made the kaiser, none

Nevertheless Muravyev and his fellow ministers reached the conclusion that Russia ought not to attempt the acquisition of new territory either in Persia or in Afghanistan, not even of the enticing province of Herat, because such action was undesirable politically and would possibly react badly upon the loosely held subject lands of central Asia, especially in the emirate of Bokhara. If no territory were wrested from the Amir of Afghanistan, hope ran high among the ministers that the maintenance of friendly relations would result in improved commercial intercourse and in some expansion of Russian political influence, which might culminate in permission to introduce Russian agents into the larger towns and trade centers.[g]

There was, to be sure, the incontestable fact that in 1872 and 1873 Russia had entered into treaties with Great Britain by which Afghanistan had freely been recognized as being outside the sphere of Russian action. These renunciations had been given a long time ago under vastly different circumstances; but treaties could be interpreted.[h] This time the Russians gave effect to their scheming in a famous memorandum of 6 February 1900, in which the old limitations upon Russian action in Afghanistan were reaffirmed, but were explained as referring only to political relationships. In the interval great changes had taken place in Russia's position in central Asia. No longer could a first rate power have no intercourse at all with a neighboring state, so the Russian government considered it indispensable to reëstablish direct frontier relations between the two countries, although assuredly these would be strictly non-political in nature.[i] This communication alarmed both the British government and the government of India, especially when it appeared that "the Russian government had no desire to enter into negotiations with the British government as to their future relations with Afghanistan, but mere-

---

too considerately, reminded Lascelles "of the prompt manner in which Lord Beaconsfield's government had purchased the Suez Canal shares." *Ibid.*, no. 311, p. 250. Langer, II, 668.

[g] *Kriegsschuldfrage*, VI, 653, 655.

[h] *B. D.*, I, no. 376, p. 306. *Kriegsschuldfrage*, VI, 653. Gwynn, I, 419.

[i] *B. D.*, I, no. 376, pp. 306-307; no. 377, enclosure, pp. 309-310.

ly made a formal notification of their intentions."[j] Such a startling innovation could not be allowed to rest, and in consequence an erratic, occasionally even an acrimonious correspondence started which never reached a satisfactory solution for more than seven years.[k]

During the Boer war Russia did not seriously consider any aggressive action against the British rule in India, although reports of increases in the Russian troops in central Asia, the conclusion of the successful military manoeuvers near Afghanistan, and the rapid extension of railroad construction to within less than one hundred miles of Herat caused many anxious moments for Great Britain.[l] On the whole Russian intentions here were unexpectedly peaceable, because the finance minister Witte was eager to obtain a commercial treaty with terms favorable for the trade which he hoped to foster between Russia and India. No success crowned his efforts, and a trade that in 1895 had had encouraging prospects for the future steadily declined, until by 1908 it had dwindled entirely away.[m] Still, the Russians were playing with the happy thought that the appointment in 1898 of Lord Curzon as viceroy of India might turn out to be of indirect benefit to Russia. He was known to be a notorious partisan of a "forward policy" in India, the actual carrying out of which, in the Russian estimation, could conceivably lead to renewed unrest, and possibly to uprisings of the native tribes, thereby weakening the British power in India.[n]

It was in the Far East in the years following the peace of Shimonoseki that Russian foreign policy had become most active. Muravyev congratulated himself in his memorandum of 1900 that the ice-free harbor of Port Arthur had been leased from China in 1898, and that in a short time it would be connected with the Transsiberian railroad by a branch line. When that should have been accomplished, he painted a fu-

---

[j] *Ibid.*, no. 377, p. 308.
[k] *Ibid.*, no. 377, enclosure, p. 311; IV, no. 465, pp. 513-515. Later phases of this correspondence over Afghanistan are given below, pp. 270-278.
[l] *B. D.*, I, no. 302, p. 244; no. 310, p. 249. *G. P.*, XV, no. 4464, footnote *, p. 508.
[m] Popov, *Krasny Arkhiv*, XIX, 57-58.
[n] *Ibid.*, pp. 56, 61-62.

ture in which Russia could participate in the affairs of the Far East and make its will forcefully felt.[o] His ardor must have been dampened by the reply of Tyrtov who pointed out that, while the possession of Port Arthur permitted Russia to exercise powerful influence in northern China and at Peking, its strategic importance vis-à-vis Japan was quite limited. This minister recommended that it should be an aim of Russian policy to obtain, either by diplomatic bargaining or by purchase, some one of the more advantageously located Korean ports, as Masampo, where of late Japan had not been paying much respect to Russian "rights."[p] Muravyev acted quickly upon this recommendation and forced the Korean government, by an agreement signed on 30 March 1900, to grant a concession of land for a Russian coal depôt and a naval hospital near Masampo, "by common consent far the finest harbor in the East."[q] Both British and Japanese opinion feared that the Russians would proceed to develop the concession into a naval base of greater importance than either Vladivostok or Port Arthur, which would consitute "a permanent menace to Japan." As a result, however, of vigorous opposition this agreement was finally thwarted.[r] Despite his animosity for Great Britain and his feverish, but inconstant efforts, Muravyev had not been able to take advantage of the embarrassment of that country to win any profit for his own. Soon afterwards he died and was succeeded by Count Lamsdorff, a more cautious and abler man.[s]

The general situation in the Far East, from the British point of view, remained "far from satisfactory" largely be-

[o] *Kriegsschuldfrage*, VI, 653-654.
[p] *Ibid.*, pp. 659-660.
[q] *B. D.*, II, no. 40, pp. 32-33.
[r] *Ibid.*, no. 39, p. 32; no. 41, p. 33; no. 117, p. 105.
[s] Lamsdorff took over Muravyev's office in midsummer 1900 and was definitely appointed foreign minister by the tsar early in 1901. He had spent his entire previous career at the foreign office, and Witte described him as "a walking archive of this ministry." Lamsdorff and Witte were close friends, and undoubtedly Witte's recommendation of him to the tsar played a rôle in the appointment. (Witte, *Vospominaniya*, I, 160.) While Lamsdorff was no genius, he was greatly superior to his predecessor, considered reliable by the Germans (Bernhard, Fürst von Bülow, *Denkwürdigkeiten*, [Berlin, 1930], II, 6), and soon won the compliment from Lord Lansdowne that he "has always impressed me favorably, and I am as ready as you [Sir Charles Scott] are to give him credit for a desire to pursue a conciliatory policy." Newton, p. 215.

cause "the influence of Russia in China was increasing." [t] A grasping policy, nominally conducted by the disapproving Lamsdorff, was forced upon him by a selfish group headed by the unprincipled concessionaires and chauvinists Bezobrazov and Abaza, and by the political-military adventurer Admiral Alexeyev, eager to exercise power in the Far East. What gave weight to the aims of this clique was the fact of their influence over the weak tsar, Nicholas II. Russia also participated fully in the international military efforts to suppress the Boxer movement around Peking, and when the disorders spread into Manchuria with the Chinese attacking the Russian railroad line during July 1900, a more private venture began with the military occupation of that province. On 4 August the town of Newchwang and its customs house were seized. [u] Lamsdorff gave assurances that no permanent conquest was contemplated, but that the Russian troops would be withdrawn following the pacification of the territory and the conclusion of an agreement with China intended to protect the railroad line from future raids, in addition to regulating the conditions of the evacuation. [v]

The terms which the Russians sought to include in the arrangement with China proved to be a new source of trouble. They were declared by some European powers and by Japan to be incompatible with the sovereignty and territorial integrity of China, besides constituting an impairment of the treaty rights of other powers. [w] In an attempt to forestall any Russian advantage and to protect their own positions Great Britain, Japan, and to a lesser degree Germany, endeavored to strengthen the back of the Chinese government by giving it the advice not to conclude any separate agreement with a single power which contained provisions of a dangerous character. [x] This supporting counsel was appreciated by the Chinese gov-

[t] *B. D.*, I, no. 311, p. 250.
[u] *Ibid.*, II, no. 1, p. 1.
[v] *Ibid.*, no. 42, and enclosure, p. 34.
[w] *Ibid.*, no. 44, p. 36; no. 45, p. 37; no. 46, p. 37; no. 71, p. 53. For the text of the first Russian demands upon China as transmitted from Peking to London on 6 March 1901, see no. 47, pp. 38-39.
[x] *Ibid.*, no. 44, p. 36; no. 60, p. 48; no. 67, p. 51. *G. P.*, XVI, no. 4812, pp. 317-318; no. 4814, p 321.

ernment and it continued to decline the Russian proposals, even when slightly modified.[y] Annoyed by the Chinese recalcitrancy, the Russian government suddenly announced, early in April 1901, that in the existing circumstances it appeared as if the efforts being made to arrive at a preliminary arrangement looking toward the restitution of Manchuria might cause serious difficulties for China rather than serve as a proof of Russia's friendly sentiments. The Russian memorandum ended on a threatening note:

Therefore the Imperial Cabinet not only does not insist on the conclusion of the arrangement with the Chinese government, but itself declines all further pourparlers on this subject and, resolutely faithful to the program which it has followed from the beginning, calmly awaits the development of events.[z]

In spite of their differences in China, the British foreign office believed that the Russians were in a friendly mood, with Nicholas II "all in favor of working on a good understanding with us." Lamsdorff seemed inclined to adopt a more conciliatory attitude, especially because he feared a future war with Japan.[a] This apparent friendliness was welcomed in London, where the generally hostile feelings of the great powers manifested during the South African war had revealed the dangers of British isolation as neither splendid nor secure. The activity of the venerable Salisbury was drawing to a close; his opinions were no longer unquestioned.[b] There was enough favorable feeling in the British government and in public opinion so that a "second attempt" was made "to arrive at a friendly understanding with Russia on Chinese questions"

[y] The Russian revised demands are summarized and commented upon by Lansdowne in *B. D.*, II, no. 60, pp. 47-48.
[z] *Ibid.*, no. 65, enclosure, p. 50. *G. P.*, XVI, no. 4838, pp. 351-352. The German comments and notes on this document clearly show that the veiled conclusion was fully appreciated. The Russian memorandum was made public on 5 April 1901.
[a] *B. D.*, II, no. 73, p. 55. Newton, p. 215.
[b] Nicolson, pp. 130-131. Grey, I, 40-41. Lee, I, note 3, p. 748; II, 727. Salisbury also had misgivings about the adequacy of British isolation, but he thought that "it would hardly be wise to incur novel and most onerous obligations, in order to guard against *a danger in whose existence we have no historical reason for believing.*" (*B. D.*, II, no. 86, p. 68.) Lansdowne admitted the force of this observation, but replied that "we may push too far the argument that, because we have in the past survived in spite of our isolation, we need have no misgivings as to the effect of that isolation in the future." *Ibid.*, no. 92, p. 77.

after the manner of that of 1898.[c] The Russians quickly made it clear that Great Britain could reach no agreement with them over the Manchurian situation, and this "second attempt" failed with hardly a trace left to show that it had ever been made.[d] Russian policy in Manchuria would concede nothing to the views of another power. Before long the demands which China must accept prior to the Russian military evacuation of the province were being pressed again. The British could do little more than to make a series of requests that Russia should promise to get out of Manchuria, in much the same manner that France had tried since 1882 to get Great Britain to withdraw from Egypt.[e]

The British were no more successful in 1901 in escaping from isolation by means of an alliance with Germany. The irrepressible Joseph Chamberlain had let the Germans know that the time had come when England must choose between the Triple or the Dual alliance, and that most of the cabinet, including himself, and the foreign office favored the first alternative, only turning to the other in the event of German unwillingness.[f] These negotiations, arising from a nebulous

[c] Newton, p. 216. Sir T. H. Sanderson, the permanent under secretary for foreign affairs, thought that "a good understanding [with Russia] . . . would be much the best plan if it could be managed." (*B. D.*, II, no. 73, p. 55.) Speaking in behalf of the opposition, on 26 July 1901 Sir Edward Grey declared that an understanding with Russia was "really vital to any satisfactory condition of affairs." (*Parliamentary Debates*, 4th series, XCVIII, 286-287.) An article by J. W. Gambier, "A Plea for Peace — an Anglo-Russian Alliance," *Fortnightly Review*, LXXIV (1900), 1002, 1006, based a desire for agreement with Russia on the grounds of commercial advantage as well as in behalf of world peace.

[d] Again during November 1901 Lansdowne suggested to Staal that Great Britain and Russia should reach an agreement in their Chinese relations. Staal replied evasively. While he personally wished to see the mutual distrust ended, he thought that Great Britain ought to make the first proposals because it had always attributed hostile intentions and malevolent plans to Russia. France, Ministère des affaires étrangères, Commission de publication des documents relatifs aux origines de la guerre de 1914, *Documents diplomatiques français (1871-1914)*, 2e série *(1901-1911)*, (Paris, 1930-), I, no. 493, p. 581; no. 523, p. 617. (Hereafter cited as *D. D. F.* All volumes used are in the second series.) Langer, II, 756-759.

[e] Newton, p. 216. *B. D.*, II, no. 1, p. 2; no. 75, pp. 56-57. It is rather surprizing to find Lansdowne calmly admitting that "Russia cannot be expected to withdraw at once and without precautions from territories which have been the scene of serious disturbances and which so closely adjoin her possessions, and the necessary provisional arrangements pending evacuation can scarcely fail to involve some derogation from the sovereign rights of China." *Ibid.*, no. 75, p. 57.

[f] *G. P.*, XVII, no. 4982, p. 19; no. 4994, p. 42. Lee, I, footnote 1, p. 798. Nicolson, p. 132. Fischer, pp. 201-202.

beginning in the spring, never became wholeheartedly intimate, languished over the summer, and were broken off entirely in December, leaving relations between the two countries only the worse for the trouble. Neither side had found the proposals of the other acceptable.[g] In both foreign offices, more especially in the German, there were ministers not in favor of an alliance. As the conversations dragged on without success, the feeling was voiced that the proper time had not yet come.[h] The British believed that the Germans demanded too much. The Germans were interested in getting the British to pay their price, and more often speculated academically how high that price ought to be than they made efforts to reach an agreement.[i] In consequence Great Britain looked in still another direction to find a partner for an alliance.

Ever since Great Britain had refused to join Russia, France and Germany in pressing Japan to reduce its demands upon China after the victorious war of 1895, British and Japanese policy towards China had followed a similar direction.[j] The Japanese government authorized its ambassador in London, Baron Hayashi, to suggest to Lord Lansdowne, on his own responsibility, that "some permanent understanding for the protection of their interests" in the Far East should be reached between them. No definite proposals were made at an interview on 17 April 1901, but after the Anglo-German discussions had lulled in midsummer, on 31 July Lansdowne hinted strongly that he would be ready to discuss Far Eastern policy "with a view to the possible establishment of an understanding

[g] B. D., II, no. 86, pp. 68-69; no. 91, p. 76; no. 92, p. 78; no. 94, p. 81. G. P., XVII, no. 4989, p. 35. For further details of this negotiation see G. P. Gooch, History of Modern Europe 1878-1919, (New York, 1923), pp. 324-330; S. B. Fay, The Origins of the World War, (New York, 1929), I, 135-141; Langer, II, 711-746; Eugene N. Anderson, The First Moroccan Crisis 1904-1906, (Chicago, 1930), pp. 52-81; Fischer, op. cit.; G. P., XVII, pp. 3-129.

[h] B. D., II, no. 81, p. 63; no. 91, pp. 73-76; no. 94, p. 82; no. 96, p. 85. G. P., XVII, no. 4983, p. 21; no. 4984, p. 22; no. 4989, p. 36; no. 4995, note 4, p. 44, for Bülow's "Kastanientheorie."

[i] Fischer, pp. ix, 201. G. P., XIV, part II, no. 4019, p. 544; XVII, no. 4991, p. 39; no. 4998, p. 49; no. 5019, pp. 86-88. Bülow believed that "British difficulties will still mount in the coming months, and therewith also the price which we can demand will increase. We must not show Great Britain any too great ardor, which would only heighten British claims and diminish our prospects for winnings." Ibid., no. 4983, p. 20.

[j] B. D., II, Editors' Note, p. 89; no. 102, p. 91; no. 124, p. 113.

between our two countries." [k] Two weeks later the Japanese acknowledged a readiness to treat, and Lansdowne told Hayashi that he should obtain definite proposals from the Japanese government, while the British foreign secretary would endeavor to be ready with a reply. The Japanese ambassador offered the first definite terms for an alliance with Great Britain on 16 October, when formal negotiations were begun.[l]

In undertaking these negotiations with an Asiatic power for the defence of British interests in Asia, British diplomacy followed established precedents.[m] The two parties easily agreed that if either were attacked in defence of their respective interests, the other needed only to maintain a strict neutrality. If, however, the attacking power were joined by an ally, (and in all probability this would be Russia aided by France), then both parties to the treaty would conduct the war henceforth in common, and would make peace in mutual agreement.[n] Each party had, however, certain bothersome special interests. The most coveted gain desired by Japan from the alliance was expressed with unmistakable frankness: the concern for the future of Korea. The Russian aggression in the Far East menaced Japanese interests not only in Manchuria, but also threatened to result in obtaining a preponderating influence in Korea, which Japan was determined to oppose.[o] The Japanese government declared that "they would certainly fight in order to prevent it, and it must be the object of their diplomacy to isolate Russia, with which power, if it stood alone, they were prepared to deal." [p] The British were well informed of the Japanese warlike attitude toward Russia, so they endeavored to avoid being drawn into a war as a sequel to any measures to which Japan might resort "however reckless or provocative,

---

[k] Pooley, *Hayashi*, p. 116. *B. D.*, II, no. 99, p. 89; no. 102, p. 91.
[l] *Ibid.*, no. 103, p. 92; no. 105, p. 97. In a memorandum of 11 November 1901, Lansdowne wrote: "In approaching the Japanese we have, indeed, virtually admitted that we do not wish to continue to stand alone." *Ibid.*, no. 92, p. 77.
[m] Dennis, p. 18.
[n] *B. D.*, II, no. 125, p. 117.
[o] *Ibid.*, no. 105, p. 97. Pooley, *Hayashi*, p. 125.
[p] *B. D.*, II, no. 102, p. 91.

in order to support her interests in Korea." [q] The best check that Great Britain could obtain in the treaty upon Japanese aggressiveness was the mutual statement in the preamble that both countries were "specially interested in maintaining the independence and territorial integrity of the Empire of China and the Empire of Korea," as well as the assertion in the first article that they both were "entirely uninfluenced by any aggressive tendencies in either country." [r]

For the purpose of getting a treaty at all Great Britain recognized the special interests of Japan in Korea. Lansdowne then wanted to extend the scope of the treaty to include British special interests in India, because it was only equitable that Japan should assist Great Britain if it became involved with two powers in a dispute originating over India. No persuasion, however, could win the acceptance of this proposal by the Japanese, and no mention of India was made in the final treaty.[s] In a diplomatic note which accompanied the treaty, the British government refused to assume an obligation to maintain a definite naval strength which would be at all times superior to that of any third power in the extreme east, but promised to maintain that superiority in so far as possible.[t] The journey of Marquis Ito to St. Petersburg at the end of 1901, however, temporarily threatened the successful issue of the alliance. In common with certain of the more venerable statesmen of Japan, he thought it would be more profitable to obtain an agreement with Russia over Korea than with Great Britain.[u] This mission to Russia caused some de-

[q] *Ibid.*, no. 110, p. 99; no. 117, p. 105. Pooley, *Hayashi*, pp. 129, 165. The *British Documents* are replete with indications of the Japanese bellicosity toward Russia.

[r] *B. D.*, II, no. 125, pp. 115-116. Hayashi had told Lansdowne that in his opinion "it was most unlikely that Japan, knowing as she must know what a war with Russia must mean, would light-heartedly involve herself in such a war for any but the most amply sufficient reasons." (*Ibid.*, no. 116, p. 104; no. 117, p. 105. Dennis, p. 6.) Nevertheless, "the Japanese, while no doubt desirous of peace, too, were careful to leave a loophole which would give them an excuse for war with Russia over Korea if necessary." Newton, p. 228.

[s] *B. D.*, II, no. 110, p. 99; no. 115, p. 102; no. 117, p. 104. Langer, II, 783. The expression "extreme east" in place of "Far East" was therefore used in the treaty to make sure of this limitation of the scope.

[t] *B. D.*, II, no. 115, p. 103; no. 121, p. 111; no. 125, pp. 119-120.

[u] Pooley, *Hayashi*, pp. 155, 158. Alexander A. Savinsky, *Recollections of a Russian Diplomat*, (London, 1927), p. 23. Newton, p. 223. K. K. Kawakami,

lay in the Anglo-Japanese negotiations and aroused suspicion in London, although the Japanese denied that his visit was responsible for the pause, or that he was in any manner authorized to discuss or to conclude an arrangement with Russia.[v] Ito did in fact nearly succeed in coming to an agreement in St. Petersburg, but when the Russians, as usual, procrastinated, he left without an answer.[w] A Japanese crown council definitely decided on 7 December for the agreement with Great Britain, after which the negotiations were hurried along so that the first alliance between Great Britain and Japan was signed on 30 January 1902.[x]

The reception of this treaty by the powers of Europe was quietly reserved, with an occasionally scornful remark because a western nation had made an alliance with one of the yellow race. The British foreign office was most interested in the reaction of Russia and France, against whom the alliance was primarily aimed. The French ambassador in London betrayed no sign to Lansdowne that he was aware that "the agreement was in any way directed against France," but he did complain of the excessive distrust in England "as to Russian designs in different parts of the world," while in Paris by the very brevity of his comments Delcassé showed how little he liked the alliance.[y] Lamsdorff sought to cloak his surprize and displeasure by seeing in the objects and terms of the treaty only those "in such complete accordance with intimate views and repeated declarations of the Russian government that he was disposed to ask permission to associate Russia

"Prince Ito's Confidential Papers," *Foreign Affairs*, XI (New York, 1933), 493-495.

[v] *B. D.*, II, no. 112, p. 100; no. 113, p. 101. Kawakami, *Foreign Affairs*, XI, 495.

[w] Savinsky, p. 23. Savinsky believes that Russia hesitated to give Japan a free hand in Korea because of the need felt for a port between Port Arthur and Vladivostok, and because Russia doubtless harbored later designs on Korea; but had the agreement been concluded with Ito there would not have been war in 1904. (*Ibid.*, p. 301.) In 1905 Witte said: "If in 1901 we had accepted Marquis Ito's proposal, Japan would not have formed an alliance with England." (I. Ya. Korostovetz, *Pre-War Diplomacy. The Russo-Japanese Problem*, [London, 1920], p. 57.) See also *G. P.*, XVII, no. 5042, pp. 144-145.

[x] *C. H. B. F. P.*, III, 292. W. L. Langer, "Die Entstehung des russisch-japanischen Kriegs," *Europäische Gespräche*, IV (1926), 300-303. Pooley, *Hayashi*, pp. 195, 206. Kawakami, *Foreign Affairs*, XI, 495-496.

[y] *B. D.*, II, no. 131, pp. 124-125; no. 137, p. 128.

with the two governments in their agreement;" but he was dissuaded from this step by his inability to understand precisely why the articles regarding the eventuality of any hostilities were included.[z] A few days later he expressed his regret that the Anglo-Japanese agreement would probably retard the realization of the desire "for a frank and friendly understanding" with Great Britain in the Far East.[a]

Lamsdorff, however, quickly and secretly set about devising a rejoinder to neutralize the effect of the Anglo-Japanese alliance, to which he hoped the nations of Europe would subscribe. After the tsar had approved his proposal, he sent it to Paris where Delcassé promptly accepted it in principle.[b] With some revision the joint Franco-Russian note of 16 March, which set forth the manner in which they regarded the recent treaty, was made ready for communication along with an invitation to the great powers to associate themselves with it. The note approved the declared purposes of the agreement to preserve peace in the Far East, to maintain the independence of China and Korea, and the "open door" for the commerce and industry of all nations, but concluded with this strong declaration:

Nevertheless, being obliged themselves also to take into consideration the case in which either the aggressive action of third powers or the recurrence of disturbances in China, jeopardizing the integrity and free development of that power, might become a menace to their own interests, the two allied governments reserve to themselves the right to consult in that contingency as to the means to be adopted for safeguarding those interests.[c]

Austria-Hungary willingly adhered, but Lamsdorff was painfully disappointed when Germany, although appreciating the substance of the statement, remained aloof because it had only commercial interests in China.[d] This counter-declaration was

---

[z] *Ibid.*, no. 130, p. 124. *G. P.*, XVII, no. 5047, p. 155.
[a] *B. D.*, II, no. 140, p. 130.
[b] *D. D. F.*, II, no. 79, p. 87; no. 97, p. 112; no. 98, p. 113. *G. P.*, XVII, no. 5049, p. 157; no. 5057, p. 170.
[c] The full text is reprinted in *D. D. F.*, II, no. 145, pp. 177-178. *G. P.*, XVII, no. 5064, Anlage, p. 180. *B. D.*, II, no. 145, enclosure, p. 135. English translation partly in Dennis, pp. 8-9.
[d] *G. P.*, XVII, no. 5050, p. 158; no. 5064, pp. 179-180. *D. D. F.*, II, no. 156, pp. 187-188.

as little to the liking of Great Britain as the treaty in reply
to which it was made had been to Russia or France. For the
immediate future Anglo-Russian relations were cool, and once
again the prospects for a general understanding went glim-
mering.[e]

Russian policy then followed its own course, but no provoking incidents upset Anglo-Russian relations during the remainder of 1902. Russia succeeded in making an agreement
with not too derogatory conditions for China by which the
Russian troops would be withdrawn from Manchuria in three
stages, to be completed by 8 October 1903, if nothing happened to alter the plans.[f] The real region of rivalry between
Great Britain and Russia in Asia was centering around Persia,
where Russian activity had progressed slowly and surely for
many years but of late had been intensified. This was partly
because with the coming of Lord Curzon's impetus, British
policy discarded its apparent indifference. Attempts were made
to retain and to regain the British paramount position in
southern Persia with some indications of success, although the
increased opposition to the expansion of Russian political and
commercial influence in the rest of the land remained futile.[g]
The British position in the Persian Gulf also seemed threatened by the plans for the Bagdad railway, so that the London
financial interests refused, early in 1903, to participate in its
construction, partly because the German terms did not guarantee equal influence to other nations in the control of the project, and partly because British public opinion was vigorously
hostile to it.[h] In order to defend British interests around the

[e] B. D., I, no. 338, p. 273; II, no. 145, minute by King Edward, p. 136. G. P.,
XVII, no. 5065, p. 181. Newton, p. 234

[f] B. D., II, no. 144, pp. 132-135; no. 225, p. 198. The text of this agreement
of 8 April 1902 is in Accounts and Papers, CXX, 172-173.

[g] D. D. F., I, no. 225, p. 265; no. 396, pp. 474-476; II, no. 256, pp. 311-312;
III, no. 232, p. 312; no. 410, pp. 548-549. B. D., IV, no. 321 (a), pp. 369-371.
Newton, pp. 234-235.

[h] Lansdowne disapproved of "the 'scuttle' of the financiers." He believed
that "although our abstention may have the effect of retarding the completion
of the line, I feel little doubt that it will eventually be made. That it should
be made without British participation would, to my mind, be a national misfortune." (B. D., II, no. 216, p. 187; no. 224, p. 196.) Russia did not approve
of the project, and France officially refused to participate. Ibid., no. 217, p.
188; no. 223, p. 194.

Gulf from Russian aggression and from a future terminus of the Bagdad railway, if not under British control, Lansdowne pronounced his famous warning in the house of lords on 5 May. Great Britain did not desire, he insisted, to exclude from the Gulf the legitimate trade of any nation, but "we should regard the establishment of a naval base or of a fortified port in the Persian Gulf by any other power as a very grave menace to British interests, and we should certainly resist it with all the means at our disposal." [i]

Anglo-Russian relations suddenly clouded over again when it became known late in April 1903 that Russia was insisting upon new conditions which China must accept before Russian troops would be finally withdrawn from Manchuria as had been stipulated. In Great Britain these additional demands, seven in number, were "considered highly objectionable, as being derogatory to the sovereignty of China and detrimental to the interests of the powers." [j] Lamsdorff denied that there was any intention "of departing from the published declarations and assurances which had been given with regard to the evacuation of Manchuria, or infringing on the treaty rights of other powers." [k] It was quickly apparent that Lamsdorff was badly informed and that this question was not being handled by the Russian foreign office, but in some more devious way. On 13 August Admiral Alexeyev was appointed viceroy of the Far Eastern provinces, and the tsar elevated Bezobrazov to be a special foreign minister, reporting directly to himself. This establishment of "two foreign offices" became well known in Europe and made Russian policy hopelessly inconsistent, and Count Lamsdorff's position ineffective. [l]

This latest Russian adventure immediately produced an exceedingly tense atmosphere in Japan, and the Japanese foreign minister, Baron Komura, spoke "with unwonted serious-

[i] *Parliamentary Debates*, 4th series, CXXI, 1348. B. D., II, no. 222, pp. 193-194; IV, no. 321 (a), pp. 370-371. G. P., XVII, no. 5364, pp. 560-561. D. D. F., IV, no. 5, pp. 10-13; no. 25, pp. 35-37.
[j] B. D., II, no. 225, p. 198; no. 226, p. 199.
[k] Ibid., no. 230, p. 203; no. 231, p. 203.
[l] Ibid., no. 244, p. 213; no. 248, p. 216; no. 250, p. 218; no. 258, p. 223. G. P., XVIII, part I, no. 5425, pp. 81-83. D. D. F., IV, no. 5, pp. 10-13; no. 25, pp. 35-37. Bompard, pp. 20-24, 31.

ness" to Sir Claude MacDonald, the British minister at Tokyo. The earliest indications of the Japanese attitude revealed a willingness to go to extreme, although as yet not precisely defined lengths. On 3 July 1903 Lansdowne was informed that Japan no longer felt safe in maintaining its "attitude of watchful reserve" or "the policy of forbearance" towards Russia, but proposed to offer to that power as a solution of the present situation "a mutual engagement to respect the independence and territorial integrity of China and Korea, and to maintain the principle of equal opportunity for the commerce and industry of all nations in those two countries."[m] The British government, with some reluctance, saw "no reason for dissuading the Japanese government" from embarking on this new departure, but reserved the right to protect its own interests, or to consider becoming a party to any successful issue, under proper conditions.[n] The Japanese government thereupon addressed proposals to the Russian foreign office and negotiations were opened, which appeared for some time as if they might lead to a satisfactory understanding.[o]

This notice of Japanese intentions to seek an agreement with Russia was followed from August onwards by a renewed effort on the part of Lansdowne to engage Russia in discussions for a friendly arrangement with Great Britain on those "other points" of clashing interests not resolved by the agreement of 1899, which now "must, of course, include the Manchurian question."[p] While never a word was written that might betray any interrelation between the two moves, no stretch of the imagination is required to perceive that British policy was trying to rival the Japanese ally in gaining the benefits to be derived from agreement with Russia. An agreement between Russia and Japan would make one with Great Britain needless

---

[m] *B. D.*, II, no. 226, p. 199; no. 237, pp. 206-207. Japan professed a desire for "an amicable adjustment" with Russia. "It was not necessary at this time to attempt to say what the result of Russia's rejection of such proposals would be, but the responsibility for whatever consequences might ensue would lie solely upon her." *Ibid.*, no. 238, p. 208.

[n] *Ibid.*, no. 239, p. 210. The best reason why Japan received British permission was expressed by Sir Claude MacDonald: "I do not think any objection we may make will deter them." *Ibid.*, no. 240, p. 211.

[o] *Ibid.*, no. 245, p. 214; no. 248, p. 216; no. 254, p. 220.

[p] *Ibid.*, no. 242, p. 212; no. 243, p. 213.

for Russia, since the British would no longer be in a position
to offer anything to Russia in Manchuria. Indeed Benckendorff had received Lansdowne's assurance that, if Great Britain and Russia should make an arrangement over that province, Russia could count on British assistance in bringing about
an arrangement with China satisfactory to Russia.[q]

The French were eager to promote good relations between
their older ally and their coming friend, and this had been a
motivating purpose in Delcassé's foreign policy during his tenure of office. Some care had also to be bestowed on Franco-
Russian relations, because the honeymoon ardor of the allies
had worn off: they were no longer self-sufficient, and sought
for other distractions and friendships.[r] While France had
taken "an extra dance" with Italy, coquetted with Spain, and
flirted across the channel, Russia had shown no jealousy but
had turned to Vienna, where a family welcome had been extended. This intimacy with Austria, which had arisen from
coöperation in Balkan affairs, had also produced improved
relations between Germany and Russia, until by 1903 talk of
the revival of something similar to the old League of the
Three Emperors echoed in the chancelleries.[s] Some suspicion
existed that Lamsdorff was not pleased with Delcassé's anglo-
philism, in consequence of which the Dual alliance "had been
penetrated by a mortal virus."[t] The French realized that
Russia must be assured that their alliance still formed the
basis for French policy, but that only the benefit of improved
relations between Russia and Great Britain would come from
a successful agreement between the latter and France. Lamsdorff seemed to agree that there were no insuperable barriers
to the realization of harmony with Great Britain, where it
was becoming realized that the full advantage of a rapprochement with France would never be enjoyed until an understanding had also been achieved with Russia.[u]

[q] *Ibid.*, no. 243, p. 213.
[r] *D. D. F.*, III, no. 370, p. 484; IV, no. 317, p. 422. Newton, p. 285.
[s] *D. D. F.*, III, no. 32, pp. 41-43; IV, no. 317, pp. 419, 421. *G. P.*, XVIII,
part II, no. 5911, pp. 839-840.
[t] *Ibid.*, no. 5888, pp. 806-807. *D. D. F.*, IV, no. 317, p. 420.
[u] *Ibid.*, III, no. 397, pp. 527-528; no. 410, pp. 547, 550. Lee, II, 281. Bencken-

Reports had already come from the German embassy in London which placed the prospect of a new three power combination of Great Britain, France and Russia before the officials of the Berlin foreign office. The British had tried to get the Russians to consider a peaceful settlement of their conflicting interests in Persia and elsewhere, but had received no encouragement. Negotiations for the composition of Anglo-French differences were, however, reputedly under way.[v] While Bülow thought that there was scant probability of the achievement of either agreement, he was not so certain of his opinion that he did not at once ask for the ripely considered views of the ambassadors in London, St. Petersburg and Paris. The replies were nearly unanimous in their conviction that far too many insurmountable obstacles still existed in the way of the creation of any such combination that could be dangerous to Germany.[w] Bülow summed up these reports as giving additional proof that there was no likelihood of a "Russian-French-English brotherhood" within any predictable time, and that "we cannot take things too coolly."[x] Once again full faith in Holstein's unalterable antagonisms was reaffirmed.

On the eve of Lamsdorff's visit to Delcassé in Paris at the end of October, Lansdowne made his greatest attempt to draw Russia into conversations by which a stop could be put to their disputes. He complained to the French ambassador that he had not been able to start negotiations with the Russian government, and that he knew neither what it desired nor what it

dorff, who replaced Staal in London in 1903, told Paul Cambon that Russia was not disturbed by the Anglo-French conversations but counted upon them to help improve Anglo-Russian relations. *D. D. F.*, III, no. 393, p. 521.

[v] *G. P.*, XVII, no. 5361, p. 557; no. 5369, p. 569.

[w] *Ibid.*, no. 5370, pp. 571-572; no. 5371, pp. 573-577, from London; no. 5372, pp. 577-580, from St. Petersburg; no. 5373, pp. 581-585, from Paris. A second report from Paris did mention that there was some belief that an Anglo-French agreement could be realized, but the German ambassador was not impressed by the sources of his information, nor was it seriously considered in Berlin. (*Ibid.*, no. 5374, pp. 585-587.) Alvensleben reported that an attaché of the British embassy in St. Petersburg had admitted that "the Russians would indeed be foolish if they let themselves in for such an understanding" with Great Britain. *Ibid.*, no. 5372, p. 578.

[x] *Ibid.*, no. 5375, pp. 588-589; XVIII, part II, no. 5911, pp. 839-840. Alvensleben advised that there was no reason why Germany should not press on with no show of weakness in the forthcoming negotiations with Russia for the renewal of the favorable commercial treaty of 1894. *Ibid.*, XVII, no. 5372, pp. 579-580.

was prepared to do. He hoped that during their meeting Delcassé would be able to prevail upon Lamsdorff to discuss matters with Great Britain in the same frank spirit as the British were carrying on the exchange of ideas with France.[y] Delcassé took full advantage of the occasion to impress upon Lamsdorff that "a little more frankness was desirable and would be calculated to smooth difficulties" in Russian relations with the British. Lamsdorff recognized that this was true and declared that Russia was ready to explain things in a most conciliatory and friendly manner through Benckendorff, who would soon receive instructions.[z] An unusually long and pleasant interview between Lansdowne and Benckendorff followed on 7 November, which "broke the ice."

Count Lamsdorff felt strongly [so Lansdowne noted] that it was of importance that an endeavor should be made to remove all sources of misunderstanding between the two governments, and that there should be "a change for the better" in our relations. Count Benckendorff was therefore instructed to discuss frankly with me the various questions outstanding between Great Britain and Russia, with the object of arriving at an agreement as to the manner in which they should be dealt with. In the meantime, the Russian government would be careful to avoid any action bearing the appearance of hostility to this country.[a]

Lansdowne expressed his real pleasure upon hearing Lamsdorff's views, as well as his readiness to contribute to the realization of an agreement.[b] A second meeting ten days later was less satisfactory because Benckendorff, willing enough to discuss the Russian attitude, was still without authority to offer specific proposals. Lansdowne was less encouraged and even "disposed to think that our discussions are not likely to

[y] B. D., II, no. 242, p. 212; no. 250, p. 218. D. D. F., IV, no. 44, pp. 66-67; see also III, no. 393, pp. 520-521. Un Diplomate, Paul Cambon, ambassadeur de France, 1843-1924, (Paris, 1937), p. 218. This volume is hereafter cited as Paul Cambon.

[z] B. D., II, no. 257, p. 221. D. D. F., IV, no. 49, p. 72; no. 58, p. 83. The German foreign office noticed that the unfriendly criticism of Great Britain in the Russian press was replaced by kindlier comments and suggestions of a possible agreement. It was believed that Lamsdorff had requested this change following his visit in Paris. G. P., XVII, no. 5366, p. 562; no. 5367, p. 563.

[a] B. D., II, no. 258, p. 222. G. P. Gooch, "Die Entstehung der Triple Entente," Berliner Monatshefte, VII (1929), 595.

[b] Lansdowne complained to Cambon that only generalities were discussed, and nothing precise was suggested. D. D. F., IV, no. 77, p. 103.

have much result." Nevertheless he explained to the ambassador in considerable detail, on 25 November, what concessions would be expected from Russia, along with what recognition would be accorded Russian interests, in any agreement for the regulation of their relations in Asia.[c]

In truth these conversations did not have much result partly because the Russian attitude remained vague, but more because the British had not been careful to avoid actions in Asia which upset the Russian government by their evident hostility.[d] To emphasize the warning given in the Persian Gulf declaration of 5 May, Curzon had already been granted the permission refused him in 1901 to make a triumphal cruise in those waters to parade the greatness of British predominance before the eyes of the impressionable natives. This pompous show went on through November with the viceroy "escorted . . . by an imposing naval force . . . in almost swashbuckling style."[e] Appearances were made in well-nigh regal circumstance at many of the port towns where speeches of welcome, often imposed textually in advance, were pronounced by humiliated natives.[f] What Lansdowne delightfully phrased as "George Curzon's prancings in the Persian puddle" worried the Russian government, while in London it was hoped that no serious consequences would follow.[g] Curzon was also sponsoring a diplomatic mission to Tibet led by Colonel Younghusband, but the Tibetans had stubbornly refused to treat with it. By the end

[c] *B. D.*, IV, no. 181 (a), pp. 183-184; no. 182, pp. 186-188. King Edward was interested in these conversations and had a long discussion with Benckendorff. (*Ibid.*, no. 181 (b), p. 186. Lee, II, 281.) Sir Charles Hardinge, an under secretary in the foreign office but soon to be ambassador in St. Petersburg, believed that Benckendorff had talked matters over with Lamsdorff so that the views he expressed, even if without instructions or details, "represent to a certain extent those of Lamsdorff, although he has very likely kept something back." *B. D.*, IV, no. 181 (b), pp. 185-186. Bompard, p. 237.

[d] Newton, p. 287.

[e] Ronaldshay, II, 314. *D. D. F.*, IV, no. 6, pp. 13-15; no. 55, p. 78. The *British Documents* are remarkably silent on this episode.

[f] *D. D. F.*, IV, no. 92, p. 119. Newton, p. 243. The French thought the whole show to be "a simple bluff in the familiar English style." (*D. D. F.*, IV, no. 55, p. 79.) M. Defrance wrote from Teheran an amusing description of the voyage, of Curzon's kidney trouble, and of his failure to arrange a sufficiently imposing reception for himself at Bushire. *Ibid.*, no. 123, pp. 178-181.

[g] Newton, p. 287. *D. D. F.*, IV, no. 92, pp. 119-120. Lansdowne assured Cambon that Curzon was making an "inspection of the consulates" run by the government of India, but that there was no intention of altering the *status quo* in the Gulf. *Ibid.*, no. 76, p. 102.

of 1903 a strong military escort was added, which virtually transformed the mission into an expeditionary corps, ostensibly to assure the protection of the commissioner, but actually to fight its way into Tibet even to the forbidden city of Lhasa, there to compel the monks to enter into negotiations.[h] As this expedition went slowly along its route, the Russian government became increasingly anxious, not only for the spread of British influence in a new region, but for the impression it would make upon a few million Buddhist Buriat subjects in Siberia, who looked upon the holy places of Lhasa as something in the nature of a Vatican. The Russian attitude was one of ominous silence, and Lansdowne took occasion to explain to Benckendorff that the expedition had been undertaken "owing to the outrageous conduct of the Tibetans . . . but that this step must not be taken as indicating any intention of annexing or even of permanently occupying Tibetan territory." [i]

What definitely put an end to Lansdowne's quest for friendly relations with Russia was the steadily growing trouble between Russia and Japan in the Far East. Their relations took a turn for the worse early in October 1903 when the ascendancy of the clique of adventurers revealed the impotence of Witte and Lamsdorff.[j] By the beginning of 1904 the negotiations had reached an impasse and the Japanese, becoming continually more warlike, had presented their last proposals which were "the irreducible minimum" that they would accept.[k] On the other hand, Russia had moderated its position until it was willing to accord nearly all Japan demanded in Korea. Of the three disputed points remaining (the unrestricted right of Japanese settlements in Manchuria, the creation of a neutral zone in Korea south of the Russian border,

---

[h] *B. D.*, IV, Editors' Note, p. 305. *D. D. F.*, IV, no. 73, p. 99. Lee, II, 369. For a more detailed description of the Younghusband expedition see below, pp. 67-70, 185-191.

[i] *B. D.*, II, no. 258, pp. 223-224. *D. D. F.*, IV, no. 129, pp. 188-189; no. 168, pp. 237-239.

[j] *Ibid.*, no. 5, pp. 10-13; no. 14, p. 25; no. 25, pp. 35-37; no. 82, pp. 108-109. *B. D.*, II, no. 263, p. 227. *G. P.*, XVIII, part I, no. 5425, pp. 81-83.

[k] *B. D.*, II, no. 265, pp. 227-228; no. 267, p. 229; no. 275, pp. 233-234. *G. P.*, XIX, part I, no. 6038, p. 187. *D. D. F.*, IV, no. 146, pp. 203-204.

and Russian recognition of Manchuria as an integral part of China), the last was the most important.[1] The Russian government refused to enter into a treaty engagement with Japan, or any other power, to recognize the sovereignty and territorial integrity of China in Manchuria, but was ready to make a simple declaration to this effect to all the powers, including Japan.[m] Most of the opposition in Russia to satisfying the Japanese demands centered around the tsar, but in January 1904 the "earnest efforts" of "powerful influences" to persuade him to give some satisfaction to Japan seemed to be succeeding. It was believed that Lamsdorff had been restored to control in Far Eastern affairs; and the British ambassador reported from St. Petersburg that the "situation appears to have changed for the better." [n]

Lamsdorff needed some time to prepare a conciliatory answer to the latest Japanese proposals, which he thought he could accomplish. Meanwhile he eagerly turned to Delcassé with requests that France should try to persuade Japan to adopt a moderate attitude, as well as asking Great Britain to associate itself with France in the task. Lamsdorff gave unmistakable hints of his personal desire for mediation, more than once directly to the British.[o] Delcassé promptly took up Lamsdorff's suggestion and worked hard to moderate Japan, but without success because ambassador Motono admitted that he had little credit with his government, while evidence

[1] *Ibid.*, no. 181, note 2, p. 254. *B. D.*, II, no. 284, p. 241. Bompard, pp. 40-44. Tyler Dennett, *Roosevelt and the Russo-Japanese War*, (New York, 1925), p. 102. The Japanese themselves did not care whether the territorial integrity of China in Manchuria was preserved or not. They were clearly concerned to keep Russia from establishing a protectorate over Manchuria, as well as a loophole for their own later penetration. (*B. D.*, II, no. 274, p. 233; no. 284, p. 240.) The last thing that the Russians would have conceded was the free right of settlement to Japan, because if that were "granted to [the] Japanese [it] would mean their swarming over Manchuria." (*Ibid.*, no. 280, p. 237.) It has taken more time for other powers to appreciate the Russian viewpoint.

[m] *Ibid.*, no. 252, p. 219; no. 283, p. 240; no. 295, p. 247. Lansdowne thought the Japanese insistence upon a treaty engagement proper because they were willing to pledge themselves in an agreement "to respect the integrity and independence of Korea." (*Ibid.*, no. 296, p. 249.) Yet he had already been informed that a successful conclusion to the negotiations with Russia "would permit the Japanese to consolidate their position in Korea, which they would strain every nerve to do." *Ibid.*, no. 254, p. 220.

[n] *Ibid.*, no. 264, p. 227; no. 281, p. 237. *D. D. F.*, IV, no. 211, p. 285.

[o] *Ibid.*, no. 171, pp. 241-242; no. 185, p. 258; no. 193, p. 270. *B. D.*, II, no. 279, p. 236. Bompard, pp. 46-49.

continued to accumulate that Japan desired and was rapidly preparing for war.[p] The French minister tried valiantly to have Great Britain join in offering "sedative advice" to its yellow ally, but Lansdowne absolutely refused to encourage Japan to modify its demands.[q] At no time throughout the crisis, not even in behalf of peace known to be endangered, did the British foreign office put any pressure upon Japan, because it knew that no mediation or interference was wanted.[r] Just when the Russian reply to the Japanese demands was nearly ready to be sent, Lansdowne first showed some willingness to advise Japan to accept it if the terms were at all reasonable.[s] Before anything happened, without waiting for the Russian reply to arrive, the Japanese broke off the negotiations on 6 February and determined to "take such independent action as they may deem best to consolidate and defend their menaced positions as well as to protect their established rights and legitimate interests. . . ."[t]

The Japanese action caught the Russians off guard. While Lamsdorff was surprized and disappointed at the rupture, he still did not expect that war would come in a hurry. He turned now with urgent appeals to the British government to use its influence, but Lansdowne "had no idea of putting pressure upon Japan."[u] Suddenly, two days in advance of the formal declaration of war, hostilities began on 8 February with the Japanese attack on Russian warships in the harbor of

[p] *D. D. F.*, IV, no. 172, pp. 242-243; no. 208, pp. 282-283; no. 222, pp. 300-301. Both the French and German documents give much clearer indications of Japan's spirit and preparations for war than do the British.
[q] *Ibid.*, no. 195, p. 272; no. 215, p. 293. *B. D.*, II, no. 283, p. 240.
[r] *Ibid.*, no. 268, p. 229; no. 280, p. 237. *D. D. F.*, IV, no. 220, p. 297; no. 246, p. 327. In a telegram of 5 February 1904 to the British ambassador in Washington, Lansdowne indicated some of "our private views" in declining to ask Japan to abate its demands: "We might, moreover, incur [the] lasting resentment of Japan if we were to stand in her way and deprive her of an opportunity which she is apparently determined to turn to account. If she were to miss her chance now she might suffer for it hereafter." *B. D.*, II, no. 288, p. 243. Newton, p. 309.
[s] *D. D. F.*, IV, no. 239, pp. 319-320. *B. D.*, II, no. 284, p. 241.
[t] *Ibid.*, no. 287, pp. 242-243; no. 292, pp. 245-246. Bompard, pp. 48-49.
[u] *B. D.*, II, no. 293, p. 246; no. 294, p. 247; no. 295, pp. 247-249. *D. D. F.*, IV, no. 245, pp. 324-325; no. 246, p. 327. It has been suggested that Great Britain acted callously "in the hope that the struggle would weaken and exhaust the Japanese just as well as the common enemy [Russia]." Langer, *Europäische Gespräche*, IV, 322.

Port Arthur.[v] For the duration of the Russo-Japanese war it was naturally impossible to expect any prolongation of the Anglo-Russian conversations for an understanding in Asia. Large groups of important opinion in Russia were, and for a long time remained, bitterly angry at Great Britain believing, with good reason, that the "race of monkeys" would never have dared move against great Russia without the surety of the British alliance.[w] Yet, for the first time since the idea of a broad understanding between Great Britain and Russia had been gingerly tossed about, this last overture was destined not to be completely forgotten. During the entire course of the war, even when incidents happened which threatened the peace between the two powers, the idea persisted with just enough life that at some more auspicious, future time, the consideration of the methods by which a compromise of their conflicting interests could be reached would be revived.[x]

The progress of Japanese soldiers into Manchuria and around Port Arthur, with the Russian troops slowly but steadily retiring, came as something of a surprize to a world not then believing in the possibility of a Japanese victory. Even Japan's first great success at the Yalu river at the beginning of May 1904, and the continued investment of Port Arthur did not seem to forecast other and greater victories in the future. Yet the steady Japanese advance had upset so many expectations that governments, and the writers of articles, cast around increasingly throughout 1904 for explanations of the illogical military situation. Upon consideration it became ob-

[v] D. D. F., IV, no. 257, pp. 338-339; no. 274, footnote 2, p. 356. Savinsky, p. 80. Bülow retails the story that, at a ball given by the tsar on the evening before the Japanese attack, the Japanese ambassador "with the immovable countenance" of the Oriental told the Countess Alvensleben, wife of the German ambassador: "The poor tsar does not know that while he speaks with me here, his squadron in Port Arthur is being sunk by us." Bülow, *Denkwürdigkeiten*, II, 22-23. H. H. Fisher, editor, *Out of My Past. The Memoirs of Count Kokovtsov*, (Stanford University, California, 1935), pp. 8-9.

[w] Bompard, p. 54. Lansdowne agreed with this judgment in a memorandum of 18 April 1904 to King Edward: "The Anglo-Japanese alliance, although not intended to encourage the Japanese government to resort to extremities, had, and was sure to have, the effect of making Japan feel that she might try conclusions with her great rival in the Far East — free from all risk of a European condition such as that which had on a previous occasion, deprived her of the fruits of victory." Newton, p. 309.

[x] Bompard, pp. 8, 237. *Paul Cambon*, p. 219.

vious that Japan had several initial advantages. It was much nearer the theater of operations and consequently could transport troops and supplies in greater numbers and quantities than could the Russians. All Russian reënforcements had to come over the single-track railroad across Siberia; and even this railroad was not completed around the mountainous southern end of Lake Baikal before 1905. Dissensions existed among the Russian generals; the disorder in the army was amazing. The warships stuck close to their anchorages at Port Arthur and Vladivostok, while the soldiers, being outnumbered and awaiting reënforcements, defended only the most favorable positions.[y] The German emperor merely expressed a generally held belief when he wrote to the tsar on 6 June 1904, that he hoped General Kuropatkin would not risk exposing his troops to a serious check "before the whole of his reserves have joined him, which are as I believe still partly on the way."[z] It was commonly thought that Time was on the side of the Russians; with time, the troops and supplies on the way from Russia would recover what had been lost.

The Russian people as a whole even from the beginning had very little interest in the war, and did not support the government in its efforts to carry on the fight. A belief quickly arose that Japan would not have gone to war had it not been encouraged by Great Britain, and secured against complications by the agreement of 1902.[a] Anglo-Russian relations were embittered, and the British government felt itself confronted by one of the greatest dangers which had threatened it in recent years.[b] The mobilization of Russian troops, the great increase of their number in central Asia and the Turkestan steppes,

[y] See the tsar's remarks on the situation to the kaiser, *G. P.*, XIX, part I, no. 6034, p. 181. In April 1904 the German General Staff believed in the eventual victory of Russia, even if it had no definite views on the matter. So too did Kuropatkin. *Ibid.*, no. 6031, p. 175; no. 6043, pp. 196-197.

[z] I. D. Levine, (edited by N. F. Grant), *The Kaiser's Letters to the Tsar*, (London, [1920]), p. 118. Hereafter cited as *Kaiser's Letters. G. P.*, XIX, part I, no. 6035, p. 183.

[a] *D. D. F.*, IV, no. 274, p. 357. Bompard, pp. 52-53, 238.

[b] *D. D. F.*, IV, no. 274, p. 357. *B. D.*, II, no. 263, p. 227. Russian public opinion in general was very uncomplimentary in its references to Great Britain at this time. *G. P.*, XIX, part I, no. 6028, p. 166; no. 6030, p. 173; no. 6033, p. 177. Gwynn, I, 403.

with the hastening of the strategic Orenburg-Tashkent railway line towards completion in the autumn, indicated that an angry Russia might attempt some retribution against the British position in Afghanistan and India. To this there was joined the fear that Russia might again try to form some continental combination of European powers, in which the attitude of an unloving Germany might become seriously menacing.[c] In these circumstances the British government endeavored to act carefully so that Russia would feel reassured that no unfair advantage of its difficult position was being taken. The British used the friendliness in Anglo-French relations to ask the French to quiet the apprehensions of their ally. Delcassé admitted that, although the task was difficult and the opposition of interests seemingly unsurmountable, he was still hopeful of bringing Russia and Great Britain together.[d]

King Edward himself had an opportunity to work for the improvement of relations with Russia when he met the Russian minister in Copenhagen, Alexander Izvolsky, at the British legation for the first time on 14 April 1904, and had a long and friendly conversation with him. This meeting has remained famous as a landmark on the slow and difficult road to an Anglo-Russian agreement. Speaking on his own initiative, without promptings from the British foreign office, the king declared to Izvolsky that the conclusion of the Anglo-French entente "gives me the hope of attaining by the same methods still more important results, that is to say, to a similar entente with Russia, — an entente which has always been and continues to be the object of my most sincere desires."[e] The king admitted that it would be most difficult to bring this about, but since an agreement was so necessary and desirable the new British ambassador, Sir Charles Hardinge, who was to replace the pessimistic and now inadequate Sir Charles Scott in St.

[c] *Ibid.*, pp. 392-395, 404, 409. *G. P.*, XIX, part I, no. 6048, pp. 214-215; part II, no. 6342, p. 645.

[d] *D. D. F.*, IV, no. 350, p. 462; no. 382, p. 527. *G. P.*, XVII, no. 5368, p. 564; XIX, part II, no. 6345, p. 648. Lansdowne wrote to Sir Charles Hardinge on 27 July: "I feel sure that the more quietly we can proceed, the better . . . and we must blacken their faces as little as possible." Newton, pp. 313-314.

[e] Lee, II, 284, 287. Izvolsky drew up the record of this conversation, showed it to King Edward at his own request, who approved it and took a copy. *Ibid.*, p. 286. *B. D.*, IV, no. 183, note 1, p. 188.

Petersburg in May, "will have as instructions to devote himself to the establishment of the most cordial relations with the Russian government and to seek the means for arriving at a full agreement on the questions which divide us in the different parts of the world." The conversation then naturally turned to the "unfortunate" and "regrettable" Russo-Japanese war. The king lamented the intensity of the anti-English sentiment it had provoked in Russia and the serious obstacle this ill-feeling placed in the way of an entente between the two countries. With astonishing exaggeration, perhaps pardonable for the occasion, the king declared that "his government had done everything that was possible to moderate Japan, which had not desired to listen to reason, and had demanded to be left free to regulate its differences [with Russia] as it pleased." [f] Izvolsky let pass the royal remark that the Anglo-Japanese alliance had been conceived for an entirely pacific purpose, indeed even to restrain Japan, but he did not hesitate to express his conviction that the alliance had in reality been one of the principle causes of hostilities. While he had been the Russian minister at Tokyo he "had been able to observe personally its effect on the psychology of the Japanese and to judge how much it had inflamed the bellicose party in Tokyo and had aided it to combat the opposition of the elder statesmen." [g] This interview between King Edward and Izvolsky did not result in any immediate action. Both the Russian and the British foreign offices were pleased with the courtesy and the sentiments expressed at Copenhagen, but understood perfectly well that the time was not suitable for discussing Anglo-Russian disputes.[h] Meanwhile nothing could be attempted except to keep the future open, and in the end this exchange of views was not without result. Izvolsky never lost the impression that it made

[f] Lee, II, 285. King Edward by this time had "little faith" in the "efficiency" of Sir Charles Scott in St. Petersburg. *Ibid.*, p. 281.

[g] *Ibid.*, pp. 285-286.

[h] *D. D. F.*, V, no. 15, pp. 17-19. *B. D.*, IV, no. 183, p. 188; no. 185, pp. 190-191. Tsar Nicholas and King Edward exchanged friendly letters with each other over this meeting. (*Ibid.*, no. 184, p. 189; no. 185, note 1, p. 190.) King Edward told the Germans the substance of this interview on his visit to the kaiser at Kiel, 26 June 1904, and described Izvolsky as "the most capable Russian diplomat." *G. P.*, XIX, part I, no. 6038, p. 188.

upon him and over two years later, when he had become foreign minister, he succeeded in smoothing out the difficulties
which made the convention of 1907 possible.[1]

As the Russo-Japanese war became more rigorous, new incidents arose to disturb Anglo-Russian relations. Great Britain, for so long unquestioned mistress of the seas and accus-
tomed to name the articles contraband in time of war, was
angered by the Russian order of 29 February 1904, and its
later extensions of 18 March and 9 May. The lists of commodities which the Russians designated in these proclamations
struck heavily against British products, particularly when coal
was finally added.[j] This question became far more acute when
the Russian Volunteer Fleet was increased by the addition of
two cruisers which had successfully passed from the Black Sea
through the straits at Constantinople, temporarily disguished
as merchantmen. The ships of this Volunteer Fleet began the
seizure of both German and British vesels, which were declared to be loaded with contraband goods.[k] In response to
protests by both governments, many of these prizes were released after protracted delays, but long after the end of the
war the British government was pressing a large bill of claims
against Russia for damages with only indifferent success.[l] The
British also considered the possibility that the Russian Black
Sea squadron might try to run through the Straits in violation
of the existing régime, while the Japanese, alarmed by rumors
of this intention, urged the British government to oppose any
attempt. The British attitude was never precisely formulated,
and Lansdowne limited himself in reply to the Japanese solici-
tations by explaining that, while he "could not undertake to
say what action we might think it necessary to take by way of
response," British policy nevertheless "in regard to this question remained . . . unchanged." He did not believe, however,

[1] Lee, II, 287. Friedrich Stieve, *Iswolski und der Weltkrieg*, (Berlin, 1925),
p. 2; English edition, *Isvolsky and the World War*, (New York, 1926), p. 10.
Alexander Izvolsky, *Recollections of a Foreign Minister*, (Garden City, N. Y.,
1921), p. 22.
[j] Gwynn, I, 389.
[k] Lee, II, 297. *C. H. B. F. P.*, III, 330. *D. D. F.*, V, no. 272, pp. 321-322.
B. D., IV, no. 49, p. 53; no. 51, p. 54; no. 53, enclosure, p. 56.
[l] *Ibid.*, no. 56, pp. 60-64. *D. D. F.*, V, no. 278, p. 326; no. 282, pp. 329-330.

that the Russian government would ever order its warships to leave the Black Sea.[m]

There were other actions by Great Britain which just as effectively hindered congenial relations with Russia. The march of the armed Younghusband expedition into Tibet had started by January 1904, and the first collision with the natives occurred on 31 March. Despite the resistance offered by the uncouth people, the expedition reached the little trading-mart of Gyangtse on 11 April. Still finding the Tibetans recalcitrant, with no one among them with whom to negotiate, the mission soon set out for Lhasa some 150 miles away, to maintain the famed British prestige and to compel the conclusion of a satisfactory treaty.[n] This last move caused more apprehension in St. Petersburg than could be safely ignored even while war was going on with Japan. No Russian government would have tranquilly watched the rise of British influence in Tibet, so the ambassador in London asked Lansdowne if some reassuring statement could not at once be made.[o] The Russian distrust was not allayed by Lansdowne's reference to past statements of British policy; but shortly thereafter he proposed a bargain which the Russians entered into with caution.[p]

[m] *B. D.*, IV, no. 40, p. 48; no. 41, p. 49; no. 45, p. 51; no. 55, p. 57. Lansdowne was most explicit on 29 April in describing the British position privately to the French ambassador Cambon: "The passage of the Straits by a Russian squadron for the purpose of attacking our ally in the Far East could not . . . be tolerated by this country." (*Ibid.*, no. 43, p. 50.) A few days before, on 22 April, King Edward and Sir Charles Hardinge took the view that "there did not appear to be any reason for preventing the passage of the Dardanelles by Russian warships as we have endeavored to do in the past," and that this "concession of an unopposed passage might prove a very useful asset in the event of the general negotiations for an arrangement with Russia being resumed. It would be a useful 'quid pro quo' to have in hand." (Lee, II, 289-290. *B. D.*, IV, no. 55, note 1, p. 60.) This may very likely explain why no outright assurance was given to Japan.

[n] Lee, II, 369. Ronaldshay, II, 345. King Edward himself took the jingoistic view of the mission, writing on 9 May: "We must be firm with the Tibetans, England's prestige must be maintained." (Lee, II, 369.) Colonel Francis Younghusband's travelogue and very partial version of his expedition is nevertheless interestingly told in *India and Tibet*, (London, 1910), pp. 84-307.

[o] *B. D.*, IV, no. 183, p. 188. *C. H. B. F. P.*, III, 325. Lessar, the Russian minister at Peking, said that Russia still possessed certain means to moderate Curzon's most recent activity if it were pushed too far. Herat, in Afghanistan, could be occupied, indeed within twenty-four hours, provided Russia had complete liberty of action in the Far East, which was not momentarily the case. *D. D. F.*, IV, no. 168, and note 1, p. 239.

[p] *B. D.*, IV, no. 183, pp. 188-189. *D. D. F.*, IV, no. 168, pp. 237-239; no. 388, p. 532. *Paul Cambon*, pp. 219-220.

In conformity with an ardent French suggestion, Lansdowne told Benckendorff that if Russia would subscribe to the terms of the Khedivial decree contained in the Anglo-French entente of 8 April, the British government would be so gratified that it would willingly give an assurance that it still adhered to its old Tibetan policy. It would not attempt to annex the land, or to establish a protectorate over it, or to control its internal administration in any way.[q] By the beginning of June the Russian approval to the Khedivial decree was given "as a friendly act towards both England and France," although it had been an unpleasant surprize to find that, besides the decree itself, there had been an additional clause which had concerned no Russian interest.[r] The British government then omitted this clause and handed over a memorandum again proclaiming the innocuousness of its intentions with regard to Tibet and the Younghusband expedition. Count Lamsdorff regretted to find in this statement the weakening qualification "that H[is] M[ajesty's] gov[ernmen]t cannot undertake that they will not depart in any eventuality from the policy which now commends itself to them," but he finally expressed his satisfaction and hoped that other bothersome questions could be as amicably settled in the future.[s] For a time it appeared that Anglo-Russian relations might regain some cordiality.[t]

The slight improvement was quickly checked when the Russian government learned of the convention concluded at Lhasa on 7 September 1904 between the British commissioner, Colonel Younghusband, and the representatives who had been compelled to act for the Dalai Lama.[u] The terms of the treaty

[q] B. D., IV, no. 184, p. 190; no. 291, p. 308. D. D. F., V, no. 41, pp. 47-48; no. 50, pp. 58-59.
[r] B. D., IV, no. 185, p. 191; no. 188, p. 194; no. 291, p. 307. D. D. F., V, no. 124, p. 141.
[s] B. D., IV, no. 188, p. 194; no. 293, p. 310; no. 295, p. 311. D. D. F., V, no. 145, p 164; no. 214, pp. 247-248.
[t] Ibid., no. 190, p. 210; no. 214, p. 248. G. P., XIX, part I, no. 6036, p. 185; part II, no. 6346, p. 649; no. 6347, p. 650. When King Edward met the kaiser at Kiel near the end of June he told Bülow that he hoped to reach an understanding over conflicting interests with Russia. (Ibid., part I, no. 6038, p. 188. Lee, II, 294.) Later in the year the British monarch accepted sponsorship for the tsar's infant heir. Ibid., pp. 300-301.
[u] B. D., IV, no. 298, pp. 314-316. D. D. F., V, no. 299, pp. 350-352; no. 340, p. 402. Younghusband gives a descriptive account of the negotiations and ceremonies in his book.

had been framed on the basis of instructions sent by the government of India, but which had not been approved by the cabinet in London.[v] Lamsdorff's first knowledge of the treaty was derived from a text published in the London *Times*, so that his remonstrances against the provisions were consequently made unofficially to Sir Charles Hardinge. He found much that was in violation of the assurances he had recently received from Lansdowne, and summed up his protest with the assertion that the treaty conferred upon Great Britain "a virtual protectorate over Tibet." The British ambassador made a sorry attempt to justify the supposed terms of the treaty and exhibited much petulance before he admitted how useless it would be "to prolong the discussion of a treaty of which neither of us knew the authentic text." [w] When the Russian chargé d'affaires in London, Sergey Sazonov, complained on 27 September about the unfavorable impression which the excessive demands in the Tibetan convention had called forth in St. Petersburg, Lansdowne also resorted to devious justifications. He asserted that the British government intended to remain faithful to its announced policy, and to the assurances given to Russia. He believed that the version of the treaty published in the *Times* was "slightly misleading in one or two passages." He attempted to reassure Sazonov that nothing would be done "to give ourselves a pretext for the permanent annexation of Tibetan territory." [x]

The excessive zeal of the government of India and of its representative had embarrassed the home government. It had not wished to become involved in Tibet for a long stay, and the objections raised by Russia to the Tibetan convention could not be wholly denied. It was privately recognized that Younghusband had far exceeded his authority and had regrettably

[v] *B. D.*, IV, no. 296, p. 312. Lee, II, 371.

[w] *B. D.*, IV, no. 299, pp. 317-318. *D. D. F.*, V, no. 345, pp. 407-409; no. 346, pp. 409-410. Although Lamsdorff's protests were made unofficially, Hardinge was mildly deceptive when he told his German colleague, Count Alvensleben, that "he had informed Count Lamsdorff of the content of the Anglo-Tibetan convention, and the minister had raised no objections against it." *G. P.*, XIX, part II, no. 6347, pp. 649-650.

[x] *B. D.*, IV, no. 301, pp. 319-320. *C. H. B. F. P.*, III, 324. *D. D. F.*, V, no. 357, pp. 427-428.

"acted in direct disobedience of orders." [y] Lansdowne was uncomfortably concerned with the existing situation and the British government, although reluctant to give up entirely the tutelary control of Tibet thus acquired, conceded that the terms of the treaty must be modified to harmonize with the promises given to Russia.[z] No changes could be made in the convention before the British mission had left Lhasa, but some modifications were contained in a declaration signed on 11 November by the acting viceroy of India, Lord Ampthill, which softened some of the most objectionable provisions. Russian remonstrances ceased after the middle of October because of the continuance of the war with Japan.[a]

Great Britain may have tried to avoid giving the appearance of taking advantage of Russian preoccupation in war, yet the knowledge that a mission under Mr. Louis Dane, foreign secretary to the government of India, was being prepared to visit the Amir of Afghanistan still further aroused the Russian government towards the end of October 1904. The Amir Habibullah, who had come to the Afghan throne in 1901, had never accepted the annual subsidy paid by Great Britain in return for control over Afghan foreign relations, and had stubbornly declined to accept invitations to visit in India. In order to clear up this uncertain conduct, so it was asserted, the Dane mission was being sent to negotiate new agreements.[b] Other nations promptly suspected greater enterprize, and the German consul-general reported from Simla that it was believed to be the chief purpose of the expedition to establish an unquestioned British supremacy of influence, both political

[y] *Ibid.*, IV, no. 388, p. 532. "The home government in fact deemed Younghusband worthy of censure. In December, however, Mr. Brodrick [the secretary of state for India] gave way to the King's urgency so far as to agree to the bestowal of a K[night]. C[ommander]. [of the] I[ndian]. E[mpire]." Lee, II, 371.

[z] *B. D.*, IV, no. 303, pp. 321-322. *D. D. F.*, V, no. 382, pp. 459-460; no. 430, pp. 507-508. Lee, II, 371. *G. P.*, XIX, part II, no. 6354, pp. 655-656. The American minister in Peking is said to have informed his government that the Anglo-Tibetan convention had injured the policy of preserving the open door, and that Great Britain made claims in Tibet to what it had reproached Russia for attempting in Manchuria. *Ibid.*, no. 6348, p. 651.

[a] *B. D.*, IV, no. 298, p. 317; Editors' Note, p. 322. *G. P.*, XIX, part II, no. 6354, p. 655.

[b] *B. D.*, IV, no. 466 (a), note 1, p. 520. *D. D. F.*, V, no. 379, pp. 454-455.

and military, in the country in order to prevent any Russian advance upon the Indian frontier from this direction. If it could be managed, it would also be most acceptable if the trade between Afghanistan and India could be increased.[c] Again in response to pressing inquiries from Russia, Lansdowne gave the customary assurances to Benckendorff on 17 February 1905, that "our present negotiations with the Amir did not portend any attempt to annex or occupy Afghan territory."[d] Lamsdorff admitted that the Russian government, in its helplessness, must "proceed with the utmost circumspection" and was not disposed to start any discussions so long as Afghanistan continued to remain a "buffer state," an expression which Lansdowne believed to be "an appropriate description of the position which both governments desired to assign to Afghanistan."[e] Nothing serious happened in any event because the Amir kept the Dane mission waiting an unconscionable time before he signed a new treaty on 21 March, which merely confirmed the agreements that had been made with his father, and granted no new concessions to British importunities. Nevertheless Russia became so deeply alarmed at British activity that large reënforcements of troops and supplies, intended for the war area, were sent instead into Turkestan where, in turn, their mounting numbers only succeeded in disquieting the British until some Russian action was thoroughly expected.[f] Even so, it remained for another incident, in another part of the world, to embitter Anglo-Russian relations almost to the breaking point, to be followed by a full year of cordiality between Germany and Russia unmatched since the best days of Bismarck and Alexander III.

During the night of 21-22 October the Russian Baltic Sea fleet was steaming through the North Sea on its long cruise to the scene of war in the Far East, where it was to regain control of the water routes by which Japanese troops and

[c] G. P., XIX, part II, no. 6355, pp. 656-657. Lovat Fraser, India under Curzon and After, (London, 3rd edition, 1911), p. 67; see Chapter II, section IV.
[d] B. D., IV, no. 466 (a), p. 520.
[e] Ibid., no. 466 (b), p. 521.
[f] G. P., XIX, part II, no. 6342, p. 645; no. 6343, p. 646; no. 6356, p. 658. Wroblewski, Kriegsschuldfrage, V, 1225.

supplies reached the mainland. This fleet had been rapidly collected, with many ill-assorted and old vessels included; manned by a crew still imperfectly trained, a deficiency to be made good through drill on the way; prematurely sent off on 11 October, impressive indeed in numbers, but utterly lacking in effectiveness.[g] The progress of the fleet through the Baltic Sea had been without incident, but the numerous warnings of the rumored presence of Japanese torpedo boats lying in wait in the North Sea to cause all possible damage had aroused considerable nervous tension in Admiral Rozhdestvensky and his sailors.[h] The day of the 21st found this overstrained fleet firing wild shots on scattered fishing boats of Swedish and Norwegian nationality, but the incidents were quickly hushed up and adjusted by the Russian government.[i] Sometime shortly after midnight as the fleet was passing the Dogger Bank, it found itself in the midst of some fifty British small fishing vessels. Suddenly the Russian fleet opened fire, which lasted only a few minutes and then as suddenly ceased, with the fleet continuing on its way without stopping. In those few minutes, however, one boat of the fishing fleet had been sunk and others damaged; two humble British fisher-folk had been killed and more wounded; and an international incident of first magnitude created.[j]

[g] Fisher, pp. 45-46. *G. P.*, XIX, part I, no. 6056, p. 223; no. 6057, p. 225. The Emperor William favored the tsar with much advice on military and naval strategy, even as he had the British government during the Boer war, and especially on this occasion. The advice was not followed. *Ibid.*, no. 6057, pp. 224-225. *Kaiser's Letters*, pp. 124-129.

[h] Korff, p. 38. *G. P.*, XIX, part I, no. 6100, and footnote *, p. 281. M. A. Taube, *Der grossen Katastrophe entgegen. Die russische Politik der Vorkriegszeit und das Ende des Zarenreiches (1904-1917). Erinnerungen*, (Berlin, 1929), p. 29. This fuller German edition is always used in preference to the French edition, *La politique russe d'avant-guerre et la fin de l'empire des tsars*, (Paris, 1928). Izvolsky, then Russian minister at Copenhagen, had arranged with the Danish government for skilled pilots to assist the passage of the Russian fleet through the Kattegat and Skagerrak. Izvolsky, footnote *, pp. 29-30.

[i] Gwynn, I, 390. Taube, pp. 30-32. Izvolsky, pp. 29-30.

[j] *B. D.*, IV, no. 5, pp. 5-6. Taube, pp. 5, 28-30. Agnes Fry, editor, *A Memoir of the Right Honourable Sir Edward Fry, G. C. B., 1827-1918*, (Oxford, [1921]), p. 181. British accounts tend to make the period of firing rather longer: "maintained for a considerable time" (*B. D.*, IV, no. 6, p. 6); "the firing lasted nearly half an hour" (*C. H. B. F. P.*, III, 332). Taube reproduces from memory details from the log-books of the Russian ships indicating a period of about three minutes. (Taube, p. 37.) The details there given make the shorter time more plausible; the damage actually done was small.

Years afterwards it was difficult for so mild a commentator as Sir Edward Grey "to understand what the Russians did think they were firing at, and why their guns went off at all." [k] At the time the effort to understand was hardly made, and the British and Russian diplomatic versions varied in the extreme. To the British it was "a most dastardly outrage" that a peaceful fishing fleet, pursuing their legitimate occupation "in accordance with international regulations, presumably well known to Russian Naval Authorities," should have been fired upon as "nothing but the most culpable negligence could have led to their being mistaken for anything but what they were." [1] The action of Admiral Rozhdestvensky was all the more reprehensible because his fleet continued on its course without having made any attempt to succor "seriously injured and defenceless people." [m] Count Lamsdorff, for the Russians, from the outset admitted that "the news had filled him with horror," which the Russian government could only believe to be the result of "some terrible misunderstanding." His government, even as that of Great Britain, had at the moment only the information that had been given by panic-stricken fishermen, which could not be accepted as entirely correct before the explanations of the admiral in command had been received. Until this report arrived, and wireless telegraphy was not then in general use, the Russian explanation for "this deplorable incident" attributed it "to a disastrous mistake due to the apprehension of an attack by Japanese vessels in disguise." [n] This assumption naturally found no credence in Great Britain. The Russians were greatly distressed and promised to hasten an investigation. The tsar and Lamsdorff at once expressed their sincere regrets, and promised that the innocent victims, or their families, would be guaranteed a most ample indemnity.[o] The Russian government had quite properly gone out of its way

[k] Grey, I, 53.
[1] B. D., IV, no. 5, minute by King Edward, p. 6; no. 6, p. 6. Taube, p. 5.
[m] B. D., IV, no. 7, p. 7; no. 8, p. 8.
[n] Ibid., no. 7, p. 7; no. 11, p. 10; no. 13, p. 12. Gwynn, I, footnote 1, p. 390. The Russian government had had trouble before in communicating with their ships.
[o] B. D., IV, no. 10, p. 9; no. 11, pp. 9-10; no. 13, enclosure 1, p. 13. D. D. F., V, no. 387, pp. 465-467. Taube, pp. 5-6. Savinsky, p. 95.

to do all in its power to atone for the indefensible action of its
nervous fleet.

Yet these expressions of regret and promises of compensation were bluntly declared by the British not to be enough.
From the first news of the wanton attack off the Dogger Bank,
British righteous indignation flared up to a remarkable degree,
and gained in heat every succeeding day, going so far as
lightheartedly to contemplate war.[p] The British government
could not, or would not, do anything to moderate the outburst
of feeling in the press and among the people, while the "pet-
ulant patriotism" of the prime minister, Mr. Balfour, is said
to have made Lansdowne's efforts for a pacific solution of the
crisis more difficult.[q] To appease popular feeling and to make
sure that the Russian fleet did not continue beyond the Spanish
harbor of Vigo before stopping, the British admiralty issued
telegraphic orders to all nearby British fleets to be ready to
stop the Baltic squadron "by persuasion if possible, but by
force if necessary." When Lansdowne called Benckendorff's
attention to this regulation he warned the ambassador that,
if the Russian admiral did not put in at Vigo, "we might find
ourselves at war before the week was over."[r]

The Russian government was eager to accord satisfaction
to most of the British demands. The British, however, urged
with unusual insistence that the Russian government should
remove from the fleet those officers responsible for the firing.
After their trial, during which the British were to be given
every facility for presenting evidence to make sure that the
investigation was thoroughly done, those found guilty were to
be appropriately punished.[s] This demand had not been acceded
to by the Russian foreign office, where it was considered
humiliating and unacceptable, when the belated report of

[p] *B. D.*, IV, no. 6, p. 6; no. 13, p. 12. *G. P.*, XIX, part I, no. 6101, p. 282; no.
6102, pp. 283-284; no. 6103, pp. 284-285. Gwynn, I, 432. Taube, pp. 5-6. Lee,
II, 302.

[q] Arnold White, "Anglo-Russian Relations," *Fortnightly Review*, LXXXII
(1904), 960. *D. D. F.*, V, no. 432, pp. 510-512.

[r] *B. D.*, IV, no. 13, p. 12; no. 19, pp. 18-19. *D. D. F.*, V, no. 388, p. 467.
Gwynn, I, 436.

[s] *B. D.*, IV, no. 12, pp. 10-11; no. 13, enclosure 2, pp. 13-14; no. 14, p. 14.
G. P., XIX, part I, no. 6104, p. 285. Lee, II, 302-303. The eagerness of King
Edward for the punishment of the responsible Russian officers is most noticeable.

Admiral Rozhdestvensky was received in St. Petersburg on 27 October. This document supposedly confirmed the Russian contention that the fire of the Baltic fleet had been directed against two Japanese torpedo boats which had suddenly appeared out of the night, and that the British fishing smacks had been struck by inadvertence. When the enemy's ships had been possibly sunk, or in any event had disappeared, the firing had stopped at once. The fleet had continued on its way, not giving assistance to the trawlers because of their apparent complicity and suspicious movements.[t] The Russian government chose to accept this version, and a new turn was given to the Dogger Bank incident. Before the British demand for the punishment of the responsible officers could be considered, the actual facts of the encounter itself must first be established, as a basis for determining whether or not any question of guilty conduct on their part existed at all.[u]

With public feeling in Great Britain continuing at fever pitch, the way out of the threatening situation came on 28 October with the proposal of Nicholas II, which crossed with a similar suggestion from Lansdowne, "to submit the scrupulous examination of this question to an international commission of enquiry as foreshadowed by the Convention of the Hague." The Russian government promised, after this commission had determined what actually had happened, that it would adequately punish any persons found guilty of having caused this regrettable incident.[v] The acceptance of this pro-

[t] B. D., IV, no. 15, p. 15; no. 16, p. 15. D. D. F., V, no. 396, pp. 473-474. C. H. B. F. P., III, 333. Taube, pp. 5-6, 12. It is quite certain that Rozhdestvensky's report was written with little regard for the truth and more to cover up a serious and ridiculous blunder. Shortly afterwards, when the log-books of the fleet were examined, it appeared from them that the two Japanese torpedo boats fired upon had really been the Russian cruisers Dmitry Donskoy and Aurora. It was suspected that the British government had also found this out. In one of his discussions with Lamsdorff, if he did not actually know that the Russians had fired on their own boats, Hardinge was extremely shrewd when he "insinuated that the torpedo boats fired on by Rozhdestvensky might belong to the Russian squadron." (Savinsky, p. 96.) The details of this discovery are interestingly related in Taube, pp. 36-38. See also Maurice Bompard, "Le Traité de Bjoerkoe," Revue de Paris, XXV (1918), 428.

[u] B. D., IV, no. 15, p. 15; no. 16, p. 16. Taube, p. 6. When the admiral's report was received, Lamsdorff is said to have exclaimed to Hardinge: "You ask for an inquest, but I insist on having one. . . . Infamous is the only term for the act committed by the Japanese." Savinsky, p. 95.

[v] B. D., IV, no. 16, p. 17; no. 18, p. 18; no. 20, pp. 20-21. G. P., XIX, part I, no. 6107, p. 288. D. D. F., V, no. 404, p. 480; no. 405, p. 481.

posal removed the alarming prospects of war, and the impetuosity of British public feeling abated as rapidly as it had arisen. Mr. Balfour, in a speech at Southampton which struck the Russians as being "needlessly caustic and offensive" in some of its passages, explained that the Russian government had given satisfactory assurances for the settlement of the trouble and against any future repetition.[w] By 4 November 1904 the Russian foreign office had accepted the British draft describing the composition and procedure of the International Commission of Enquiry. The firing of the Baltic fleet on the British fisherfolk was thereupon consigned to the formality of an unspectacular settlement by a commission of admirals with their legal advisers.[x]

The affair of the Dogger Bank, however, pushed Russia away from any thought of an agreement with Great Britain to a closer friendship with Germany. The tsar had summoned Hardinge on 30 October for one of the infrequent audiences that he granted. In this long interview the tsar expressed his great pleasure that war had been avoided, although he defended the Russian viewpoint with more than usual steadfastness. He remarked that the late unpleasantness had undoubtedly provoked new bitterness which would endure for some time, but he thought that the improvement in Anglo-Russian relations could be revived.[y] The tsar had really hidden

---

[w] B. D., IV, no. 22, p. 23; no. 23, p. 23. D. D. F., V, no. 409, pp. 484-485. It is interesting to note how completely King Edward's own attitude had moderated by this time. He now felt that the "unbridled language of the press" had unnecessarily "egged on" public opinion which might have led to war which, in turn, "would be a dire calamity for this country . . . after all for the sake of the heirs of two harmless fishermen." He also reversed his insistence on punishment of the Russian admiral and officers which he now "strongly deprecated" as "Russia could not accept such a humiliation." (Lee, II, 303-304.) The French worked diligently throughout the crisis to preserve peace. In St. Petersburg they urged the Russians to be prompt and conciliatory, while in London they insistently admonished the British to control the excessive clamor of the press and public opinion. D. D. F., V, no. 390, p. 468; no. 399, pp. 476-477; no. 403, p. 480; no. 413, p. 489; no. 432, pp. 509-512. Paul Cambon, p. 222. Bompard, p. 71.

[x] B. D., IV, no. 22, p. 23; no. 25, enclosure 1, pp. 30-31. There was a slight hitch in November when Lamsdorff successfully revised the wording of one article to gain a better juridical position for Russia. (Ibid., Editors' Notes, pp. 31, 36, 38; no. 27, p. 36; no. 28, pp. 36-37. D. D. F., V, no. 446, pp. 533-534; no. 449, pp. 535-540; no. 458, pp. 552-553. Taube, pp. 12-16.) The German ambassador in London predicted a peaceful outcome from the beginning. G. P., XIX, part I, no. 6101, p. 282; no. 6102, pp. 283-284; no. 6111, p. 291.

[y] B. D., IV, no. 24, pp. 25-28. D. D. F., V, no. 414, p. 489; no. 416, p. 491.

his true feelings from the ambassador, but had confided them to the pages of his diary where he was less restrained over the "impudent behavior" of his "scabby enemy." [z] Of much greater significance was the rapid rise in the friendliness of the tsar and of important groups of Russian public opinion for the kaiser and his country. The kaiser almost alone, often for only selfish reasons, had praised the tsar's entrance into the war with Japan, had sympathized with him, encouraged and counselled him from the time of the first Russian reverses.[a] Such an attitude on the part of Germany aroused grateful satisfaction in the Russian government, the more so because France was still in the "eighth honeymoon" with Great Britain after the signature of the entente cordiale. The Franco-Russian alliance was suffering temporarily from the anglophil policies of Delcassé and France had given no aid and little comfort to its older ally, a fact which the kaiser never ceased to cast up before the tsar.[b] Benckendorff assured his German colleague in London that the position maintained by the kaiser's government had made a deep impression in Russia, which would lead in "due course of time necessarily to a further rapprochement of the three imperial powers." [c]

Witte had been in Berlin during the latter half of July 1904 to negotiate the renewal of the 1894 commercial treaty between Germany and Russia which, the kaiser complained, had not yet been done because of the lazy "Geheim-Räthe and chinovniks." Witte had also explained how much the influence of the kaiser had mounted with the tsar in recent years. Shortly before that Nicholas had distrusted his cousin and had been uneasy in his presence, but a great change had taken place since then, which had continued to grow until now the former

[z] Taube, pp. 6-7. *D. D. F.,* V, no. 422, pp. 496-499; no. 468, p. 565.

[a] *G. P.,* XIX, part I, no. 6035, p. 183; no. 6047, kaiser's note 3, pp. 211-212. *D. D. F.,* V, no. 450, pp. 540-541.

[b] The expression "eighth honeymoon" is Delcassé's; see Taube, p. 27. *G. P.,* XIX, part I, no. 6028, pp. 166-167; no. 6035, p. 183; no. 6037, p. 186; no. 6120, p. 307. *Kaiser's Letters,* pp. 118, 132. The French were worried for fear that Russia was slipping away, thus weakening the military efficacy of the Dual alliance against Germany. Nelidov, the Russian ambassador in Paris, suggested that France should furnish some evident proof to Russia that the entente with Great Britain had not weakened regard for Russia. *D. D. F.,* IV, no. 366, p. 507; no. 390, pp. 543-544. Bompard, pp. 71-72.

[c] *G. P.,* XIX, part I, no. 6029, p. 168.

suspicion had been replaced by full confidence.[d] William II
was pleased with the warmth of this new appreciation of himself by the tsar.[e] The first tangible result of this more cordial
relationship, as well as an indication of the helplessness of the
Russian international position, came with the conclusion of the
negotiations on 28 July for the renewal of the commercial
treaty. This treaty conferred considerable preferences on
Germany, although these were deprecated, as the fortunate
party so often can afford to do.[f]

The Dogger Bank incident created both an opportunity and
a necessity for proposing some kind of an alliance on the part
of Germany to Russia. The necessity sprang from the sudden,
but imaginary fear that a war might be forced upon Germany
by Great Britain over the question of the supply of coal to the
Baltic fleet by German ships, which might further involve "a
reckoning with France on land" because of its greater friendliness for Great Britain than for its old ally.[g] The opportunity
came because the anger in Russia against the attitude of Great
Britain was extreme, and the tsar could not find words "to
express my indignation with England's conduct." [h] The calculated mildness of recent German policy towards Russia had
been in sharp contrast to the harsh actions of Great Britain,
and had won a still mounting appreciation.[i] The German effort
commenced on 24 October in favorable circumstances when
Holstein proposed an entente between Russia, Germany and
France, and assured Osten-Sacken that Germany intended to

[d] *Ibid.*, no. 6034, footnote *, p. 182; no. 6043, pp. 199-200. *Kaiser's Letters*,
p. 116. *D. D. F.*, V, no. 269, p. 318.
[e] Bülow, still the impeccable courtier, congratulated his master on his "deserved reward for [his] knightly and intelligent bearing." *G. P.*, XIX, part I,
no. 6049, p. 216; no. 6050, p. 217.
[f] *Ibid.*, no. 6042, p. 195; no. 6043, footnote *, p. 203. *Kaiser's Letters*, p. 119.
B. D., IV, no. 4, pp. 4-5; no. 69, p. 77. *D. D. F.*, V, no. 291, pp. 343-344.
[g] *G. P.*, XIX, part I, no. 6084, pp. 257-258. Max Montgelas, "Russland und
Europa 1904-1914," *Berliner Monatshefte*, VIII (1930), 241. Savinsky, p. 97.
The contract for coaling the Russian squadron had been arranged by a private
Russian company with the Hamburg-American line, which had let a subcontract
to a British concern for both the coal and ship transportation. *G. P.*, XIX,
part I, chapter 133. Bernhard Huldermann, *Albert Ballin*, (Berlin, 1922),
p. 146.
[h] *G. P.*, XIX, part I, no. 6119, p. 305. *Kaiser's Letters*, p. 138. Bompard, p. 83.
[i] *D. D. F.*, V, no. 106, p. 119; no. 283, p. 331; no. 310, pp. 371-372. *G. P.*,
XIX, part I, no. 6068, p. 238.

stand by Russia should Great Britain participate in the war on the side of Japan. On the 27th the kaiser also sent a telegram directly to the tsar wherein he depicted the danger which he fancied threatened Germany, and adroitly sketched as a solution the same powerful combination which Holstein had laid before the Russian ambasador, a group so strong that Great Britain and Japan "would think twice before acting."[j]

When these two telegrams arrived in St. Petersburg the impression they made on their two recipients was not identical. The cautious Lamsdorff submitted his opinion to the tsar that, while in general he agreed that the time had come for a closer relationship between Russia and Germany, he perceived in this latest proposal the continued wiles of the German government to disturb the friendly relations existing between Russia and France. The foreign minister thought that it was not the right time to antagonize France, and his conception of a correct foreign policy for Russia suggested that no rigid alliances should be made with any country, taking no step nearer Berlin than towards Buckingham palace.[k] Nicholas II, on the other hand, held quite different views and believed that it was "certainly high time" to make it clear to Great Britain that all its arrogant demands could not be fulfilled, while its excessive impudence must be restrained. Such a three-power continental alliance as was now outlined, the tsar asserted, had long lain close to his heart, and Lamsdorff would see from his answer already telegraphed to the kaiser that the latter had been asked: "Would you like to lay down and frame the outlines of such a treaty and let me know it?"[l]

Would the kaiser like to frame the outlines of such a treaty!

[j] Ibid., no. 6118, pp. 303-304, and footnote **, p. 303. Montgelas, Berliner Monatshefte, VIII, 241. Kaiser's Letters, p. 138. Taube, p. 43. "Der in Björkoe abgeschlossene russisch-deutsche Vertrag vom Jahre 1905," Kriegsschuldfrage, II (1924), pp. 456-458. The Russian original documents are in Krasny Arkhiv, V (1924). For a more detailed account of this negotiation see J.-P. Reinach, Le traité de Bjoerkoë (1905). Un essai d'alliance de l'Allemagne, la Russie et la France, (Paris, 1935), pp. 76-98.

[k] G. P., XIX, part I, no. 6118, footnote **, p. 303. Taube, pp. 41, 44, 56. Savinsky, p. 97. A. A. Savinsky, "Guillaume II et la Russie. Ses dépêches à Nicolas II, 1903-1905," Revue des deux mondes, XII (1922), 7ᵉ période, 790-791.

[l] G. P., XIX, part I, no. 6109, pp. 289-290; no. 6118, footnote **, p. 303; no. 6119, p. 305. Kaiser's Letters, p. 139. Taube, pp. 44-45.

He sent a telegram in answer to the tsar on the folowing day, to tell him that a letter with a draft treaty had already been despatched.[m] This joyful letter found the kaiser expediently modest: "Be it as you say. Let us stand together." With the coöperation of Bülow, a purely defensive treaty had been composed "in the form of a mutual fire insurance company against incendiarism" which France was to join, and which would serve to warn Great Britain to maintain peace. The only reservation was an afterthought that the North Sea incident must be closed before the treaty should become valid, or France approached.[n] In this draft treaty the two emperors entered into a defensive alliance for the announced purpose of localizing the Russo-Japanese war as much as possible. The *casus foederis* was set out in the first article and was to arise "in the event of one of the two empires being attacked by a European power," whereupon "its ally will help it with all its land and sea forces." In case a war arose the two allies would act together "to remind France of the obligations she has assumed by the terms of the Franco-Russian treaty of alliance." The second article was a conventional stipulation that no separate peace would be made with a common enemy. An awkward attempt was made in the third and last article to arrange for assistance in the event that certain actions done by one ally during the war, "such as the delivery of coal to a belligerent," as Germany was then engaged in doing for the Russian Baltic fleet, should give occasion to a third nation to complain regarding "pretended violations of the rights of neutrals." [o]

The tsar and Lamsdorff accepted this draft as a satisfactory start and throughout November proceeded to make small alterations in its wording. After other changes had been made in Berlin the purpose of the alliance in the last version made was transformed to read "to assure the maintenance of peace in Europe." No alteration was made in the *casus foederis* of the first article, nor of the provision against a separate peace

[m] *G. P.*, XIX, part I, no. 6121, p. 308. *Kaiser's Letters*, p. 139.

[n] *G. P.*, XIX, part I, no. 6120, Anlage I, pp. 306-307; no. 6123, p. 310. *Kaiser's Letters*, pp. 130-133.

[o] *G. P.*, XIX, part I, no. 6120, Anlage II, p. 308. *Kaiser's Letters*, pp. 135-137. Taube, pp. 45-46.

in the second. With regard to the action to be taken towards France, the tsar insisted that this part of the first article must be altered to read: "His Majesty the Emperor of all the Russias will take the necessary steps to inform France of this agreement, and to invite her to associate herself with it as an ally." [p] A new third article, prepared in Berlin, provided that this treaty should remain in force until denounced a year in advance.[q] The question of coaling the Russian fleet offered more difficulty, and was being considered as material for a separate and secret article to the treaty. Both parties agreed to make common cause against any complaints brought by a third power relative to alleged violations of neutrality in the instances mentioned in the kaiser's original draft. This troublesome question, arising out of the German fear of war with Great Britain, had not been settled before it was pushed into the background by a far more serious difference of opinion.[r]

The kaiser made no attempt to conceal his annoyance when he received a telegram from Nicholas II on 23 November, in which the desire was clearly expressed that the Russian government should acquaint France with the text of the treaty before it should be approved by the two rulers.[s] He diagnosed the tsar's concern as a case of "cold feet," and correctly suspected Lamsdorff of having insisted upon consultation with France in advance of signature. Witte was also believed to have joined Lamsdorff's opposition, motivated by his anxiety for French loans, so that these were the two persons who, as William II wrote, "had spit in the soup." [t] The kaiser tried to stiffen the tsar's courage by explaining that he considered it absolutely dangerous to inform France before the treaty had first been concluded between themselves, and that it would be better to make no treaty at all if it could not be done in

[p] G. P., XIX, part I, no. 6124, Anlage, p. 311. Kaiser's Letters, pp. 134-136.

[q] G. P., XIX, part I, no. 6125, Anlage, pp. 313-314. Kaiser's Letters, pp. 135-136.

[r] The latest formulation of the treaty is in Kaiser's Letters, pp. 135-137. Another text of the treaty is in G. P., XIX, part I, no. 6124, Anlage, p. 312; see also no. 6126, p. 316. Taube, p. 47.

[s] G. P., XIX, part I, no. 6126, Anlage, p. 317.

[t] Ibid., no. 6126, p. 316. Kriegsschuldfrage, II, 471-472. Savinsky, Revue des deux mondes, XII, 790.

this order. Lamsdorff persuaded the tsar not to change his opinion, but in his letter of 7 December Nicholas did remark to the kaiser that if France refused to join, then only that part of the treaty referring to it need be eliminated.[u] This opportunity to make a dual alliance, similar in conception to Bismarck's reinsurance treaty of 1887, was never taken up in Berlin. The German foreign office determined to come to some binding agreement before everything else on the limited subject of the coaling question.[v] Nicholas readily agreed to do this, which would relieve the German alarm over a war with Great Britain, as well as continuing to make certain of the coaling of the Baltic fleet. On 12 December Lamsdorff gave Count Alvensleben a formal note of assurance that the Russian government would make common cause with Germany in all the difficulties which might arise from this undertaking during the period of the Russo-Japanese war.[w] The negotiations for a triple continental alliance of Germany, Russia and France were dropped with the acceptance of this note by Germany. The kaiser again wrote the tsar on 21 December still insisting that any treaty must first be accepted by them before France could be informed, but eagerly promising that "we shall under all circumstances remain true and loyal friends." [x] Count Lamsdorff had won out in his policy of making no definite alliances fully as much because of German methods as from his own efforts upon the tsar; and he had won also the enduring distrust of the kaiser.[y]

The German foreign office determined that no signs of displeasure or irritation over the failure should be disclosed to

[u] *G. P.*, XIX, part I, no. 6127, Anlage, pp. 318-319; no. 6131, p. 323. *Kriegsschuldfrage*, II, 473-474. Savinsky, pp. 104-106.

[v] *G. P.*, XIX, part I, no. 6129, p. 321; no. 6130, p. 322; no. 6132, p. 325. *Kaiser's Letters*, pp. 149-150.

[w] *G. P.*, XIX, part I, no. 6133, p. 325; no. 6136, p. 328; no. 6137, p. 329. The coaling of the Russian fleet was successfully continued. (*Kaiser's Letters*, footnote 2, p. 149.) Lamsdorff was doubtless more willing to give this note because he did not believe that either Great Britain or Japan would make war upon Germany over this question. *G. P.*, XIX, part I, no. 6134, p. 326; no. 6136, p. 328.

[x] *Ibid.*, no. 6141, pp. 340-341. *Kaiser's Letters*, pp. 151-152. The kaiser was bitterly disappointed when no further mention of the treaty appeared in the tsar's answer of 25 December, and he lamented his "first failure" to Bülow. *G. P.*, XIX, part I, no. 6145, p. 346; no. 6146, pp. 346-347.

[y] A critical review of German policy is in Taube, pp. 47-50.

Russia, but that on the contrary an effort should be made to maintain agreeable relations so that Russia should not be forced into the arms of Great Britain.[z] The German government suspected that France and Great Britain had heard something about the negotiations which had taken place, and knew that Delcassé was endeavoring to bring about a friendlier feeling between Great Britain and Russia.[a] At this time the International Commission of Enquiry had just begun its sittings in Paris to investigate the true facts of the episode off the Dogger Bank. Russia was being courted by two opposing groups out of which a new three-power European alignment could be formed, and Lamsdorff could tell the Russian legal adviser that Russia was still "for certain people in Europe 'a rich bride' which one would unwillingly see in the arms of another." [b]

Under the conciliatory influence of the French government the long intermittent sessions of this commission ended surprizingly well for the Russian position. The final award of 25 February 1905 declared that there had been no Japanese torpedo boats anywhere in the vicinity of the Dogger Bank, and that there had been consequently no justification for the Russian fire. As British trawlers had been damaged, with two of the fisherfolk killed besides others wounded, the Russian government was called upon to pay an indemnity of £65,000 in compensation. The commission glossed over the failure of Admiral Rozhdestvensky to render aid because of the uncertainty of the danger, so no discredit was cast upon either the valor or the humanity of the Russian navy. Nothing at all was said about the earlier violent demand for the punishment of the Russian officers responsible for the dastardly outrage. Now, however, this mild solution of the incident was received with satisfaction in England.[c] Delcassé had done much to

---

[z] G. P., XIX, part I, no. 6127, p. 318; no. 6143, p. 343. Bülow, Denkwürdigkeiten, II, 66.

[a] G. P., XIX, part I, no. 6114, pp. 296-297; no. 6146, p. 347; no. 6148, p. 349. Bompard, pp. 80-83. Taube, p. 48.

[b] Ibid., p. 18.

[c] D. D. F., VI, no. 144, p. 191. C. H. B. F. P., III, 334. Taube, p. 39. Lee, II, 304. The racy and interesting Russian version of the labors of the commission, written by the Russian legal adviser is in Taube, pp. 19-41; the prosaic and

bring about the peaceful settlement, even to "predisposing"
Russia and Great Britain "toward greater friendship in the
future." [d] At an official luncheon at the Quai d'Orsay, Delcassé frankly told the Russian legal adviser that he hoped
the friendly solution of the commission's task would be "a
turning point in the history of the future, where former
enemies take the first step to understand each other better and,
perhaps, to go along together thenceforth." While the time
was not yet ripe to make a natural extension of the entente
cordiale into a three-power understanding, Delcassé admitted
that he had already undertaken to peg out its boundary posts.[e]
In the early spring of 1905 there appeared to be just as much
chance for an entente between Russia, France and Great Britain as for the continental grouping of three powers which the
kaiser's recent efforts for a treaty with Russia had outlined.
Yet with Lamsdorff's clinging to his particular version of a
"free hand" policy, wanting no alliances with any other nations, some new and decisive alteration in Russia's international standing had to occur before either of these two nebulous constellations could become a reality.[f]

This change in the importance and authority of Russia
among the states of Europe was not long in coming. The fall
of Port Arthur on 2 January initiated the train of disasters
that was to mark the year 1905 as one of the most dismal in
Russian history, and rapidly to reduce the eastern colossus to
a position of helplessness. Nowhere more than in Germany
did this create concern for the future, and the kaiser forthwith
wrote of the "great commotion" caused by the news. He
inquired of the tsar what plans he had in mind "so that, if
possible, I may make myself useful to you and be enabled to
shape the course of my policy." [g] Even more humiliating for

slight account of the British legal adviser is in Fry, pp. 180-193. President
Roosevelt wrote to Spring Rice on 27 December 1904 that he had "reason to
believe that the Japanese were disappointed and unfavorably impressed by the
English vehemence of speech and exceeding moderation of action in the Hull
fishing fleet affair." Gwynn, I, 442.
  [d] Izvolsky, footnote *, pp. 29-30. Bompard, pp. 114-115.
  [e] Taube, pp. 27, 40.
  [f] Ibid., pp. 41, 50-51. G. P., XIX, part I, no. 6033, p. 179.
  [g] Ibid., no. 6180, p. 404. Kaiser's Letters, pp. 154-155. D. D. F., VI, no. 19,
pp. 22-23.

Russia was the massacre on Bloody Sunday, 9/22 January, which was followed by numerous strikes in the cities and revolutionary disorders throughout the countryside, arising from the paralysis of the government's internal policy and the wretched economic condition of the nation, which Witte had so penetratingly described to Bülow in July 1904.[h] The impotency of Russia steadily became more evident as each passing month saw the internal excesses not only not stopped but spreading, and the military forces slowly pushed backwards on the war front. Public opinion in Russia was becoming more united in favor of peace without victory, indeed in some sections favoring an alliance with Japan after the peace. Only the tsar and the war clique surrounding him stubbornly insisted on prosecuting the war to a hopefully successful conclusion.[i] The uncertainty of the Russian situation was deeply disquieting to the German government in March 1905. Bülow feared that the disappearance of the monarchy and the end of the tsar would be a great danger for monarchical Germany, so he sought means for working upon the tsar to strengthen the latter's determination to suppress all revolutionary disorders and to continue the war, because time was on the side of the Russians.[j]

During the first half of 1905 there was no pronounced tendency in Russia to lean in the direction of either Great Britain or Germany. Some of the sting had gone out of Anglo-Russian animosity as a result of the settlement of the Dogger Bank affair. British policy had subsequently been closely modelled on Sir Charles Hardinge's caution against "the great risk which may at any moment be incurred of a long and costly war by an action having the semblance of menace or humiliation, the Russian government being at the present moment exceptionally sensitive as to their dignity as a great power."[k] The irritation produced by the Younghusband expedition into Tibet and the Dane mission to Afghanistan had subsided, and

[h] G. P., XIX, part I, no. 6043, pp. 197-198. D. D. F., VI, no. 53, pp. 69-70.
[i] B. D., IV, no. 31, p. 40; no. 67, pp. 75-76. Gwynn, I, 467.
[j] G. P., XIX, part II, no. 6191, pp. 417-419.
[k] B. D., IV, no. 26, p. 35. Bompard, pp. 237-238. Gwynn, I, 422-423.

nothing new was undertaken by Great Britain which might drive Russia any farther along the road toward Germany. On the other hand the increasing distraction of the Russian government had enabled the kaiser to shape the course of his policy to have a reckoning with France by seizing upon the Morocco question, and to test the strength of the entente cordiale.[1] Many Russians had noticed how Germany had taken advantage of their inability to resent actions which had netted so much profit "without losing a man or spending a sou," yet the tsar could still write his cousin on 31 May: "Let me thank you, dear Willy, for the true and loyal friendship you and your country have shown us during this unfortunate war." [m]

Foreign relations, however, received only a minor share of Russian governmental attention in the first half of 1905, being overshadowed by the unsuccessful efforts to suppress strikes and disorders, as well as to carry on the war until the Baltic fleet could win the expected decisive engagement against the Japanese navy in the China sea. When, at last, the sickening news of the almost total destruction of Rozhdestvensky's squadron in the straits of Tsushima on 27-28 May gradually seeped out, the general reaction of the country, in opposition to the tsar and the war party, advocated the conclusion of peace with Japan, while the demands for the reform of the system of government took on additional vigor.[n] The kaiser lost no time in writing again to the tsar, to advise him to make peace at once since now all was honorably lost. It would be dangerous to prolong an unpopular war which no longer had a prospect of success, and the kaiser offered his services, especially under American leadership, "for the preparatory steps intended to bring about peace." [o] President Roosevelt

[1] *Ibid.*, pp. 469, 477. Anderson, pp. 397-398. Spring Rice wrote to Mrs. Roosevelt in a letter of 26 April 1905, intended for the president to see: "It [the impotence of Russia] is just like the departure of a big bully from a school. The other bullies have such a good time and kick the little boys. Did you realize that France really is a little boy in comparison with Germany, simply from not having children enough?" Gwynn, I, 469.

[m] *B. D.*, IV, no. 69, pp. 77-78; no. 190, p. 197. *G. P.*, XIX, part II, no. 6193, footnote *, p. 419. Gwynn, II, 53. Dennett, pp. 87, 172-175. Bompard, *Revue de Paris*, XXV, 432.

[n] *B. D.*, IV, no. 76, pp. 83-84. *D. D. F.*, VI, no. 481, p. 574; no. 489, pp. 581-582; no. 490, pp. 583-585.

[o] *G. P.*, XIX, part II, no. 6193, pp. 419-422. *Kaiser's Letters*, pp. 183-190.

had for some time been anxious to bring about peace between Russia and Japan. His efforts were made easier by the real need of peace by Japan, which had been feeling around for an end of the war since the late months of 1904.[p] In Russia the greatest obstacle to peace was to win the reluctant consent of the emperor, which was finally obtained by the president, with the secondary assistance of the kaiser, on 7 June 1905, and by the 12th both belligerents had agreed to send their plenipotentiaries to Washington.[q] With the end of the war in the Far East, the Russian government was enabled to devote some larger consideration to the remains of its diplomatic position in Europe. Although "the Russian diplomatic currency has become debased and discredited" as Lansdowne said, Russia still remained the "rich bride" with whom France, Great Britain, and Germany wished to stand in closer relationship.[r]

The first advantage in position came to the benefit of Germany. After the proposed treaty of alliance between Germany and Russia had lapsed since Christmas 1904 because of the impossibility of gaining French adhesion, the kaiser had continued to write his lively and affectionate letters to the tsar in undiminished quantities, which maintained his influence upon the latter at its effective peak. Towards the end of July 1905 both the kaiser and the tsar were cruising nearby in the waters and bays of the Baltic Sea and the Gulf of Finland. It was hardly surprizing that the self-extended invitation of the kaiser to pay his cousin a visit, "coming as a simple tourist without any fêtes," won a delighted acceptance. Nicholas proposed that they should meet on their yachts in the Björkö sound near Viborg, "quite singly and homely." [s] In anticipa-

---

Bülow now thought it essential for the best interests of Germany that Russia should conclude peace so that the monarchy in Russia, and the position of Russia as a world power, should not for long be weakened. *G. P.*, XIX, part II, no. 6197, pp. 425-426.

[p] *B. D.*, IV, Editors' Note, p. 73; no. 57, p. 64. *G. P.*, XIX, part II, no. 6178, p. 401. Pooley, *Hayashi*, p. 226. Dennett, footnote 1, p. 214; p. 260.

[q] *Ibid.*, pp. 192-198, 221-226. This is a supremely good account of the entire peace negotiations, especially for President Roosevelt's share. See also *B. D.*, IV, no. 78, p. 85; no. 80, p. 86; no. 83, p. 87. *G. P.*, XIX, part II, no. 6196, footnote *, p. 425. *D. D. F.*, VII, no. 46, pp. 53-54; no. 67, p. 73.

[r] Newton, pp. 339-340. *G. P.*, XIX, part II, no. 6358, p. 659.

[s] *Ibid.*, no. 6202, and footnote *, p. 435. For a longer account of the meeting at Björkö and its aftermath, see J.-P. Reinach, pp. 109-182.

tion of this meeting, which was to be kept strictly secret, the
kaiser at once telegraphed to his foreign office for a copy of
the text of the alliance project of the previous year. This
request was eagerly complied with, and Bülow and Holstein
collaborated in framing advice for the emperor's use. The
opportunity was deemed most valuable because it permitted
Germany to make sure of Russia before Great Britain could
renew its efforts to reach an agreement over Asiatic disputes,
and before Lamsdorff and Witte could bring about the Anglo-
French-Russian entente which, in Berlin, they were suspected
of desiring.[t] In an attempt to prevent a repetition of the
failure of the previous winter, the German foreign office hoped
that Lamsdorff would not be present; but if he did appear, the
kaiser was to paralyze his influence upon the tsar by killing
him with kindness.[u] It now seemed permissible to let Russia
sound out the French government, in the first place because it
was somehow believed that the new French cabinet under
Rouvier would not be so opposed to joining the alliance as Delcassé had been, as well as because it was realized that the need
of a loan by Russia made that government unwilling to take so
serious a step without the agreement of France.[v]

Thus carefully loaded in advance with the text of the proposed treaty and with cues for his actions, the kaiser steamed
towards Björkö to meet the tsar. It is not possible to do full
justice to William's rapture over the interview, and his elegaic
description of it was seldom equalled in all his writing. At the
first conversation with Nicholas, the kaiser declared that the
Morocco crisis with France was calming down and that Germany desired to be on good and lasting terms of friendship with
the Gallican neighbor; while the tsar, striking the table with
his fist in rare determination, vehemently denied that King
Edward would ever get "a little agreement" out of him that
would be directed against Germany.[w] So well did the conversations and entertainment of the first day prepare the way

[t] *G. P.*, XIX, part II, no. 6202, p. 436; no. 6203, p. 438; and following
documents.
[u] *Ibid.*, no. 6208, p. 445.
[v] *Ibid.*, no. 6207, pp. 441-442.
[w] *Ibid.*, no. 6218, p. 455; no. 6220, p. 460.

that on the next morning, 24 July, the kaiser stuck the copy of
the treaty in his pocket to be ready for any eventuality.[x] After
breakfast aboard the tsar's yacht the conversation picked up
where it had left off the day before, and when the tsar again
complained of King Edward's *penchant* for "little agreements," the kaiser felt his time had surely come to suggest
that such a transaction should be made between Russia and
Germany, as had been considered last year. The tsar was
properly impressed, but regretted that he did not have a copy
of the treaty, whereupon the kaiser replied that "so entirely
by chance" he had it with him. After the tsar had read the
draft and approved of it, William pulled himself together to
ask: "Should you like to sign it? It would be a very nice
souvenir of our entrevue."[y] When the two emperors had
signed the document, and a member from each of their suites
had countersigned, the treaty of Björkö entered upon its short
and unsuccessful existence.

The treaty signed at Björkö was nearly unchanged from the
project considered in the foregoing year.[z] The preamble expressed the purpose of the two monarchs in concluding this
defensive treaty as being in order to maintain the peace in
Europe. The *casus foederis* in the first article declared that
when one of the two empires should be attacked by another
European power, its ally would aid it with all its forces by
land and by sea in Europe. Only the words "in Europe" had
been inserted by the kaiser into the draft as telegraphed from
Berlin, and this was done so that Germany should not be
called upon to aid Russia in Asia, while no great worth was
laid upon a fanciful Russian march against India in the event
of war with Great Britain, either by William or by the Ger-

[x] *Ibid.*, no. 6220, p. 462.
[y] *Ibid.*, no. 6220, p. 463. Tschirschky's sober report to the foreign office is in
general agreement with the kaiser's emotional letter. *Ibid.*, no. 6218, p. 455.
[z] The French text of the Björkö agreement is in *ibid.*, no. 6220, Anlage, p.
465. A facsimile of the treaty, on a folio of paper bearing the seal of the
kaiser's yacht "Hohenzollern" is reproduced in Bülow's *Denkwürdigkeiten*, II,
140. The copy from which Baron Taube made his translation (*op. cit.*, p. 52)
was written on the paper of the tsar's yacht "Polar Star" and is probably the
one written by the tsar's brother, Grand Duke Michael Alexandrovich, at the
time of the signature. See *G. P.*, XIX, part II, no. 6220, p. 464. Bompard,
Revue de Paris, XXV, 425.

man chief of staff.[a] In the second article of the treaty, the two allies engaged not to conclude a separate peace with any common enemy. The treaty was not to come into force, so the third article read, until Russia had succeeded in making peace with Japan, and was thereafter to remain valid until a year's notice in advance had been given. The fourth and last article left the task to the emperor of Russia to inform France of the treaty, and to obtain its adhesion as an ally sometime after the document should come into force. By this treaty it was anticipated that British arrogance would be checked; that the poison of the Alsace-Lorraine question would at last be removed from Franco-German relations; that in the face of so powerful a triple continental European alliance all the lesser powers would necessarily fall into line, and the peace of Europe would be secured.[b] It may be doubtful whether these benefits would have resulted from the treaty signed at Björkö; but the early years of the twentieth century never saw any other arrangement fabricated that would have come so near.

The bare information that the treaty had been signed was pleasurably received at the German foreign office, and Bülow at once telegraphed his praise to the kaiser for his efforts in bringing about so great a success, which the kaiser, in a moment of elevated generosity, ascribed to an act of God.[c] Only after his glowing account had been received, accompanied by the text of the treaty, was the insertion noticed of the words limiting the scope of the treaty to "in Europe," and Bülow felt that this spontaneous modification introduced by his master made the treaty worthless for Germany.[d] The chancellor thereupon began a whirlwind campaign to convince the kaiser of the sinfulness of his action, and to search for expedients to get the offending phrase either entirely out of the treaty, or

[a] *G. P.*, XIX, part II, no. 6220, p. 458; no. 6225, p. 471; no. 6229, pp. 477-478; no. 6233, p. 485.
[b] *Ibid.*, no. 6203, p. 438; no. 6208, p. 444; no. 6220, p. 460; no. 6221, p. 466.
[c] *Ibid.*, no. 6216, p. 452; no. 6220, p. 459.
[d] *Ibid.*, no. 6222, p. 467. O. Hammann, *Deutsche Weltpolitik*, p. 144. Erich Brandenburg, *Von Bismarck zum Weltkriege*, (Berlin, 1925), p. 202. In his recent *Denkwürdigkeiten* (II, 143), Bülow wrote: "This addition took a high trump out of our hand, while Russia retained its trick and England no longer had to fear the opponent's ace." Bülow must have played bridge badly to have written such nonsense.

lse satisfactorily explained so as to insure the participation of
Russian troops in Asia in the event of a war with Great Britain.[e] William II, however, was reluctant to admit that he
had erred and defended his position with ardor, even with
larity until phantasy spurred on the flow of his rhetoric.[f] To
win his point and to make his sovereign knuckle down, Bülow
alleged his inability to take responsibility for such unbridled
action. He wrote out his resignation on 3 August and for-
warded it to the unsuspecting kaiser, still enjoying his vacation
n the Baltic. This manoeuver quickly brought the kaiser to
time, who thereupon gave up his defence and in unseemly
abjection begged his chancellor and friend to retain his post.[g]
Bülow also came fairly close to stampeding Holstein into
sharing his point of view, but the great authority of the foreign office regained his ascendancy. By 14 August he definitely
expressed his opinion that the Björkö treaty, whatever its
imperfections, ought to be left alone. A great measure of
profit remained in it for Germany, while to tamper with its
provisions in any manner could only furnish Lamsdorff with
an opportunity to ruin the whole accomplishment. Now that
Bülow had won his stand against the uncontrolled action of
his master, he accepted Holstein's advice, and for some indefinite time no German efforts to bring about either an interpretation or a revision of the treaty were undertaken.[h]

No signs of Russian activity in regard to the treaty of
Björkö were noticed, undoubtedly because the weak tsar had
not yet revealed what he had done to his foreign minister, and
because the final struggle in the peace negotiations with Japan
at Portsmouth was just approaching.[i] At this peace conference Witte had been surprizingly successful in drawing sympathy to the Russian side, while the Japanese were steadily

[e] *G. P.,* XIX, part II, no. 6225, p. 471; no. 6228, p. 476; no. 6229, p. 480.
[f] *Ibid.,* no. 6229, pp. 477-479; no. 6233, p. 485.
[g] *Ibid.,* no. 6230, p. 481; no. 6235, p. 489; no. 6237, pp. 496-498.
[h] *Ibid.,* no. 6227, pp. 474-476; no. 6232, pp. 483-484; no. 6234, pp. 487-488;
no. 6239, p. 501; no. 6240, p. 502.
[i] The French were naturally much concerned about what happened at
Björkö. Several instances in volumes VII and VIII of the *Documents diplomatiques français* reveal how eagerly rumors were investigated and precise
information was sought, without notable success.

finding themselves in an ever more precarious position. They were finally confronted by an ultimatum offering either the choice of accepting the last Russian concessions, or of resuming a war which could no longer with certainty bring them added profit.[j] The Japanese acceded and Witte, disregarding the tsar's last-minute instructions to break off the negotiations,[k] concluded peace on 23 August / 5 September on terms so favorable for a defeated country that Russia appeared as the victor in the peace, yet also with such skill that a period of friendly relations could soon be instituted with the disappointed victor in the war.[l] The immediate reception of the treaty in both Russia and Japan was unfavorable, but displeasure in the latter country was quickly mollified by the publication of the treaty renewing the Anglo-Japanese alliance in advance of the normal time.[m]

Towards the end of December 1904 the Japanese prime minister had expressed the satisfaction felt by his government for "the particularly friendly manner" in which Great Britain had fulfilled its obligations as an ally. He hoped that if the Russo-Japanese war should result in victory for Japan, "the present Anglo-Japanese alliance might be strengthened and extended."[n] In the early months of 1905 these sentiments were repeated, and Lansdowne suggested to Viscount Hayashi that he obtain instructions from his government relative to the terms and scope of a new treaty. By 19 April Hayashi replied that his government would favor a new treaty with a longer duration, but that it should not be extended beyond the present limits.[o] The British cabinet was quite willing to renew the

[j] Korostovetz, pp. 102-103. Pooley, *Hayashi*, p. 226. Gwynn, I, 498-499. Dennett, pp. 260, 297-301.

[k] C. Nabokov, "Why Russian Statesmanship Failed," *Contemporary Review*, CLXXXIII (1923), 182. The order sent to Witte read: "Convey to Witte my order in any case to terminate the negotiations." In later official Russian publications the word "terminate" was changed to "conclude."

[l] *D. D. F.*, VII, no. 395, p. 486. Izvolsky, pp. 125-126. Izvolsky gives some excellent sketches of Witte (pp. 107-136), and his statement that "no career diplomat could have made such a treaty" (p. 125), exactly expressed what Witte thought of himself. The text of the treaty of Portsmouth is in *B. D.*, IV, no. 101, pp. 107-111. It was ratified by Russia and Japan on 1/14 October 1905.

[m] *D. D. F.*, VII, no. 396, p. 487; no. 427, p. 531. Dennis, pp. 26-27. Gwynn, I, 486, 496. *C. H. B. F. P.*, III, 336.

[n] *B. D.*, IV, no. 31, pp. 40-41.

[o] *Ibid.*, no. 112, p. 122.

agreement for a longer period of time, but also believed that it would be opportune to increase its scope in order to strengthen the alliance. It would be useful to have some modification of the former provisions whereby the premature renewal could be more easily, publicly justified. Lansdowne therefore suggested that each party should come to the aid of the other in the event that it had been attacked without provocation by any single power, whereas the 1902 agreement required that there should be an attack by one hostile power supported by a second before the *casus foederis* arose. Great Britain proposed to assist Japan with the full strength of its navy, although not assuming any new military obligations on land, if in return Japan would help Great Britain both on land and sea "within certain geographical limits" eventually defined as "the regions of Eastern Asia and of India." [p] These two regions were patently offsets for each other.[q] As each embraced the gain most cherished by Great Britain and Japan in renewing the alliance, the negotiations were rapidly terminated, and the treaty of renewal was signed at London on 12 August 1905.[r]

The British government soon decided to furnish the French and Russian governments with advance copies of this treaty, along with explanatory and reassuring statements calculated to lessen the painful impression which the communication was certain to produce.[s] The British ambassadors carried out their duty on 8 September, three days after the treaty of Portsmouth had been signed. In Paris the renewal was regretted

[p] *Ibid.*, no. 116, p. 125; no. 131, p. 144; no. 136, p. 150; no. 155, p. 165.

[q] Lansdowne wanted Japanese aid for the defence of India because he thought Russia "would almost certainly turn her attention to other parts of the Asiatic continent" rather than plan for revenge against Japan. (*Ibid.*, no. 115, p. 124; no. 151, pp. 161-162. D. D. F., VII, no. 375, pp. 451-452. Lee, II, 311. Dennis, pp. 25-26, 68.) Nevertheless the British general staff feared that even if Japan did send troops to India, Great Britain "might lose rather than gain by their help," which Lansdowne characterized as an "extremely important expression." (*B. D.*, IV, no. 127, pp. 139-140, and minute on p. 140. For a similar statement by Lord Roberts see *Annual Register*, [1905], p. 229.) In Eastern Asia the Japanese admitted that the freedom "to establish a protectorate over Korea" after the war "was the real object of the whole alliance" for them. *B. D.*, IV, no. 129, p. 142; no. 132, p. 145.

[r] *Ibid.*, no. 154, p. 164. The text of the treaty is in no. 155, pp. 165-169. Lansdowne declared that there were no secret articles. *Ibid.*, no. 163, p. 172; no. 169, p. 175. *Annual Register*, [1905], p. 228.

[s] *B. D.*, IV, no. 160, p. 171; no. 167, p. 175.

because "Russia could not be expected to like it," although
the hope was expressed that Russia and Great Britain could
be brought together, in which France was ready to assist.
Lamsdorff was outwardly serene when Hardinge called the
treaty to his attention and attempted to explain how harmless
it all really was to Russia, since it was a purely defensive alliance, and that by the very renewal of this agreement the
conclusion of peace between Russia and Japan had been
facilitated.[u] The Russian minister declared his willingness to
work with the British ambassador to remove all the causes of
dissension between their countries, but now deprecated any
too early renewal of negotiations for a friendly understanding
as this could possibly defeat the object in view, because Russian public opinion was not yet reconciled to such a step.[v]
Although the Russian press took the publication of this treaty
quite reasonably, and was speaking of Great Britain in tem-
perate language, Hardinge again spoke with Lamsdorff on 4
October, this time to inquire explicitly what the real attitude
of the Russian government was toward the renewal of the
Anglo-Japanese alliance and the resumption of negotiations
with Great Britain. In reply Lamsdorff chose to speak unofficially and privately; what he had to say was disappointing.[w]
He plainly admitted that the renewal of the alliance with
Japan was resented in Russia and had left an unpleasant impression, so that he considered "it would be a mistake to
attempt at the present moment the resumption of the previous
negotiations." He warned Sir Charles that, while personally
he was sincerely desirous of good relations with Great Britain,
"systematic and untiring efforts" were being made in St.
Petersburg to prevent their realization.[x]

Something about these systematic and untiring efforts was

[t] *Ibid.*, no. 172 (a), p. 177. *D. D. F.*, VII, no. 428, pp. 532-536.
[u] *B. D.*, IV, Editors' Note, p. 172; no. 172 (b), p. 178. Gwynn, I, 501.
[v] *B. D.*, IV, no. 172 (b), p. 179.
[w] *G. P.*, XIX, part II, no. 6358, p. 660; no. 6359, p. 661. *D. D. F.*, VII, no
433, pp. 540-543; no. 449, p. 565. *B. D.*, IV, no. 193, pp. 203-204. Taube, pp
65-66. Gwynn, I, 501. Bompard, p. 170.
[x] *B. D.*, IV, no. 195, pp. 206-207. Benckendorff told Lansdowne in London
practically the same thing on the next day, concluding that "it would be better
to give time for the effect [of the Anglo-Japanese alliance renewal] to pass
off." *Ibid.*, no. 196, p. 208. *D. D. F.*, VIII, no. 19, pp. 32-33; no. 44, pp. 62-65

suspected in London and Paris. After the Björkö meeting of
the kaiser and the tsar, Hardinge was forced to report that he
knew "nothing authentic" except that Nicholas II had
returned "thoroughly pleased with his interview." [y] Almost
a month afterwards the kaiser relayed to the tsar that King
Edward had been hard at work trying to find out what had
been going at Björkö, and had been disgusted with his lack of
success. [z] The French government also had become anxious as
to the possibility of a rapprochement between their Russian
ally and German enemy. As a result of this anxiety the French
ambassador in St. Petersburg, Maurice Bompard, confided to
his British colleague on 4 October that "he had been obliged
to defer taking leave," while his government was hoping that
Great Britain would make an attempt to establish better relations with Russia, in which France would be able to coöperate. [a]
While the definite details were not known, it was clear to the
French and the British that, at the end of the Russo-Japanese
war, Germany occupied a more favorable position with the
Russian government than they did; and some grounds existed
for suspecting a closer friendship between Russia and Germany after the Björkö meeting.

Russian foreign policy did not take on any clear direction
until after Witte returned from Portsmouth, when certain
incidents happened to him on his homeward journey which
were to have some bearing upon it. After disembarking at
Cherbourg, Witte came first to Paris. He was careful not to
antagonize the French with his ideas on foreign combinations
which Russia might join, because of the approaching need for
a loan. [b] To the German ambassador, Prince Radolin, Witte
was less reserved, and declared his conviction that the renewal
of the Anglo-Japanese alliance had barred the way to an understanding between Russia and Great Britain for many years. In
these circumstances, Witte went on, the three greatest con-

---

[y] B. D., IV, no. 91, p. 95.
[z] Kaiser's Letters, pp. 198-200, 202. Lee, II, 357.
[a] B. D., IV, no. 195, pp. 205-206. D. D. F., VIII, no. 32, p. 48; no. 65, pp.
97-98. Bompard, pp. 141, 170, 179.
[b] Bompard, p. 150. In a conversation of 25 July Rouvier had told Witte
that there was no possibility of France joining in a combination with Russia
and Germany: "you forget '70." D. D. F., VII, no. 258, p. 300.

tinental powers should stick together in order to restrain Great Britain. There had never been a better time, nor a more favorably disposed French cabinet than that of M. Rouvier, to bring France and Germany together, provided the opportunity was not lost by pressing the difficulties over Morocco too far.[c] Present also in Paris to see Witte was the first secretary of the Russian embassy in London, Poklevsky-Kozell, bearing an invitation from the British government, which King Edward approved, asking Witte to come to England.[d] Poklevsky spoke of the king's wish to have friendly relations with Russia by removing the misunderstandings between the two countries in Persia, Afghanistan and Tibet.[e] Witte made no effort to obtain the tsar's permission to make the visit, but told Poklevsky that he believed good relations between the two nations were desirable, in behalf of which he would work on his return to Russia, if he was then to have influence or power. He feared, however, that any treaty would cause trouble with Germany, and Russia should do nothing to harm its standing with the continental powers. While in Paris Witte's opinion was that Russia needed years of peace without alliances with other nations.[f]

Witte did, however, receive the tsar's command to betake himself to the German emperor's hunting lodge at Rominten, where his presence had been requested.[g] On his way, Witte stopped over in Berlin. He had a meeting with Prince Bülow on 25 September, to whom he explained his opinions, again portrayed the necessity of a combination against Great Britain, and asked that greater consideration be shown in the Moroccan question in order to win over France to this continental scheme, for which some time would be needed.[h] The interview

---

[c] G. P., XIX, part II, no. 6241, p. 504.

[d] Lee, II, 307-308. Witte, *Vospominaniya*, I, 407; II, 406. Dillon, p. 350.

[e] Lee, II, 308. Witte, *Vospominaniya*, II, 406; see English edition, p. 433. There is no substantiation for Witte's declaration that Poklevsky held in his hand a written document proposing an agreement in the same general fashion as the convention signed by Izvolsky in 1907.

[f] Lee, II, 308. Witte, *Vospominaniya*, I, 406-407; II, 407. Witte, always making claims for himself, later asserted that it was because of his objections that an Anglo-Russian treaty did not come before 1907. *Ibid.*, I, 432.

[g] G. P., XIX, part II, no. 6241, footnote *, p. 503.

[h] *Ibid.*, no. 6243, p. 506. Bülow, *Denkwürdigkeiten*, II, 170. Despite his

at Rominten the following day passed off favorably for both William II and Witte. On the afternoon of his arrival Witte had a political conversation with the emperor, at which he dilated once more with fervor on his theme of a three-power continental alliance which should include France. Thereupon the kaiser, with the previous consent of the tsar, "described" in detail to Witte the Björkö rendezvous and "communicated" the accomplishment of the alliance which had been made there, so well in accord with the hopes Witte had just expressed.[1] The latter was amazed by this information and declared that the first task was to gain French acceptance. Partly as the result of Witte's intercession the kaiser did command the issuance of the necessary instructions to overcome the last difficulties in the way of an agreement upon the program of the international conference which was to settle the dispute over Morocco.[j] With a German decoration and an autograph portrait of William with the cryptic inscription "Portsmouth-Björkö-Rominten" in his baggage, Witte set out for St. Petersburg with an undoubtedly exaggerated idea of

variability, the belief in an alliance of Russia, Germany and France was doubtless Witte's firmest conviction. It betokened no particular sympathy for the Germans; it represented a way to keep Great Britain under control. If Russia were allied with the military power of Germany the outbreak of a European war would be more effectively prevented. With France included, Russia would benefit from its money power, and also not become the satellite of Germany. Finally, a close connection with Germany was required to preserve the monarchical idea and the ruling house in Russia. Witte, *Vospominaniya*, I, 412. Bülow, *Denkwürdigkeiten*, II, 44. Izvolsky, p. 53. See also *D. D. F.*, III, no. 416, pp. 556-559. Bompard, *Revue de Paris*, XXV, 436-437.

[1] *G. P.*, XIX, part II, no. 6244, p. 507; no. 6246, pp. 508-510. At this time Witte did not know much more about the Björkö meeting than that it had taken place. (Witte, *Vospominaniya*, I, 421, 427. *G. P.*, XIX, part II, no. 6242, footnote *, p. 505. *D. D. F.*, VII, no. 255, p. 295; VIII, no. 244, p. 331.) The kaiser did not show him the text of the treaty, and it is also impossible to tell how accurately it was described. (Witte, *Vospominaniya*, I, 414; English edition, p. 420. *G. P.*, XIX, part II, no. 6246, footnote ***, p. 510.) After the conversation with the kaiser, Witte told Prince Eulenburg, who accompanied him to his quarters, "Björkö is the greatest comfort of my life!" Bülow, *Denkwürdigkeiten*, II, 172.

[j] *G. P.*, XIX, part II, no. 6245, p. 508; no. 6246, pp. 509-511. *D. D. F.*, VII, no. 466, and note 2, p. 585; VIII, no. 19, p. 23. Bompard, pp. 153, 155. Witte had not the slightest ground for saying that his intercession prevented a Franco-German war over Morocco. (Witte, *Vospominaniya*, I, 419; English edition, pp. 424-425.) Franco-German tension was relieved because the Björkö treaty provided for the eventual adherence of France. To gain this objective both Bülow and Holstein were ready to go easy with France over the Moroccan troubles. (*G. P.*, XX, no. 6782, pp. 531-532.) When the Björkö treaty failed, Germany caused plenty of trouble during the Algeciras conference.

the accomplishments he had won for his country, for France, and for the peace of Europe.[k]

Even before Witte reached Russia, the treaty of Björkö had there fallen upon evil days. Nicholas had delayed showing its text to Lamsdorff until at the close of an audience on 30 August / 12 September.[l] This revelation caused Lamsdorff to return to his ministry where he burned his light throughout the evening. Before he had finished he had written out two notes, one for the tsar, which summarized all the reasons which made the treaty objectionable for Russia, and the other for Nelidov, the Russian ambassador in Paris, to apprize him of the situation and to obtain his advice whether or not to sound out the French government respecting its eventual association with the Björkö agreement.[m] On the next morning the foreign minister wrung the tsar's approval of both, although Nicholas insisted that he did not believe the treaty could be turned against France, or that William had been insincere during the interview.[n] The letter to Nelidov was sent by special courier, and the ambassador's prompt reply so thoroughly excluded the advisability of approaching France on the subject that Lamsdorff determined to undo his sovereign's work.[o]

It was at this point that Witte arrived home and had his audience with Nicholas, who conferred upon him the title of "Count", but only when he visited his old friend Lamsdorff did he have the chance to read for the first time precisely what the treaty of Björkö contained.[p] Because Witte still insisted that a continental alliance was the best policy for Russia and spoke favorably of its realization at Björkö, Lamsdorff asked him whether he had ever read it. When Witte admitted that neither William nor Nicholas had showed him the text, Lamsdorff shoved it over and urged him to read this wondrous docu-

---

[k] *Ibid.*, XIX, part II, no. 6244, p. 507. Witte, *Vospominaniya*, I, 416. Taube, p. 57. *B. D.*, IV, no. 193, p. 202; no. 195, p. 205.
[l] Savinsky, p. 114. Savinsky, *Revue des deux mondes*, XII, 798. Taube, pp. 55-56. Bompard, pp. 155-157.
[m] Savinsky, *Revue des deux mondes*, XII, 799-800. Bompard, pp. 156-157.
[n] Savinsky, *Revue des deux mondes*, XII, 801. Taube, pp. 55-56.
[o] Bompard, pp. 157-158. Savinsky, *Revue des deux mondes*, XII, 801. *Kriegsschuldfrage*, II, 478-480.
[p] Witte, *Vospominaniya*, I, 421-422, 426-427; see English edition, p. 425. Bompard, pp. 158-159. *B. D.*, IV, no. 193, p. 202.

ment.[q] From his own inexact reproduction of the provisions of the treaty it is clear that he "could hardly realize what the words implied," entirely missed the declaration that it was a defensive arrangement, so that he came to the conclusion that the treaty of Björkö was incompatible with the Franco-Russian alliance.[r] Whether or not this was the correct interpretation, the two counts seized upon it as the means for getting out of an alliance that Lamsdorff never wanted and which Witte threw over completely.[s] Strengthened by the presence of Grand Duke Nicholas Nicholayevich, the ministers went to Peterhof early in October, where they persuaded the reluctant tsar to recover the honor of Russia by forsaking his private venture in diplomacy.[t]

The Russian efforts to get out of the Björkö arrangement began with the personal letter of Nicholas to William of 7 October.[u] The kaiser sent an impassioned appeal to keep the treaty alive, but his plea was ignored.[v] Nelidov continued to admonish Lamsdorff that, even although the Rouvier cabinet

[q] Witte, *Vospominaniya*, I, 421, 426-427. Taube, pp. 56, 60. Dillon gives a lengthy account (pp. 354-367) of what Witte told him, but admits that during their acquaintance Witte related several versions varying in details.

[r] Witte, *Vospominaniya*, I, 426-427; see English edition, p. 426. Taube, pp. 60-61.

[s] Witte, *Vospominaniya*, I, 427. Taube, pp. 57, 61. It is difficult to explain Witte's *volte face*. Possibly he did misinterpret the treaty, although this is disputed. Izvolsky declares (p. 44) that his action was motivated by the "deep-seated dislike which he felt towards Emperor Nicholas." Baron Taube suggests (pp. 57-59) that Witte's conduct is explicable on the grounds of wounded vanity. Hammann (*Deutsche Weltpolitik*, p. 145) believes that Witte's idea for a continental alliance was one for economic union, but not for political or military purposes. Bompard offers the opinion (pp. 169, 175) that Witte was concerned to retain the French money market. In a conversation with the French ambassador in St. Petersburg on 10 September 1914, Witte left the impression that something else influenced him: "I'm sworn to secrecy on this matter." (Maurice Paléologue, *An Ambassador's Memoirs*, [New York, 6th edition, n. d.], I, 124-125.) It is likewise difficult to explain Lamsdorff's acceptance of the argument that the Björkö treaty conflicted with the French alliance. He had characterized the former to Nelidov as "strictly defensive" and "entirely pacific." (Bompard, pp. 157, 165.) Taube believes that Lamsdorff knew better, but agreed with Witte in order to gain his help to keep Russia free of "the German yoke." Taube, pp. 57, 61. See also *Kriegsschuldfrage*, II, 480-481. Bülow, *Denkwürdigkeiten*, II, 133.

[t] Witte, *Vospominaniya*, I, 428-430; see English edition, pp. 427-429. Taube, p. 63. Savinsky, *Revue des deux mondes*, XII, 801. *Kriegsschuldfrage*, II, 487.

[u] G. P., XIX, part II, no. 6247, pp. 512-513. Witte wrote a letter to Eulenburg intended for the kaiser to see. (*Ibid.*, no. 6250, Anlage, pp. 519-520.) Osten-Sacken also transmitted an informal communication to Bülow which contained Lamsdorff's objections. Izvolsky, p. 56.

[v] G. P., XIX, part II, no. 6248, pp. 513-514. *Kaiser's Letters*, pp. 216-217.

had been more pliant in its policy to Germany, the Russian government ought not to make any proposals to France to join the continental combination, because the French premier had already warned him that "there could be no question of French participation in such a project." [w] As it became increasingly apparent that the three-power grouping would not materialize, Lamsdorff let Nicholas propose a declaration in his letter of 23 November to the kaiser that could have transformed the Björkö treaty into a dual alliance between Russia and Germany, not operative only in the event of a war with France.[x] This suggestion, however, was not enticing enough to gain either an acknowledgment or a counter-proposal from Berlin. At last, with the tsar's letter of 2 December, and a formal communication through Osten-Sacken that Russia considered the treaty of Björkö inoperative, the affair was dropped and Russia escaped from the orbit of strong German influence.[y]

Meanwhile the British government persevered in its efforts to win favor with Russia, in which it received the active support of France, especially because of French alarm at the possibility of an arrangement between Russia and Germany.[z] In St. Petersburg, twice within the first week of October, Bompard had suggested to Hardinge:

His Majesty's government should make some advance to the Russian government in order to show their conciliatory disposition. . . . The object of this step . . . would be to forestall any action on the part of Germany and to frustrate any overtures for a Russo-German combination in the Far East which the Russian government might be disposed

[w] *B. D.*, IV, no. 203, p. 217. Bompard, pp. 164-169. *Kriegsschuldfrage*, II, 489-490. Taube, p. 63. See also *D. D. F.*, VIII, no. 47, pp. 68-69. In St. Petersburg, Bompard frequently expressed his fears to Hardinge that "Germany was making a serious endeavor to inveigle Russia into some sort of agreement or undertaking to which Count Lamsdorff was personally unfavorably disposed." By 21 October, however, Hardinge could write: "I am reliably informed that the idea of any combination with Germany has now been definitely dropped." *B. D.*, IV, no. 198, p. 212; no. 201, p. 214.

[x] *G. P.*, XIX, part II, no. 6254, Anlage, p. 524. Taube, p. 64.

[y] *G. P.*, XIX, part II, no. 6258, p. 527, and footnote **, p. 528; XXII, no. 7376, p. 61. Taube, pp. 64-65, 129-130. Montgelas, *Berliner Monatshefte*, VIII, 243. Bülow, *Denkwürdigkeiten*, II, 150. Izvolsky, pp. 55-56.

[z] Newton, p. 328. Bompard, *Revue de Paris*, XXV, 426-427. Indications of the French alarm are evident in *D. D. F.*, VII, no. 323, p. 392; no. 401, p. 497; no. 434, p. 546; and *B. D.*, IV, no. 197, p. 209; no. 198, p. 212; no. 201, p. 214; no. 203, p. 217.

to accept as a salve to their wounded *amour-propre* if His Majesty's government held aloof.[a]

Hardinge did accede to the proposal of his French colleague and offered some ideas to Lansdowne on the manner in which "a friendly advance" might be made to Russia. He mentioned the fact that Russia was trying to place part of its forthcoming loan on the English market. While Lansdowne felt that such financial negotiations should "take their course independently of any negotiations having reference to political affairs," Hardinge could cite to the tsar some two weeks later "the presence in St. Petersburg of Lord Revelstoke who, with the countenance of His Majesty's government, was endeavoring to negotiate with an international group of bankers a loan to the Russian government." [b]

There was no lack of desire on the part of the British foreign office to reach an Asiatic agreement with Russia. It would be easier to agree with Russia over disputed interests than to face possible attempts made by Russian agents to assert claims to local domination which had long lain dormant, but which had never been entirely abandoned. An agreement would finally lay the ghost of a Russian attack upon India, and at the same time prevent too great an ascendancy of Germany over Russia.[c] Fear of Germany was becoming genuine in Great Britain. The continued progress of the German commercial penetration of Turkey had already occasioned Lord Ellenborough's remark in 1904 that it would be far better to see Russia at Constantinople than a German military depôt on the Persian Gulf; and this seemed always more likely as each further mile of the Bagdad railway was constructed without benefit of international control.[d] The steady increase

[a] *Ibid.*, no. 197, p. 209. Bompard, p. 239. See also *D. D. F.*, VIII, no. 32, p. 48; no. 65, pp. 97-98.

[b] *B. D.*, IV, no. 197, minute, p. 210; no. 202, p. 215. King Edward wanted the tsar to know of his "earnest desire that the best and most durable relations should be established between the two countries." Lee, II, 310.

[c] Gwynn, I, 422-423, 497-498; II, 77. Nicolson, p. 234. *G. P.*, XIX, part II, no. 6359, p. 661. *D. D. F.*, VII, no. 401, p. 497; no. 445, pp. 561-562.

[d] I. Reisner, "Anglo-russkaya konventsiya 1907 goda i razdel Afganistana," [The Anglo-Russian Convention of 1907 and the Partition of Afghanistan], *Krasny Arkhiv*, X (1925), 57. Wroblewski, *Kriegsschuldfrage*, V, 1226.

of the German navy was yearly more disconcerting.[e] In the English press, shortly after the conclusion of peace between Russia and Japan, the possibility of reaching an agreement with Russia became increasingly popular. Hardinge did not so unfairly exaggerate when he pointed out to the tsar on 24 October that "complete unanimity prevailed in England on this subject, since it constitutes part of the policy not only of the government but also of the opposition, while the press without exception was favorably disposed towards the idea."[f] Yet in seeking to bring about more friendly relations with Russia, the British insisted from the outset that an agreement regulating their interests in Asia must not be considered as having a point aggressively directed against any other country. "It was not a question of getting Russia to join England against Germany: it was solely a question of preventing Russia from joining Germany against England."[g]

This trend in British policy to court pleasanter relations with Russia did not escape unnoticed in Berlin. By the middle of September it was no secret that efforts were being made in London to start the discussion of an Anglo-Russian agreement.[h] A month later Benckendorff positively admitted to Metternich that Lansdowne wished for an understanding with Russia on local differences, but no political entente. He now awaited concrete proposals from Great Britain, although none had yet been made.[i] This development was not to Bülow's liking. He had hoped to keep Russia so much involved in the Far East that Russian attention would be distracted from the Balkan peninsula, and the Russian army kept away from the

[e] Bernadotte E. Schmitt, *England and Germany, 1740-1914*, (Princeton, 1916), p. 180. Gwynn, I, 422-423.

[f] *B. D.*, IV, no. 202, p. 215. The return of Russian influence in European affairs, in a manner friendly to Great Britain and France, was steadily more appealing in London. (Prince G. Trubetzkoy, *Russland als Grossmacht*, [Stuttgart and Berlin, 2nd edition, 1917], p. 92.) See also René Marchand, editor, *Un livre noir. Diplomatie d'avant-guerre d'après les documents des archives russes, novembre 1910-juillet 1914*, (Paris, 1922-1923), I, 14, where Neklyudov, in a despatch of 14/27 December 1910, recalled how the French had dreaded the weakened condition of Russia as a source of danger to themselves, and worked for an Anglo-Russian agreement as added security for France.

[g] *B. D.*, IV, no. 194, p. 204; no. 196, p. 208. Nicolson, pp. 234-235. Gwynn, I, 501.

[h] *G. P.*, XIX, part II, no. 6357, p. 658; no. 6358, p. 659; no. 6362, p. 666.
[i] *Ibid.*, no. 6360, p. 663. *D. D. F.*, VIII, no. 37, p. 55; no. 87, p. 124.

German and Austrian frontiers.[j] If Great Britain thought to push Russia on at Constantinople, that was only less objectionable in the German estimation than the sharp rivalry which it would engender between the Austrian and Russian empires, which would not be to the advantage of either.[k] The Austrian and German ambassadors in London, however, were not particularly disquieted by the prospect of an Anglo-Russian reconciliation, which to them was still something nebulously far away; but Bülow had become more skeptical and felt that "we must keep our eyes wide open . . . precisely in this direction."[l] The repeated professions from both the British and Russian governments that no agreement that might be contemplated would be directed against Germany were not sufficiently reassuring. In a remarkable sentence Bülow combined a statement of the German attitude toward the prospect with a prediction of its future sequel: "If Russia goes with England, then that necessarily means a point against us, and this would lead within a reasonable length of time to a great international war."[m] Although such a possible combination was judged to be "necessarily" directed against Germany, Bülow devised no moves to obstruct its progress.

The discussions for better relations between Russia and Great Britain picked up quickly from the middle of October 1905, after the Russo-German treaty of Björkö was definitely headed to its grave. Hardinge was able to report that the political situation in Russia had improved, and that at an interview on 20 October the change in Lamsdorff's attitude "was very marked and his manner was far more friendly than it has been since the communication of the text of the Anglo-

[j] Bülow, *Denkwürdigkeiten*, II, 130.
[k] *G. P.*, XIX, part II, no. 6364, p. 672. See also no. 6361, p. 665 for Metternich's remark drawing the attention of Mensdorff, his Austrian colleague in London, to this danger, and Bülow's marginal note 5 in which he expressed his approval, p. 666.
[l] *Ibid.*, no. 6361, Bülow's marginal note 6, p. 666.
[m] *Ibid.*, no. 6359, p. 661; no. 6360, p. 663; no. 6361, p. 665; no. 6364, p. 672. The *Hamburger Nachrichten* at this time printed an article according to which Benckendorff was setting "heaven and hell in motion" to bring Russia over from Germany to the side of Great Britain; and rather brilliantly remarked that the existing international situation was rushing on to a diplomatic revolution comparable to that which had begun in 1756. *Ibid.*, footnote *, p. 674.

Japanese agreement." [n] Lamsdorff even referred with satisfaction to the friendliness of the former discussions on the
questions at issue between the two countries, which he was
pleased to think indicated "the friendly intentions actuating
both governments and was of happy augury for the future." [o]
The British ambassador was considerably encouraged and
asked for an audience with the emperor before leaving for
England on the eve of the parliamentary elections in November. The audience was arranged for 24 October, and King
Edward was called upon for a few kindly words to be given
to Nicholas. The king graciously responded by telegraph, and
Hardinge was able to convey the message at the beginning of
his reception. [p] After this bit of pleasantry, which the tsar
reciprocated, the way was cleared for Hardinge to explain
that Lansdowne had proposed, and Lamsdorff had agreed,
that it would be better not to set out in quest of one grand
agreement settling the differences between the two countries,
which were really few in number, but to solve each question
separately, in piecemeal fashion, until all had been cleared
away. [q] Both Hardinge and the tsar hoped that no foreign
power would choose to regard any agreement as directed
against itself, since friendship was actually wanted with all
nations. [r]

This interview marked the zenith of the progress for reaching an understanding with Russia which was attained during
1905, and by the Conservative government of Great Britain.
No further ventures were attempted before the parliamentary
elections, the outcome of which was the coming into power of
the Liberal party after ten full years in the wilderness of
opposition. The main outlines of British foreign policy con-

---

[n] B. D., IV, no. 201, pp. 214-215.
[o] Ibid., p. 215. D. D. F., VIII, no. 75, pp. 107-108.
[p] Lee, II, 310. B. D., IV, no. 202, p. 215.
[q] Ibid., no. 194, p. 205; no. 195, p. 207; no. 202, p. 215.
[r] Ibid., no. 202, p. 216. Gwynn, II, 7. D. D. F., VIII, no. 77, p. 110; no. 87,
p. 125. The Russian government was making it quite clear that it could not
afford to find itself faced with bad relations with Germany as a result of any
Anglo-Russian agreement; and to realize the latter more easily, Great Britain
needed to improve its own relations with Germany. B. D., IV, no. 192, p. 200;
no. 196, p. 208. G. P., XIX, part II, no. 6253, pp. 521-522; no. 6359, p. 661;
no. 6361, p. 665.

tinued, and the Conservatives bequeathed a considerable heritage to their successors in the improvement of relations with Russia. Some seven years before, in an early excursion away from splendid isolation, Salisbury had seen the desirability of an Anglo-Russian agreement which would eliminate the friction in Asia. The limited agreement of 1899 had been merely a faint beginning with little cordiality, which had soon disappeared in the doubtful Russian attitude during the Boer war. Lansdowne once more picked up the broken thread and, from the end of 1902, tried consistently to persuade Russia to renew the conversations looking towards an Asiatic settlement. His efforts met with such success, so far as the general idea was concerned, that on the eve of the Russo-Japanese war, while no specific proposals had yet been exchanged, it could truthfully be said that "a point of hopefulness" had been reached.[s] When again the negotiations were interrupted by the Russo-Japanese war, it was only with the mutual and oft-repeated assurances that their checkered course would be resumed after the peace. Many unforeseen incidents, however, threatened that resumption, and the foreign policy of Russia turned deeply into German channels before it veered back with the failure of Björkö towards Great Britain. In the brief time left Lansdowne in charge of the direction of British foreign affairs, the renewal of his assiduous courtship of improved relations with Russia had not only regained that earlier point of hopefulness, but had gone on with such success as to become "of happy augury for the future." This was the Russian inheritance that the Liberals were given: nothing of positive proposals, but a kindlier spirit between two long and bitter enemies, with a future in which the animosities and rivalry of the past need not be perpetuated.[t] No one more succinctly or fairly

[s] Gwynn, II, 77.

[t] *B. D.*, IV, no. 201, p. 215. In a speech before the Junior Constitutional Club on 6 November, Lansdowne declared that he would be happy to conclude a "simple, loyal, and practical" entente with Russia. (*D. D. F.*, VIII, no. 115, p. 156.) Lansdowne's biographer evaluates his subject's achievement rather well, except for the overstatement in the first clause: "By the end of 1905 Germany was almost completely isolated, and Russia and England were on more amicable terms than they had been for a century. Lord Lansdowne had contributed not a little to the cordiality of Anglo-Russian relations. . . ." Newton, p. 339.

characterized this legacy than did Sir Charles Hardinge, who labored with much of the skill and persuasiveness that had made it real: "The improvement which has already shown itself in the relations between England and Russia only requires careful fostering to bear fruit in due season." [u]

[u] *B. D.,* IV, no. 202, p. 216.

CHAPTER THREE

THE NEGOTIATION OF THE CONVENTION,
1905-1907

THE new British secretary of state for foreign affairs in the Liberal cabinet which replaced the Conservatives took over his office on 11 December 1905. Since become world-renowned, at the time of his appointment Sir Edward Grey was not known for any particular achievements from the past, nor for pronounced views or abilities. His preparation for his new post had come entirely from subordinate positions at the foreign office and, as had been true of Count Lamsdorff, he had never held an appointment abroad. His designation as the foreign secretary in the Liberal government had not come as a surprise; as early as 22 October 1905, before the elections, Count Metternich had told the German foreign office that Sir Edward "had the best chances" for the position.[a] Since the 'nineties it had been known that the new minister had been favorably disposed to the idea of a reconciliation with Russia as a way out of British isolation, and early in 1899, "in the impartiality of his spirit," had spoken so effectively in behalf of an entente in the Far East with the old adversary, that the Russian ambassador in London recommended to his chief that the speech "merited being read in its entirety."[b] As the years continued, Grey kept this viewpoint with such moderation that no diplomat had characterized him as a Russophil statesman. By the time he became minister he had reached the conclusion that "an agreement with Russia was the natural complement of the agreement with France; it was also the only practical alternative to the old policy of drift, with its continual complaints, bickerings, and dangerous friction."[c] On 20 October, in one of his few speeches which foreign representatives in England bothered to note, Grey

[a] *G. P.*, XIX, part II, no. 6360, p. 664.
[b] Grey, I, 4. Meyendorff, II, no. 6, p. 416.
[c] Grey, I, 148.

had declared that "there was, indeed, no British government that would not gladly let Russia have a free hand in the Near East if it should come to a general Anglo-Russian agreement." This remark did not escape Metternich's attention, and William II singled it out for comment.[d] Unlike Baron de Staal in 1899, neither commented on the impartiality of Sir Edward's spirit.

The Liberal cabinet decided early in its course to obtain an agreement with Russia. The recent military defeat of that country had materially altered the importance and the weight of its position in European affairs, and it struck John Morley as reasonable to "suppose even that we held the upper hand in the negotiation" of an understanding. He therefore asked Lord Minto, then the viceroy of India, to advise the home government "what would be the terms that you would exact from Russia as essential to the bargain."[e] In his own first conversation with Count Benckendorff on 13 December, Grey frankly expressed the hope "that an agreement might be reached between Great Britain and Russia with regard to outstanding questions in which both countries were interested." Unfortunately, the ambassador could only respond that "it was quite impossible to make any progress" with the discussions while the internal revolutionary conditions in Russia remained an open humiliation for the monarchy. Sir Edward considerately declared that he realized that some delay was inevitable, and explained that it would be Great Britain's policy "not to do anything which would make the resumption of negotiations or a settlement more difficult later on," which Sir Charles Hardinge, soon after New Year's, summed up in one word as a policy of "inaction."[f] The Liberals were making it clear to Russia, right from the start, that they were fully as eager for a friendly arrangement as their predecessors had been.

[d] *G. P.*, XIX, part II, no. 6360, p. 664, and the kaiser's marginal note 5, p. 665. The kaiser felt that the change of ministry would be good for both Anglo-German and Anglo-Russian relations. *Ibid.*, XXV, part I, no. 8502, p. 5.

[e] John, Viscount Morley, *Recollections*, (New York, 1917), II, 167. *C. H. B. F. P.*, III, 357.

[f] *B. D.*, IV, no. 204, p. 218; Appendix III, p. 623. See also *D. D. F.*, VIII, no. 378, pp. 496-499.

Also like their predecessors, the Liberal ministers were to discover during the first half of the year 1906 that there was a series of unavoidable hindrances, which compelled a continuance of the policy of inaction. Hardinge had a final audience with the Emperor Nicholas on 10 January, at which time he presented a letter from King Edward announcing his recall to London as permanent under secretary for foreign affairs. The interview passed off cordially with expressions of satisfaction over the recent improvement in Anglo-Russian relations, as well as of the conviction that the future would find them better still. Nicholas admitted the seriousness of the Russian internal situation, but declared that the government was taking vigorous measures to prevent the repetition of the December Moscow uprising and to restore order, although "it could hardly be expected that the series of outrages would cease at once." [g] By this change in the diplomatic personnel, Russia gained one friend more at the British foreign office. The newly appointed ambassador, Sir Arthur Nicolson, was himself "most anxious to see removed all causes of difference between us and Russia." [h] Nicolson, however, did not at once enter upon his duties and, while the pessimistic, letter-writing Spring Rice took charge of the British embassy, no attempts were made to carry on the negotiations further.

The new British ambassador did not proceed to his post and the negotiations were not resumed because the international conference over the Morocco question opened on 16 January at Algeciras, where Nicolson was first sent as the British representative. This conference offered an opportunity for Anglo-Russian coöperation in support of France, and for effective improvement in the relations between themselves. [i] The tsar had promised Hardinge, at the time of his leave-taking, that Great Britain and Russia would work together for a favorable conclusion of the gathering "since Russia would also loyally support France." [j] The powers had not been long at

[g] B. D., IV, no. 206, p. 221; no. 208, p. 223. G. P., XXV, part I, no. 8501, and footnote *, p. 3. Lee, II, 310.
[h] B. D., IV, no. 520, p. 580. Nicolson, pp. 206-207.
[i] B. D., III, no. 223, p. 204.
[j] Ibid., IV, no. 206, p. 220. While in Paris at the end of January 1906 Lams-

work before it was agreed that the coöperation of Nicolson and Cassini, the Russian representative, formed another indication of "good augury for future good feeling" between their respective governments.[k] While Lamsdorff avoided any sign of an aggressive policy in Europe, and Cassini was content to report that it was Nicolson's "zeal" which backed up France at Algeciras, the foreign minister declared it to be "a source of satisfaction to him" that both Great Britain and Russia were "working side by side for the maintenance of peace." It was becoming clear that the old animosities really were not unsurmountable, and that the "atmosphere," as Benckendorff described it, was changing to one of willingness for a better understanding.[1]

The policy of inaction was not entirely dominant at the beginning of 1906. So far as Witte was concerned, the time had come when a treaty could be quickly arranged. After his return from Portsmouth he had been appointed the tsar's chief minister, not from preference but from necessity, because he was the one man in Russia most capable of preserving the monarchy from the revolutionary disorders. Now again in power, and weaned from his continental combine, Witte "had suddenly made a new departure," shifting from one grouping to another with a dexterity which Chamberlain had earlier possessed. On New Year's day 1906, using his good friend Dr. E. J. Dillon, a British press correspondent well versed in Russian affairs, as intermediary, Witte explained that Russia had needed during war times a strong military friend on its western border, which Germany had been; but in the present circumstances Russia preferred as a friend some liberal and commercial power, and British sympathy would be admirably calculated to strengthen the party of order in Russia. In his estimate of the existing situation Witte was sure that "Germany could give a finger's length of help and England an arm's length." It was his idea that "if England could see her

---

dorff, with the approval of the tsar, publicly proclaimed: "Les amis de nos amis sont nos amis." *Ibid.*, III, no. 272, p. 246.

[k] *Ibid.*, IV, no. 208, p. 223.

[1] *Ibid.*, pp. 223-224. *C. H. B. F. P.*, III, 356.

way to such an open and evident sign of sympathy he himself could undertake to arrange permanently for the settlement of all difficulties between the two countries in the form of a satisfactory treaty." The method of attaining this result was characteristic of the egotistic impatience of the man: he wished to avoid the delays of diplomatic channels and "much preferred to send a messenger straight from himself who knew his inmost thoughts and could express them as he wished them to be expressed." [m] When Hardinge returned temporarily a few days afterwards to St. Petersburg, Witte called in hot haste to defend his idea. He insisted that negotiations through Lamsdorff and the regular diplomatic corps offered no guarantee of success, but were certain to be protracted, with a golden opportunity lost as the result. Now Witte "opened fire" with the bolder proposal that King Edward should come at once, winter and revolution notwithstanding, to St. Petersburg, there to "arrange directly with the emperor for an agreement," a most feasible method because Nicholas was, so Witte credited him for his purpose, "the only government in Russia and that nothing else was any real good." [n]

Of course it was most unlikely that Witte could have carried out his scheme even at home, but he never had the opportunity because his proposal was so undiplomatic and abrupt that no British statesman would have entered into it. Hardinge returned the call on the following day and raised up many objections. Witte's disappointment was plain to see; "the conversation then drifted off to secondary topics [and] the attempt had failed." [o] His proposal had not been to the British liking anyhow because it was suspected, and Witte candidly admitted, that the "open and evident sign of sympathy" which Great Britain should show to Russia could only be in the form of a loan. There was no doubt that the granting of a loan would immensely strengthen the Russian government's position before the duma which was soon to assemble, but the wisdom of doing so "before it was certain whether

[m] B. D., IV, no. 205, p. 219. Gwynn, II, 54-56.
[n] B. D., IV, no. 207, p. 221. Gwynn, II, 57. Bompard, pp. 240-241.
[o] B. D., IV, no. 207, p. 221.

the government was about to renew the old order of things or seriously to inaugurate reforms" was questioned.[p] Spring Rice was skeptical as usual. He believed that Great Britain would have to advance the money immediately, in return for which Russia would promise readily enough to begin negotiations. An agreement, however, would come after long delays, if at all, because once having the money, Russia might not appear disposed "to make any serious or permanent concessions."[q] The British attitude in general did not favor buying Russian good will through the grant of a loan, and King Edward later decided that even the suggestion of his visit was calculated only to enable Witte to float this loan, — "an extraordinary idea! and one that does not appeal to me in any way."[r]

In face of the internal disorders in Russia and the importance of the Morocco conference to European chancelleries, only informal conversations and exchanges of views continued between Russian and British diplomats. At the end of January 1906 Spring Rice wrote that "the Russians still think that we are dying to have an arrangement with them and would pay anything to have one."[s] All the attempts up to then had come from the British side, but Benckendorff had just told Spring Rice that for Russia to sign a treaty with Great Britain in the unfavorable situation of the moment might be regarded as a sign of weakness, unless provisions advantageous to Russia were included. Benckendorff did admit that an agreement would be popular in Russia if some concessions were written in for "publication." In his personal opinion these could be a dual arrangement over the Bosphorus and the Dardanelles, which he judged Great Britain might now be willing to accept, and the granting to Russia of "the longed-for commercial access to the Persian Gulf." The Russian foreign office, Benckendorff was sure, strongly desired to receive definite proposals from Great Britain which would start things going. Once negotiations had been initiated, an

[p] *Ibid.*, no. 205, p. 219.
[q] *Ibid.*, p. 220.
[r] Lee, II, 565.
[s] Gwynn, II, 61.

"entente" could be carefully framed in its main outlines in secret; then "clinched" during personal conversations at a meeting between King Edward and the tsar.[t] Russian interest in the matter was picking up; Benckendorff was freely using the word "entente" and hoping for generous British proposals since "a beginning must be made by someone," but which would be embarrassing for Russia to attempt. Spring Rice remained skeptical: about a dual arrangement for the Straits, "we ought to say that it is impossible." The Russians "want us to declare what we will give them, in order, as before, to count it as given." [u]

The proposal that the king should visit the emperor in Russia was less easily shelved than Witte's method for concluding a treaty. Nicholas himself was eager for the meeting and suggested how perfectly feasible and pleasurable it would be to have it at the palace in Tsarskoye Selo, which would avoid all the objections to a land journey to Russia and a stay in St. Petersburg while the internal condition of the nation remained unsettled.[v] Despite persistent opposition on the score of the risk involved, the possibility of the visit hung fire until after the middle of March. It was admitted that the moment was opportune except for the unrest in Russia, and Nicholas was certain to be sensitive to a refusal.[w] King Edward practically settled the matter when he noted on 22 March that he could see no particular object in going, because he could do nothing to improve the state of affairs in Russia and because British public opinion would probably not approve of the journey. On 28 March, Sir Edward Grey agreed that "for the present it is impossible to come to any decision and we must wait upon events;" and this marked the end of the suggestion.[x]

[t] B. D., IV, no. 208, pp. 222-223.
[u] Gwynn, II, 61.
[v] B. D., IV, no. 208, p. 223.
[w] Ibid., no. 211, p. 227. Witte now believed that an early visit by King Edward "would have a much greater effect than if it was put off till all danger had passed, or until there was no court to visit."
[x] King Edward had "no desire to play the part of the German Emperor, who always meddles in other people's business." Lee, II, 565. B. D., IV, Editors' Note, p. 231.

Anglo-Russian relations continued to be "entirely indefinite," unguided in their course by any specific commitment, but they were becoming filled with a spirit of friendly coöperation. Both sides remarked upon this with pleasure. Lamsdorff and Benckendorff expressed their satisfaction that Great Britain was tending to go along with Russia in settling the political and religious troubles in Crete, and in the chronic effort to cause Turkey to institute effective reforms in Macedonia.[y] "Nothing could exceed the friendliness of the [Russian] foreign office" when it was known there that Great Britain was not inclined to make a loan to the tottering Persian government, because no money could be lent unaccompanied by political conditions, which would alter the situation in Persia.[z] To strengthen the British position there by means of money-lending coupled with political conditions was "an extension of responsibility" which Grey did not desire. He was entirely unwilling to prejudice future good relations with Russia, including some arrangement on Asiatic questions, by attempting to prevent any break-up of the government in Persia.[a] When the Russian government, late in March 1906, revealed a number of documents to the British foreign office purporting to show the existence of a secret agreement by which Great Britain and Japan had promised to guarantee the territorial integrity of the Turkish possessions in Asia Minor, Grey noticed that "now for the first time the Russians are giving us the opportunity of exposing the lies," while the Liberal prime minister Sir Henry Campbell-Bannerman, in an excess of sentiment, opined that "this last fact is worth all the lies put together."[b] The British repudiation of these documents and warm acknowledgment of their communication caused Lamsdorff, nearing the close of his career, to explain that "he was convinced by experience that the wisest policy in diplomatic dealings was a policy of frankness."[c]

Anglo-Russian coöperation was most appreciatively shown

[y] *Ibid.,* III, no. 272, p. 246; IV, no. 212, p. 228.
[z] *Ibid.,* no. 210, p. 226; no. 212, p. 228.
[a] Gwynn, II, 65.
[b] *B. D.,* IV, no. 213, and minutes, pp. 228-229.
[c] *Ibid.,* no. 215, p. 230.

early in 1906 at the Morocco conference, where the two powers shared their information and worked together for a peaceful settlemeri, which would also be satisfactory to France.[d] Although the disorders within Russia combined with the recent loss of international prestige to prevent giving much effective assistance, Lamsdorff declared later that his government "had never deviated for a moment from her policy of supporting her ally."[e] As time passed, however, Grey believed in the recovery of Russia which "would change the situation in Europe to the advantage of France," and hoped that then Great Britain would be and remain on friendly terms with Russia.[f] With this in mind, Grey worked to keep open the door that would lead to a reconciliation with Russia, because thereafter "an *entente* between Russia, France and ourselves would be absolutely secure." He felt that the Algeciras conference was a "most unfavorable moment" for an attempt to check Germany, but with an entente of the three abused powers "it could then be done."[g] Still with perfect sincerity on his part he insisted that such an entente must not be considered as conceived in a hostile sense against any other power, nor to create unfair difficulties for Germany.[h] This early it was becoming a fine-spun distinction that this entente could hold Germany in check by making aggressive interference in the preserves of others less likely, at the same time that it in no way was to hamper Germany's own rightful enterprizes.[i]

The tendency toward friendly coöperation between Great Britain and Russia was worth encouraging, and Grey admitted in the house of commons that if it continued the growing harmony "will naturally result in the progressive settlement of questions in which each country has an interest."[j] It was amazingly difficult to advance this progressive settlement of questions because of the unstable political conditions within

[d] *Ibid.*, III, no. 283, p. 253; IV, no. 212, p. 228.
[e] *Ibid.*, III, no. 373, p. 316. See also Bompard, pp. 192-193. Fisher, pp. 90, 94.
[f] *B. D.*, III, no. 278, p. 249; no. 373, p. 316.
[g] *Ibid.*, no. 299, p. 267.
[h] *Ibid.*, IV, no. 216, p. 232.
[i] Grey's memorandum of 20 February 1906 is worth reading in full. *Ibid.*, III, no. 299, pp. 266-267.
[j] *Ibid.*, IV, no. 217, p. 232.

Russia. Lamsdorff was disinclined to offer proposals which might be used against his government, but he would be glad to know what England was prepared to suggest, whereupon Grey also discovered that proposals were really "not easy to formulate." It was unpleasant to anticipate, in turn, that "they may simply be used against us by the next man," if Lamsdorff should relinquish the direction of Russian foreign affairs.[k] The attitude of the emperor was naturally of importance. Spring Rice declared that Nicholas had neither initiative nor active courage, although the French ambassador believed that "he was *not* under the kaiser's influence at all," which he wisely qualified by adding, "or at least not at the moment of talking." Grey had offered by the end of May no general conditions upon which an entente could be constructed.[l] To suggest them would be useless until the tsar ordered discussions and took a hand in them; "and that," Grey said, "brings us back to the king's visit." [m]

How reactionary the Russian monarchy might be in completing the suppression of the late revolutionary disorders, thereby alienating liberal British sympathy from Russia, was as yet uncertain; but Spring Rice was for once optimistic and wrote that "our relations will very much improve as soon as the duma is a working institution." [n] The time that must pass before the first duma should meet, and before a government that would be stable under the new conditions could be formed, meant further delay in the attempt to negotiate an understanding with Russia. It had also been anticipated, ever since the October manifesto of 1905 had limited the full autocratic power of the monarch, that in all likelihood some other person would be foreign minister in place of the aristocratic Lamsdorff. Never at any time truly popular, increasing dissatisfaction with his handling of foreign relations was being expressed by the Russian press, and his position was steadily weakening.[o] All his life long he had firmly believed and supported the

[k] *Ibid.*, no. 208, p. 222; no. 212, p. 228. Gwynn, II, 71-72.
[l] *Ibid.*, II, 36. *B. D.*, IV, no. 210, pp. 226-227; no. 216, p. 232.
[m] Gwynn, II, 72. *B. D.*, IV, no. 214, p. 230.
[n] *Ibid.*, no. 210, p. 226. Gwynn, II, 70.
[o] *B. D.*, IV, no. 209, and minute, pp. 224-225. Taube, p. 83.

autocratic idea. With the coming of an elected, even if almost powerless duma, he neither could nor would fit into the new order. His contempt for the amateur representatives of the people he expressed clearly to the German ambassador Schoen, whom he told that he "could wait a long time before I will demean myself to talk with these people." [p] The first meeting of the new institution took place on 10 May 1906; and, as good as his word, Lamsdorff was no longer in office.

The choice of a successor to Count Lamsdorff had been determined in advance in the mind of the tsar, and in what little there was of informed Russian public opinion. The new minister, Alexander Petrovich Izvolsky, was summoned from Copenhagen where he had been Russian minister at the court of the Danish royal relatives of the house of Romanov.[q] This advancement was rather a disappointment to the future arbiter of Russian foreign policy, who had personally hoped to be sent to one of the more important embassies; and to have replaced the ailing Osten-Sacken in Berlin would have crowned his aspirations.[r] In the closing days of 1905, however, it would have been hard to find among the members of the Russian foreign service a better choice for foreign secretary than Izvolsky.[s] The damage done to his reputation, in considerable measure unfairly, in recent years by German writers, has no connection with Izvolsky's appointment, nor with his conduct of Russian foreign relations during the first year and a half of his ministry. In 1906 Izvolsky was well received in his new position in European diplomatic circles, German included. The French minister at Copenhagen was actually "distrustful" of Izvolsky's "sympathy with, and leanings toward Germany," although his British associate concluded that "Izvolsky had held the scales pretty evenly balanced between his French and

[p] *G. P.*, XXII, no. 7355, p. 22; no. 7356, p. 25. Taube, p. 83.
[q] *Ibid.*, pp. 83-84. Witte, *Vospominaniya*, II, 302. Bompard, pp. 206-209. While Witte was in Berlin negotiating the commercial treaty, he prophesied to Bülow, on 15 July 1904, that Lamsdorff's "successor would surely sometime be Izvolsky. Izvolsky was more brilliant than Lamsdorff, but less objective." (*G. P.*, XIX, part I, no. 6043, p. 199.) The French government remarked upon the possible replacement of Lamsdorff by Izvolsky in November 1903. *D. D. F.*, IV, no. 82, pp. 109-110.
[r] Izvolsky, pp. 7, 14-15, 25-26. Taube, p. 86. *G. P.*, XXII, no. 7355, p. 23.
[s] Taube, p. 84.

German colleagues, both of whom have possibly informed
their governments of the friendship felt by His Excellency to
their respective countries." [t] The kaiser himself thought well
of Izvolsky, once early in 1905 having ventured to ask the tsar
to send him to Berlin if Osten-Sacken were to be replaced,
because "he is one of the best men in your foreign service,"
an intimate friend of Bülow "who would be overpleased at
having him here . . . as he cherishes Izvolsky much." [u] In his
letter to Nicholas of 14 June 1906, William explained that
he had expected Izvolsky's selection and hoped, as he was "a
most clever man," that the German government "will be able
to continue working with him on the base [sic] of mutual
confidence arising out of the community of interests." [v] The
German ambassador in St. Petersburg was particularly well
acquainted with Izvolsky. He regarded him as "a very well
grounded, versatile and gifted diplomat and an upright and
reliable colleague," who, without being "a proven friend of
Germany," still valued highly enough "the worth of a close
and sincere friendship between Russia and Germany out of
regard for external as well as internal policy." [w] There were
few serious objections to Izvolsky expressed at the time by
German diplomats. While Schoen's friendly opinions were
somewhat minimized, more especially in later years, others in
turn suspected that Schoen and Germany would have the inside track in St. Petersburg with the new Russian foreign
minister. [x] Prince Bülow's judgment is far more correct than
that of the subsequent, bitter German detractors, when he
declared that Izvolsky was not at all anti-German in the beginning, but only became so, gradually at first, as the result
of abuse. [y]

Among other qualities Izvolsky was judged to be motivated
by intense national patriotism, and possessed of ability enough

---

[t] *B. D.*, IV, no. 219, p. 235. Bompard, p. 273.
[u] *Kaiser's Letters*, p. 158. Dillon, p. 365. *D. D. F.*, VII, no. 434, p. 545.
[v] *Kaiser's Letters*, pp. 230-231.
[w] *G. P.*, XXII, no. 7355, p. 22.
[x] *Ibid.*, no. 7355, footnote **, p. 22; footnote *, p. 23. *B. D.*, IV, no. 219,
p. 235.
[y] Bülow, *Denkwürdigkeiten*, II, 295.

to work for the advantage of Russia.[z] His political outlook was accepted as being liberal, but Benckendorff pointed out that Izvolsky had never openly committed himself and could consequently be expected to survive changes in ministries. Baron Aehrenthal, while still Austrian ambassador to Russia, with an early tinge of malice would not believe the liberalism genuine, but considered Izvolsky to be an opportunist liable to be found anywhere if it would help him to retain his position.[a] His concern for his position, both in politics and in high society, escaped no one, and Izvolsky's vanity and sensitiveness to criticism were his most evident defects of character, so that others had often to handle him with patience and circumspection.[b] While his capabilities were praised, his past activities were not calculated to have prepared him for prompt handling of European questions, which his cautious and sometimes annoying delays during his first year as minister verified.[c] His stay at Edinburgh, where he had attended the university, led to his admiration for English institutions, his knowledge of the language, and his interest in English literature and history, all of which was credited with influencing Izvolsky to his timid liberal views.[d] From London the German foreign office learned that Sir Charles Hardinge had told Mensdorff that Izvolsky, at an early opportunity, was expected to show friendliness to England, which made the Austrian ambassador regret all the more the departure of the "good Lamsdorff."[e] At the same time it was known that Izvolsky was properly impressed by the power of Germany, and that he did not wish any cooling off of relations with the western neighbor, a fact which his conduct during his first year also eloquently attested.[f]

[z] *B. D.*, IV, no. 219, p. 236. *G. P.*, XXII, no. 7355, footnote **, p. 22.

[a] *Ibid.*, XXV, part I, no. 8517, p. 22. See also, XXII, no. 7357, p. 29. Fisher, pp. 160, 165. Hélène Iswolski, editor, (with introduction and notes by Georges Chklaver), *Au service de la Russie. Alexandre Iswolsky. Correspondance diplomatique, 1906-1911*, (Paris, 1937), I, 12-13. Subsequently referred to as: Izvolsky, *Correspondance diplomatique*.

[b] A detailed and rather sharp sketch of these weaknesses of Izvolsky is given in a word picture by Taube, pp. 96-105. Nicolson, p. 217. *G. P.*, XXV, part I, no. 8517, p. 22. Gwynn, II, 73.

[c] *G. P.*, XXII, no. 7355, p. 23.

[d] *B. D.*, IV, no. 219, p. 236. Nicolson, p. 217. *G. P.*, XXV, part I, no. 8517, p. 22.

[e] *Ibid.*, XXII, no. 7356, p. 25.

[f] *Ibid.*, XXV, part I, no. 8517, p. 22. Nicolson, p. 217. Taube, pp. 107-108.

Izvolsky entered upon his duties with a program which was more clearly thought out than was at first apparent. In March 1906, after he had known that he was soon to become foreign minister, Izvolsky had journeyed to Paris and London, meeting with the ambassadors Benckendorff, Nelidov, and Muravyev from Rome, all of whom were opposed to Witte's recent efforts to bring Russia into an alliance with continental European powers, especially Germany.[g] Izvolsky believed that it was necessary to prevent Germany from obtaining too great an ascendancy which would reduce Russia to a vassal of Germany. He reached "a communion of ideas" with the worthy ambassadors that "Russia's foreign policy must continue to rest on the indestructible basis of her alliance with France, but that this alliance should be reinforced by agreements with Great Britain and Japan." [h] While Izvolsky had been minister at Tokyo he had constantly opposed the schemes of the clique of adventurers that had culminated in the Russo-Japanese war. Then his views had brought him disfavor, but when the Russian defeats had served to justify his warnings, Izvolsky's reputation had been enhanced.[i] He belonged with those who viewed the Far Eastern gamble as a regrettable interlude in Russia's true foreign policy. He wanted to direct that policy back into the course where it belonged, to Russia's historic interests in the Balkans and at the Straits, where Constantinople would repay with interest the losses in the Far East, and of Port Arthur.[j] Because of the weakening of Russia through military defeat and the ensuing internal troubles, nothing could be done alone in the Near East until the muddle in the Far East had been liquidated in a reconciliation with Japan, and until the disputes in central Asia with Great Britain had been resolved by an arrangement, whereby British diplomatic support, in some undefined degree, could be expected in Europe.[k]

[g] Izvolsky, pp. 21-22. Taube, pp. 91-92. Stieve, *Isvolsky and the World War*, p. 10.

[h] Izvolsky, pp. 21-22, 72-73. Stieve, p. 12. G. P., XXII, no. 7355, footnote *, p. 23. B. D., III, no. 414, p. 356.

[i] Stieve, pp. 2-3. Izvolsky, pp. 5-6.

[j] Reisner, *Krasny Arkhiv*, X, 54. B. D., IV, no. 219, p. 235.

[k] Reisner, *Krasny Arkhiv*, X, 54-55. Nicolson, p. 217. Taube, p. 92.

When Izvolsky became the minister of foreign affairs on 12 May 1906, it was with the assurance "of the emperor's entire conformity" with these views.[1] In the first place, the Russian international position was such that the maintenance, even the strengthening, of the old Franco-Russian alliance was fundamental in the new foreign policy. Then must come the resolution "of the heritage of Count Lamsdorff in Asia" in a reconciliation with the late enemy Japan. This should be supplemented by an entente, and possibly an alliance, with Great Britain by which the conflicting interests of Russia and that power in Asia should be settled as sincerely and satisfactorily as were the differences that had made the entente cordiale a reality in 1904.[m] There was still a third point in Izvolsky's program for a foreign policy: despite his English sympathies and his intention to achieve a genuine rapprochement, Russia was too powerless to become involved in any international complications, and the revolutionary disorders made the Russian government look to the constitutional, yet strongly monarchical structure of Germany as the ideal model for its own reconstruction. Therefore these real necessities of the moment compelled Izvolsky to hold as an equally important part of his policy the retention of the best possible relations with Germany. He did not want to be drawn into any entanglement similar to the old Holy Alliance, nor to the treaty signed at Björkö; but neither could he afford to sacrifice good relations with Germany for the sake of getting a general agreement with Great Britain. His solicitude not to do anything that would offend the strong western neighbor acted as an effective restraint on his personal predilection for a friendly understanding with Great Britain.[n]

No sooner had Izvolsky become foreign minister than rumors of an impending agreement between Russia and Great Britain emerged. Some of these figments were picked out for an article in the London *Standard* on 19 May, which proceeded

---

[1] Izvolsky, p. 73. Izvolsky, *Correspondance diplomatique*, I, 14-19.
[m] Taube, pp. 92, 94-95, 105-106. Nicolson, pp. 237-238. B. D., III, no. 414, p. 356.
[n] Taube, pp. 95-96, 106-108. G. P., XXII, no. 7355, footnote *, p. 23.

somewhat sensationally to sketch the probable provisions of the "expected Anglo-Russian convention." [o] This article made it appear as if the negotiations had reached an advanced stage in settling the conflicting interests of the two countries in Turkey, Persia, Afghanistan, and Tibet, and that a concerted attitude on the projects of the Bagdad railway, with its branch lines, had been agreed upon.[p] The German government was disturbed by this article and ordered Schoen to make inquiry of Izvolsky concerning it. At the same time Bülow briefly formulated the way in which his government would regard an Anglo-Russian understanding:

We will welcome such an arrangement between the two powers, so far as it has for its object exclusively Anglo-Russian interests, and promotes the general peace through the removal of Anglo-Russian grounds for dispute. We expect of the Russian government, however, that it will not make decisions without our coöperation in questions which touch German interests, and place before us a *fait accompli.* We regard the Bagdad railway as such a question, because it has become an object of value to Germany through concession of the sultan.[q]

Izvolsky gave the German ambassador a preliminary answer to his official inquiry on 20 May; and requested two days time to study the subject thoroughly before making a definite and considered reply. He could at once deny the newspaper statement that actual negotiations for an agreement with Great Britain had taken place, other than to preserve the existing situation in Asia. So far as the Bagdad railway was concerned, nothing had been done, nor would be done, without German agreement.[r] With the approval of the tsar, Izvolsky made his frank and straightforward reply within the agreed time, repeating his previous denials, which he followed with an official explanation of the direction which Russian policy could be expected to take:

[o] *B. D.*, IV, no. 218, and footnote 1, p. 233. *G. P.*, XXV, part I, no. 8507, footnote *, p. 11. Izvolsky, *Correspondance diplomatique*, I, 43.

[p] *B. D.*, IV, no. 216, p. 231. *G. P.*, XXV, part I, no. 8507, pp. 11-12. The Persian chargé d'affaires in St. Petersburg claimed to have heard that the account in the *Standard* had sprung from German inspiration. Even he did not believe his information. *Ibid.*, no. 8511, p. 15.

[q] *Ibid.*, no. 8507, p. 12.

[r] *Ibid.*, no. 8508, p. 13.

After all there can quite naturally develop out of this a concrete agreement [with Great Britain] on the basis of mutual interests. The Russian government has taken note, therefore, with especial satisfaction that the German government will cheerfully welcome an arrangement of that nature, in the event that it shall come into existence. The Russian government recognizes the interests of Germany in all respects in the very important question of the Bagdad railway, and will not reach any kind of a decision which could affect this same question without previously having come to an understanding in absolute candor with the German government.[8]

Schoen immediately thanked Izvolsky warmly for this "loyal, thorough and conciliatory declaration," while on the next day Bülow telegraphed his personal thanks for having heard what he had expected to hear from Izvolsky, whose opinions and high statesmanlike discernment were known to him.[t] Izvolsky completed his first act of loyalty and frankness by communicating to London the substance of his reply to the German interrogation. Grey admitted that Izvolsky "had described the situation and the feeling between Russia and England in terms with which I entirely agreed." Since he knew that he must soon answer a question in parliament about the reports of an agreement, he had determined to "adjust" the language of his answer to conform with that chosen by Izvolsky.[u] In his statement on 24 May, Grey denied the existence of an agreement, but added that the growing tendency of the two countries "to deal in a friendly way with questions concerning them both as they arise" could lead to a progressive settlement and the "strengthening of friendly relations between them." [v]

The British government agreed that the Bagdad railway was a German interest, and there was no disposition to create difficulties in an arrangement which was not intended to disturb any other power. The British were willing to discuss financial participation and coöperation with Germany in the railroad, in common with France and Russia, should the latter

[8] *Ibid.*, no. 8509, p. 14; no. 8511, p. 15. *B. D.*, IV, no. 216, p. 231.
[t] *G. P.*, XXV, part I, no. 8509, p. 14; no. 8510, p. 14. Izvolsky, *Correspondance diplomatique*, I, 41, 297.
[u] *B. D.*, IV, no. 216, p. 231.
[v] *Ibid.*, no. 217, p. 232.

withdraw earlier objections, and if the German proposals were satisfactory.[w] So far as the negotiations for an Anglo-Russian agreement were involved, the question of the Bagdad railway was thenceforward of no direct interest, and constituted a separate matter for diplomatic treatment. After the Algeciras conference there were signs that Germany desired to establish friendlier relations with Great Britain. It did not wish to be left out of the developing "ring" of friendly association that had already been formed between Great Britain and France, and was now being fostered with Russia.[x] Grey privately thought that "all that is necessary is for the Germans to realize that they have got nothing to complain of," and that "England has always drifted or deliberately gone into opposition to any power which establishes a hegemony in Europe."[y] By the end of July 1906 Grey was explaining to Metternich that "it was not the sentimental friendship, but the practical results of an understanding with Russia that we valued," while to improve relations further with Germany "time was all that was required, provided of course that things went quietly and no new cause of trouble arose."[z]

Those who were to become the "chief artificers" of the future Anglo-Russian convention were not in their places until Sir Arthur Nicolson arrived in St. Petersburg on 28 May. Hardinge became the permanent under secretary at the foreign office to give detailed knowledge to Sir Edward Grey, who pressed forward "in the cause of European stability and peace." There was little further delay before negotiations were opened in earnest with Izvolsky, who favored them and hoped to recover something of the prestige Russia had lost in the course of the last two years.[a] Nicolson came fresh from his triumphs at Algeciras, where he had worked in harmony with Count Cassini of Russia, but where he had also laid the basis for the German belief that he was an intriguer and a foe.

[w] *Ibid.*, no. 216, p. 232; no. 218, pp. 233-234.
[x] *Ibid.*, III, no. 416, p. 357; no. 422, pp. 363-364; no. 423, p. 365; no. 425, p. 370.
[y] *Ibid.*, no. 416, minute, p. 358; no. 418, p. 359.
[z] *Ibid.*, no. 422, p. 364.
[a] Gwynn, II, 82. Nicolson, pp. 203-204. Onslow, *Slavonic Review*, VII, 548. Bompard, p. 241.

He himself thought that his work at the conference had increased his reputation at home, and would give him the authority necessary and desirable if he were to have any weighty negotiations to do while ambassador to Russia. Nicolson, however, was not an uncritical admirer of the Russians, and he afterwards wrote that he "undertook the post with great diffidence and considerable misgivings," although he was anxious to "see removed all causes of difference between us and Russia." [b] Like many other Britishers of the day, Nicolson had convinced himself that Germany was more determined to expand, and less to be trusted, than Russia. The German unfriendliness during the Boer war had galled more than the Russian. The growing hold being gained in Turkey and the Near East through an active policy, the menace envisaged in the rapid rise of the German navy, and the recent experience in the Morocco dispute with what Lord Salisbury long ago had dubbed German "bad manners," all constituted important reasons for feeling that "England must cease to be the enemy of all the world," but should supplement the entente with France by something similar with Russia.[c] For doing this the time seemed now more likely to permit success than ever before.

Nicolson assumed his post with the determination to attain the long-coveted general agreement with Russia which would settle the disputed interests in Asia. It was his opinion that such a reconciliation would probably not be pleasing to Germany, where it was regarded as almost a certain impossibility, but at the same time "there was no question of 'encircling' Germany." [d] He was convinced that

[b] *C. H. B. F. P.*, III, 356. *D. D. F.*, VIII, no. 185, pp. 252-253. Trubetzkoy, p. 92. Onslow, *Slavonic Review*, VII, 548. Nicolson, pp. 197, 206-207. Lord Onslow, in his appreciation of Nicolson (*Slavonic Review*, VII, 550), claimed: "He knew the Russians and he knew their limitations. He knew that they were the weakest link in the chain of the entente, and he knew that without Russia, England and France could never make any headway against Germany."

[c] Nicolson, pp. xi-xii, 235-236. Anderson, pp. 114, 404-405. "The German historians are perfectly correct," so writes Nicolson's son and biographer, "in regarding him as a protagonist in the so-called policy of encirclement. They are apt, however, to attribute his efforts and convictions to an envious desire to destroy the growing might of Germany. In this they are mistaken." Nicolson, p. xii.

[d] *Ibid.*, p. 235.

in dealing both with France and Russia, we had honestly no other object than to place our relations on a safer and more secure basis in the general interests of peace, yet the subconscious feeling did exist that thereby we were securing some defensive guarantees against the overbearing domination of one power. We were trending towards a regrouping of the states of Europe.[e]

This reasonable confession of faith, with which Grey had agreed, was rounded out with an assertion of peaceful intentions.

It can be safely postulated and admitted [Nicolson wrote, a bit pompously] that neither France nor Russia nor Great Britain had the remotest desire to disturb the peace or to impair the relations between themselves and Germany, Austria and Italy. It can be asserted with absolute truth that there was not an aggressive or bellicose feeling or aim existing among members of what came to be called the Triple Entente.[f]

It is quite impossible to find a more balanced or milder declaration of the intentions of those powers that felt compelled, in 1906, to seek a new grouping among the states of Europe.

The British embassy in St. Petersburg was occupied as well by its regular routine, in reporting upon the internal condition of Russia, the pacification of the revolution, and the working of the government under the changes produced by the new electoral regulations. In order to be assisted in these tasks, and doubtless to be free to devote his best energies in quest of the general understanding, Nicolson sent for his friend, the publicist Sir Donald Mackenzie Wallace, who had a good knowledge of the country.[g] Sir Donald resided at the embassy for nearly seven months and devoted his attention to contemporary affairs, acquiring much valuable information from varied sources, from personal interviews, from party meetings of many political hues, as well as from revolutionary pamph-

---

[e] *Ibid.*, p. 236.

[f] *Ibid.* In words that Sir Edward Grey would undoubtedly have made his own, Nicolson also wrote: "I am by no means overstating the case for the Triple Entente when I assert that unless the powers composing it were exposed to aggression, or to a wilful invasion of cherished interests and rights, they were resolved that peace should be maintained throughout Europe. It was indeed their hope, though not perhaps their expectation, that, as time proceeded, a general unity of all the great powers might eventually be attained. *Ibid.*, p. 237.

[g] Onslow, *Slavonic Review*, VII, 549.

lets.[h] Nicolson called upon Izvolsky on 29 May and told him that Grey had instructed him "to exchange views on several important matters, such as Tibet and others, and [Nicolson] understood that the Russian government were desirous of entering upon a discussion which might lead to a satisfactory conclusion."[1] They agreed that the Bagdad railway was a question which ought to be handled separately from the others which they were to consider. Izvolsky assured the British ambassador that "he would cordially take part" in the conversations, with all the more satisfaction because he had recently learned from Germany that he could "set his mind at rest in regard to any possible difficulties" in the way of an agreement from that quarter. Nicolson concluded his interview with the proposal to inaugurate the conversations after a few days with an exchange of views concerning Tibet.[j] At last after many years, and the discouraging failures and procrastinations that they had witnessed, a Russian foreign minister had agreed cordially to discuss several important matters with a satisfactory conclusion as the ultimate goal. While Russia had appeared to be a strong power nothing had really ever happened; but in 1906, after two disastrous years, a humbled position among the great powers of Europe and an uncertain situation at home had destroyed the reasons for pride. Now years of quiet were vitally needed to recuperate and to reorganize; but to recover a lost international prestige might require both French and British assistance, besides freedom from German domination.[k]

[h] Nicolson, p. 212. Izvolsky, *Correspondance diplomatique*, I, 341. Count Witte, who was the close friend of another English correspondent, E. J. Dillon, but hardly of Wallace, has belittled the latter. He rightly pointed out the aristocratic weakness of Sir Donald's viewpoint and social relations, but Witte was merely spiteful in saying that Wallace "was not taken seriously in England." (Witte, *Vospominaniya*, I, 372; English edition, p. 138.) Well over a year later, the German chargé d'affaires in London, Wilhelm von Stumm, reported on 22 August 1907 that he had it on good information that both Wallace and "a Mr. Baring" had undertaken "to win over the Russian press for the idea of an entente, and indeed even with financial arguments so far as necessary." It appeared that the *Novoye Vremya* had been reached by "such arguments." (*G. P.*, XXV, part I, no. 8533, p. 38.) Many Russian papers, for some reason or other, were favoring an Anglo-Russian agreement.
[i] *B. D.*, IV, no. 221, p. 237. Nicolson, p. 215.
[j] *B. D.*, IV, no. 221, p. 237. Izvolsky, *Correspondance diplomatique*, I, 298, 303.
[k] Nicolson, pp. 235, 250. Gwynn, II, 53. Trubetzkoy, p. 92. Taube, pp. 92, 94-95.

The British overture to start discussions that would terminate in a settlement of the outstanding differences in Asia
with Russia was also earnestly approved by Nicholas II during
the course of the audience which he granted to the new British
ambassador on 4 June 1906.[1] Nicolson was properly impressed
by the cordiality of the tsar, who repeated his desire for a
satisfactory understanding "not only in the interests of the two
countries but in those of the peace of the world." Nicolson
believed the tsar would facilitate the task and "doubtless exercise a useful influence over the attitude of the minister for
foreign affairs."[m] To both the tsar and Izvolsky, Nicolson
proposed that the interchanges should be kept strictly confidential, because the questions at issue concerned only their own
countries. He wanted to prevent, if possible, any Russian
consultation with other powers, particularly with Germany.
He was not sanguine, however, that Izvolsky would keep his
promised discretion, as he evidently had one eye cocked on
Berlin and might take his friend, the German ambassador
Schoen, more into his confidence than would be desirable.[n]
Since all the initiative had come hitherto from the side of the
British, Nicolson remarked that both nations stood on an
equal footing during the negotiations, in an attempt to ward
off any likelihood of the Russians considering the British as
suppliants, consequently setting up more exacting demands.[o]

In his first interview with Izvolsky, when proposing to open
the discussions with an exchange of views over Tibet, Nicolson
had declared that he preferred to wait a few days before examining them, which turned out to be a suggestion, in dealing with
Russians, that he needed never to repeat. On 7 June, he came
to recount to Izvolsky the various treaties that Great Britain
had with Tibet and China, and explained the five points of the
British demands deemed necessary for securing the proper

---

[1] For the remainder of the chapter only the steps in the negotiation of the
convention, and the attitudes taken by other powers towards it during this
time, are described. The actual difficulties encountered, and the settlements
finally arranged respecting Tibet, Afghanistan and Persia, are left to the three
following chapters.
[m] *B. D.*, IV, no. 222, p. 238. Nicolson, pp. 215-216.
[n] *B. D.*, IV, no. 221, pp. 237-238. Nicolson, p. 215.
[o] *B. D.*, IV, no. 223, p. 239.

enjoyment of the position then held in Tibet.[p] Izvolsky had already confessed that "his mind . . . was a blank on the questions with which we should deal," but promised to study the entire past correspondence before another meeting.[q] In response to his query as to the mode of procedure, Nicolson laid down the method that was to be followed during the course of the negotiations. Because of the hardiness of the old suspicions, the proceedings must be thoroughly business-like, with the discussions purely matter of fact concerning opposing interests within specific and strictly defined regions. Only after a virtual agreement had been reached on one question should another be taken up. When all subjects had been examined, and their discussion terminated, a convention should be drawn up and signed which comprised everything, "but that settlement of each question must depend on a general understanding being arrived at."[r] Izvolsky agreed to this suggested method of procedure and did not later seek to change it, although how much he may have deliberately delayed to cause the prior revelation of British views cannot be told.

Nevertheless, throughout the whole of the coming summer the conversations over Tibet failed to make real headway, which is explained by several factors besides the need of diplomats for vacations. No doubt Nicolson overestimated the sincerity that he ascribed to the tsar's desire for an agreement, for the emperor had written to the kaiser shortly after Nicolson's audience that the British were "fiddling around" about Asia, but that their proposals were being calmly awaited.[s] Izvolsky from the outset had been dilatory in taking up the discussions, alleging that he was not yet well enough versed in

[p] *Ibid.*, no. 224, p. 239. The five demands are printed in no. 311, enclosure 2, p. 333. Nicolson, pp. 217-219.

[q] *B. D.*, IV, no. 223, p. 239; no. 224, p. 240.

[r] *Ibid.*, no. 224, p. 240. Nicolson, p. 207. Grey was ready to reveal the British desires in Tibet and in Afghanistan, but thought that Russia should declare its demands about Persia where Russian interests were paramount. Nicolson was to see to it that "as far as possible the disclosure of the Russian point of view on each question should be equivalent to our own." *B. D.*, IV, no. 224, Grey's minute, and footnote 1, p. 240; no. 226, p. 241; no. 227, p. 241.

[s] In his reply of 14 June the kaiser wrote that, if the British offers were acceptable, "an understanding with them would remove many elements of friction and conflict which would also give me satisfaction." *Kaiser's Letters*, p. 231.

the subjects and needed time for study.[t] When he came to the
foreign ministry he had not found its organization nor its
personnel to his liking, and his efforts to remedy these defects
consumed his time and largely distracted his attention from
political considerations.[u] One of Izvolsky's personal weaknesses, his concern to build up a secure and important social
position, annoyed Nicolson, especially when the foreign minister neglected his official duties to pay ceremonial visits to
Russian grand dukes who lived at a distance from the capital,
and whose importance Nicolson did not appreciate.[v] Two
incidents also arose during the summer, of no lasting importance to be sure, but which produced momentary touchiness in
Russia, and served to keep mutual relations distant and cool.

Towards the end of May, a practice cruise of a part of the
British fleet into the Baltic Sea had been ordered, and the
Russian government had been asked if it would be convenient
to receive a visit from a naval squadron at Kronstadt and
other Baltic ports.[w] This suggestion was made "with a view
to easing the relations between the two countries;" but an
affirmative answer was returned reluctantly by the Russian
government. The British request was badly timed, and both
Izvolsky and the tsar spoke of it as being in the nature of
unwelcome self-invitation.[x] Izvolsky objected because the visit
was calculated to indicate a greater degree of warmth in Anglo-Russian relations than the actual circumstances warranted.
It came unwelcomely at a time when the country was still
troubled with internal disturbances, with its fleet almost non-
existent after the losses in the Japanese war, and consequently
in no position to return the visit in corresponding style within
a predictable time.[y] The projected visit which became steadily

[t] B. D., IV, no. 223, p. 239.
[u] G. P., XXV, part I, no. 8508, p. 13. Taube, pp. 86-87, 100-104.
[v] Onslow, Slavonic Review, VII, 549. Taube, pp. 104-105.
[w] B. D., IV, Editors' Note, p. 241. G. P., XXV, part I, no. 8513, p. 17. Grey, I, 150.
[x] Lee, II, 565. G. P., XXV, part I, no. 8512, p. 17; no. 8513, p. 17. The kaiser wrote to the tsar on 14 June that he was "fully convinced of your feelings of indignation" respecting this "self-invited visit." William availed himself of the chance to keep Nicholas suspicious of Great Britain by warning him that the British "will certainly try to strengthen the backs of your ultra liberal party." Kaiser's Letters, pp. 231-232.
[y] G. P., XXV, part I, no. 8513, pp. 17-18.

more unpleasant to the Russians also "aroused dislike and opposition among Liberals in the House of Commons." This caused embarrassment in the British foreign office, which hesitated to cancel the trip for fear that it would be construed as a rebuff to Russia. The troublesome question was solved when a request came from St. Petersburg on 12 July that the visit should not take place. Izvolsky explained, with discretion and tactfulness, that it would be better if the British fleet stayed away, since its presence could lead to unpleasant demonstrations while the internal situation in Russia remained unstable.[z] The tsar also sent a personal telegram to King Edward in which he pointedly expressed his anxiety: "To have to receive foreign guests when one's country is in a state of acute unrest is more than painful and inappropriate." The king at once replied that he fully understood and appreciated the objections, but hoped that the visit might take place the following year.[a] The British proposal was doubtless well-intentioned but over-hasty, and succeeded only in irritating the Russian government. By Izvolsky's own admission it resulted in a temporary lull in the drawing together of Russia and Great Britain.[b]

The second incident which wounded Russian feelings happened in London at the opening of the sessions of the Inter-Parliamentary Union, where the representatives of all the European parliaments had foregathered. The British prime minister, Sir Henry Campbell-Bannerman, was almost ready to give the address of welcome on the morning of 23 July 1906, just as word was received that the first Russian duma had been dissolved in displeasure by an ukaz of the tsar two days previously.[c] This momentous event could not be ignored in his speech, and Sir Henry hurriedly bethought himself of a few French sentences which seemed to him felicitous, so he incorporated them into his address, although they had been

[z] Grey, I, 150. *G. P.*, XXV, part I, no. 8514, p. 19; no. 8515, p. 20. Izvolsky, *Correspondance diploma.ique*, I, 320, 327, 331, 333.

[a] Lee, II, 565-566. Izvolsky, *Correspondance diplomatique*, I, 332, 338.

[b] *G. P.*, XXV, part I, no. 8515, p. 20.

[c] *Ibid.*, no. 8517, footnote *, p. 21. J. A. Spender, *The Life of the Right Honourable Sir Henry Campbell-Bannerman, G. C. B.*, (London, 1923), II, 261-262.

written "rather too late" to be passed upon by the foreign office. When he came to this passage in his remarks, the prime minister adroitly disclaimed any intention of casting either blame or praise on the dissolution. He asserted that new institutions often were known to have troubled youths, but that the duma would be revived in some form or other. His happiest inspiration he saved to the end in the adaptation of a familiar cry: "La Douma est morte, Vive la Douma!" [d] This brought rousing cheers from the parliamentary delegates, but inquiries from the Russian government, and anxious moments to the British cabinet. Sir Henry declared himself "desolated" to understand that his words were considered as a rebuke to the tsar and an interference in the internal affairs of Russia. This second misadventure in British attempts to be friendly was only closed after the most conciliatory assurances had been tendered both by the prime minister and Sir Edward Grey.[e] Anglo-Russian relations retained a temporary dullness, and an article in the London *Times*, abusing the Russian emperor, poured no soothing oil on sensitive feelings. It irritated Nicolson to realize that these were minor incidents of no vital concern, but in his diary he had to note for 6 August: "Izvolsky's former eagerness has been replaced by silence and apparent indifference. The emperor is wounded. Two months ago there was every hope, and now very little." [f]

As the summer waned and the Anglo-Russian negotiations lagged, the British foreign office plodded serenely along doing the necessary spade-work to be ready for the future. The British plan for a settlement in Tibet had long been in Russian hands, and a counterscheme had been promised which was not yet forthcoming. The British government knew fairly definitely what it wanted in Afghanistan, and near the middle of August Grey hoped that he had sufficiently prepared his instructions to enable Nicolson to take up this subject.[g] Very likely the dilatory pace set by the Russians had not been

[d] *Ibid.*, pp. 262-263. Izvolsky, *Correspondance diplomatique*, I, 336, 338.
[e] *G. P.*, XXV, part I, no. 8517, pp. 21-22. Spender, II, 264. Izvolsky, pp. 204-205.
[f] Nicolson, p. 222.
[g] *B. D.*, IV, no. 227, p. 241.

NEGOTIATION OF THE CONVENTION, 1905-1907   133

entirely unwelcome in London, because the views of the government of India in regard to Afghanistan had been so intemperate that they were likely to be rejected by the India office at home.[h] The essential terms for which the government of India spoke were so staggering that they would have made any discussion with Russia futile. Although Morley was not surprized by "the frowns of incredulity, suspicion, and dislike with which the idea of an Anglo-Russian agreement was greeted at Simla," he had to exercise a moderating influence early and often, which he started to do in his reply of 6 July 1906. He declared explicitly that "the policy of a Russian entente was not open to question, that the home government were definitely decided on an entente, and that there could not be two foreign policies, one at Whitehall and the other at Simla."[i] The Indian government persisted tenaciously in its recalcitrant viewpoint and Grey had to admit that "it takes a little time to lead them to the waters of conciliation and get them to agree that they are wholesome."[j]

Sir Edward Grey was not impatient with the slow movement of the conversations and cared to go no faster than was necessary to keep them alive for the time that Russia remained, in his opinion, on the brink of revolution. Only by 7 September did he despatch to Nicolson the authorization to open discussions on Afghanistan, as well as to receive any proposals concerning Persia that Izvolsky should choose to put forward.[k] Yet Nicolson could only reply that there was no evident eagerness to pursue the negotiations; no counterdraft was forthcoming on the Tibetan question; Izvolsky listlessly agreed to discuss Afghanistan, but made no effort to do so; and when Nicolson hinted that he would like to hear the Russian views on Persia, Izvolsky looked at him blankly and replied that he had no views at all.[l] The minister was then much more worried about the loan desired from impecunious Russia by the

[h] *Ibid.*, no. 226, p. 241. Habberton, p. 77.
[i] Morley, II, 151, 176. Lee, II, 569. Even King Edward urged that there should be greater "coöperation."
[j] *B. D.*, IV, no. 227, p. 241.
[k] *Ibid.*, no. 227, p. 242; no. 341, p. 389.
[l] *Ibid.*, no. 228, p. 242.

Persian government, and wished for British participation in order to be able to forestall any solicitation being sent to Germany.[m] The reports that Persia had recently offered a concession for a German bank in Teheran further alarmed Izvolsky, even despite the assertions that the bank would serve only commercial and no political German interests.[n] All this Nicolson found "a little discouraging," and he suggested that it would be better to help settle these more pressing special questions, and to leave Izvolsky alone for a while on the major subjects.[o]

By the last week of September, Izvolsky had made "a step or two in advance" and showed more interest in the course taken by the negotiations than lately he had, but even so he had expressed only his personal views in the vaguest outline.[p] It was becoming clear, however, where the difficulties were to be found. Izvolsky's early initiative had been diminished, so it was suspected, by the objections of the military party in the Russian government, whose desires for a port upon the Indian Ocean, connected by a railroad with Russia, and for greater control in the strategic Persian province of Seistan would not harmonize with the idea of an agreement with Great Britain. The real attitude of Nicholas II would be a deciding factor which, despite his pleasant assurances, was really something unknown.[q] Nicolson assumed that the Russians were proceeding more cautiously than was usual because they realized the weakness of the country and feared that Great Britain would take advantage of it.[r] Most of all, however, the delay sprang from the recent activity of Germany in Persia, which alarmed Izvolsky both because it was an invasion into a region where

[m] *Ibid.*, no. 336, pp. 386-387; no. 340, p. 389. Izvolsky, *Correspondance diplomatique*, I, 359, 362, 368, 375.

[n] *B. D.*, IV, no. 351, p. 396; no. 356, p. 401. *G. P.*, XXII, no. 7362, p. 36.

[o] *B. D.*, IV, no. 228, p. 242.

[p] *Ibid.*, no. 229, p. 242. This veering towards Great Britain was reported to the German foreign office, and in an annotation the kaiser described excellently the future possibilities: "A nice outlook! One can, therefore, in the future count upon the Franco-Russian alliance, the Franco-British entente cordiale, and the Anglo-Russian entente, with Spain, Italy and Portugal as onhangers thereto in the second rank!" *G. P.*, XXV, part I, no. 8518, p. 23.

[q] Izvolsky, *Correspondance diplomatique*, I, 367, 377-378. Gwynn, II, 85. *B. D.*, IV, no. 229, p. 242; no. 233, p. 246; no. 234, p. 247.

[r] *Ibid.*, no. 229, p. 243.

Russian domination had been hitherto unquestioned, and because this forward movement weakened the assurances obtained from Germany in May that no objection would be raised against an Anglo-Russian agreement which did not injure the interests of other powers. During October 1906 Izvolsky made a journey to western Europe, essentially for a vacation and to select apparel for himself and his wife as would be fitting for their new position, with some lesser time devoted to the cares and perplexities of state.[s] At a meeting in Paris on 22 October with the British ambassador Sir Francis Bertie, Izvolsky explained his attitude and purpose with notable frankness:

Before coming to arrangements with England, I must find out at Berlin what interests the German emperor and his government consider that Germany has in Persia, not necessarily in order to allow them to stand in the way of an agreement with England, but in order to avoid a repetition by Germany of her attitude in the Morocco question and Russia being placed in the dilemma of France. . . . I require all this information in order to enable me to judge how far I can go without the risk of meeting with German opposition. In the present position of Russia it is essential to consider German susceptibilities.[t]

On his way to Paris Izvolsky had stopped off in Berlin where, on 12 October, he told Schoen that on his return he would take the opportunity to discuss with the chancellor and the emperor his general policies and special questions. In particular he would consider friendly and neighborly relations with Germany in keeping with the good, old tradition. He would explain frankly and fully the aims, the bounds and the progress of the attempt for a reconciliation with Great Britain. He would also speak about the recently disquieting reports of German interests developing within Persia, where Russian political and commercial influence occupied a privileged position.[u] British and French statesmen paid close attention to Izvolsky while he remained in Paris, where he revealed to them how important it was for Russia not to become involved

[s] *G. P.*, XXII, no. 7362, p. 35; no. 7364, p. 38. Taube, pp. 108-109. Izvolsky, *Correspondance diplomatique*, I, 47-48, 55-56, 367.
[t] *B. D.*, IV, no. 230, p. 243.
[u] *G. P.*, XXII, no. 7362, pp. 35-36. See also *B. D.*, IV, no. 233, p. 246.

in any unfriendly way, and that anything like the Morocco crisis must be avoided as a result of an agreement between Russia and Great Britain.[v] King Edward extended an invitation to Izvolsky to include London in his tour, but this was declined, although the French seemed to think that Izvolsky had altered his previous intentions.[w] When he explained that this visit had not been planned and that his remaining time was fully occupied; that the negotiations were not sufficiently advanced nor the occasion propitious before he had discovered the real German attitude to them, or their intentions in Persia, King Edward was able to "understand and appreciate the reasons given," although he would "*always* regret that M. Izvolsky was unable to come to London this year." [x]

The second stay Izvolsky made in Berlin, between 28 and 30 October, was marked by straightforward discussions at the foreign office and with the kaiser. Izvolsky explained how necessary it was for his country to reach a settlement of the differences with Great Britain. The unfavorable position of Russia in the Far East left no other choice, as the renewal of the Anglo-Japanese alliance was a standing menace, all the more threatening because Izvolsky could foresee no direct reconciliation with Japan for many years. The regions wherein Russia contemplated reaching an agreement with the century-old enemy comprised Tibet, Afghanistan and Persia, but there was to be absolutely no point in the agreement directed against Germany, as the rights and interests of third parties were to be scrupulously preserved. Contrary to the trend of the articles and rumors published by the press, particularly the English, Izvolsky gave the honest assurance that the negotiations were only in an elementary stage and were progressing slowly.[y] He spoke forcefully respecting the recent German moves in Persia and declared that Russia could not look with equanimity upon the establishment of a German

[v] *Ibid.*, no. 230, p. 243; no. 231, p. 244; no. 233, p. 246.
[w] *Ibid.*, no. 230, p. 243; no. 233, p. 246; no. 237, p. 251. Izvolsky, *Correspondance diplomatique*, I, 379-382.
[x] *B. D.*, IV, no. 230, and minute, p. 243; no. 233, and minute, p. 246. Izvolsky, *Correspondance diplomatique*, I, 382-387. See also *G. P.*, XXII, no. 7364, p. 40.
[y] *Ibid.*, p. 39.

bank in Persia, empowered to grant loans to the local government or to undertake the construction of railroads or telegraph lines. These were matters reserved in part to Great
Britain and to Russia which, because of their financial and
political obligations, must be respected. On this point Izvolsky
was at once reassured: the concession for a German bank in
Teheran was far from reality. If it did ever materialize it
would be a commercial bank to assist the developing German
trade with Persia, (in itself displeasing to Russia), but all
political plans were entirely beyond its compass.[z] So far as his
attitude to the Bagdad railway was expressed, Izvolsky had
no personal objection to it so long as any Persian connections
would not endanger the Russian position in northern Persia,
and he agreed to attempt to overcome traditional Russian
opposition against an understanding on this question acceptable
to Germany.[a] Before quitting Berlin, Izvolsky called upon the
British ambassador, Sir Frank Lascelles, to tell him that he
believed he had convinced Bülow that an Anglo-Russian understanding would not be directed against Germany. He now had
hopes of reaching a complete agreement with Great Britain,
although time would be required to allay important and long-
enduring Russian suspicions.[b]

The Berlin sojourn restored to Izvolsky the contentment
of the May interchange, and he was pleased in the highest
degree with the reception of himself and his explanations.[c]
When he was back in the Russian capital, Schoen told him that
the kaiser had been impressed by his unreserved frankness and
loyalty, which had moderated the painful memories of recent
Russian-German relations, whereupon Izvolsky assured him
that Germany "could be certain not to experience any disappointment through him."[d] Nicolson also was witness to
Izvolsky's renewed spirits and described him as "evidently
relieved at the removal of the fear which was haunting him

[z] *Ibid.*, p. 40. Izvolsky, *Correspondance diplomatique*, I, 215-217.
[a] *G. P.*, XXV, part I, no. 8649, pp. 231-232.
[b] *B. D.*, IV, no. 234, pp. 247-248.
[c] *G. P.*, XXII, no. 7364, p. 41. Izvolsky, *Correspondance diplomatique*, I, 68,
70, 391-395.
[d] *G. P.*, XXII, no. 7366, p. 43.

that Germany would step in at a given moment and make matters uncomfortable for Russia," and believed that "the assurances which he has received have stimulated him to take up the discussions more actively than he has hitherto done." [e] Izvolsky in turn succeeded in quieting German anxiety over exaggerated rumors appearing in the press concerning the nature of the Anglo-Russian conversations. Bülow gave a long address in the German Reichstag on 14 November, in which he asserted that the Anglo-Russian negotiations were fraught with no danger to Germany. "We have no thought," said the chancellor, "of wishing to push ourselves in between France and Russia or France and England. . . . We have no reason at all to disturb these [Anglo-Russian] negotiations, or to regard their probable result with mistrustful eyes." [f]

In other places Izvolsky's reception in Berlin, and the assurances that he gave there, did encounter mistrustful eyes. To Baron Aehrenthal, who had been appointed minister of foreign affairs for Austria-Hungary while Izvolsky had been away, and who was lingering on in St. Petersburg only to take his leave, Izvolsky spontaneously repeated the assurances that had quieted the extreme sensitiveness of the Germans about the Anglo-Russian negotiations. [g] Aehrenthal had, from the first rumors, desired to obstruct the possible conclusion of any such agreement. He was now less contented with the explanations. His own opinion was that Russia would have done more wisely to have conciliated Japan, and plant the seed of distrust between that empire and Great Britain, consequently remaining free to participate in some renewal of the old League of the Three Emperors. [h] Aehrenthal realized that the time was not suited for this, but he also remained skeptical that Izvolsky would act as much in harmony with Austria in the Balkans as Lamsdorff had done, or that his will power was strong enough to keep him from gravitating toward Great Britain, for this

[e] B. D., IV, no. 236, p. 250.
[f] G. P., XXII, no. 7362, p. 35; no. 7366, p. 43; no. 7368, p. 48. Izvolsky, Correspondance diplomatique, I, 74, 219, 394-395.
[g] G. P., XXII, no. 7366, p. 44; no. 7367, p. 46.
[h] Ibid., no. 7366, p. 44; no. 7367, p. 46; XXV, part I, no. 8506, pp. 10-11.

would be popular among the liberal element in Russian politics.[1]

The French government was also worried over Izvolsky's reception in Berlin. Latterly Franco-Russian relations had lost considerable cordiality and the two countries had been tied closely together mostly because of the serious need of Russia for loans supplied by French investors in search of what appealed to them as good security for their savings.[j] The French ambassador in St. Petersburg had communed with Nicolson shortly after Izvolsky's return from Berlin. Bompard admitted that there had been some uneasiness in France, where it was believed that Izvolsky had been forced to promise that no Anglo-Russian agreement would be made that could be turned to the disadvantage of Germany. The Frenchman had been calmed by Izvolsky's declaration that recent reports of the contemplated revival of the Three Emperors' League were "pure myths," and that the French alliance still stood as the cornerstone of Russian foreign policy.[k]

Despite the careful explanations already received from Izvolsky while he had been in Paris, Grey had remained suspicious of the intimate meetings which the Russian minister had had with the Germans. He let Nicolson know that the British would expect some frank statements as to what had passed between Izvolsky and his hosts, as well as some progress in the negotiations with England to serve as a proof "that the Germans are not putting spokes in the wheel." [l] Early in November, Nicolson found out from Izvolsky that no details of the Anglo-Russian conversations had been disclosed by him in Berlin, but that he had allayed the misgivings in the German mind that an effort was in progress to isolate Germany and to confine that nation within a ring of hostile powers.[m] In return Izvolsky was at ease in his own mind that Germany would put no obstacles in the way of an arrangement

[1] *Ibid.*, XXII, no. 7367, p. 45; no. 7369, p. 50.
[j] *Ibid.*, no. 7366, pp. 44-45. *B. D.*, IV, no. 243, pp. 255-256.
[k] *Ibid.*, no. 240, pp. 253-254. Bompard, pp. 241-242, 244. Izvolsky, *Correspondance diplomatique*, I, 217, 393.
[l] *B. D.*, IV, no. 235, pp. 249-250.
[m] *Ibid.*, no. 369, pp. 412-413. Bompard, p. 242.

that would remove the causes of friction between Great Britain and Russia in Asia, wherefore "laying his hand on his heart" he pledged to use "all his energies" to accomplish his task, and to attain that understanding which he "honestly and sincerely" desired, being convinced that it was "the right policy for Russia to pursue." Nicolson expected that Izvolsky would still move slowly and plead for time because of the strong opposition that persisted in the government against his plans. In one respect it appeared that the critics of Izvolsky were on strong ground, and would force him to obtain compensations, for which Nicolson suggested that the British government should be prepared. When the bargaining should begin over Persia, if Russia then promised to retire from the strategically valuable region of Seistan alongside the Afghan frontier, the demand was certain to arise for something adequate in return for Russia. To propose giving Russia a free hand in the north of Persia would not satisfy, because Russian influence was already supreme there. Nicolson recognized that "in the present case we are not in a position either in Persia, Afghanistan or Tibet, to make any great concessions or as our hostile critics say any at all." [n] Izvolsky, however, had hinted that he would probably need some balancing gain, and Nicolson thought that sometime there would come "some proposals as to a deal over the Near East," for Great Britain either to "support or, in any case, not oppose Russia in obtaining some modifications of certain treaty clauses which hamper and restrict her liberty of action." [o] It was clear that the negotiations would not gain any encouraging speed unless Russia got some rewards for leaving positions coveted by Great Britain, and Nicolson's warning that the Near East would play a part in the course of the conversations was timely, enabling the foreign office to prepare to entertain the subject.[p]

[n] Izvolsky, *Correspondance diplomatique*, I, 395, 407. *B. D.*, IV, no. 236, p. 250.

[o] *Ibid.*, p. 251.

[p] Sir Edward Grey in his reply to Nicolson enclosed a departmental memorandum on the question. (*Ibid.*, pp. 58-60.) Grey also agreed that some satisfaction would have to be given Russia in the Near East, "the original cause of

As the year 1906 drew to a close something like the outline of an agreement respecting Tibet took shape. There had been many notes interchanged since midsummer, and no conflict of interests had proven permanently insurmountable.[q] The difficulties had been considered leisurely and in a conciliatory spirit by both sides, and the time was not far off when "the reluctant compromise was embodied in a convention which is a masterpiece of drafting."[r] In the face of approaching harmony Grey had authorized, as far back as September, that Afghan questions could be examined and that Russian proposals on Persia should be requested. Afghanistan, however, was hopelessly lost in the tangle of more pressing problems, and no discussions were attempted before February 1907. Izvolsky alleged that he was unprepared to talk about a Persian settlement, and besides was deeply exercised by German attempts to increase its commercial influence in northern Persia.[s] His most immediate concern was to win the prompt association of Great Britain in making a joint loan to the impoverished Persian government in order to prevent German participation, because it would be difficult for the Russian government in its straightened financial circumstances to find the money for the first advance on the loan.[t] In the discussion of this question Nicolson had mentioned that the British desired the southeastern part of Persia, behind a line between the towns of Birjand and Bandar Abbas, as their special region; and on 17 September 1906 Izvolsky had agreed that "we should delimitate our respective spheres of influence as soon as possible," but that the process should not be associated with the making of a loan.[u] Izvolsky recognized that the mention of spheres of influence opened up the whole question of Persia, and the reconciliation of the con-

the hostility and friction between Russia and us." He then indicated what British policy would be: "But it is not for us to propose changes with regard to the treaty conditions of the Dardanelles. I think some change in the direction desired by Russia would be admissible, and we should be prepared to discuss the question if Russia introduces it." (*Ibid.*, no. 370, p. 414.) The Russian embassy in London also put out feelers on the Near East. *Ibid.*, no. 241, p. 254. Nicolson, p. 243. Izvolsky, *Correspondance diplomatique*, I, 24, 400-402.

[q] *B. D.*, IV, no. 314, pp. 336-345.
[r] Nicolson, p. 239.
[s] *B. D.*, IV, no. 228, p. 242; Editors' Note, p. 522.
[t] *Ibid.*, no. 344, p. 391; no. 348, p. 393.
[u] *Ibid.*, no. 347, p. 392. Izvolsky, *Correspondance diplomatique*, I, 377.

flicting interests in this part of Asia was to be one of the most important tasks on the way to any agreement.

The idea of partitioning Persia into Russian and British spheres of influence was not at all new, but it had not frequently been greeted with mutual approval. To go no further back than the autumn of 1903, when Lansdowne began his supreme bid for a rapprochement with Russia, Benckendorff had "let fall the observation" that his government would not favor any arrangement which would place northern Persia under Russian or southern Persia under British influence.[v] The Russian government, he said, "saw no reason why their commercial development should be limited to the northern half," and while willing to recognize British predominance in the Persian Gulf, a commercial outlet there would probably be demanded for Russia, although without a naval base or a garrison of troops.[w] This authoritative language had been delivered before the war with Japan had humbled Russia; and almost two years afterwards, as Lansdowne resumed his quest for a reconciliation with Russia, Benckendorff believed that the Persian question offered most difficulty, but that it could be solved. Lamsdorff himself declared that, since the integrity of Persia was to be upheld, the technical difficulties in the way of an agreement, among which was the delimitation of spheres of influence, should be easily adjusted.[x] Nearly a year later, on 19 September 1906, Izvolsky had agreed that this was the sole method "of solving the Persian question so far as Russia and England were concerned."[y]

In "his humble duty to the king" of 24 September, Grey proposed to demand of the Russians a sphere in southeastern Persia which should include the strategic Seistan district in order to minimize the danger of military invasion into India, releasing to Russia large regions in the north and west. The government of India desired a much vaster extent for Great Britain, which the foreign secretary rejected because it could

[v] B. D., IV, no. 181 (a), p. 183.
[w] Ibid., no. 181 (b), p. 185. Benckendorff blythely remarked to Lansdowne, "You may guard it if you like!"
[x] Ibid., no. 196, p. 208; no. 202, p. 216.
[y] Ibid., no. 348, p. 393.

not be obtained by diplomacy.[z] He did not intend to relinquish all of Persia outside of the British sphere into Russian hands, but first brought out the suggestion that "there will have to be a sphere open to general or common interests."[a] With somewhat surprizing complaisance, Izvolsky found the tentative description of the British region perfectly acceptable. He gave no sign of the limits desired for the Russian region except that it would be considerably removed from the British, thereby independently reaching the view that most of the middle of Persia would be left open to general enterprize. While he declared this to be his own firm conviction, Izvolsky did not hide the fact that he would have a strong opposition to overcome, or that when the Russian sphere had been finally allotted, they might then do in it pretty much as they pleased.[b]

No sooner had this general agreement been reached than trouble arose. The British foreign office became impatient to obtain the definitive recognition of the limits of their sphere of influence "as a starting point for common action," and as a condition for making the joint advance to Persia. Izvolsky was upset and devoted some energy to elucidating for Nicolson's benefit how British impetuousness would render negotiations exceedingly difficult. "The question of spheres of influence in Persia was not a matter to be settled off-hand at twenty-four hours notice. It was an extremely delicate question requiring much thought and consideration."[c] It would cause him trouble enough to gain the acquiescence of others who approved of it far less than he did. It was also too important a matter to be tied up with another so relatively small as a loan to Persia. Izvolsky repeated his earlier objections to this association, and capped his exposition with the promise that Russia would find the small sum necessary for its share in a Persian loan out of its own resources, however inconvenient that might temporarily be, if the British government persisted in its attitude.[d] Nicolson accordingly advised London

[z] *Ibid.*, no. 350, p. 395.
[a] *Ibid.*, no. 347, minute, p. 393.
[b] *Ibid.*, no. 349, p. 394.
[c] *Ibid.*, no. 352, p. 397. Nicolson, p. 242.
[d] Izvolsky, *Correspondance diplomatique*, I, 377. B. D., IV, no. 352, pp. 397-398.

not to rush Izvolsky with the negotiations, nor to tie on impossible conditions, because "we may frighten him off the whole question." There was suspicion enough that Britain was taking advantage of Russian difficulties to force matters, and if the negotiations were to be ultimately successful, it would be prudent to remove this suspicion from Russian minds.[e] Nicolson's advice was taken in London and remembered.[f] For one of the few times during the negotiation the timid, hesitating Izvolsky had spoken his mind with sharp clearness, and got his way.

No advance in the conversations could be expected during the October days when Izvolsky took his vacation, and made his visits to Paris and Berlin. In London, Grey thought of a slight extension in the British region in Persia, and wished to avoid using the term sphere of influence in the coming negotiations.[g] Nicolson found Izvolsky troubled at their first meeting in November by technical difficulties in the way of defining those spheres of influence, a term which he also wished not to mention. He was puzzled how to accomplish this purpose, which appeared to be a bald division of Persia, and yet reconcile it with an inescapable profession of a mutual desire to respect the integrity and independence of Persia. Both parties would affirm that there was no departure from the principle of equal opportunity, yet neither Great Britain nor Russia intended to let another power obtain concessions within its sphere. There would be no temptation for Germany to seek concessions in the area envisaged for Great Britain; but there could be made no sphere for Russia in northern Persia in which Germany might not want all kinds of concessions, practically forcing Russia to come to terms with Germany.[h] In some degree Nicolson knew how to assuage these doubts, although

---

[e] *Ibid.*, p. 398. Nicolson, p. 242. See also Izvolsky, *Correspondance diplomatique*, I, 402, 407.

[f] Hardinge summoned his long acquaintance with the Russian character in order to minute: "The Russians always move slowly and do not like being 'rushed'." (*B. D.*, IV, no. 352, minute, p. 339.) In the middle of November 1906, Grey was repeating back to Nicolson: "We must avoid raising in M. Izvolsky's mind the suspicion that we wish to force the pace in order to take advantage of Russia's present situation." *Ibid.*, no. 370, p. 414.

[g] *Ibid.*, no. 366, p. 407.

[h] *Ibid.*, no. 367, pp. 408-409; see also no. 231, p. 244.

he had no "ready drawn formula to submit." Something could
be done to explain away the appearance of a partition of
Persia, and the "open door" would be left ajar to the legitimate commerce of other nations in both the spheres of influence, "and in any case throughout the whole of the rest of
Persia" in every respect.[1] Nicolson had full confidence in
Izvolsky's intentions and desires for an understanding, but
believed that he would proceed with such "extreme and deliberate caution" as would "unduly prolong the negotiations," so
that he did not wish to wait for Russian proposals. He suggested that a draft of an article be sent to him that would
serve as a preamble to a Persian agreement, besides stimu-
lating Izvolsky to greater zeal.[j]

As a result Grey had prepared and despatched a sketch of
an agreement for Nicolson to present to Izvolsky. This sketch
was not in treaty form, but was intended to serve as an *aide-
mémoire* of what had been talked over. It had a rudimentary
preamble in which the respect for the integrity and independence of Persia, and the assurance of equal opportunity for the
commerce of all nations were placed. The line within which
the British government would expect to have a free hand in
seeking concessions of whatever nature was precisely specified,
while the corresponding engagement offered for a Russian
region was left undefined.[k] The British region included the
district of Seistan, which would free India from the apprehension of an attack by Russia. Grey recognized that Russia
would obtain no equivalent gain for this in the northern part
of Persia, and anticipated that Izvolsky would seek for a
counterbalance somewhere else, most probably at the Dar-

[1] *Ibid.*, no. 367, p. 409, and minute, p. 411. The phrase "the whole of the rest
of Persia" was a happy one! In the famous "Curzon Despatch" of the government of India of 21 September 1899, the whole of the rest of Persia is described
as being "deserts that form a natural barrier of division between northern and
southern Persia. . . ." (*Ibid.*, no. 319, pp. 358, 360.) In April 1907, Sir Charles
Hardinge was to contribute his description of what had become the "neutral
zone" as "of such a barren and mountainous character, chain after chain of
mountains rising diagonally across any railway route from the north, that
there need be no fear of any company or gov[ernmen]t attempting such a
gigantic task as a railway to the s[outh] of Persia." *Ibid.*, no. 411, enclosure
and minute, p. 457.
[j] *Ibid.*, no. 367, p. 410.
[k] *Ibid.*, no. 371, enclosure, pp. 415-416.

danelles. Nicolson was instructed that because this question was a Russian interest in which the other powers of Europe were concerned, Izvolsky must "say what he wants," but that he should receive these requests and refer them home.[1] When the substance of this was handed to Izvolsky in an *aide-mémoire* of 3 December, it marked the first written proposal offered for the Persian discussions. Izvolsky read the copy with care, and his only immediate criticism, which Nicolson did not share, was the honest recognition "that even as drawn up others might regard it as a division ('partage') of Persia into spheres of influence." Since an off-hand answer was not required at the moment, Izvolsky requested to be permitted "to study carefully" the document in hand.[m] Whenever Izvolsky desired to study anything carefully it was sure to consume time; but it also needed time for him to overcome his scruples to a partition of Persia only thinly concealed, and the objections of others to any partition at all.

Sir Edward Grey by now had a better comprehension of the opposition the Russian foreign minister had to meet. He no longer was inclined to force the pace, only wishing that the negotiations should not "go to sleep."[n] What afterwards could be described as "an amicable and expectant pause," but which at the time was a delay with which Nicolson "was not wholly satisfied," stopped the discussion of Anglo-Russian interests in central Asia from the beginning of December 1906 until into February 1907.[o] In this interval Izvolsky made considerable progress in negotiations with Japan, to carry out the provisions of the peace of Portsmouth which had been left for future settlement, and to form a basis for safer relations with Japan in the Far East. The seriousness of these negotiations which, with the help of France, were just passing out of a threatening stage, claimed Izvolsky's earnest attention.[p] Benckendorff stated that there was so little likelihood of a prompt

[1] *Ibid.*, no. 370, p. 414. Grey, I, 156-158. Nicolson, p. 243.
[m] *B. D.*, IV, no. 373, p. 417.
[n] *Ibid.*, no. 370, p. 414.
[o] Nicolson, p. 243.
[p] Izvolsky, *Correspondance diplomatique*, I, 288, 414-415. The French government prevented a loan to Japan until after the success of the Japanese-Russian treaty negotiations was assured. Bompard, pp. 250, 253-254.

renewal of the discussions with England that he expected to prolong his vacation in St. Petersburg for several weeks.[q] Yet Nicolson, in his annual report for 1906, believed Izvolsky to be sincerely in favor of an understanding with Great Britain. It was true that relations between Russia and Germany were "intimate and cordial," and that "a suave, conciliatory attitude and a gentle solicitude are the characteristics of German diplomacy in this capital." It was unfortunate that the Dual alliance had suffered a temporary eclipse with "many influential quarters" feeling that "the union between Socialistic freethinking France and Orthodox Russia is not a sympathetic one." The attitude of the court and the military party was doubtless inimical to the negotiations, but the Russian cabinet on the whole seemed willing to conclude a fair bargain, so Nicolson could view the coming year with hope.[r]

The first days of 1907 were, nevertheless, clouded with doubts for Sir Arthur. He hoped that the dismal Russian winter had not affected his judgment, but he confessed to some misgivings as to the speed of the negotiations, as well as to recent changes in Izvolsky's attitude. The occupation of the Chumbi valley in Tibet after 1905 was a touchy question because the British were reluctant to promise that it would not be extended under any circumstances, while Izvolsky expressed the fear, whether genuinely his own or, as Nicolson preferred to believe, insinuated to him by the Russian general staff, that Great Britain "might indirectly instigate incidents in order to justify a prolonged occupation." The discussion of the differences in Tibet had progressed the farthest of any, but Nicolson was still uneasy because Izvolsky persisted in speaking "as if our interests in Tibet were no more than those of Russia," although Izvolsky's viewpoint was nearly correct. In regard to Persian affairs, it was distressing to observe the reversal in the Russian minister's attitude. Until lately Russia had been eager for British association in a loan to the Persian government and Great Britain had originally been reluctant

    [q] G. P., XXV, part I, no. 8521, pp. 27-28; no. 8522, and footnote *, pp. 28-29; no. 8523, pp. 29-30. Izvolsky, Correspondance diplomatique, I, 414.
    [r] B. D., IV, no. 243, pp. 255-260. Nicolson, p. 243.

to participate, whereas now Izvolsky was anxious to withdraw
the advance at precisely the same time that reports from
Spring Rice at Teheran revealed a growing disinclination of
the Russian colleague to work in harmony. This time it was
Nicolson who wished not to lose the association which had
been "of such admirable augury for a general arrangement,"
because "if we unlink our arms on this question, we may find
difficulty in hooking him on again." [s] The French ambassador
Bompard, an interested spectator, while not wishing to be
indiscreet, "feared our negotiations were unduly dragging"
and in need of "some little more stimulus." [t] He was uneasy
because Izvolsky was extremely sensitive in his "regard for
German susceptibilities," but Nicolson did not attribute the
existing slowness to any German action after the assurance
of "benevolent indifference" that had been given to Izvolsky
in Berlin. The lagging was better attributable to the necessity
of overcoming opposition in Russia, in addition to the fact
that Great Britain "had several different and widely separated
authorities to consult: and all this caused some unavoidable
delay." [u]

The treaty discussions with Japan, although progressing,
were another cause for delay. It perplexed Nicolson to understand why this should be so; but his explanations had the merit
of being rational. It might be that Japan would make some
demands to which Russia could not effectively object, yet which
would be seriously disadvantageous to Russia. It would hardly
do for a new foreign minister in his first two agreements to
show nothing but concessions to Japan in the Far East, and to
Great Britain in middle Asia. Nicolson and the Japanese
ambassador agreed that it would be "an admirable consummation" if both countries could succeed in obtaining such
understandings with Russia as could only make for peace in
their relations throughout Asia.[v] Izvolsky was earnestly seeking an agreement that would end the danger of a second war

[s] B. D., IV, no. 244, p. 266.
[t] Nicolson, p. 243. Bompard, pp. 255-256. B. D., IV, no. 245, p. 267.
[u] Ibid., no. 244, p. 266; no. 245, pp. 267-268; no. 247, p. 269.
[v] Ibid., no. 246, pp. 268-269. Nicolson, p. 243. Izvolsky, Correspondance
diplomatique, I, 418.

with Japan; while Count Witte, although out of power but not without influence, approved the policy that "Russia should endeavor to make terms with Great Britain and Japan rather than be cajoled by the allurements which might emanate from Berlin." [w] As the Russo-Japanese negotiations developed ever more favorably through February and March, Izvolsky hoped to attain something that, if not actually constituting an entente, would at least produce "des relations," while Grey desired Russian friendliness with Britain's ally Japan, so that his object of getting on good terms with Russia would not be frustrated or minimized.[x] As the prospects of success seemed ever more certain of crowning his labors with Japan, Bompard found Izvolsky at last becoming "radiant and sanguine." [y]

Nicolson's hopes were in the ascendant again before January was gone. Izvolsky had returned to an earlier suggestion that Benckendorff should join their conversations while he remained in St. Petersburg. This was thoroughly acceptable, not alone because of Benckendorff's pleasant company, but also because he was a cordial proponent of an agreement, whose more decided opinions might stimulate Izvolsky's, besides cutting down the opposition in military and court circles.[z] Benckendorff declared that the tsar had been "sincerely desirous that an arrangement should be reached" when last he had been received in audience, while it was surely encouraging to listen to him say that "he did not consider the opposition of the military party would be so strenuous as was feared." There had been some feeling that Great Britain had originated the negotiations at the close of the Japanese war for the purpose of benefitting from the weakened condition of Russia, but Benckendorff had taken pains to explain that these conversa-

[w] *B. D.*, IV, no. 250, p. 273; no. 251, p. 274. Nicolson, p. 250.

[x] *B. D.*, IV, no. 253, p. 275; no. 256, p. 279; no. 388, p. 430. Dennis, p. 29. Pooley, *Hayashi*, pp. 230-232. On 27 February / 11 March 1908, Izvolsky explained in the duma that the agreements with Japan were made with the approval of the tsar, and to institute friendly relations with Japan following the peace of Portsmouth. *Stenograficheskey otchet: Gosudarstvennaya duma*, [Stenographic Report: Imperial Duma], third convocation, first session, (1908), pp. 112-115, 117.

[y] *B. D.*, IV, no. 252, p. 275; no. 388, p. 430. France was contemporaneously engaged in making an agreement with Japan. Dennis, p. 28. André Tardieu, *France and the Alliances*, (New York, 1908), pp. 234-237.

[z] *B. D.*, IV, no. 248, pp. 269-270; no. 467, p. 522.

tions had commenced long ago, and had only been resumed upon the close of the war.[a] On 9 February Benckendorff again brought Nicolson interesting news to the effect that the much dreaded attitude of the Russian general staff had moderated enough to accept in principle the desirability of an agreement with Great Britain if "some concessions of a political nature should be made to Russia in return for her projected withdrawal from a 'military position'." While Benckendorff professed not to know what concessions were meant by this statement, he did let fall an observation about the Dardanelles, which neither Nicolson nor the British foreign office failed to note.[b] Fully as encouraging were the statements by Izvolsky and Benckendorff that "a small commission" or "inter-departmental committee" of the government was to meet shortly to discuss some of the matters about which the negotiations were concerned, after which the Russian views could be presented to Nicolson more precisely. This body of dignitaries did meet on 1/14 February, and Nicolson's first indications of the results came through Bompard, who had found Izvolsky more animated in spirit, and "satisfied with the outlook of his negotiations" with Great Britain, with whom he now possessed "a good prospect of coming to terms." [c]

The meeting of 1/14 February had really been a Russian ministerial council, assembled to discuss the advisability of entering into a treaty with Great Britain on Persian affairs.[d] Izvolsky had declared that it was necessary for the council to

[a] *Ibid.*, no. 249, p. 272. Sir Charles Hardinge made a very curious minute to this despatch: "C[ount] Benckendorff might also add that after the war the initiative in the resumption of negotiations was taken by the Russian government." This is at variance with the published British documents which show Hardinge himself, then British ambassador to Russia, eagerly doing his part during the war to keep the future open for a resumption, and after the war in endeavoring to overcome Russian reluctance to resume, induced particularly by the displeasure caused by the premature renewal of the Anglo-Japanese agreement. See also Izvolsky, *Correspondance diplomatique*, I, 401.

[b] *Ibid.*, no. 250, p. 272.

[c] *Ibid.*, no. 248, p. 270; no. 250, p. 273; no. 252, pp. 274-275. Bompard, p. 274.

[d] The minutes of this session first partially appeared in B. de Siebert, (George Abel Schreiner, editor), *Entente Diplomacy and the World*, (New York, 1921), no. 548, pp. 474-477. This is reprinted in *B. D.*, IV, pp. 270-271. The entire document was subsequently published in *Graf Benckendorffs diplomatischer Schriftwechsel*, (Berlin and Leipzig, 1928), I, no. 1, pp. 1-9, hereafter cited as Benckendorff.

come to a decision respecting "the proposal of the British government to divide Persia into spheres of influence." He reminded the ministers that such a proposal would not have had an agreeable reception until recently, because it had been Russian opinion that all of Persia would come under Russian influence. The conditions under which this would have been possible had meanwhile disappeared.

The events of the past few years, however, have shown this plan to be impossible of realization and that everything must be avoided that might lead to a conflict with England. The best means for achieving this purpose is the demarcation of the spheres of influence in Persia.

Later in the session other ministers suggested certain changes to be made in the British draft, to make certain that no concessions in either the British or Russian sphere should be available to the subjects of third powers, as well as that these "concessions of a political and commercial nature" should be more precisely set forth in the articles of a treaty. So far as Seistan was mentioned, the representative of the general staff was reluctant to see such a natural route out of Persia into India go over to British control, although it was pointed out that at the present time it would be impossible to prevent a British occupation of the region. In return for so important a concession, corresponding compensations should be obtained from Great Britain. The close connection of Seistan with Afghanistan should not be ignored, while the latter state must be preserved as a buffer, in order to prevent the passage of Indian troops through the country, or the use of Seistan as a concentration region for troops in the defence of India. The military reorganization of the Indian army, which Lord Kitchener was actively effecting, had thoroughly disquieted the Russians.[e] Izvolsky summed up that the opportunity to reach an agreement with Great Britain was at hand, by which the possibility of a conflict would be obviated. Therefore it would be wise not to be too unyielding in demarcating the lines of the spheres of influence, and to gain as much compensation as possible elsewhere for relinquishing the strategic district of

[e] See Grey, I, 155. Reisner, *Krasny Arkhiv*, X, 56.

Seistan to the British sphere. The council of ministers in the end "accepted the principle of spheres of influence as the only basis possible" for an agreement with England.

Thereupon Izvolsky turned to an equally weighty and closely connected subject. The full value of a treaty with Great Britain would accrue to Russia only in the event that Germany raised no objections to it. Assurances had already been tendered, and accepted, that no agreement concluded would injure any German interest. To be completely at ease, however, Russia would have to arrive at a definite understanding with Germany whereby their mutual interests were satisfied. Izvolsky posed the question before the council whether the previous opposition to the construction of the Bagdad railway should be exchanged for a recognition of the Russian sphere of influence in the north of Persia, where German banking and commercial interests were expanding uncomfortably for Russia. The minister of finance, Kokovtsov, while he believed the German penetration into Persia was greatly exaggerated, and that the disturbed condition of the country made the undertaking of any new ventures unlikely, approved of an understanding since he could not deny that German interests did exist. The council frowned upon the prospect of the Bagdad railway, and bemoaned the fact that Russia had not the power to prevent its construction, nor even to postpone it for any length of time. It was an unavoidable menace to the existence of which Russia must become reconciled. Not that the transit trade from Europe to the Persian Gulf really mattered, for Russia had never shared in that, but the financial position of the government was too uncertain to permit of decent participation, and any fictitious influence behind French capitalists offered no great attraction. From the military angle, the Bagdad railway was a total loss to Russia, and could only be equalized by burdensome extensions of the existing Russian lines in the Caucasus, including a large increase in the number of troops maintained in that area. No military compensations could be obtained from other nations because there was none to give.[f] There was no hope for building a competing line to

---

[f] Siebert, no. 548, pp. 474-477. Benckendorff, I, no. 1, pp. 1-9.

India through Russian connections, because Great Britain would probably dread such a railroad even more.[g] In fact, the Russian position was so unenviable that concessions of any real worth could hardly be hoped for at all. Nevertheless the council realized that Russia could not block the Bagdad route, and that such compensations as could be secured should be sought in return for no future obstruction. Possibly one of the worst of all menaces, the construction of branch lines leading to the Persian frontier, which would open all the north Persian markets to foreign enterprize where Russia had so far monopolized them, could be prevented by agreement with Germany. The support of both Great Britain and Germany might be won for securing the renewal or extension of old treaties with Persia and Turkey which conveyed virtual control of railroad building in northern Persia, and in the region along the south shore of the Black Sea, into Russian hands. Under such conditions Russian consent to the existence of a Bagdad railway might regretfully be given to Germany, since nothing else could be done.[h]

The first Russian step in carrying out the recommendations agreed upon by the council of ministers came when Benckendorff informed Nicolson that "considerable progress has been made," and voiced the belief that the "time was approaching when the whole convention would be concluded." [i] When Nicolson next met Izvolsky himself on 18 February his hopes touched a new "high" for the year. In the first place, the last British draft respecting Tibet was practically accepted except for a few additional explanations. Izvolsky then read portions of the proposals from the first complete Russian draft on the Persian question, and explained that the military party had

[g] In March 1908 the idea of a competing line through Russia, Persia and Afghanistan, connecting with British roads to India, was still unaccepted, although being thought about. On the 17th Hardinge wrote to Nicolson: "The government of India is far too suspicious to regard any such scheme with complacency. A few years more are required to remove prejudices which have existed for more than fifty years. . . . The idea of through connection with India was negatived as premature. . . , but the great thing is to cut out the Bagdad R[ailwa]y in the meantime." *B. D.*, VI, no. 254, p. 359.
[h] Siebert, no. 548, pp. 476-477. Benckendorff, I, no. 1, pp. 3-4. *B. D.*, IV, no. 256, p. 278.
[i] *Ibid.*, no. 469, p. 523.

virtually conceded the inclusion of the strategic district of Seistan within the British zone. At the end of the conversation Izvolsky disclosed his anxiety to learn the conditions Great Britain had in mind for an arrangement in Afghanistan, which he felt he needed to know because of its close relation to the Persian question, which made it impossible to settle the one independently of the other.[j] Izvolsky did not disguise his concern lest British influence in Afghanistan might be increased beyond anything hitherto enjoyed, against which some guarantee would be required. When Nicolson asked if that meant that "Russia desired the maintenance of [the] political *status quo*," Izvolsky assented and suggested that "some arrangement should be made as to relations of local frontier officers and as to trade." Nicolson, however, remained silent and gave no indication of what Great Britain intended to propose.[k] Two days later Izvolsky turned over the full Russian draft proposals for a Persian agreement, with appropriate comments.[l] At last he gave indications of wanting to push on with the negotiations, which so impressed Nicolson that he strongly recommended to the foreign office that "the favorable conditions which now prevail in regard to our negotiations should not be allowed to disappear," nor long silences to interrupt the continuous flow of the discussions.[m]

Nicolson had wanted to run the risk of an early revelation of the British Afghan proposals in order to take advantage of Benckendorff's presence in St. Petersburg. Because of their "moderate and conciliatory character" Nicolson had thought that their disclosure would help the sympathetic members in the Russian council of ministers to strengthen the chances for an Anglo-Russian understanding.[n] These demands had been sent to Nicolson in September 1906, but he had continued "to sit upon them in the meanwhile" because Russia had not made any openings relating to Persia.[o] When the first Russian draft

[j] *Ibid.*, no. 388, p. 429.
[k] *Ibid.*, no. 253, p. 275.
[l] *Ibid.*, no. 254, p. 276; no. 389, pp. 431-433.
[m] *Ibid.*, no. 388, pp. 430, 431; no. 469, p. 523; no. 470, p. 524.
[n] *Ibid.*, no. 467, p. 522.
[o] *Ibid.*, no. 339, p. 388; no. 341, p. 389; no. 468, p. 523.

on this question had been handed over, Nicolson was authorized on 22 February 1907 to communicate the British views
about Afghanistan. On the next day Nicolson gave Izvolsky a
paper containing five headings which "merely represented in
outline" the British position, and wished to draw in reply the
"full details of the views of the Russian government." For
the first time the three major topics existing between Great
Britain and Russia were all uncovered, and the negotiations
for an agreement were in full swing.[p]

The negotiations did go on at a lively pace, with draft
bringing counterdraft and long discussions, careful and polite
even when over small points, and a grammarian's funeral on
matters of phraseology. Tsar Nicholas was quoted as having
said with emphasis that "the agreement *must* be made," which
was encouraging because "his good will to that end will naturally be a weighty factor with the Russian government." [q] The
same feeling had been entertained before without subsequent
signs of success, but once again all was pleasure regarding the
progress being made. The main difficulties left for settlement
were in the arrangement over Afghanistan, where Great
Britain wanted to make sure of its existing favored position,

[p] *Ibid.*, no. 390, p. 433; no. 472, p. 526. Rumors of the resumption of Anglo-
Russian relations quickly appeared in the press. Mr. Cartwright wrote from
Munich on 13 March: "If one is to judge of public opinion in England as
expressed in her newspapers, it must be evident to everyone that the British
public are determined to arrive at an understanding with Russia, and they
will in no way be influenced by the manner in which the internal affairs of
Russia may be eventually settled." (*Ibid.*, VI, no. 5, p. 16. See also *G. P.*, XXV,
part I, no. 8523, and footnote *, pp. 29-30.) Earlier in the month Metternich
inquired of Grey whether the press reports were true. Grey admitted that
they were, but emphasized the fact that no German interests were affected
in any way. Anglo-German relations were momentarily touchy, but Metternich
wrote privately and with understanding on the 28th to his friend Tschirschky,
the German foreign secretary: "The Anglo-Russian compromise, within the
limits already frequently sketched, stands on the threshhold. Here they will
seek to make much capital out of it, for the most part because of fear of us.
They wish here to secure themselves from us. Consequently the new search for
friendships. Nevertheless I still insist that they do not wish to be aggressive
here." (*Ibid.*, no. 8526, footnote *, p. 32.) Prince Kinsky, a former Austrian
diplomat, shrewdly predicted the nature of the coming convention to Metternich: "The entire agreement would be of a purely negative nature, — promises
not to encroach upon the preserves of the other." (*Ibid.*, no. 8525, p. 31.) The
semi-official *Novoye Vremya* declared that "the international ill-feeling towards
Germany is explicable, not by the envy of her neighbors, but by . . . the un-
broken record of German aggressiveness. . . . It is this method of action that
accounts for the moral isolation in which Germany finds herself." *Annual
Register*, (1907), p. 330.
[q] *B. D.*, IV, no. 255, pp. 276-277.

where Russia wanted to make sure that it would not increase and, perhaps after all, to keep the future open.[r] It was inevitable that the question of the Straits would be brought up sometime before any Anglo-Russian negotiation could be concluded, and for a year the Russians had, on occasion, unmistakably hinted that British concurrence with a new interpretation of the régime of the Straits was desired.[s] On 15 March Benckendorff intruded the subject by way of the side door of his own personal views, when "he wished to point out that the opening of the Straits to Russia would strengthen and ensure a good disposition in that country, and complete the success of the arrangements we were now discussing." He stated the present Russian position as based on the preference that "the Straits should remain closed to all powers than that they should be opened to all powers." There would be no objection that access to Constantinople be on the same terms for all, but if Russia could not obtain egress from the Black Sea without permitting ingress to others, it would be better not to raise the question at all. Benckendorff suspected that any arrangement made with Great Britain would have to be "platonic" in its nature, because other nations were involved in the question, although even this much would have a great, beneficial effect on Russian public opinion.[t]

Sir Edward Grey was prepared for this question and graciously replied:

I had felt all through these negotiations that good relations with Russia meant that our old policy of closing the Straits against her, and throwing our weight against her at any conference of the powers must be abandoned. It was this old policy which, in my opinion, had been the root of the difficulties between the two countries for two generations. And, for us and Russia to settle our difficulties in Asia, and then to find ourselves afterwards in opposition on some other important matter, would be to undo the good which would be done by the present negotiations as to Asiatic frontiers.

Right at that moment, however, "it would be difficult for us

<hr/>

[r] *Ibid.*, no. 256, pp. 277-278; no. 473, p. 527. *G. P.*, XXV, part I, no. 8525, p. 31.
[s] Bompard, pp. 269-270. *B. D.*, IV, no. 210, p. 226.
[t] *Ibid.*, no. 257, p. 279.

to put anything concerning the Straits in the form of an engagement," so Grey "wanted, therefore, to have a little time to consider the question." With the gentlest irony he concluded that if Izvolsky was expecting to hear something on this subject, which Benckendorff had broached without instructions, "I should not like him to infer from silence that the mention of it had been unfavorably received." [u] No great period of time was needed to consider the British attitude towards the Straits question, because already before 1904 the leaders in the foreign office no longer professed to pursue the old anti-Russian policy in Turkish affairs, but believed that it was "if desirable, possible to make an important concession to Russia in relation to the Dardanelles without fundamentally altering the present strategic position in the Mediterranean." [v] While this theoretical change in British policy had not been revealed to Russia, it had been recognized in London that some satisfaction must doubtless be granted in return for the surrender of valuable regions, and previous policies, in central Asia. As long ago as 28 November 1906 the Russians had been informed that "we would be very glad to consider any proposals which the Russian gov[ernmen]t might submit to us but that they must emanate from them." [w] By the time Benckendorff touched upon the question in the following March, Grey had cogent reasons ready for not wishing to include any engagement on that subject in an Asiatic agreement.

On 19 March Grey reverted to the two days' old conversation and repeated the views of the British government, because he "thought it better to give Benckendorff [his] record of that conversation, to avoid misunderstandings afterwards." [x] He brought up three points to buttress his opinion that no definite provisions regarding the Straits should be written into the forthcoming agreement. To begin with, the time was not yet ripe:

[u] *Ibid.*, p. 280.
[v] *Ibid.*, Editors' Note, p. 60; no. 199, p. 213. See also *G. P.*, XIX, part II, no. 6359, p. 662; no. 6360, p. 664; no. 6362, p. 667.
[w] *B. D.*, IV, no. 241, p. 254; no. 370, p. 414. Grey, I, 156-158. Nicolson, pp. 243, 250. Gwynn, II, 53.
[x] *B. D.*, IV, no. 258, p. 280. Grey, I, 158.

It might be that some important sections of public opinion would be very critical of a particular engagement on this question. I had no doubt the house of commons would accept whatever we proposed, but it would be better to propose something which secured general acceptance than to make a proposal which would cause party feeling though commanding a majority.

Then he explained that Great Britain would naturally expect, in return for such an important concession, "Russia's support about some Egyptian and other kindred things in the Near East, which matter to us and are not important to her." [y] Lastly, Grey reminded Benckendorff that Germany had been promised many times that nothing was to be in the agreement which touched the interests of a third power:

If our agreement was to include an article about the Dardanelles and the Bosphorus, it would be necessary to tell Germany beforehand that the original scope of the negotiations had been widened; otherwise I should be open to a charge of having mislead [sic] the German ambassador intentionally.

Yet with all these serious limitations, Grey ended his explanation on an encouraging note: "I wish it to be understood that the question was one which we were prepared to discuss. If, however, the Russian government desired a discussion now, it would be for them to take the initiative." [z]

For once Sir Edward had said something that aroused the Russians to spirited action. Only a few hours after the conversation the counsellor of the Russian embassy, Poklevsky-Kozell, was on his way to St. Petersburg, and Metternich observed that his view of the negotiations was "very rosy." [a] After Izvolsky had heard Poklevsky's report, Nicolson found him "beaming with pleasure" and "rarely . . . so contented and satisfied." [b] Izvolsky was enraptured by the vista that Grey's attitude seemed to let open, and he accounted it as "a great

[y] *B. D.*, IV, no. 258, p. 281. Grey, I, 158. Russian support would be wanted in relation to the capitulations in Egypt and the Bagdad railway in the Near East.

[z] *B. D.*, IV, no. 258, p. 281.

[a] *G. P.*, XXV, part I, no. 8525, p. 31.

[b] *B. D.*, IV, no. 259, p. 282; no. 261, p. 283. Bompard, p. 270. Nicolson, p. 243. Nicolson's biographer has Izvolsky "beaming with pleasure" over Hardinge's intimation of 28 November 1906, rather than over Poklevsky's report of March 1907, when Nicolson actually reported Izvolsky's beaming.

evolution in our relations and a historical event." [c] He pledged the most careful consideration from all points of view, "especially as to the method and moment of advancing further in the question." [d] Izvolsky did not complete his study before 14 April, when he agreed that it would be inopportune to complicate the existing negotiations with a special arrangement as to the Straits, and submitted a memorandum on the Russian attitude towards a revision of the treaty stipulations concerning the passage of the Straits on some more favorable occasion.[e] This memorandum essentially reaffirmed the declarations that Grey had made to Benckendorff, and only gave detailed expression upon one point which Grey had not himself specified. Izvolsky had written in his version:

We also attach the greatest importance to the fact that Sir E. Grey has not made any objection in principle to a plan of arrangement which will give to Russian warships the exclusive right to pass the Straits in both directions, while the naval forces of other powers will not be permitted to enter the Black Sea.[f]

Possibly it was fortunate that Izvolsky did not know the manner in which Lord Fitzmaurice, the parliamentary under-secretary of state for foreign affairs, pounced upon this declaration. Fitzmaurice, typically illustrating that critical, partisan feeling which Grey had already warned still existed, vigorously objected that "the Russian government are taking a most unfair advantage of the expressions used by Sir E. Grey. . . . I hope a clear and emphatic caveat will be at once put in against the language of the Russian foreign office and their covert insinuations." [g] Sir Edward gave Benckendorff another memorandum on 27 April, commenting upon the Russian reply, in which his attitude was more chilling than it had been.

The original [British] proposal did not exclude a right of exit from the Black Sea and the Straits being allowed to other limitrophe powers on the Black Sea. And the [Russian] memorandum makes no definite mention of the fact that the proposal contemplated the passage of the

[c] *B. D.*, IV, no. 261, p. 284.
[d] *Ibid.*, no. 259, p. 281.
[e] *Ibid.*, no. 264, p. 286.
[f] *Ibid.*, no. 265, enclosure, p. 287.
[g] *Ibid.*, minute, p. 288.

Dardanelles and the rest of the Straits being made available for other powers as far as the entrance to the Black Sea on the same terms for all, although it is clearly implied.

I do not wish, however, to discuss the particular conditions under which the existing arrangements with regard to the Straits might be altered . . . and I do not wish to be regarded as committed to any particular proposal, though, on the other hand, I do not wish to attach conditions now which would prevent any particular proposals from being discussed when the time comes.

I am glad that the Russian government have agreed to let the matter rest for the present. . . . If the negotiations now in progress between the two governments with regard to Asiatic questions had a satisfactory result, the effect upon British public opinion would be such as very much to facilitate a discussion of the Straits question if it came up later on. I have no doubt whatever that, if as a result of the present negotiations, the British and Russian governments remained on good terms in Asia, the effect on British public opinion and on any British government with regard to other questions, including this, would be very great.[h]

So far as can be discovered, this memorandum did not noticeably disturb Izvolsky by its limitations, nor impair his estimate of the great evolution this modified British outlook had brought about in Anglo-Russian relations. His own final memorandum, delayed until 10 July, then merely acknowledged the receipt of Grey's and the "reservations" contained in it, combined with the declaration that Russia would wait for a more opportune moment before commencing any discussions.[i] Grey found nothing in this reply to which to take exception as placing a wrong construction on any British statements, and for the duration of the general negotiations the question of the Straits was touched upon no more.[j] A new British attitude had been indicated to Russian aspirations for a more favorable régime at the Straits which, if sincerely applied, justified Izvolsky's radiance and contentment; but not one definite commitment had been given, and after the first fair start Grey had been putting in reservations, the force of which Izvolsky had possibly not sufficiently appreciated.

[h] *Ibid.*, no. 268, enclosure, p. 291. See also no. 276, p. 296.
[i] *Ibid.*, no. 275, pp. 295-296.
[j] *Ibid.*, minute, p. 296.

The original effect of this interchange of ideas about the Straits was beneficial to the course of the Anglo-Russian negotiations. Nicolson discerned that "the atmosphere from that moment became more favorable [and] the opposition of the Russian [general] staff diminished." [k] The conversations were taken up with renewed, and at last sustained determination. The problems encountered over Tibet were settled, and those arising out of the conflicting interests in Persia and Afghanistan were laid into with unprecedented vigor. [l] As a gesture of friendliness, King Edward extended an invitation to a group of officers and sailors from a Russian squadron of three vessels which had put in at Portsmouth to visit London. On 26 March the delegation was entertained at a theater, with a banquet in the evening followed by a gala performance in the Alhambra variety theater, which was also attended by dignitaries of the British government, among whom was Sir Edward Grey. [m] Such unusual display of cordiality was not overlooked, and newspapers carried articles suggesting that a return visit of British warships to the Russian Baltic ports was possible later in the year, but nothing ever came of the rumors, very likely because the time was still inopportune and the Russian fleet not yet of respectable size. [n] This exhibition of courtesy, but far more the unconcealable increase in the speed of the negotiations, unleashed a number of press accounts, with each succeeding week becoming more particular in describing the presumed contents of the forthcoming understanding. [o] All this aroused the curiosity of other powers, which sometimes proved unwelcome to the two contracting parties.

The French ambassador came to warn Nicolson that he

[k] Nicolson, p. 243.

[l] *B. D.*, IV, no. 314, p. 348; no. 404, pp. 445-447; no. 474, p. 528.

[m] *G. P.*, XXV, part I, no. 8526, p. 32. Metternich found it "indeed unprecedented that an English foreign minister will go to a variety theater for the welcoming of strange guests." *Ibid.*, footnote *, p. 32.

[n] *Ibid.*, no. 8528, p. 34.

[o] *B. D.*, IV, no. 260, p. 282; no. 267, p. 289. *G. P.*, XXV, part I, no. 8527, pp. 32-33. The tsar's idea of the value of the press remained typical of him, but he expressed it with considerable truth. "The control of these irresponsible people who compose the newspapers, is one of the most difficult questions of the present time." *B. D.*, IV, no. 266, p. 289.

suspected Izvolsky was becoming disquieted over the attitude of the German press, which was cutting up nastily with warnings to the public that attempts were under way to isolate Germany. Bompard presumed that Izvolsky was sensitive to the possibility that "Germany was contemplating some intervention in the Anglo-Russian negotiations of a disagreeable nature." [p] The excited ambassador urged that the pending negotiations be quickly concluded, to prevent the introduction of unhappy obstacles from the outside. Nicolson, on the contrary, was serenely calm and believed that Russia had gone too far and was too eager to conclude an arrangement in order to be free to regain European prestige, to forsake the policy followed for the last year. Nor did he close his eyes to the intimate relations existing between the Russian and the German courts, yet he felt that it would take more than personal sympathy to draw Russia into the orbit of Berlin. Like any cautious man, however, Nicolson was "strongly of opinion that it will be well to terminate the negotiations without undue delay and to bring the convention safely into port." [q] London also remained placid and unruffled, and found real solace in the speech Bülow gave in his genially reassuring manner before the Reichstag on 30 April. [r] The chancellor attempted to allay the criticism that he took the Anglo-Russian rapprochement too nonchalantly. He explained that repeated promises had been received that the two nations desired to reconcile their conflicting interests in Asia, but that those of no other power would be impaired. Bülow took especial pains to dissociate himself from any belief in Holstein's old dogma, and declaimed that "we cannot introduce the opposition between the whale and the elephant as an unalterable factor in our political calculation." There was no enmity between two nations which Germany could constantly use as an opportunity for itself, and there was no cause to look with pessimism upon the attempt of

[p] *Ibid.*, no. 260, p. 282. Bompard, p. 255.
[q] *B. D.*, IV, no. 260, p. 283; no. 271, p. 293.
[r] *Ibid.*, no. 269, p. 291. Grey only understated the German predicament when he told Benckendorff: "It seemed to me that Germany was jealous of the way in which other powers were settling their differences with each other and improving their relations, while she was not settling any difficulties with anyone."

Great Britain and Russia to compose their old quarrel; but also not with any lightheartedness.[s]

From another direction there came prying queries as to the extent of the Anglo-Russian negotiations, this time in behalf of the sultan of Turkey, who "was perplexed and somewhat disturbed at the reports he had heard." The British ambassador, Sir Nicholas O'Conor, was called upon for such general information as he could give. On 8 April he explained the nature of the conversations as being concerned with conflicting interests in Asia, in no way molesting any Turkish territory. Sir Nicholas had not at the time known that there had been any communications dealing with the passage of the Straits, but when he was informed of that interchange he was "rather inclined to believe that the suspicions of the sultan have . . . been aroused and that it is probable that he has spoken with greater freedom to the German ambassador on the subject." It was not the fact that the Straits question had been considered secretly by Great Britain and Russia which gave Sir Nicholas pause, nor his opinion that there was "nothing the present sultan would more dislike or would more strenuously oppose than the opening of the straits of the Dardanelles to foreign men-of-war." He did fear that somehow Germany would find out, either from Izvolsky directly, or in some subterranean manner, and then fill the sultan's mind "with still further distrust of British policy while at the same time advancing their own interests." [t] The British foreign office appreciated fully the force of this warning, and determined "to urge upon [the] Russian gov[ernmen]t the necessity of observing the strictest secrecy in the matter for the present," which Grey admitted, a bit ruefully, was "all we can do." [u] Both Benckendorff and Izvolsky were advised of "the undesirable consequences which might ensue" should any revelation occur, even to the length of driving Turkey into an alliance with Germany. Izvolsky, however, took the matter quite

[s] G. P., XXV, part I, no. 8531, footnote **, p. 35. Izvolsky, Correspondance diplomatique, I, 88.
[t] B. D., IV, no. 267, p. 289.
[u] Ibid., minutes, p. 290.

easily and assured the British that no "leakage" had or would come from him.[v] Nothing further happened to warrant any worry that Germany had learned about the exchanges of views regarding the Straits, and the incident was simply indicative of the distrust in which the great powers of Europe commonly held each other.

From far distant Teheran came an unwelcome despatch, dated 11 April, from the testy Sir Cecil Spring Rice. He had just received, in a leisurely manner, a copy of Izvolsky's first Persian proposals of the previous 20 February. "It is clear from the date and manner of the communication that my opinion on this proposed arrangement is neither invited nor desired." [w] Nevertheless Spring Rice's moral indignation spurred on his pen over many eloquent pages wherein he did his duty by reporting on "the strong current of public opinion which now prevails" in Persia, and delineated the severe loss British prestige and influence would sustain upon the publication of such an agreement, which would "simply be regarded as a treaty for the partition of Persia." [x] He bitterly pointed out that the proposals sent to him would be taken by the Persians as a full admission "that England will be held to have abandoned their cause." In prophetic words Sir Cecil summed up:

Although in a sense the convention only recognizes what already exists, and what we cannot prevent, namely the immense preponderance of Russia in northern Persia and in the capital, its publication will I think produce a considerable effect on the general situation. It will imply the definite withdrawal of England from the diplomatic struggle at Teheran on which the Persians have so long relied as the safeguard of their independence.[y]

The irate minister was right in his estimate of Persian opinion of British actions; but he did not see clearly enough that the foreign office had decided that it was not worth the candle to support the flea-bitten government of Persia against Russian advances, when an agreement with Russia, with a division of

[v] *Ibid.*, no. 272, p. 294; no. 273, p. 294.
[w] *Ibid.*, no. 389, enclosure, p. 432; no. 409, p. 450.
[x] *Ibid.*, no. 409, p. 451. Nicolson, p. 252.
[y] *B. D.*, IV, no. 409, p. 452.

the spoils in Persia, could more easily be had.[z] Before Grey's reply written "in pained reproof" could reach him, the Persian arrangement was practically settled. Spring Rice's opinion had not been especially wanted.[a]

The Russian government had, in fact, determined to pursue a mild policy in Asia, intent only on strengthening the defence of the existing position rather than to prepare for new aggressions or extensions. Another council of ministers was held in St. Petersburg on 14/27 April, some fragmentary traces of the existence of which have since come to light, again to consider the proposals for an agreement with Great Britain.[b] The combined thought of the ministers was centered upon a determination of the Russian viewpoint toward Afghanistan, in addition to an investigation of the recent British proposals for the settlement of the conflicting interests of the two countries in central Asia. A memorandum, composed by the Russian ambassador at Constantinople, I. A. Zinovyev, was read in which this shrewd authority set forth that nothing could be more immediately desired than to release the Black Sea fleet from its inactivity by opening up the Straits, thereby permitting egress into the Mediterranean. To obtain this privilege the sincere support of Great Britain was a prime requisite; and if that power was disposed to coöperate, then Russia should be prepared to make equivalent concessions in central Asia.[c] In his turn Kokovtsov, the minister of finance, spoke in favor of concessions in return for an agreement with Great Britain. Afghanistan, he asserted realistically, was too far distant and inaccessible to fall handily within the sphere of Russian influence. Russia might well, therefore, quiet British alarm by renouncing pretensions in this direction, which would guarantee the security of the Indian frontier, without which Great Britain would conclude no convention.[d] The council concluded that the British proposals were for the most part

[z] *Ibid.*, no. 421, p. 471.
[a] Nicolson, p. 252.
[b] *B. D.*, IV, no. 260, p. 283; no. 271, p. 293; no. 476, p. 529. Reisner, *Krasny Arkhiv*, X, 55-56.
[c] *Ibid.*, p. 55.
[d] *Ibid.*, pp. 55-56.

acceptable for Russia. These were eventually written into the final treaty with only one minor reservation which the Emperor Nicholas soon thereafter described blandly as "necessary in order to enable the neighboring people to live in amity with each other," but which was really inserted to permit arrangements for the direct settlement of local frontier questions, and the regulation of trade between Russia and Afghanistan.[e]

There was little more left to be done to complete the Persian agreement because, by the end of April, both parties "were now of one mind as regards Persian affairs," and it appeared evident that the tsar considered this question as settled. Yet not quite, for Great Britain expended some efforts during May to push back the line of the Russian sphere in Persia to the town of Zulfikar. This was done in order to keep Russia away from any part of the Afghan frontier which touched eastern Persia. Although brought up regrettably late in the day, no great opposition was offered, and by 27 May the alteration was accepted by Russia.[f] In the following month, however, when the British tried to make good for what had been "an afterthought on our part" by having the Russians agree to the insertion of a clause in the preamble "referring to the special interests which Great Britain had in the maintenance of the status quo in the Persian Gulf," no success whatever resulted.[g] Plead and explain as he did, Nicolson could not persuade Izvolsky to accept this addition. Izvolsky found sound refuge for his stand behind the same argument Grey had used before in order to keep all mention of the Straits out of the agreement: it was a subject which would widen the scope of the negotiations, because it touched upon a question in which other powers could claim an interest. Consequently Izvolsky refused to consider the Persian Gulf in order to be certain that he should cause no friction between Russia and Germany.[h] So adamantly did he stick to his opinion that Nicolson willingly gave up the quest, because any insistence "would

[e] *Ibid.*, p. 56. *B. D.*, IV, no. 266, p. 288.

[f] *Ibid.*, no. 266, p. 288; no. 270, p. 292; no. 411, enclosure, pp. 455-456; no. 414, p. 460.

[g] *Ibid.*, no. 428, minutes, p. 476; no. 429, p. 477.

[h] *Ibid.*, no. 429, pp. 478-479; no. 431, pp. 482-483. Nicolson, p. 253.

have in the first place suspended a continuance of the negotiations for a long period, and in the second place would have very possibly endangered their ultimate success." Izvolsky was "immensely relieved . . . and promised to hasten on the termination of our affairs." [1] Grey decided that he could issue instead a public statement which "would reaffirm the declaration of Lord Lansdowne in 1903," and the Persian agreement with Russia was safely in the outer harbor of the port.[j]

The last difficulties in the way of a full reconciliation came out of the bitter feelings existing between Russia and Great Britain in their positions towards Afghanistan. Nicolson had first declared his readiness to discuss this Asiatic squabble late in February 1907, but little more than a beginning had been made two months afterwards. The first of May found Grey complaining that the Russians were taking a long time about Afghanistan.[k] That month was filled with serious, technical exchanges, with the Russians trying hard to win promises that no change in the political status of Afghanistan would subsequently be made by Great Britain without previous consultation with Russia, while Great Britain endeavored to close all openings whereby Russia could deal directly with Afghanistan, whether over political or commercial affairs.[l] The truly dessicating discussions grew in volume through the early summer, yet on 10 July Grey lamented to Nicolson:

Your recent telegrams on Afghanistan are not reassuring. We cannot admit the possibility of Russian intervention in Afghanistan nor the limitation of our own right of intervention. They must trust us to act in a friendly way to them in our relations with the Amir and to honestly endeavor to carry out the engagements which we have undertaken.[m]

The British had come to suspect that, with the improvement of the internal affairs of Russia, the military party was again in the ascendant, and that an agreement with Great Britain

[1] B. D., IV, no. 280, p. 299; no. 432, p. 483; no. 435, p. 485; no. 439, p. 489; no. 440, p. 489. In his manuscript *Diplomatic Narrative* Nicolson wrote: "I am quite sure that I should not have overcome his [Izvolsky's] objections." Nicolson, p. 253.
[j] B. D., IV, no. 439, p. 488; see also no. 428, minutes, p. 477.
[k] *Ibid.*, no. 266, pp. 288-289; no. 270, p. 292.
[l] *Ibid.*, no. 479, p. 536; no. 480, p. 537. G. P., XXV, part I, no. 8529, p. 34.
[m] B. D., IV, no. 274, p. 294.

was no longer as essential as it had been. Anxious as the British foreign office was to terminate these long negotiations, it feared that it would likely require some very plain speaking to obtain an Afghan solution.[n] Nicolson hung on with dogged tenacity, and Izvolsky was entirely friendly as well as eager to finish with the business. Nicolson finally wormed out of him an unofficial memorandum on the Russian attitude and objectives regarding Afghanistan, which he took along on his trip to London for some three weeks during July and August, to discuss in full detail at the foreign office. In that interval, the Anglo-Russian negotiations passed through their last, but expectant lull.[o]

In accordance with the new spirit of relations developing between Great Britain, Russia and France, there was the need of coming to terms with Britain's ally, and Russia's late enemy, Japan. The conclusion of political treaties between France and Japan on 10 June, and between Russia and Japan on 30 July 1907, at least insured toleration if not cordiality.[p] The Franco-Japanese treaty negotiations had been going on with Russian knowledge and approval in direct connection with those between Russia and Japan.[q] The German government

[n] *Ibid.*, no. 274, p. 294; no. 487, pp. 549, 550.
[o] *Ibid.*, no. 490, footnote 1, p. 551; no. 491, enclosure, pp. 553-554. *G. P.*, XXV, part I, no. 8530, p. 35.
[p] The text of the French treaty is given in English in Pooley, *Hayashi*, pp. 321-322; the essential passages in French are in *G. P.*, XXV, part I, no. 8547, footnote **, p. 67. The Russian treaty text is given in English in Pooley, *Hayashi*, pp. 323-324; in French in *G. P.*, XXV, part I, no. 8545, footnote *, p. 62. Russia and Japan also had signed an agreement regulating railroad lines in Manchuria on 13 June 1907, and over fishery concessions in Far Eastern waters, including the use of land for drying and preparations to Japan on 28 July. Both the political treaties provided for the strengthening (in the case of France) or the consolidation (in the case of Russia) of peaceful and friendly relations, as well as for the removal of all cause of future misunderstanding. Both mentioned respect for the existing territorial integrity of China, and declared belief in the principle of equal opportunity for the commerce and industry of all nations within the Celestial empire. France and Japan agreed to maintain by all peaceful means their respective positions and territorial rights on the continent of Asia, and for order and peace in Chinese territory adjacent to their own. Russia and Japan agreed similarly to respect the existing positions of each other as well as all rights accruing to each from any treaties made with China not violating the principle of equal opportunity. By a secret agreement Russia recognized Japanese special interests in Korea; Japan recognized that Russia had interests in Mongolia; and drew a line of demarcation in Manchuria virtually creating spheres of influence, in which each would keep out of the way of the other. See Dennis, pp. 28-29. Tardieu, pp. 231-237. Bompard, pp. 276-277. Fisher, p. 572.
[q] *G. P.*, XXV, part I, no. 8541, p. 53.

obtained wind of these negotiations and took some stock in the rumors of a possible quadruple alliance in the Far East directed against German enterprizes. Izvolsky was warned that Russia should not join any such hostile combination unless that country was ready to be classed thereafter among the enemies of Germany.[r] Izvolsky sincerely denied all possibility of that, and often and fervently explained that the negotiations were no evidence of love, but were dictated by compelling and bitter necessity. The perilous condition of Russia made it essential that all complications must be avoided with Japan which might lead to another war, while the treaty of Portsmouth had deliberately left some questions for future agreement which only now, after much difficulty, were being arranged.[s] In very truth, Izvolsky declared, the treaty did not contemplate fabricating an alliance against Germany, but far more was intended to hold Japan to the status quo, and to circumscribe further its aspirations for expansion.[t] This first step in a marriage of unlovely convenience between Russia and Japan, with France appearing in a supporting rôle, was bitterly yet helplessly resented by China. This Chinese hostility was expected in Berlin to improve the position of, and the trust reposed in, Germany at Peking.[u] For a brief moment the idea of a more righteous counter-alliance of the United States, Germany and China appeared; but however salutary it might have been, it quickly vanished because the United States could not be inveigled into any combination.[v]

The Emperor Nicholas, in his acceptance of a cordial invi-

[r] *Ibid.*, no. 8542, p. 58.

[s] *Ibid.*, no. 8527, p. 33; no. 8541, pp. 53-55; no. 8543, p. 59. Witte, *Vospominaniya*, II, 403. Izvolsky also gave this explanation in his speech to the members of the duma on 27 February / 11 March 1908. *Stenograficheshy otchet: Gosudarstvennaya duma*, third convocation, first session, (1908), pp. 112-115, 117.

[t] *G. P.*, XXV, part I, no. 8543, p. 59; no. 8544, p. 61.

[u] *Ibid.*, no. 8547, pp. 67-68; no. 8548, pp. 69-71. Chinese press organs fully appreciated the respect these treaties professed for China. "Our newspapers can see nothing to congratulate China on in the agreement, and cannot say with any show of unction that the integrity of our country is more strongly assured by the consummation of the entente or that the peace of the Far East is rendered more secure." Pooley, *Hayashi*, pp. 217-219.

[v] For the details of this project engineered by the kaiser see Luella J. Hall, "Germany, America, and China, 1907-8," *Journal of Modern History*, I (1929), 219-235.

tation, notified the kaiser on 12 July that he could be expected
at Swinemünde on 3 August for a three days' meeting, to
review the German navy, on the occasion of his first visit away
from Russia since the start of the disasters of the past two
years.[w] Aside from naval officials, the tsar was to be accompanied by Izvolsky, whose pleasure in associating with such
royal society can be presumed. Schoen contributed in advance
of the gathering a résumé of Izvolsky's conduct of Russian
foreign policy, and pointed out that this minister, despite difficulties and some failures in minor instances, still strove to be
loyal to Germany and to work for more cordial and neighborly
relations. In particular Schoen emphasized that Izvolsky had
kept his year old assurances that no German interests would
be molested in the Anglo-Russian negotiations and, while not
denying that he was much more liberal than Russian ministers
had formerly been, insisted that he was by no means pro-
English. Schoen rightly reminded the foreign office that the
quest for an understanding with Great Britain was begun in
Lamsdorff's days, which Izvolsky had continued out of necessity, although the ambassador in plain truth should not have
covered up Izvolsky's readiness.[x] The days at Swinemünde
passed happily in monarchical solidarity, in accordance with
the spirit of Björkö even if the treaty itself was not alive.[y]
Here Izvolsky gave a copy of the recent Russian-Japanese
agreement to the German chancellor, to the accompaniment
of the dire necessity explanation, and of the need to clear up
the many obscurities of the Portsmouth peace. Bülow expressed his entire concurrence with the provisions of the
agreement, which was said to be in harmony with the aims of
German policy in the Far East.[z] Nothing in detail was told
of the contents of the Anglo-Russian negotiations, as Izvolsky

[w] G. P., XXII, no. 7374, pp. 56-57; no. 7380, p. 72.
[x] Ibid., no. 7377, pp. 61-66. With exceptional dispassionateness the kaiser
noted: "On the whole quite right, perhaps somewhat too favorable for Izvolsky."
(Ibid., p. 66.) Earlier the kaiser had written of Izvolsky: "Aha! He was and
is anglophil." (Ibid., XXV, part I, no. 8527, marginal note 1, p. 33.) The German critical attitude towards Izvolsky first became earnest only when the
convention of 1907 appeared certain. Ibid., no. 8533, pp. 38-39. Izvolsky, Correspondance diplomatique, I, 93, 95.
[y] G. P., XXII, no. 7378, p. 67; no. 7379, p. 69.
[z] Ibid., no. 7378, pp. 67-68. Bülow, Denkwürdigkeiten, II, 295-296.

only declared that the agreement was soon to be completed, and concerned such Asiatic affairs in which no German rights or interests were harmed, with not a word said about the Bagdad railway.[a] Throughout the meeting the tsar was in good humor, and Izvolsky enjoyed the opportunity to have profound conversations on all subjects in order to win mutual confidence. On his return to St. Petersburg, Izvolsky appeared greatly contented; to the British chargé his description of the Swinemünde visit "was excessively *couleur de rose*." [b]

The British and French representatives in Russia, however, looked upon this interview in no roseate light. The announcement of the royal meeting had been carefully concealed until a few days before it was to be held. The news sent the French ambassador scurrying to Izvolsky in a state of nervous excitement, mildly reproachful because of the secrecy used. Izvolsky could hardly have soothed his ruffled disposition when he remarked that "one could also have good friends alongside of allies." The British embassy was likewise discomfitted, and the undying suspicion of a renewal of something like the Three Emperors' League momentarily plagued excited minds.[c] Some rumors were being bandied about which suggested that Germany was actively engaged in blocking a reconciliation between Russia and Great Britain, but this was promptly denied, and Nicolson later assured Schoen that nothing of the kind was believed by the British government.[d] Immediately after the Swinemünde gathering the Russians took great pains to contradict rumors that Izvolsky had revealed to Bülow the terms of the Anglo-Russian agreement soon to be signed, or that anything had transpired that would prove in any way prejudicial to the conclusion of an understanding, or to the future improvement of relations. Sir Edward Grey gladly accepted all the assurances, while he explained how he relied on the Russian government not to be influenced by Germany to the

[a] *G. P.*, XXII, no. 7378, p. 68; no. 7379, p. 70.
[b] *Ibid.*, no. 7378, p. 67; no. 7379, pp. 69, 71-72; XXV, part I, no. 8533, p. 37. *B. D.*, IV, no. 279, p. 298. Izvolsky, *Correspondance diplomatique*, I, 97-98, 227. Bompard, p. 277.
[c] *G. P.*, XXII, no. 7379, pp. 68-69. Bompard, p. 274. Izvolsky, *Correspondance diplomatique*, I, 93, 157.
[d] *G. P.*, XXV, part I, no. 8530, p. 35; no. 8531, p. 35; no. 8532, p. 37.

disadvantage of Great Britain "in matters which affected Russia and ourselves alone." [e] All bad impressions were finally dispelled in London following the successful meeting on 14 August at Wilhelmshöhe between the kaiser and King Edward. [f]

Before the middle of August Nicolson was back in St. Petersburg, having brought with him the well-considered concessions that the British foreign office was prepared to offer for an Afghan settlement. These latest proposals had been arrived at without consulting the government of India, the objections of which would have blocked every chance of agreement. [g] Nicolson warned Izvolsky that this offering was as far as his government was prepared to go in meeting Russian wishes. Izvolsky was encouraging in his reception, for he admitted that "certainly a great step had been made towards an agreement." Although his first impressions were distinctly favorable, and he promised to do his utmost to hasten a conclusion, he would need to study these drafts carefully, besides obtaining the sanction of the tsar. [h] In London it was believed that Izvolsky's present cordial disposition was attributable to the favorable outcome of his conversations with Bülow at Swinemünde, and that agreement had at last been reached with Russia over the main difficulties, leaving the time-robbing labor of formulating the texts the most important task yet to complete. [i] The weightiest dialectical problem centered around what the final treaty should be styled; whether, as the British desired, it should be described as a convention, the most formal way possible; or, as Izvolsky vigorously contended, as anything else, such as an arrangement, agreement or a declaration, although both parties admitted that these forms had equal validity in international law, and were just as binding. Izvolsky based his argument

[e] B. D., IV, no. 277, p. 297; no. 278, p. 297; no. 279, p. 298.
[f] G. P., XXV, part I, no. 8533, p. 38. B. D., VI, no. 25, pp. 43-44; no. 28, p. 48.
[g] Ibid., IV, no. 274, p. 294. Grey, I, 160.
[h] B. D., IV, no. 493, p. 556.
[i] G. P., XXII, no. 7380, p. 74; XXV, part I, no. 8530, p. 35. B. D., IV, no. 280, p. 299.

for an arrangement concerning Tibet and Persia on the ground that, as Great Britain and Russia were simply defining their line of conduct in both places, an arrangement "would not have [the] character of an encroachment on [the] sovereign rights" of Persia, an independent nation, or of China as the suzerain power of its vassal Tibet. On the other hand Izvolsky professed to believe that formal conventions would certainly excite the suspicion of both the Persian and Chinese governments; but he had no scruples against calling the Afghan settlement a convention, because of the special relationship in which Afghanistan stood to Great Britain.[j]

Although the British foreign office preferred to have its way, it was recognized with philosophical resignation that "if a power wishes to disregard her obligations she will be just as ready to do so whatever they are called." Since it was "undesirable to argue about what is really only a matter of form . . . Sir A. Nicolson . . . may be safely left to settle the details." [k] In the end both parties received satisfaction because of an idea which Izvolsky had on 23 August and which, even although unprecedented, Nicolson thought "seems a good one." To avoid three separate ratifications, and to cast all the agreements into one instrument, Izvolsky proposed to have a general preamble preceding the three parts and a single ratification for all.[l] The following day Nicolson despatched the French texts of the agreements to London in the belief that no vital modifications would follow, and that the final Russian approval was near at hand.[m] With commendable alacrity the foreign office took up Izvolsky's idea, and Grey sent back the twist to it that satisfied every viewpoint as to the title by which the understanding should be known. "We agree," he telegraphed to Nicolson on 27 August, "to one general preamble and one ratification, but in that case there must be one instrument styled a convention since it includes one of that category" and two arrangements. On the next day Izvolsky accepted this

[j] *Ibid.*, no. 281, pp. 299-300; no. 282, enclosure, pp. 300-301 ; no. 452, enclosure, pp. 499-500.
[k] *Ibid.*, no. 281, minute, p. 300.
[l] *Ibid.*, no. 283, pp. 301-302.
[m] *Ibid.*, no. 284, pp. 302-303 ; no. 508, p. 566.

style for the Anglo-Russian understanding — if there was to be one.[n]

The long-sought general understanding between the two old enemies retained its elusiveness until the end. Even the last British proposals touching upon Afghanistan still did not meet with Russian approval. The issue that encountered the last full measure of objection was the British insistence that Russia should promise "not to annex or to occupy any part of Afghanistan, nor to take any measures involving interference with the internal government of the territories of the Amir."[o] Such an unconditional undertaking on its part the Russian government had always opposed since Great Britain would not give a similar promise in return; but Nicolson had come back with a British proposal, to use only if necessary, that "should any change occur in the political status of Afghanistan the two governments will enter into a friendly interchange of views on the subject."[p] If the Russian government preferred to leave out their unconditional guarantee, then to match this the British formula was also to have no place in the final agreement.[q] Izvolsky candidly explained that the Russian government wanted to be sure that should Great Britain cause any alteration in the political status of Afghanistan, there would be an amicable exchange of views on the situation "so that the equilibrium in central Asia should be maintained."[r] Izvolsky was ready to accept the British additional statement on 23 August, promising to give an official reply on the morrow after obtaining the assent of his colleagues.[s]

On the 22nd Izvolsky had won the tsar's limited consent to the treaty, but he had insisted that a council of ministers must

[n] *Ibid.*, no. 285, p. 303; no. 286, p. 304.
[o] *Ibid.*, no. 483, p. 543, last sentence of article II of the British counterdraft. For details of this last dispute see below pp. 295-304.
[p] B. D., IV, no. 492, pp. 554-555. Grey, I, 159-160.
[q] B. D., IV, no. 494, p. 557; no. 496, p. 558; no. 506, p. 564.
[r] *Ibid.*, no. 504, p. 563. Izvolsky had himself proposed that Great Britain should include the engagement to consult with Russia should the political status of Afghanistan be changed; or else to write "a despatch to the Russian ambassador in London to be published with the convention saying that if [the] political situation were changed Russia was freed from her obligations." Nicolson at once replied that this alternative "would never do." *Ibid.*, no. 494, p. 557.
[s] *Ibid.*, no. 505, pp. 563-564; no. 508, p. 566.

unanimously agree to all of the texts. The council held its
session on the night of the 24th, which lasted well into the
morning hours because strong opposition developed, leaving
Izvolsky and his supporters in a minority. Nicolson telegraphed his disappointment and doubts on the 25th, stating
briefly: "An unexpected and serious hitch has occurred." [t]
The trouble centered mainly in the unfair attitude of the
majority of the council, who demanded that Russia be freed
from its own unconditional promise, yet with the British
formula for consultation in the event of the alteration of the
political position of Afghanistan inserted. Nicolson knew that
there was no need to argue with Izvolsky, who understood the
British position, for he appreciated the fact that the majority
had taken the opportunity to embarrass Izvolsky because of
their disapproval of his policy. [u] The British foreign office
was "much disappointed at this unexpected difficulty," but had
no more concessions to offer. Grey hoped that the Russian
government would yield not only because these agreements
regarding Asia would otherwise fail, but also because the
friendly relations for which they prepared the way would
never come. Without those friendly relations there was little
chance that Great Britain would coöperate advantageously
with Russia on questions which might arise elsewhere in the
world. This benefit was worth more than the agreements
themselves, and he wished that the Russian government would
keep this fact in mind. [v] Izvolsky must have labored well, for
on 28 August the council of ministers decided to give up both
the unconditional promise of Russia respecting Afghanistan,
and the insistence on an exchange of views with Great Britain
should the political status of the country undergo any change.
After wearisome months Nicolson could finally declare accomplished what had often seemed hopeless: "the negotiations are
now concluded." [w]

British and Russian approval of all the agreements came

[t] *Ibid.*, no. 506, p. 564. Nicolson, p. 254.
[u] *B. D.*, IV, no. 506, pp. 564-565.
[v] *Ibid.*, no. 507, p. 565.
[w] *Ibid.*, no. 511, p. 572; no. 512, p. 573.

without delay, and Nicolson and Izvolsky signed at St. Petersburg on 31 August 1907 the full text of the convention between Great Britain and Russia relating to Persia, Afghanistan and Tibet.[x] Mutual congratulations on the accomplishment, and flattering paeans for kind support and guidance during arduous labors, were promptly interchanged.[y] Izvolsky himself was the grateful recipient of a kindly message from Grey; and Nicolson, while not concealing his desire that the Russian had a stiffer spine and was less sensitive to criticism, paid him the deserved compliment: "He has acted most loyally to us throughout, and I have not detected the slightest attempt to take an unfair advantage. The game has been played most fairly." [z] Izvolsky, indeed, had just reason for his buoyant feelings. It was not many foreign ministers who, in their first full year of service, could point with pride to two successful major operations. One cleaned up the wreckage of the Russo-Japanese war, the gaps in the treaty of Portsmouth, and instituted orderly relations with the late enemy. The other was an almost miraculous achievement to settle century old differences, and even more potent suspicions, with a rival great power, out of which tolerance for a time would at least arise and, so it had been hinted, possibly also profit "elsewhere." August 1907 found Izvolsky's fame at its peak, his vanity adequately appeased: it was his good fortune then that the future is closed to man's knowledge.[a] Almost to the finish it had not seemed possible that the game could be played fairly enough for Russia and Great Britain ever to agree, and to find a similarly great diplomatic revolution one must go back in time a goodly hundred and fifty years.

[x] *Ibid.,* no. 287, p. 304. See also *G. P.,* XXV, part I, no. 8534, p. 40. The French text of the convention of 1907 is in *B. D.,* IV, Appendix I, pp. 618-621.
  [y] *Ibid.,* no. 288, p. 304; no. 520, p. 580; no. 537, p. 596. Grey, I, 160. Nicolson, p. 255.
  [z] *B. D.,* IV, no. 288, p. 304.
  [a] *G. P.,* XXV, part I, no. 8520, p. 26; no. 8533, p. 39. Taube, pp. 107, 133. It was German belief that Izvolsky wished to perform great deeds quickly and escape from the ministry with a reputation into an ambassadorship, a place more in keeping with his personal fortune. What these "deeds" were, was only of secondary importance to him.

CHAPTER FOUR

THE ARRANGEMENT RESPECTING TIBET

I F Great Britain and Russia had been content to mind their own business, this chapter, like many another, would never have been written. Early in this century purely imperialistic motives had brought first Great Britain and then Russia into unsavory relations in Tibet, where neither country belonged, and whom the half wild, unsociable natives had kept at proper distance as long as their stubbornness had saved them from their own weakness to defend their land by force. While neither Great Britain nor Russia had won any security of tenure before 1900, the serious efforts to acquire influence and control in Tibet undertaken after that year were simply additional reasons for being bad friends with each other. An almost inaccessible country, hard to reach because of the necessity of crossing the highest and most unfriendly mountains in the world, it was harder still for small bands of adventurers to get into after the frontiers were reached, because the Tibetans were inhospitable people who belligerently desired only to be let alone. They had no wish to become a white man's burden. Their rudimentary life had nothing enchanting to offer, unless it could be a queer kind of Buddhistic religion. The land itself long remained uncharted; still is in parts only poorly known. Until contemporary times its wealth remained undivined, therefore unenticing, while even yet the quantity is estimated with no degree of accuracy.[a] After a while, however, Great Britain and Russia came to the conclusion that it would be better for them if they became friends in spite of Tibet. Even although animated by so noble a sentiment, it was not easy to agree to be friends because of their intense mutual distrust, and each wanted to be sure that no opportunity would be left open to the other to steal a march in the future despite their arrangement. Consequently it took a long time and much

[a] Fraser, pp. 135-136.

wearisome argument to settle several remarkably unimportant disputes.

If one wishes to become excited, and some do,[b] in a fine frenzy of moral indignation, it can be shown that Great Britain started to cast glances in the direction of Tibet late in the eighteenth century, slowly slithering closer throughout the next, fastening its tentacles around independent Nepal (by 1816), Bhutan (by 1865), and Sikkim (by 1861), both once dependencies of Tibet, even while the Chinese empire was formally recognized as the suzerain power of the land of the lamas. Hereafter the way to Tibet itself was easier, for the best route for penetration led through Sikkim into the narrow Chumbi valley and across the Himalayas, inhabitable by white men with some comfort. By 1890 the British encroachments on Tibet picked up in pace. Hitherto no explanations by way of justification had been needed; lack of success required none. From the last decade of the nineteenth century, as successes began to crown British enterprise, the fabrication of excuses also commenced in order to put a decent and reassuring touch to its activity. It was a misfortune that it seemed requisite to make them; for, after all, no harm was really caused to Tibet (it was too worthless), and Chinese suzerainty had been for years little more than a politeness of speech. The harm that was to result from the British expansion into Tibet came when it created another region in which the culture of Anglo-Russian suspicion could thrive. As yet, however, Russia had hardly become possessively conscious of Tibet. Only within recent times had huge chunks of central Asia been absorbed; and Tibet lay still too far distant to make any more exertion desirable. Once British designs upon Tibet became clear, then Russia entered the scramble with no other excuse than jealousy; and another bitter rivalry had its petty origin, which had to be resolved as part of the convention of 1907.

Shortly before 1890 the Tibetans became involved in trivial disputes with the population of Sikkim, and their primitive

---

[b] The complaining attitude of Indian subjects of Great Britain is especially well known. Taraknath Das' volume on *British Expansion in Tibet* is an example.

military inroads which followed were held to be a challenge
to British authority as the suzerain power of Sikkim. This
British claim ran directly counter to older Tibetan rights, but
a British punitive force drove out the Tibetans, who retreated
without attempting to fight. Their "aggression and unneigh-
borly conduct" in a country formerly their vassal prompted
Great Britain to open up diplomatic communication with
China, as the suzerain of Tibet, but a year was frittered away
in desultory negotiation until "the stock of British patience
was exhausted." [c] Only then did the Chinese stop exasper-
ating delays, and the Chinese Resident in Lhasa hastened down
to Calcutta, there to conclude on 17 March 1890 a convention
with Lord Lansdowne, the viceroy of India. The encroachments of the British upon Sikkim at last won a legal reward
as China recognized the protectorate of Great Britain over
the small mountain country, which conferred "direct and
exclusive control over the internal administration and foreign
relations of that state" upon the British government. The
convention reserved for later, mutually satisfactory settlement
several local, bucolic questions, most important among which
was "the question of providing increased facilities for trade
across the Sikkim-Tibet frontier." [d] The regulations for these
reserved questions were only signed, after much dawdling, by
the British and Chinese commissioners on 5 December 1893.
So far as concerned the facilities for trade, a mart was to be
set up in Yatung, within the frontiers of Tibet, to which all
British traders were to have free access, full protection, and
every convenience, with no duty to pay for five years and with
British officers resident in the town at will to watch the conditions for the British trade. Nothing was stipulated that in any
way could benefit Tibetan traders. There was also an additional political demand regulating the interchange of official
despatches, this to be accomplished with as much speed as
possible and the letters to be "treated with due respect," a
condition of later importance.[e]

[c] B. D., IV, Editors' Note, p. 305. Das, pp. 17-18.
[d] B. D., IV, Editors' Note, p. 305. Accounts and Papers, LXVII (1904), 793.
Younghusband, pp. 439-440.
[e] Accounts and Papers, LXVII, 808-809. Younghusband, pp. 440-441.

The relations between the Tibetans and the British power
in India remained unimproved despite the convention and the
trade regulations. It would not have been difficult to have
established increased facilities for trade, because none had
previously existed. In fact, that there was any trade at all
which ought to be facilitated or protected was essentially a
myth, one of the first to do noble duty as a cloak for less hon-
orable ambitions. The science of statistics for the movement
of trade had already become so perfected that all but unimportant rivulets could be classified. Yet there are no official,
independent itemizations to prove the important extent or the
value of British trade with Tibet at the time of the regulations
of 1893, nor since the regulations to the conclusion of the
convention of 1907, and after.[t] Of course some little swapping
must have taken place, but solicitude for an expanding, or even
an existing trade with Tibet never was a bona fide factor in
British relations and difficulties with China or with Russia.
After 1895 the efforts to delimit an actual boundary between
Tibet and India encountered the enmity of angry Tibetans,
who overturned boundary pillars with perverse regularity.
They furthermore violated the regulations of 1893, continuing
as of old to drive their flocks to pasture on lands within
Sikkim; and obdurately persisted in refusing to trade, as well
as obstructing the smooth flow of whatever trade there was.
Worst of all, they did not treat with due respect official letters
from the viceroy of India, the same remaining unanswered
and even being returned, on occasion, unopened. Neither the
British government nor the government of India, for a while,
took any extreme measures; but with the arrival of Lord

----

[t] The *Annual Statement of the Trade of the United Kingdom with Foreign
Countries and British Possessions*, Compiled at the Customs House from documents collected by that Department, (London, annually), contains no separate
statistics for trade with Tibet in the volumes from 1895 to 1912, both inclusive.
This work is later referred to as *Annual Statement of Trade*. The Russian
Obzor vnyeshney torgovli Rossiy po Yevropeyskoy i Aziatskoy granitsam, [Sur-
vey of the Foreign Trade of Russia over the European and Asiatic Frontiers],
a Work of the Statistical Division of the Department of Customs House Duties,
(St. Petersburg, annually), also contains no separate statistics for trade with
Tibet in the volumes from 1895 to 1912, both inclusive. The Russians, however,
at no time laid claim to any valuable trade with Tibet. This work is later
abbreviated as *Obzor vnyeshney torgovli Rossiy*. See also Fraser, p. 146.

Curzon as viceroy in 1898, British policy was forced out of
its lethargy.[g]

Lord Curzon's nervous excitability, and determination to
maintain and enhance the grandeur of Great Britain in strange
parts of the world, did not permit him to view unsatisfactory
relations with Tibet with equanimity. The Sino-Japanese war
had revealed the military powerlessness of China, and the lack
of control over Tibet had been proved by the past futility of
all negotiations through China as the intermediary. With an
unkind realism admirably adapted to his purpose, Curzon
explained that, because Chinese suzerainty over Tibet was
merely an outworn constitutional fiction, future communication with Tibet should be by direct correspondence, and this
proposal to remove China from the way was approved by the
British government at home.[h] No more success with the
Tibetans greeted his literary efforts than his predecessors had
won, but Curzon felt the rebuffs as personal insults to his own
dignity equally as much as to British prestige. It was without
parallel that so important a personage should be "foiled by
the contemptuous silence of the Dalai Lama" as though "he
were the representative of the pettiest of petty potentates,
with whom it was beneath the dignity of the Dalai Lama to
converse."[i] The failure of his diplomatic endeavors served
only to convince him of the need to use more forceful ways
of persuasion to bring the Tibetans to a decent respect of the
power which he represented. His conviction was intensified
by the first suspicious actions of Russia in Tibet, and Curzon
never could abide the presence of Russians in close proximity
to British interests or pretensions.

Russia had become interested in Tibet as a result of the
conquests of territories in central Asia, and of peaceful pene-

[g] B. D., IV, Editors' Note, p. 305. Ronaldshay, II, 204. Das, p. 27.
[h] Ronaldshay, II, 205. Das, pp. 33, 56. At this same period, but in reference
to Persia, Curzon excellently explained the nature of a "constitutional fiction":
"Within the limits of a nominally still existing integrity and independence so
many encroachments upon both these attributes are possible, that by almost
imperceptible degrees they pass into the realm of constitutional fiction, where
they may continue to provide an exercise for the speculations of the jurist,
long after they have been contemptuously ignored by statesmen." B. D., IV,
no. 319, p. 359.
[i] Ronaldshay, II, 205.

tration into both Mongolia and Manchuria in satisfaction of
services rendered to China in the revision of the terms of the
peace of Shimonoseki of 1895 with Japan. It so happened that
large numbers of the native population in the regions recently
acquired or ardently coveted belonged to that particular brand
of Buddhism dispensed by the lamas and monks from Lhasa.
Russia then began to take an interest in Tibet, and based the
justification for it on purely religious motives, "due solely,"
as Count Lamsdorff still could assert in 1904, "to the large
number of Russian Buriats who regarded the Dalai Lama as
their Pope." [j] It was accurately, although less piously presumed that the newly discovered Russian interest in Tibet
could be traced to the influence of the lamas upon the Buddhist believers in those parts of Asia not yet effectively controlled, and that that influence was not solely religious; for, if
Russia could win the favor of the lamas, these could materially
assist the Russian efforts to make placid subjects of the empire
the natives already snared, and to develop Russian influence
in those outlying provinces of the Celestial empire, lately
found so tempting. Russian foreign policy began to oppose
any change in the political position of Tibet, lest some other
nation should gain influence or control over the Buddhist lamas
to the detriment of Russian prospects outside Tibet. [k] The
greater activity shown by Great Britain in regard to Tibetan
affairs from the coming of Lord Curzon forthwith became a
matter of concern and suspicion to Russia.

Russian active interference in Tibet came only by 1898,
disguised in the person of a Siberian Buriat Buddhist belong-
ing to a monastic order in Lhasa, one Dorzhev by name. He
was often resident in Lhasa and kept in close relationship
with the Dalai Lama, and possibly may have come to be an
unofficial agent of the Russian government, although any
authorized connection was always denied. Everything that
Dorzhev may have attempted remains imperfectly known and
probably of little consequence, but he did work upon the Dalai
Lama in a sense favorable to Russia by means of valuable

[j] *B. D.*, IV, no. 295, p. 311.
[k] *Ibid.*, no. 307, pp. 327-328. Gwynn, I, 392, 415-416.

presents, political advice, and alluring suggestions for religious proselytizing in the Russian empire, and in the royal family. His success culminated in a Tibetan spiritual mission to Russia where it was received by the emperor and the empress. The suspected deeper implications of the incident greatly disquieted Great Britain, particularly because of the simultaneous inability of the government of India to obtain replies to communications sent to Lhasa.[1] In the years before 1902 Curzon had prepared plans for the despatch of a mission to Tibet, empowered to resort to force, to compel negotiations with the Tibetans who had clearly shown that they desired none, to reëstablish British prestige, and to act as balm for his wounded dignity.[m] The Russian solicitude for Tibet, itself in large measure the result of the British activity, only gave rise to additional distrust, and the rumors of secret agreements between Russia and Tibet and China increased the existing tension throughout 1902. In his letter of 13 November to the secretary of state for India, Curzon eagerly described himself as a "firm believer in the existence of a secret understanding, if not a secret treaty . . . and, as I have said before, I regard it as a duty to frustrate this little game while there is yet time. . . . I would not on any ground withdraw the mission. I would inform China and Tibet that it was going; and go it should." [n]

There were wiser and more cautious minds in the government in London who did not relish the awkward relations with Tibet, but who also were convinced of "the growing dislike, if not abhorence, of any forward move, or of any action likely to entail military operations." Lord George Hamilton, the secretary of state for India, reminded the viceroy that a war in Asia would be too costly, especially with the increasing expense of naval construction in Europe, and that Great Britain could not afford to be also in opposition to the strongest continental land power. Like gall and wormwood must Lord George's observation have been that, if the matter were

[1] Gwynn, I, 362. *B. D.*, IV, no. 295, p. 311. Das, pp. 36-41.
[m] Ronaldshay, II, 208.
[n] *Ibid.*, p. 273.

put to a vote, "there would be a disposition to abandon all our present obligations, and to substitute nothing in their place except an attempt to come to an understanding with Russia." [o] No such weakness ever daunted Lord Curzon's tenacity, and another despatch had already been sent by him to London on 8 January 1903, to urge his forward policy to protect the "seriously imperilled" British interests by means of an armed commercial mission to Tibet, and the appointment of a permanent British Resident in the capital.[p] The home government would have none of such chauvinism and on 19 February, almost unanimously, not wishing to incur the dangers of war, the cabinet refused sanction to Curzon's proposals. The next day, when Lansdowne wrote this decision to the viceroy, for the latter's guidance he added the admonition that "it seems to me, therefore, that the decision which was arrived at must be taken, not only as regulating a particular transaction, but to a large extent as governing our future policy in central Asia." [q] This was followed on the 27th by the further explanation that the scheme could not then be sanctioned because the British government was in communication with Russia, trying to obtain a further definition of Russian policy in that part of the world.[r] When the request for a categorical statement of the Russian intentions in Tibet was thrown up to him, Lamsdorff was caught unprepared to make an immediate reply, and only after some hesitation Count Benckendorff was authorized to declare on 8 April that Russia had no "convention about Tibet, either with Tibet itself, or with China, or with any one else, nor had the Russian government any agents in that country, or any intention of sending agents or missions there." [s] This clear disclaimer of Russian designs upon Tibet sufficiently removed British doubts so that the government in London declined to accede to the request from the Indian government that a permanent political agent should be stationed in Tibet.[t]

[o] *Ibid.*, pp. 268-269.
[p] *B. D.*, IV, Editors' Note, p. 305.
[q] Ronaldshay, II, 275.
[r] *Ibid.*, p. 278. *B. D.*, IV, Editors' Note, p. 305.
[s] *Ibid.*, Editors' Notes, pp. 305, 313; no. 295, p. 311.
[t] *Ibid.*, Editors' Note, p. 313.

Before the end of the year Lansdowne was engaged in his serious, but also luckless attempt to reach a general understanding with Russia in Asia.

Lord Curzon's government of India never for a moment wavered or changed its views, persisted in believing in the steady endeavors of Russia to gain political influence in Tibet by unofficial ruses, and prepared specific plans for a mission into Tibet under the leadership of Colonel Francis Younghusband. With the British position strengthened against complications by the Anglo-Japanese alliance, and with Russia becoming dangerously entangled with Japan over their Far Eastern rivalry, the British cabinet, now reorganized after the defection of Chamberlain and his followers, no longer seemed able to resist Curzon's unabated insistence upon an advance into Tibet.[u] In the face of Tibetan refusals to enter any negotiations, and the failure of the Chinese official to put in an appearance, His Majesty's government felt that it would be impossible not to take some action. Therefore, on 6 November 1903, the sanction for the advance of the mission which Curzon had hatched was reluctantly telegraphed, qualified by these clear limitations:

This step should be taken purely for the purpose of obtaining satisfaction, that it should not be allowed to lead to occupation, or any form of permanent intervention in Tibetan affairs, and that it should withdraw as soon as reparation is obtained . . . and His Majesty's government are not prepared to establish a permanent mission in Tibet.[v]

The Younghusband expedition, already at the frontier, was quickly underway; but enough has already been mentioned of the career of this aggressively "grandiose project" and of the Russian consternation when the news of it leaked out.[w] The

[u] Ronaldshay, II, 280. *B. D.*, IV, Editors' Note, p. 313. *D. D. F.*, IV, no. 388, p. 532. Das, p. 64.
[v] *B. D.*, IV, the secretary of state for India to the government of India, p. 305. Ronaldshay, II, 280. Lee, II, 369.
[w] Tardieu, pp. 249-250. *C. H. B F. P.*, III, 324. See above, pp. 67-70. Spring Rice believed that British influence should have been wielded in Tibet through gifts and through the lamas. He regretted Curzon's "more resounding method" because "to win now we have to use a great amount of force and make Russia the protector of Tibet against the foreign aggressor." (Gwynn, I, 409.) "The cardinal consideration with [the government of India] was to prevent Tibet from falling under Russian influence." ("The Durbar and After," *Round*

British cabinet experienced many anxious moments and feared dangerous complications from the bold undertaking, from which they were saved by the greater preoccupations, and the paralysis of the power of Russia.[x]

The Younghusband expedition reached Lhasa in ample time to spend the summer, marvelling at the quaint customs and buildings, shipping generous quantities of valuable plunder back to India, while waiting to start negotiations for satisfaction and reparation with persons properly qualified to act for the Dalai Lama. This personage had sought safety in flight to the neighborhood of the lesser religious center of Urga in Mongolia, where prudence bade him remain.[y] It made no impression on the government of India that Lansdowne had emphatically promised the Russian government that Great Britain would not attempt to annex Tibet, or to establish a protectorate over it, or to control its internal administration in any way so long as no other power tried to intervene on its own account.[z] No other power was trying; but the government of India persisted in its plans for acquiring as great an influence over Tibetan affairs as it possibly could, once again slipping out from the control of the home government to go further than had been either desired or authorized.[a] By mid-

---

Table, II [1911-1912], 415.) "What . . . Lord Curzon wanted [was] an agent at Lhasa." Younghusband, p. vii.

[x] *B. D.*, IV, no. 289, pp. 306-307; no. 290, p. 307; no. 293, p. 310. *C. H. B. F. P.*, III, 325. On 4 March 1904, Lady Curzon wrote from London these revealing lines to Lord Curzon: "I think it would be very grave if a crisis happened in India now, as they [the cabinet] would tie your hands absolutely here and you would have to resign. Tibet has frightened the whole cabinet, and they think it rash and are frightened to death. People talk of it more than of Russia, and their ignorance is amazing." Ronaldshay, II, 344.

[y] Gwynn, II, 74. See Younghusband's descriptive account of the expedition, pp. 84-307. A correspondent of the London *Daily Chronicle* is quoted as writing: "The expedition has looted monasteries, and for weeks past bales of plunder have been coming over the passes into India. Their contents have brought joy to the officers' wives and friends, whose houses in the hill stations began to look as some of them looked after the sack of Peking four years ago." Das, p. 65.

[z] *B. D.*, IV, no. 293, p. 310.

[a] Colonel Younghusband perfectly described the habit: "That strange force which has so often driven the English forward against their will appears to be in operation once more. It is certain that neither the British government nor the British people wished to go to Lhasa. . . . We have intended, and we have publicly and solemnly declared our intention, not to intervene, or, if we have to intervene, to withdraw immediately. . . . Somehow we have to intervene; somehow we have to stay." Younghusband, pp. 430, 437.

summer 1904 the government of India had framed what
suited its estimation of the proper demands to make in the
conversations with Tibet. It sent them to the India office in
London as well as to Colonel Younghusband in Tibet, who
was to find out with what reception they would meet without
committing the government in any way, because the proposals
had not as yet been approved by the British government.
These demands entirely violated the solemn promises that
had been given to Russia, and they did not receive the assent
of the cabinet; but the government of India and its commissioner were so wedded to the determination to stay in Tibet
and effectively to control its policy, that only one of the proposals escaped inclusion in the treaty pressed upon Tibet.[b]

By dint of much strong language, Colonel Younghusband
successfully rounded up a quota of representatives of the
Tibetan government and from the three leading monasteries,
with a sufficiently important official to affix the seal of the
Dalai Lama, absent on tour. From this motley array he
extorted a convention signed on "the 27th day of the
seventh month of the Wood Dragon year," prosaically on
7 September 1904. There was still enough present to
throw together a disarming preamble proclaiming a desire
"to restore peace and amicable relations, and to resolve and
determine the doubts and difficulties" which of late "have
tended towards a disturbance of the relations of friendship
and good understanding which have existed." Ten articles
followed which compelled such concessions from, and imposed
such restrictions upon Tibet as would insure the predominance
of British influence.[c] The Tibetans were first required to reaffirm respect for the convention of 1890, and of the frontier
between Tibet and Sikkim, the effective starting point of
British aggression. In ardent pursuit of an elusive trade, new
Tibetan markets were to be opened forthwith in other towns,
and all the privileges and facilities conferred upon the British

[b] *B. D.*, IV, no. 296, p. 312; Editors' Note, pp. 313-314. Lee, II, 371. The
demand which failed envisaged a British Resident posted at Lhasa, or at worst
at Gyangtse, "to discuss matters" with Chinese or Tibetan officials.
[c] The negotiations are recounted in Younghusband, pp. 231-307. The text of
the Lhasa convention is in *B. D.*, IV, no. 298, pp. 314-316.

merchants by the regulations of 1893 were to be maintained. An indemnity of £500,000, the equivalent of seventy-five lakhs of rupees, was exacted "for the expense incurred in the despatch of armed troops to Lhasa to exact reparation for breaches of treaty obligations and for the insults offered to and attacks upon the British Commissioner and his following and escort," a sum calculated in accordance with a rate suggested by the government of India.[d] This huge sum for an impecunious people to pay was divided into seventy-five annual instalments of rupees one lakh each on the first day of January, commencing in 1906; while as security "the British government shall continue to occupy the Chumbi valley until the indemnity has been paid and until the trade marts have been effectively opened for three years, whichever date may be the later." Lastly of importance came an article which tied Tibet in a straight-jacket in its relations with foreign powers. No other state was to be let to intervene in Tibetan affairs, to acquire or to occupy any territory, to gain a right to any revenues, to send any representatives or agents into the country, or to obtain for itself or any of its subjects any concessions or rights whatsoever, without the previous consent of Great Britain.[e]

In everything except in name a British protectorate would be established, and the Chinese government was properly concerned lest its claim to suzerainty over Tibet should disappear. The British government was willing to let a shadowy suzerainty remain, but distinctly warned China that it was not expected that those rights would be exercised with extreme effectiveness.[f] The Chinese were presented with the text of an adhesion convention during 1905 by Great Britain, and this action was held to show that the fact of Chinese suzerainty was thereby recognized, although it was not emphasized that its signature would also make valid the provisions of the Lhasa agreement. Wearisome negotiations lasting to the end of the year did not win Chinese acquiescence, and the British foreign

[d] *Ibid.*, no. 298, p. 315; no. 296, p. 312.
[e] *Ibid.*, no. 298, p. 316.
[f] *Ibid.*, no. 300, and footnote 1, p. 318; no. 302, p. 321.

office announced that it was not deemed worth while to continue them.[g] Possibly fearing the loss of position in Tibet, in January 1906 the Chinese government offered to resume the negotiations, which led to the convention signed at Peking on 27 April, whereby China agreed to the terms of the Lhasa convention concerning Tibet with no important modification, in return for a British engagement not to annex any Tibetan territory, nor to interfere in the administration of Tibet. An explicit recognition of the suzerainty of China may be hunted in vain, and another stage in the wasting away of the Celestial kingdom was confirmed.[h]

That the Russian government immediately took alarm at the first rumors of the provisions of the Lhasa convention of 1904, which both Lansdowne and Hardinge had attempted to minimize, has already been described. The British government privately recognized that Younghusband had lost all restraint, and that the agreement he concluded must be altered, because the honor and the public policy of the nation were involved.[i] The Russians were assuaged by Lansdowne who explained that there would be no permanent occupation of Tibet, no attempt made to deprive other powers of whatever rights they possessed under existing treaties, and that the Chumbi valley would be held only temporarily as a guarantee for the payment of the reparations which had been demanded from the outset. No sum would be stipulated that would be more than the Tibetans could pay, and it was said in this connection that "the indemnity of half a million sterling could hardly be smaller."[j] Nevertheless, now that so strong a position had been obtained for Great Britain in Tibet, even if by

[g] *Ibid.*, no. 300, footnote 2, p. 319.
[h] Gwynn, II, 72. *B. D.*, IV, Editors' Note, p. 322. The text of the Peking convention of 1906 is in *ibid.*, no. 305, and enclosures, pp. 323-326. The negotiation of this convention was of little moment in Anglo-Russian relations; Russia was then in no condition to object effectively. Early in January Lamsdorff had inquired about some rumors of Anglo-Chinese conversations, but allowed his mild concern to be lulled by British characterizations of his information as "purely imaginary," which was momentarily true because the negotiations with China happened to be suspended. *Ibid.*, Editors' Note, pp. 322-323; Appendix III, p. 622.
[i] Lee, II, 371.
[j] *B. D.*, IV, no. 299, p. 318; no. 301, p. 320; no. 303, pp. 321-322.

broken promises to Russia and violated instructions, once gained the government was reluctant to give up any more than was compulsory. It would be "a convenient means of disarming the opposition of other powers" to maintain in a general way that the privileges actually won by Great Britain did not harm their rights which had been previously secured.[k] Lansdowne pointed out that the assurances given Russia "must be interpreted in a reasonable manner" because the Tibetans had, indeed, behaved very badly.[l] Recourse was had once more to a glittering concept, that of geographical propinquity, to bolster British contentions; and it sounded quite well if the isolation of Tibet from other countries, and the difficulty of crossing the world's tallest mountains in order to travel between India and Tibet were ignored. That this idea was henceforth to be the prime justification for a privileged British position was stated in an official formulation:

It would . . . probably be better to defend the agreement [of 1904] on the ground that the only special privileges which it secures for Great Britain are those which she has a right to claim as the power whose geographical position entitles her to a preponderating political influence in Tibet, and that the exercise of these privileges . . . is not likely to have results injurious to other powers.[m]

In the end Great Britain had to relinquish very little of the profits accruing from the forward policy of Lord Curzon and

[k] *Ibid.*, no. 303, p. 321.
[l] *Ibid.*, no. 301, p. 320.
[m] *Ibid.*, no. 303, p. 322. It was more than a thousand miles from the nearest boundary, across dangerous country, before the Russians could reach the southern frontier of Tibet and threaten the British power in India. There, "north of Hindustan the greatest of mountain systems stretches for hundreds of miles across inner Asia. Here, from table-lands that themselves overtop the highest mountains of Europe, the titanic Himalayan peaks begin their rise into the sky. . . . From northern India through Sikkim and southern Tibet the route leads. In that broken land of mile-deep gorges the travelers trudge from the tropics to the subarctic in a few hours; from valleys where gorgeous flowers bloom and vivid parrots flash, to snowy passes where colossal icy sentinals like Chomulhari stand guard. . . .
"On the wind-swept plateau of Tibet they march in winter garb, though summer is so close behind. When the trail rises to hilltops they see mountain splendor as men's eyes seldom know, and at last, one morning, they see the glory of the Everest group far ahead and get the first glimpse of that "rock fang in the sky" where men before them have died." L. H. Robbins, "Titanic Peaks that Fling out Challenge," *New York Times*, Magazine section, 26 March 1933, pp. 10, 11.

the disregard of instructions by Colonel Younghusband when
he imposed the Lhasa convention of 1904. In a declaration
appended to it when ratified on 11 November by Lord Ampthill, the acting viceroy of India, that indemnity of seventy-five
lakhs of rupees, which "could hardly be smaller," was reduced
to twenty-five, now payable in only three annual instalments
from funds which the Chinese government could advance for
Tibet. After the last payment had been received, the occupation of the Chumbi valley was to cease, provided that the trade
marts specified in the convention should meanwhile have been
effectively opened for three years.[n] There were no other
modifications. Although Younghusband and other adherents
of the militant group bitterly lamented this concession, the
touchy incident of the Tibetan expedition sank into a welcome
quiescence, and no more protests came from the Russian government.[o] The next year was practically free of Anglo-Russian
interchanges over Tibet, and witnessed the resumption of the
attempts for an understanding in Asia by the Conservative
government in England, carried onward even more heartily
in the early months of 1906 by the Liberal successors. On 10
April, nearing the end of his own career, Lamsdorff characterized the policy of his government towards Tibet as "one of
absolute non-intervention." Russia desired that Great Britain,
and all other nations, should leave Tibet alone, "tranquil both
externally and internally."[p] The declaration that Russia did
not wish to interfere in Tibet made enjoyable reading in the
British foreign office, but the implication that Great Britain
"should be equally debarred from all interference" was not
relished, because it was not believed that the government of
India would appreciate such a limit on future action. The
British government was likewise unwilling to agree with Lamsdorff's views, because to do so would place Russia on an absolute equality of position. This prospect made it really difficult
to try for an agreement with Russia concerning Tibet, because

[n] *B. D.*, IV, no. 298, p. 317; no. 310, p. 331.
[o] *C. H. B. F. P.*, III, 325. Das, pp. 68-70.
[p] *B. D.*, IV, no. 306, p. 326; no. 309, pp. 329-330.

it seemed evident that the Russians would approach any negotiation from that standpoint, which would be totally inadmissable.[q]

Nevertheless the Liberal government and its foreign secretary, Sir Edward Grey, had no love for the recent aggression in Tibet, and preferred to reach a more enduring relationship with Russia, for the realization of which the time seemed ripe.[r] The Chinese adhesion to the Tibetan convention, which would regularize the position that Great Britain had won in Tibet, was nearly ready and would constitute a base from which to begin the negotiations with Russia. By 16 April Grey had decided that when Chinese adhesion was a reality, he could then tell the Russians what had been done, what the existing position was, "and suggest that it is very undesirable to disturb Tibet, which is one of the few places in the world where to leave things alone causes no inconvenience to anybody."[s] This was just as true in 1904 as when Grey wrote it, except that the British influence had since been desirably extended and no inconvenience would be caused to maintain it, if Russia could be persuaded to leave things alone in Tibet forevermore. After Izvolsky had become Russian foreign minister towards the middle of May, and Sir Arthur Nicolson had reached St. Petersburg near the end of the month, the British government had ready a set of draft instructions for attaining an arrangement respecting Tibet, by which the negotiations for a general understanding with Russia should be initiated. The instructions proceeded from the position that Great Britain had sought no new advantages from Tibet during the late disorders "except such as are necessary to secure the full enjoyment of the rights" previously granted, and that the government was "most anxious to complete the evacuation of Tibet;" but "it must be equally recognized that His Majesty's government could not admit the presence in Tibet of Russian officials in any capacity whatever."[t] Armed with

---

[q] *Ibid.*, no. 307, minutes, p. 328.
[r] *C. H. B. F. P.*, III, 365. Gwynn, II, 74.
[s] *Ibid.*, p. 72. *B. D.*, IV, no. 307, minute, p. 328.
[t] *Ibid.*, no. 310, p. 331.

these instructions, Nicolson proposed to Izvolsky that they should "exchange views on several important matters, such as Tibet and others," and Izvolsky cordially agreed.[u]

The Tibetan discussions were opened by Nicolson on 7 June 1906 when, after some preliminary explanations of the existing position, he disclosed the five points upon which he was empowered to treat with Izvolsky. In the first place Russia was expected to recognize, as Great Britain by implication already had, the suzerainty of China over Tibet; to promise to respect the territorial integrity of Tibet, and to refrain from any meddling with its internal administration. Secondly, the argument of geographical propinquity was pressed into duty as the reason why Great Britain would expect Russian recognition of its "special interest in seeing that the external relations of Tibet are not disturbed by any other power." This was the one demand that dogged the conversations the longest. The third point was a mutual engagement not to send any representatives to Lhasa, subsequently made more explicit to read that no Russian officials should be permitted in Tibet in any capacity whatsoever. This was followed by a reciprocal self-denial of any attempt either to seek or to obtain any concessions, commercial or otherwise, in Tibet on behalf of the British or Russian governments, or for their subjects. Lastly, both were to agree in the same manner that none of the revenues of Tibet, in cash or also in kind, should be pledged or assigned away. Izvolsky asked to be supplied with some statement in writing of these points because it would be difficult for him to recall them precisely, and he craved the indulgence of some little time to study the past records of a question in which he was not well versed, in preparation for his reply at a later meeting.[v]

Izvolsky's study of the past records was fruitful, and on 13 June he was able to tell the British ambassador that the

[u] *Ibid.*, no. 221, p. 237. Nicolson, pp. 215-217. Izvolsky, *Correspondance diplomatique*, I, 303.

[v] *B. D.*, IV, no. 311, pp. 332-333; see also no. 224, p. 240. Nicolson, p. 219. At the outset of the negotiations, Izvolsky apparently consulted with Benckendorff over the terms of the Russian proposals for Tibet. Later on this method was discontinued, and Benckendorff had to request information on the course of the Persian conversations. Izvolsky, *Correspondance diplomatique*, I, 310, 409.

emperor himself had fully appreciated the liberal nature of the British demands, which were satisfactory bases upon which to proceed with the negotiations. Izvolsky expressed his belief that there would be no serious difficulty in reaching agreement on four of the five demands presented by Great Britain. He felt uncertain, however, about the meaning of the second point wherein Great Britain claimed as a special interest, because of the geographical nearness to India, that the foreign relations of Tibet should not be "disturbed" by any other nation. Izvolsky said that "the word 'disturbed' somewhat puzzled him," and he inquired for an explanation as to how much of a commotion would constitute a disturbance.[w] It also appeared that Izvolsky had found among the past records a couple of points of interest to Russia not covered in the British draft. He suggested that if Russia should recognize British special interests, it would only be fair that the "spiritual" interest of Russia in Tibet should be acknowledged. He then dilated on the orthodox Russian expression of this necessity: that there was an important section of Buddhist subjects of Russia who, "in view of their habitat and of their military aptitude, looked to the Dalai Lama as their spiritual chief," so that Izvolsky "did not see how it would be possible for Russia to engage to abstain from all intercourse with the Dalai Lama without offending, and possibly estranging, her Buddhist subjects." It was desirable, therefore, that some loophole should be left for Russia to communicate with whomever should be the Dalai Lama "on matters strictly and solely pertaining to religious questions," permitting the Buriats to reach their chief, and letting an occasional Tibetan religious mission go to St. Petersburg.[x] Izvolsky had unearthed another point, namely, that in recent years the Russian Geographical Society had sent scientific parties into Tibet, which found out most of what was known of Tibetan geography. Now Great Britain proposed to exclude all Russian officials from Tibet, whereas

---

[w] *B. D.*, IV, no. 313, p. 335; no. 314, p. 337. Nicolson, p. 219.
[x] On the Tibetan lamaism, customs and physical plant, see the descriptions in Younghusband, *op. cit.*, and C. Eliot, "The Buddhism of Tibet," *Quarterly Review*, CCIII (1905), 192-220.

"every one of any note was an official of some sort in Russia." Surely the British did not desire to seclude Tibet from all out-side contact, nor to bar men of learning from pursuing an interest in Tibetan geography, which was "a perfectly non-political and solely scientific object." ᵧ With this rejoinder by Izvolsky, the important questions to be resolved concerning Tibet in the coming conversations were disclosed.

Izvolsky's reply gave Nicolson plenty to think about, and he promised to refer to London for the views of his govern-ment. He advised the foreign office that he expected the Rus-sian minister would insist upon leaving the way clear for some kind of relations with the Dalai Lama, as being something in the nature of an equivalent for the British demand for the right to regulate foreign affairs, and to determine the facilities for commercial intercourse with Tibet. On the other hand, Nicolson did not believe that the question of sending scientific expeditions into Tibet would be pressed with equal insistence. He suggested the attitude which the British government should take towards this matter, which was eventually to be accepted by the Russians and included in the final agreement. Rather than to oppose the entrance of all such missions it could be suggested that, for a specified term of years, both govern-ments should agree not to send any scientific parties into Tibet, thereby leaving the entire question open for definitive regula-tion at some future time when "the situation in Tibet was more settled and satisfactory." Before any further conversations advanced the agreement, on 20 June Izvolsky turned up with one last problem: they were proposing to make a settlement of difficulties in Tibet, in which Great Britain demanded that no Russian officials should appear. Hence it seemed essential to come to an understanding of just what was comprised in Tibet. During his researches Izvolsky had discovered that Tibet was an inexact term, that it might be an expression used to indicate geographical limits, or to describe an administrative unit. Now the former was the more inclusive interpretation, "as there were certain districts in the northern and western parts of

ᵧ B. D., IV, no. 314, pp. 337-338.

Tibet which lay within the boundaries of Tibet, but were not under Tibetan administration." [z] In order to obviate any later disagreement, Izvolsky wanted to know in what sense the British government would interpret the expression Tibet; although he could as well have guessed that this would be in the most extended sense.

The discussions respecting Tibet were relatively easy to handle, and the few difficulties encountered were settled in a conciliatory spirit, even if at a sluggardly pace, so that "the reluctant compromise was embodied in a convention which is a masterpiece of drafting." [a] The definition of the extent of Tibet was not well known in London, so the government of India was consulted by telegraph in what sense the expression should be used, and was requested to advise how much territory was contained in the geographical area. That government promptly answered with a description of the bounds of geographical Tibet, and claimed:

The whole tract thus defined was within the plenary and autonomous jurisdiction of the Tibetan authorities, so far as any jurisdiction could be exercised over the northern portion, which is uninhabited during the greater part of the year save by wandering hunters and gold-seekers.

The Indian government would have none of Izvolsky's notion of Tibet as an administrative unit, as one of the ordinary provinces of China, especially because they held Tibet to be a feudatory state under the suzerainty of China, already only a constitutional fiction. In their presentation of the matter, Tibet had large autonomous powers, among which was the power "to conclude treaties with coterminous states" on questions of the frontier and mutual trade. Nicolson was, therefore, instructed that in the conversations with Izvolsky, Tibet was to be employed in a geographical sense.[b]

When this decision was told to Izvolsky in the middle of

[z] *Ibid.*, p. 338.
[a] Nicolson, p. 239. The correspondence relating to the negotiations on the subject of Tibet is compressed for the greater part by the Editors of the *British Documents* into one summary memorandum drawn up by 18 April 1907, in striking contrast to the fulsome detail lavished upon the more vital difficulties offered by Persia and Afghanistan. *B. D.*, IV, no. 314, pp. 336-349.
[b] *Ibid.*, p. 341.

July, he only suggested that the geographical extent of Tibet should be such as was recognized by China, whereupon the matter was dropped until early in January 1907. At that time Izvolsky reopened the subject because, "in order to know what was forbidden ground and what not," the boundaries of Tibet would need to be described. Nicolson responded that he thought it had been previously settled as consisting of the territory which China considered to be Tibet, to which Izvolsky rejoined that it appeared that even the Chinese "did not seem to have very clear and positive ideas on the subject." His assertion survived British investigation for, after making inquiries, the Chinese could not discover any precise information regarding the boundaries on the north and east of Tibet, a failure which ought to have indicated a special urgency for more of the scientific parties sent out by the Russian Geographical Society rather than for their suspension, as Great Britain demanded. In the face of this lack of knowledge on the part of the authorities most entitled to possess it, the British government fell back upon the Tibetan frontiers as formulated by the government of India.[c] To these, however, Izvolsky was opposed because, as could be anticipated, "in his opinion these limits were rather extended," but he repeated his own unsatisfactory proposal that the Chinese boundaries delimiting the area should be accepted, as another opportunity for inquiring about this problem from China would present itself later.[d] Nothing more, however, seems to have been done with this question, and it may be an illustration of the "masterpiece of drafting" that the arrangement respecting Tibet nowhere described the geographical area of that which was Tibet.

The being styled the Dalai Lama, and the accessibility of

[c] *Ibid.*, pp. 341, 346.
[d] *Ibid.*, p. 349. When China was informed of the conclusion of the Anglo-Russian agreement respecting Tibet, a request was made that China should define the boundaries of Tibet. The Chinese reply of 4 October 1907 was extremely touchy and ill-humored: "As regards the limits of Tibet . . . no change has ever been made in them, and the old limits should be regarded as authoritative. There is no necessity to send a definition of them. Nor is there any need for a note on this subject." After this display of temper, the question was not taken up again with the Chinese government; and those authoritative, old limits of Tibet, which it was unnecessary to define, remained "long and little known." *Ibid.*, no. 543, pp. 603-604.

his sacred person in Tibet to Russian Buddhist pilgrims, bulked large in the conversations between Great Britain and Russia. Since his flight from Tibet in 1904, His Holiness the Supreme Head of the Tibetan people had passed, not unhappily, two years in Mongolia as a guest of the local princes. A young man around thirty-five he became, at last, restless to return to the scenes of his supremacy, the more so because the Tashi Lama, little his inferior and possessed of a religious administration of his own, had flourished at Lhasa in his absence, and had just been accorded a flattering reception in India by his English and Hindu friends. The Russians also would like to see him back in Lhasa, using his influence to promote Russian ambitions in Mongolia and among its Buddhist subjects, and counteracting the English-mindedness of his subordinate rival. The Grand Lama expressed fears for his life on such a journey to his Russian friends.[e] The Russian government wanted the Dalai Lama to return, but once in Lhasa not to stir up trouble, because he could count on no support or aid from Russian sources.[f] Something had to be done to screw up his courage, and to dispel his fears for his safety; so the emperor of Russia sent him a cordial telegram on 23 March / 5 April 1906, possessed of no political significance, but intended to reassure the lama and Buddhist communities within the empire.[g] More tangible encouragement was offered by some Buriats, who banded together and armed themselves to furnish an escort to conduct the Dalai Lama on the return route to Lhasa. Only two weeks before he left office, Lamsdorff admitted that the escort was approved by his government, and the British quickly countered that this escort "would give rise to trouble."[h]

The British protest complained that the armed escort would

[e] *Ibid.*, no. 306, pp. 326-327; no. 307, pp. 327-328. Gwynn, II, 74.
[f] *B. D.*, IV, no. 306, p. 327; no. 309, p. 330.
[g] *Ibid.*, no. 306, p. 327; no. 307, p. 327. The words were: "My numerous subjects, professing the Buddhist faith, won the happiness of saluting their spiritual chief during his sojourn in the north of Mongolia contiguous to the Russian empire. Rejoicing that my subjects were able to receive a beneficent, spiritual influence from Your Holiness, I beg you to believe my feeling of sincere gratitude and esteem towards you." *Ibid.*, no. 306, enclosure, p. 327.
[h] *Ibid.*, no. 308, and footnotes 1, 2, and 3, p. 328.

create disorders in Tibet, and was considered to be an intervention in the internal affairs of the country now prohibited
by treaties, while the despatch of a new expedition was openly
threatened, however reluctant the British government would
be to undertake it. Grey proposed that the Russians should
issue the necessary orders to prevent the Buriats from crossing
over the Tibetan border, or to accompany the lama further on
his way.[i] Lamsdorff was willing to be conciliatory; there was
no wish on the part of Russia to interfere in Tibet, but the
Dalai Lama ought to return to Lhasa for the good of his
religious subjects of northern Asia. The Russian government
was not able to promise him a safe journey, nor could it well
refuse the request of loyal Buddhist disciples to guard the
sacred person of their master on his dangerous way home. It
was Lamsdorff's personal impression that the escort intended
to return as soon as the frontier was reached, but anyhow
"there never had been any question of the Buriats remaining
at Lhasa." If he could do so by telegraph, he would try to
stop the escort at the frontier after it had turned over its
precious cargo to Tibetan coreligionists.[j] By the time Izvolsky
became foreign minister the whereabouts of the Dalai Lama
had become uncertain, but strict orders had been sent to keep
the Buriats out of Tibet if at all possible.[k]

The affairs of the Dalai Lama caused Izvolsky evident concern, and his vacillation in handling it at times irked Sir Arthur
Nicolson.[l] Izvolsky realized the importance to Russia of having the favorably disposed Dalai Lama return to Tibet but,
because he was conscious of British distrust, he asked whether
the presence of any Dalai Lama, or only of this one in particular, was opposed; and then at once requested this matter not

[i] *Ibid.*, no. 309, enclosure, p. 330.
[j] *Ibid.*, no. 309, p. 329. The Russian government had sanctioned the armed
escort, "acting on the advice of the officials who had special knowledge of the
temper of the Siberian Buriats."
[k] *Ibid.*, no. 311, p. 333.
[l] *Ibid.*, no. 312, p. 334. Nicolson, p. 219. Benckendorff steadily advised
Izvolsky not to support the Dalai Lama or his desire to return to Tibet, where
his activity might give the British a pretext to send another expedition into the
country. Izvolsky determined to end Russian intrigues in Tibet so that the
negotiations with Great Britain could be conducted on firm ground. Izvolsky,
Correspondance diplomatique, I, 300, 309, 319.

to be mentioned to the British government.[m] The British foreign office did not desire the immediate return of this unfriendly person whose actions, so Hardinge explained, had once provoked a war, although in principle there would be no objection to his return at some later, quieter time. Next, in July 1906, Izvolsky veered around, as a result of further study of the personality of the Dalai Lama, going so far as to propose the determination of his future career by mutual agreement, which was acceptable to the British government. Nothing ever came of this suggestion, while the Chinese government during the autumn concerned itself with his wanderings. In October the British learned that the Chinese did not want the lama to go back to Lhasa, and had taken him to the town of Kanchan to keep him away from Russian influence. A month later, on the contrary, Izvolsky announced that the Chinese government were finding the holy man an "inconvenient guest" and were urging him to resume his residence in Tibet. The Dalai Lama was then stopping over in Gumbum, where he had been informed that the Russian government thought it was undesirable for him to return to Lhasa for the present.[n] British sources discovered that the influence of Dorzhev was active again, and suspected that the Russians actually were trying to keep the Dalai Lama at Gumbum in order to gain the benefit of his influence over the Mongol population, as Russian designs progressed for the control of that still unexploited country.[o] The solicitude lavished upon the person and the movements of this little known potentate rapidly declined with the success of the conversations over other Tibetan problems, and by the time that the Dalai Lama

---

[m] *B. D.*, IV, no. 311, p. 333.

[n] *Ibid.*, no. 314, p. 339.

[o] *Ibid.*, p. 342. For a few fleeting moments the Russians brought up the question of their aggressive action in Mongolia, subsequent to the Russo-Japanese war. The government would have been pleased if the British could, in some way, agree to the maintenance of the *status quo* in Mongolia, which would by then have favored the Russian position as against the lawful rights of China. The British government was quite casual about the proposal, simply stating that any approach of this nature which the Russian government might choose to make would receive careful consideration. A Mongolian frontier formula was afterwards bandied about during the spring of 1907, but eventually the entire question was forgotten. *Ibid.*, no. 262, and Editors' Notes, pp. 284-286; no. 280, p. 299; no. 314, pp. 341-342.

did reappear in Lhasa, where he received a good greeting, he had ceased to trouble Anglo-Russian relations.[p]

Above every other consideration it was essential that there should be a Dalai Lama in Tibet in order to justify the Russian contention of spiritual interest in the country. Izvolsky laid great emphasis on the maintenance of this spiritual connection in behalf of the Buddhist population, and thought that this argument should be accepted by Great Britain, if the alleged special British interests arising out of the geographical nearness of India to Tibet were to be admitted by Russia.[q] In his remarkable studies on the Tibetan question, Izvolsky ascertained in due time:

There was also a Tashi Lama, who had almost equal prerogatives, and, as he understood, a separate administrative district. It was possible that, in certain cases, the Russian Buddhists might find it necessary to be in relations with the latter also.[r]

This was a perfectly true discovery, which bolstered the Russian proposal for direct religious communication and pilgrimages into Tibet, whether or not a Dalai Lama should reside within its boundaries. The advice of the government of India was solicited from London, and in the reply of 13 July 1906 no desire was expressed to prevent the visitations of honest, faithful pilgrims to the holy places as they had commonly done in the past. No Russian representatives, however, were to be allowed in Tibet since this would only lead to trouble, because it would be impossible to draw a distinction between political and religious matters. The Russians at once repeated that only the preservation of the old relations had been requested, whereby pilgrims brought money and presents to the Dalai Lama, and pointed out that no wish had been mentioned to have an agent at Lhasa.[s]

The first Russian draft for an arrangement respecting Tibet was handed to Nicolson on 8 October.[t] In this, at the end of

[p] Gwynn, II, 74. This is the Dalai Lama, potent in after years, who died at Lhasa in December 1933.

[q] B. D., IV, no. 313, p. 335; no. 314, p. 337.

[r] Ibid., no. 314, p. 338.

[s] Ibid., p. 340.

[t] Objections by the Russian general staff had delayed its submission nearly a month. Izvolsky, Correspondance diplomatique, I, 367.

the second article, Izvolsky had included the Russian version
of the spiritual concern for Tibet, while including no reference
to the British claim of special interests in the field of Tibetan
foreign relations.[u] In its phraseology the article gave equal
privileges to British Buddhists, although the brand of the
religion in India was not entirely the same. The British
reception of this particular point was not unfriendly, objection
being limited to a desire to see inserted some provision whereby the two governments would try to prevent any visits from
taking on a political complexion. It was quite naturally suspected that the effort might sometime be made to pass political
communications under the guise of a religious mission but,
with this act explicitly opposed, the British government felt it
would be in a stronger position to protest against any violation.[v] In order to give effect to this view, Nicolson prepared
a revision of the second article in which he incorporated a long
addition designed to prevent any religious relations from
becoming political in character, and to promise that no political communications would pass through religious hands into
Tibet. After this revised article had been approved in London,
Nicolson presented it to Izvolsky on 5 January 1907.[w] The
latter, however, demurred against accepting this specific statement, and countered ten days afterwards with his own rewor-
ing, which provided in much weaker form that the two governments engaged not to permit these religious relations to injure
the other stipulations of the accord in so far as they could
prevent it. Izvolsky's reason for refusing to agree to the
explicit British form was well founded: the Russian government had elsewhere previously undertaken to negotiate with
Tibet only through the Chinese government, so that no use
could be made of religious pilgrims for passing political communications if the terms of the agreement were observed. Sir
Edward Grey accepted Izvolsky's version and considered that

    [u] B. D., IV, footnote 6, p. 342; p. 343. This part of the article read: "It is
clearly understood that Buddhists, whether Russian or British subjects, retain
the right of having direct relations on religious matters with the Dalai Lama
and other representatives of Buddhism in Tibet."
    [v] Ibid., p. 344.
    [w] Ibid., footnote 8, p. 345.

it gave adequate security against possible Russian political designs in Tibet.[x] No further arguments resulted, and Izvolsky's text found its way into the final arrangement. The Buriats could still have access to the sacred person of the Dalai Lama, and Tibet was not hermetically sealed against the entrance of all subjects of the Russian empire.

The determination of Great Britain to keep all Russian influence out of Tibet had been clearly revealed, but the Russians were equally eager to close all ways by which British interests could be advanced. The right of occupation of the Chumbi valley for at least three years, and possibly for a longer period if the Tibetans did not fulfil the terms of the 1904 convention, suggested possibilities which the Russians wished to destroy. At the time of handing over the first draft for a Tibetan accord, Izvolsky submitted a memorandum to Nicolson in which he explained that it would be useful to declare the temporary character of the British occupation expressly in the agreement between the two governments.[y] The government of India was consulted and it could neither see any objection to repeating in the Russian agreement the provisions of the viceroy's amending declaration of 11 November 1904 and the Chinese acceptance in the adhesion convention of 1906, nor any necessity for doing this in view of the explicit statements already given to Russia of the intentions of the British government.[z] The attitude of Izvolsky on this question partly explained Nicolson's pessimistic misgivings at the start of 1907. The foreign minister no longer seemed to be content with a formal reassertion of the provisional nature of the occupation of the Chumbi valley, but wished to have an admission that the Lhasa convention should be revised if the occupied valley were to be held for any reason beyond the three years. Especially objectionable to Nicolson was the insinuation that the British might indirectly instigate incidents to justify the prolongation, and the fact that Izvolsky talked as if Russian interests in Tibet were fully the equal of the

[x] *Ibid.*, footnote 9, pp. 345-346; no. 549, p. 615.
[y] *Ibid.*, no. 314, footnote 7, p. 343.
[z] *Ibid.*, p. 344.

British; and doubtless Izvolsky felt that they were equally real and justifiable.[a]

The British government authorized Nicolson to assure Izvolsky that the statements regarding the occupation of the little valley could be repeated in the agreement with Russia, whereupon he wrote out a formula reciting the essential portions of the viceroy's declaration annexed to the Lhasa convention, which he proposed should also be annexed to the present agreement.[b] This procedure was approved both in London and in India, while Nicolson's formula was acceptable, as far as it went, to Izvolsky; but it did not adequately provide for future contingencies. Izvolsky, therefore, brought forth a supplementary clause which read that "in the event of anything occurring to prevent the evacuation, the definitive term of the evacuation should be the subject of friendly negotiation between the two governments." More than the Russian government possibly realized, the Liberal cabinet had not approved of the Tibetan policy of the last few years, and were really anxious to get out of Tibet on scheduled time. Izvolsky's proposal was only inacceptable to them where a discussion was contemplated for setting a definite term to the occupation: that depended solely upon the fulfilment of the conditions imposed upon Tibet; but it would be quite impossible to discuss with Russia whether these stipulations had been satisfactorily kept.[c] The British government did, however, express its willingness to enter into an amicable exchange of views with Russia if the occupation of the Chumbi valley were continued for any reason, provided no definite time limit was demanded within which the evacuation should be carried out.[d] When Izvolsky accepted, on 3 May 1907, this offer of a general friendly discussion, the question of the Chumbi valley was relegated to an annex to the proposed arrangement on Tibet.[e] Doubtless Izvolsky felt satisfied that he had secured concession enough to prevent an extended British occupation,

[a] *Ibid.*, no. 244, p. 266. Izvolsky, *Correspondance diplomatique*, I, 412.
[b] *B. D.*, IV, no. 314, p. 345; footnote 10, p. 346.
[c] *Ibid.*, p. 349.
[d] *Ibid.*, no. 315, enclosure, p. 350.
[e] *Ibid.*, no. 316, pp. 350-352; no. 317, p. 353.

from which it would be easier for British influence to outstrip that of Russia in Tibet.

In a way, it was a misfortune that Anglo-Russian suspicion led to the exclusion of geographical and scientific parties of exploration in Tibet. Little enough was known of this part of the world. Expeditions into it would always be costly; the knowledge brought back primarily of academic interest. Geographical discoveries could have embellished the cartographer's art; new examples of flora and fauna might have graced a few esoteric pages in the little-read book of some natural scientist; while the accurate determination of the suspected quantities of valuable minerals would for long have remained worthless information, because of the inaccessibility of the treasures. Izvolsky thought that the veto of such missions, mostly undertaken by Russians, would be undesirable because the objects were "perfectly non-political and solely scientific." [f] The British, however, were not so altruistic; doubtless it could be a strain to determine with proper nicety when a scientific mission slipped over into one for political, or commercial purposes, and anyhow British missions had already been prohibited, by their own government, for reasons not readily apparent.[g] Yet in July 1906, in the course of a conversation with Grey, Benckendorff explained that his government might agree not to permit either Russian or British scientific missions to enter Tibet for a term of five years. At the end of this period, when conditions in Tibet had settled into some tranquillity, the question could again be considered and the prohibition prolonged, if it then appeared desirable. The government of India objected to any arrangement which would "hamper their dealings" in Tibet; but the more conciliatory men in London pointed out that such an attitude was not conducive to successful negotiations with Russia, and that this suggestion had come from the Russian side. Nicolson was accordingly instructed to make the formal proposal to Izvolsky.[h]

[f] *Ibid.*, no. 313, p. 335; no. 314, p. 338.
[g] *Ibid.*, no. 314, p. 340.
[h] *Ibid.*, pp. 340-341. Izvolsky, *Correspondance diplomatique*, I, 343.

The Russian foreign minister now admitted that he thought it was advisable to exclude all scientific expeditions from Tibet for the present. He knew that he would be severely attacked for this prohibition because it would, he had found out, arouse much opposition in Russia. To obviate too formal announcement of this restriction, the British had readily agreed that the question of the scientific missions should not form an article of the treaty proper, but should be treated in an exchange of separate notes, to be done at the same time.[i] In February 1907 Nicolson gave a British draft for the note to Izvolsky, in which Benckendorff's original suggestion was worked out in detail, with the prohibited period retained at five years.[j] This note was left practically unaltered in the Russian reply, except that Izvolsky reduced the time from five to three years within which no scientific parties should cross the Tibetan frontiers, and the problem was settled when the British government accepted this formulation in its *aide-mémoire* of 4 May.[k] Both governments also agreed to approach the Chinese government with a request that it should join with them in the effort to prevent the entry of scientific missions into Tibet for the same three years. On 28 September the ministers of the two contracting powers broached the matter to the Chinese. In its reply of 4 October the Chinese government asserted that no foreigners were permitted to travel in Tibet and that there was every intention of pursuing this policy in the future, although the British and Russian governments anticipated that the futility of Chinese administrative control would make perfect realization unlikely.[l]

The really vital subject of this arrangement was the second point of the original British proposals of 7 June 1906, wherein Great Britain used the excuse of the geographical proximity of India to justify "a special interest in seeing that the external relations of Tibet are not disturbed by any other power."[m] After Izvolsky had admitted that he did not quite "grasp the

[i] *B. D.*, IV, no. 314, pp. 345, 347.
[j] *Ibid.*, footnote 11, p. 347.
[k] *Ibid.*, p. 348; no. 316, and enclosures 3 and 5, pp. 350-352.
[l] *Ibid.*, no. 543, p. 603.
[m] *Ibid.*, no. 314, p. 336.

bearing" of the demand, nor the precise meaning of the external relations of Tibet being "disturbed" by another power,
Nicolson was instructed, on 16 July, that this word would be
clarified by the insertion of additional words so that "disturbed" meant "by the intervention of any other power such
as the establishment of a protectorate or special treaty relations." This explanation rendered the meaning perfectly clear
to Izvolsky, but he preferred to recast the entire sentence,
because in other places Russia had readily subscribed to limitations which would sufficiently safeguard any attempt to obtain
a protectorate, or any special treaty regulations.[n] Accordingly,
after a long delay, in the first Russian draft of 8 October, he
handed over a new second article with a phraseology that bore
not the remotest similarity to the British original. Izvolsky
made this part of the article read:

In conformity with the recognized principle of the suzerainty of China
over Tibet, Russia and Great Britain mutually engage not to treat with
Tibet except through the medium of the Chinese government. This
engagement does not exclude the direct relations between the British
commercial agents and the local Tibetan authorities provided for by the
convention of 1904 between Great Britain and Tibet.[o]

Naturally this wording did not satisfy the British. Nicolson at once remarked that it contained no allusion to the
special interests which Great Britain professed to have in the
foreign relations of Tibet. The India office also commented
upon this, and further complained that the clause which declared that communications should only be through the Chinese
government as intermediary for everything except local matters, placed a restriction upon the liberty of British action
not specified in the Tibet convention, nor in the Chinese adhesion thereto of 1906: for these permitted direct relations with
the Tibetan government in the event of infringement of the
terms of the earlier document.[p] The British government insisted that direct relations of this nature should be clearly
expressed to leave no room for future misunderstanding, and

[n] *Ibid.*, no. 313, p. 335; no. 314, p. 340. Nicolson, p. 219.
[o] *B. D.*, IV, no. 314, footnote 6, p. 342; p. 343.
[p] *Ibid.*, p. 343.

attached importance to the recognition of its special interest
in the foreign affairs of Tibet. Nicolson was ordered to explain
these objections to Izvolsky, and to propose the excision of the
adjective "local" from modifying the "Tibetan authorities,"
and the inclusion of a reference to the provision of the adhesion convention of 1906 with China, to maintain the possibility
of direct access to the Tibetan authorities should they fail to
carry out the obligations laid upon them by the Lhasa treaty.[q]
Nicolson prepared a revised draft of the second article which
took account of these criticisms, as well as reintroduced the
original statement of the geographical basis for the special
interest of Great Britain in the external relations of Tibet.
When this formulation had been approved both by the foreign
and India offices, Nicolson submitted it to Izvolsky, whose attitude was generally satisfactory, but who demurred especially
against the specific recognition of the British special interests.[r]
Once again he tried his hand at fabricating a revision, this
time by composing a preamble, and with modifications in both
the original untouched first article and the much mauled second. The preamble recited that both Great Britain and Russia
recognized the suzerain rights of China over Tibet, originally
a part of the first article, to which was joined the statement
of Britain's special interest, because of the geographical situation, in seeing the foreign relations of Tibet maintained *in
statu quo.* The overhauled first article now simply stated
that both parties mutually engaged to respect the territorial
integrity of Tibet, and to abstain from all interference in
the internal administration. In the second article there reposed
the common undertaking not to treat with Tibetan authorities
except through the suzerain power, although the British contention that they were permitted direct communication, in case
the convention of 1904 was not properly executed, was accepted.[s] The British foreign office was fairly well pleased with
Izvolsky's labor and recommended it to the India office for
acceptance, which agreed that the first two articles would do,

[q] *Ibid.,* p. 344.
[r] *Ibid.,* p. 345, and footnote 8.
[s] *Ibid.,* footnote 9, pp. 345-346; p. 346.

but asked for a change in the preamble. The distinction was drawn that Izvolsky's version indicated that Great Britain "possessed a special interest in the maintenance of the *status quo* in Tibet," whereas the British claim was for "a special interest in the external relations of Tibet generally" because of geographical location. No Russian objections were raised to this alteration in the preamble, so Nicolson telegraphed on 21 February 1907. Thus "the whole [Tibetan] convention was agreed to by both sides." [t]

The arrangement respecting Tibet thus agreed to was one of the three parts finally comprised in the Anglo-Russian convention signed on 31 August 1907 at St. Petersburg. The negotiation had been leisurely paced, with some fencing for position, each side endeavoring to obtain the acceptance of its most cherished demands. In recapitulation, this Tibetan arrangement started off with a preamble in approved diplomatic style which recognized, in words, the suzerain rights of China over whatever was Tibet, while immediately specifying that Great Britain, thanks to its geographical situation, had a special interest in seeing the external relations of Tibet preserved entirely as they then were. The first formal article developed this idea, in that both the contracting parties engaged to respect the territorial integrity of Tibet, and to abstain from all interference in the internal administration of the country. In the first part of the important second article, both parties promised not to communicate with Tibet in any other way than through the intermediation of the Chinese government. However, this engagement was not to prevent direct relations between British commercial agents and the Tibetan authorities, if the obligations imposed by the Lhasa convention of 1904, confirmed by the convention of 1906 with China, were not faithfully observed. In return, the rest of the article recognized the necessity of Russian and Buddhist subjects to have direct relations of a strictly spiritual nature with the Dalai Lama and the other representatives of that religion customarily located somewhere in Tibet, although the precau-

[t] *Ibid.*, pp. 346, 347. Nicolson, p. 239.

tion was taken to specify that these relations should not be permitted to infringe the other stipulations of the treaty. The following article succinctly declared that neither Great Britain nor Russia could send any representatives to Lhasa. By reciprocal renunciation in the fourth article, both powers agreed neither to seek nor to obtain for themselves or their subjects any kind of commercial concession, or other rights, within Tibet; and in the last of the articles promised to forego any pledges or assignments of all Tibetan revenues, in kind or in specie, made in their favor. As an annex to the arrangement, Great Britain reiterated the intention to withdraw from the occupation of the Chumbi valley upon the payment of three annual instalments on the indemnity of the twenty-five lakhs of rupees assessed against Tibet in 1904, provided that the trade marts had been effectively opened for three years, and that the Tibetans had strictly conformed with the other provisions of the Lhasa convention in the meanwhile. If the British occupation should be prolonged for any reason beyond the envisaged period, then the two contracting powers were to enter upon a friendly exchange of views on the subject. By means of an exchange of notes outside of the arrangement itself, Great Britain and Russia agreed not to permit, and to ask China not to permit, the entrance of scientific missions of any sort into Tibet for a period of three years after 31 August 1907. When this time had passed, the two governments were to advise with each other, should the necessity arise, to determine what further measures ought to be taken to regulate the entrance of scientific expeditions into the wilds of Tibet.[u]

In this fashion, then, were settled the minor matters in dispute between two great powers, each suspicious of the presence and the intentions of the other in a scantily known land. For some time before the arrangement respecting Tibet was actually accepted, the chief efforts of the negotiators had been concentrated upon the resolution of the vastly more difficult,

[u] The text of the arrangement respecting Tibet is in *B. D.*, IV, no. 317, pp. 352-354, and Appendix I, p. 620. The exchange of notes on scientific missions is in *ibid.*, no. 318 (a), p. 354; no. 318 (b), pp. 354-355. An English translation of the convention of 1907 is in *British and Foreign State Papers*, C (London, 1911), pp. 555-560.

and really conflicting interests which divided Great Britain and Russia against each other in the kingdom of Persia; but as for Tibet, it was one of the few places in the world where "to leave things alone causes no inconvenience to anybody."

CHAPTER FIVE

THE ARRANGEMENT RESPECTING PERSIA

THE opprobrium that might have been associated with the Russian and British imperialistic penetration of Persia had been mellowed by time. In the first decade of the twentieth century, on the eve of the making of the Anglo-Russian convention, this expansion had been hallowed by a hundred years of success. The slowness of the progress, the adroitness and bloodlessness with which it had commonly been accomplished, joined with the forgetfulness of passing time in forestalling righteous rebukes. What possibly still more disarmed critics was the fact that Persia was one of the few countries into which it had been at all profitable to go. Its trade was at least of calculable worth, its location of strategic importance, both to Great Britain and to Russia. The progressive deterioration of the shahs of Persia, and of their government, seemed almost to render the presence of the representatives of the two European monarchies a blessing, for the protection of the lives and the property of adventurous foreigners, whom the lure of profits had drawn to this field. At the time when the revolutionary movement broke through the inhabited parts of the country for a few years after 1905, then too did a few crusading spirits plead for enlightened governments to rectify the weaknesses in the character of the Persian officials and the government, for the development of which they were in part responsible.[a]

By the beginning of the present century the relative position of Russia and Great Britain within Persia was more sharply defined than ever before; Russia was undeniably in the lead.

[a] The pamphlets and books by the Rev. Edward G. Browne, especially *The Persian Revolution, 1905-1909*, (Cambridge, 1910), are the worthiest of the writings put out by those who mixed sentiment with their politics. The crusading American, Morgan Shuster, in *The Strangling of Persia*, (New York, 1912), liberally sprayed envenomed criticism upon the activities of Russian and British officials in Persia, while recounting his own well-intentioned but maladroit exertions in behalf of the rehabilitation of Persia.

In the early days Great Britain had exercised important influence in Persia and had gone "hand in hand" with Russia; but Russian control in northern Persia grew with the years, engendering the long, subsequent rivalry which Britain originally sought to oppose by a policy of "alternate threat and scuttle." [b] Only after the failure at the congress of Berlin, when the door seemed effectively banged shut against the old aspirations in the Near East, did Russia resolutely turn to central Asia, and then to the Pacific coast, to make up for its frustrated hopes. The rapid progress of Russian penetration in and around Persia during the 'eighties and 'nineties produced the gains which set off the Russian position to so favorable an advantage over that which Great Britain had managed to occupy.[c] By the end of the nineteenth century Russia was dominant politically at Teheran, and its commerce was supreme throughout a generous expanse of northern Persia. With however great regret, informed British officials were compelled to admit that this part of the world was lost, and that it would be a waste of energy to try to dispute the influence of Russia within that preserve.[d] At Teheran, in 1899, Spring Rice "knew for the first time a sense of powerlessness;" while another British representative of that same epoch told Lord Curzon that all the time he was at the Persian capital "he felt like a jellyfish in a whirlpool." [e] Curzon himself declared, on 5 April 1901, that a situation already bad was becoming materially worse, and his grudging admission that "within the last twenty-five years British prestige and influence have never sunk so low" ought to be climactic testimony to the preferential position that Russia had acquired in the councils of the shah.[f]

---

[b] Calchas, *Fortnightly Review*, LXXXVIII, 539. Onslow, *Slavonic Review*, VII, 543.

[c] Gwynn, I, 278. Tardieu, 243-244.

[d] Nicolson, p. 65. Grey relates that a British minister years before remonstrated with the shah for not standing out against the Russian encroachments. He was stopped by the shah who, "making the sign of a bow-string round his own neck to express the position of Russia with regard to himself," then inquired of the minister, "What can *you* do?" Grey, I, 148.

[e] Gwynn, I, 278. Newton, p. 232.

[f] *Ibid.*, p. 230. A month earlier Sir Arthur Hardinge, the British minister in Teheran, described the strong position of the Russians. "The Russians rather take the line of being 'at home' in Persia, . . . Everybody felt the need of 'standing well' with the Russian legation." *Ibid.*, p. 232.

Persia was, however, of such physical size that even Russian control was by no means effective throughout the whole of the land. Already by 1888 a British ambassador to Russia, Sir Robert Morier, was repeating that "England and Russia had each their sphere of commercial interests," the Russians in the north and the British in the south.[g] This regional supremacy was an undisputed fact long before any negotiations for an Anglo-Russian agreement were undertaken. The fastening of Russian influence upon northern Persia was recognized as unshakable and its exercise had been considered natural. In Lord Curzon's famous despatch of 1899 this influence was admitted to be "already predominant" there and at Teheran, and almost certain to become supreme. The British government in its reply of 1900 conceded this to be a true description, and concluded that Russia "could annex that part of Persia without our being able to offer any effective resistance."[h] British officialdom no longer made serious moves to oppose Russia in the north, unless occasionally in the interest of supporting the tottering independence of the country, as well as for the sake of maintaining the British ascendancy in the south, which was a job in itself requiring the full modicum of that attention which Great Britain seemed disposed to expend in Persia.[i]

Besides the natural advantages conferred by ready accessibility, the Russians had long been in the habit of improving their interests by other measures which the British, who could not successfully match them, found reprehensible. The Russians had supported the work of their diplomats by a lavish expenditure, freely loaning money to the reckless shah, whose prodigality, along with the greedy capacity of his retainers, kept him always in need of more; and through loans Russia regularly took a closer grip on the political and financial affairs of the government.[j] In Teheran the only regularly paid, consequently disciplined force were a thousand Cossacks or so,

[g] Meyendorff, I, no. 68, p. 444.
[h] B. D., IV, no. 319, pp. 361-362; no. 320, p. 364; no. 321, p. 367. Onslow, Slavonic Review, VII, 543.
[i] B. D., IV, no. 321 (a), p. 369. Nicolson, p. 65.
[j] B. D., IV, no. 321, p. 367; no. 322, p. 375. Langer, II, 668.

armed and officered by Russians, and naturally amenable to
Russian use; while lurking in the background was the likelihood of Russian military intervention across the frontier in
the event of any disorders, with the eventual result of Persia
becoming a marionette, Russia pulling the strings.[k] In order to
prevent any possible rejuvenation of the country, or threat
against the favorable position which they enjoyed, the Russians by a treaty in 1889, renewed ten years later, bound
Persia to grant no concessions for the building of railways to
any other power without Russian consent. Russia had notions
of connecting Persia with the newly developed Transcaspian
lines. Huge sums of money had been spent in the construction
of roads leading from northern Persia to the Russian border,
over which a motor car service was in operation by 1905. By
these means Russian commerce was assisted in the region
where it was already nearly a monopoly.[l] As additional
security the Russians often gave preferential rates and generous bounties to their Persian export trade, against which
practices the British futilely complained. If nothing more
could be done in behalf of their own commerce, the Russians
imposed burdens on that of other nations. The free port of
Batum had been closed since 1886; for an even longer time
the Caucasus had been virtually shut to all non-Russian transit
trade with Asia; the salt Caspian was a Russian lake; and
through protective sanitary quarantines the effort was made to
strangle the trade from India to Persia over the Nushki-
Seistan route, long closed, but reopened in 1896.[m]

Not at all content with what was already controlled, Russia
exhibited marked tendencies to expand through the wastes of
central Persia into the south, where Great Britain held an
advantage. The British position was for the most part locally
maintained, for no longer was there enough influence wielded
at Teheran to help in its preservation. The vital interests
were those of protecting the Indian border from invasion,
and the British control in the waters of the Persian Gulf from

[k] Gwynn, I, 289, 319. *B. D.*, IV, no. 322, pp. 375-376.
[l] *Ibid.*, no. 319, pp. 359, 361-362; no. 321, p. 367.
[m] *Ibid.*, no. 319, p. 358; no. 321, pp. 367-368.

impairment. The greater activity, and more of the expense, were shouldered by the government of India which, being closer by, better appreciated the dangers than did the authorities in London.[n] There "a wider and less local view" prevailed, and the continued progress of Russia in the middle east was expected, and not considered worth the attempt to frustrate, since it could be done only by forceful means.[o] The Russian aspirations for acquiring a port on the Persian Gulf, or somewhere in southeastern Persia directly on the Indian ocean which could be connected with a railroad from the north, were well known, and in so far as this should remain a venture for legitimate commerce, not always opposed.[p] What bothered was the suspicion that this was not all that Russia would try to acquire.[q] The evident signs of this policy, the establishment of new consulates and the improvement of old, the increasing presence of Russian ships plying in the Gulf and putting in for business at the ports, the frequency with which Russian alleged scientific expeditions were spying out the country, seemed to portend the coming of still more serious moves, which by 1899 had made Lord Curzon contemplate with pure dismay "the prospect of Russian neighborhood in eastern or southern Persia, the inevitable consequence of which must be a great increase of our own burdens." [r]

Great Britain was resigned to the growth of Russian influence in the north of Persia and in the government at Teheran, but was prepared to oppose any threatening moves to the south where, as Lansdowne wrote early in January 1902, "for fully a century our efforts have been successfully devoted to building up a substantial and preëminent mercantile position, with the result that we have acquired an altogether exceptional

[n] *Ibid.*, no. 321, p. 366; no. 321 (c), p. 374. Grey, I, 148.
[o] *B. D.*, IV, no. 321 (c), p. 374. Ronaldshay, II, 99.
[p] *B. D.*, IV, no. 321, p. 368; no. 321 (a), p. 370. Russia really wanted the port of Chahbar on the Indian ocean. *D. D. F.*, III, no. 410, p. 549.
[q] In Muravyev's memorandum of 1900 there was, indeed, no disposition to admit the British rights in the southern region, thereby setting a limit to Russian expansion. On the contrary there was the determination to support Russian trade and to push on Russian influence without stint. Wroblewski, *Kriegsschuldfrage*, VI, 651-652.
[r] *B. D.*, IV, no. 319, p. 358; no. 320, p. 364; no. 321, p. 368. *D. D. F.*, I, no. 225, p. 265; no. 396, pp. 474-476.

interest in that part of Persia."[s] This substantial mercantile preëminence rested upon British control of the Persian Gulf, some ninety percent of the shipping on which remained British despite the subsidized competition of other nations, and upon the important trade routes from India leading through Seistan in the extreme east of Persia.[t] By 1899 the encroachments upon the British monopoly in the Gulf, particularly by Germany and Russia, caused the government of India to complain of the complexities added to an already difficult situation. In its reply the British government did not deny that the earlier "unchallenged supremacy both naval and commercial" had been modified to such a degree that access to the ports along the shores could not henceforth be denied to the trade of civilized powers.[u] Although the home government tried to be philosophical towards the change, nevertheless measures were taken, and warnings given, to safeguard the security of the remaining British power in and around the Persian Gulf.

The first of these steps was taken in October 1897, when a promise in writing was obtained from Teheran which pledged that "the customs of southern Persia should never be placed under foreign control and supervision."[v] This was followed in 1899 by a warning from Salisbury that the British government "felt it to be their duty to renew the intimation that it would not be compatible with the interests of the British empire that any European power should exercise control or jurisdiction over the ports of the Persian Gulf."[w] Again, during 1901, the Persian government was reminded that Great Britain did not intend to abandon "a position attained by so many years of constant effort," nor would it peacefully assent to the grant of a military or naval station on the Gulf to Russia. Further

---

[s] *B. D.*, IV, no. 321 (a), p. 369.
[t] *Ibid.*, no. 320, p. 364; no. 321, p. 366; no. 321 (a), p. 370.
[u] *Ibid.*, no. 319, p. 357; no. 320, p. 364.
[v] *Ibid.*, no. 321 (a), p. 370.
[w] *Ibid.*, no. 319, p. 358; no. 320, p. 365. There was much foolish concern over the possibility that Russia might try to establish a naval base on the Persian Gulf, which would endanger British control in India and in the seas nearby. Spring Rice took a much saner view: "Besides, a [Russian] port on the Gulf would be a convenient object for us to attack if necessary." Gwynn, I, 318.

to assist the Persians to keep this in mind, the declaration was accompanied by a threat that any such concession would provoke measures in return for the protection of British interests, "measures which, in view of [British] naval strength in those waters, would be attended with no serious difficulty." [x] The equivocal attitude of Russia, and the growing doubt of German intentions with respect to the Bagdad railway, caused Lansdowne in May 1903 to reword Salisbury's warning in a bristling declaration that, while there would be no efforts to exclude the legitimate trade of other nations, Great Britain would, nevertheless, "regard the establishment of a naval base or of a fortified port in the Persian Gulf by any other power as a very grave menace to British interests, and we should certainly resist it with all the means at our disposal." [y] To give ocular indication of the British strength to the impressionable Persians, the long sought permission was given Curzon that autumn for his viceregal "prancings in the Persian puddle." [z] One warning was ready to be delivered to Russia in January 1905, when it was feared that the Baltic fleet might possibly break its voyage to the Far East to enter the Persian port of Chahbar. There had been a few indications previously that Great Britain might look with sympathy upon a Russian plea for a warm water port on the Gulf; but the whole world knew that Britain would not stand tamely aside and let its naval and strategic control of those waters be threatened by anyone. [a]

The liberality with which Russia subventioned its own undertakings, and obstructed those of rivals, necessitated additional and unwelcome expenditures by Great Britain to keep in the race. Despite objections that the volume of trade hardly justified this outlay, it still remained a smaller amount than

[x] B. D., IV, no. 321 (a), p. 370.

[y] Ibid., no. 321, p. 371; no. 444, minutes, p. 493. Parliamentary Debates, 4th series, CXXI, 1348.

[z] See above, p. 58.

[a] B. D., IV, no. 321, p. 371; no. 321 (a), p. 370. When Lansdowne was making his bid for an agreement with Russia in November 1903, he told Benckendorff that his government was not insisting upon the denial to Russia of "commercial facilities in the south of Persia, or on the Persian Gulf." Ibid., no. 182, p. 187.

the Russian government expended without whimpering.[b] There was some evidence that Great Britain was holding its own in the south, and even advancing into the central desert of Persia. In the Gulf region a renewed examination of the ports, the harbors and the islands had been conducted; the government of India had been reviewing improved plans for military preparations in the scheme for the defence and protection of Indian interests; while the government in London promised to exercise all vigilance in closely watching developments in Persia.[c] That government had done all possible "to foster British trade and influence by every means at [its] disposal." Both from London and from Simla money had been loaned to the Persian government, for which control over certain customs and revenues had been pledged as security.[d] Large sums had been applied to equalizing Russian consular advances by a corresponding improvement of British consulates already existing, by the creation of new establishments, and by the transference of others into the more active surveillance and more generous pay of the government of India.[e] A telegraphic system had been introduced and developed, which had helped commercial progress, means of communication, the consolidation of the authority of the shah (so it was said), and the strength of British influence in the south and center of Persia.[f] Ever since March 1889 the British had a written promise that offset the Russian control over railroad construction in the north. If there was to be in the future a railroad to Teheran from the southern parts of Persia, Great Britain should have priority in the building of it, while in any event no concessions for southern railroads should be granted to other foreign companies without previous consultation with the British government.[g]

[b] *Ibid.*, no. 321, pp. 367, 368.
[c] *Ibid.*, no. 320, p. 365. *D. D. F.*, II, no. 73, p. 77; no. 256, pp. 311-312; no. 403, p. 483; III, no. 410, pp. 548-549. Newton, pp. 234-235.
[d] *B. D.*, IV, no. 321, p. 371.
[e] *Ibid.*, no. 320, p. 365; no. 321, p. 368; no. 321 (c), p. 374. *D. D. F.*, III, no. 232, p. 312; VI, no. 269, pp. 336-337.
[f] *B. D.*, IV, no. 321 (a), pp. 369-370; no. 321, p. 371. *D. D. F.*, III, no. 232, p. 312.
[g] *B. D.*, IV, no. 321 (a), p. 370; see also no. 320, p. 365.

In one final place British ambitions clashed head on with those of Russia. This was in the triangular district of Seistan, directly on the Afghan border, the mountain passes of which permitted the overland trade routes to reach India the most conveniently, at the same time that they made possible the threat of military invasion by Russia. From the early days of Curzon's viceroyalty it became an axiom that Seistan must absolutely be included in any delimited British sphere in Persia.[h] The simplest explanation was the necessity for protecting the Indian trade with Persia; but this was not sufficient to justify the intensity of the British insistence. The real reason was that the retention of no other place would as effectively safeguard the British position in the south of Persia, or so well secure the Indian frontier from a Russian attack.[i] The Russians knew the commercial importance and the strategic value of Seistan in their own possession, and Curzon thought, in 1899, that it would be "exceedingly doubtful . . . whether Russia would . . . forgo [sic] her designs upon Seistan." The enormity of the British boldness in bidding for this district was all the more astounding because it lay "not to the south but to the north of the great desert," and was "severed by no clear line of division" from the province of Khorasan, well within the area of Russian predominance.[j] Nothing daunted, on 9 July 1901, Lansdowne had directed that the attention of the Persian government be called "to the interest which this district has for Great Britain . . . and to state that we regard it as of the utmost importance that it should remain free from the intrusion of foreign authority in any shape."[k] At the close of his discussions of 1903 with Benckendorff on the

[h] *Ibid.*, no. 319, pp. 360, 361.
[i] The control of Seistan in British hands would deprive Russia of the power to interfere with the trade routes; of a strategical position from which to commence any invasion of Afghanistan and India, over which the British did appear worried; of the most favorable route from the north to the ports in the south of Persia and on the eastern end of the Gulf, which could be of value to Russia only if connected by rail with the north, "and any railway must pass through Meshed and Seistan" to avoid the central desert and the numerous high mountain ranges across any route through the west and southwest of Persia. *Ibid.*, no. 321, p. 368; no. 322, p. 376; no. 411, minutes, pp. 456-457.
[j] *Ibid.*, no. 319, pp. 360, 361.
[k] *Ibid.*, no. 321 (a), p. 370.

theme of an Asiatic understanding, Lansdowne courageously demanded that Russia would be expected to recognize that Seistan "was entirely under British influence, and to abstain from interfering with the trade routes leading through it." [1] Russia was, indeed, in a more favorable position generally throughout Persia, and intended to improve upon that; but, after some earlier despair, Great Britain was again pushing forward in actual rivalry, at the same time that it voiced still more sweeping claims.

Both Russia and Great Britain had declared that the value of the commercial relations had occasioned the measures taken in northern and southern Persia to protect and maintain their positions. More often than has usually been true, something could be said in behalf of such assertions. The actual volume of trade that Russia and Great Britain enjoyed with Persia, worth something as it actually was, was frequently spoken about in magnified terms, or in figures dressed up for the purpose of supporting extravagant pretensions. It would appear that most of the Russian trade passed over the 852 versts of the common border with Persia, with a smaller amount over 393 versts of the southwestern shore line of the Caspian Sea.[m] Some Russian steamers had lately sought to establish themselves in the Persian Gulf trade, but with no discoverable profit.[n] Russian trade over the Asiatic frontiers was really increasing at a rapid rate in the last decade of the nineteenth century and in the first years of the next, until there came a temporary setback between 1906 and 1909, for which the revolutionary disorders and acts of God, in withholding normal grain harvests, must bear the chief blame.[o] Even so, only a small part, scarcely six percent in 1907, of the total Russian trade passed over the Asiatic frontiers.[p] Since 1895 the trade with Persia always occupied a place among the half dozen

[1] Ibid., no. 182, p. 188.
[m] Obzor vnyeshney torgovli Rossiy, (1897), Introduction, p. 1.
[n] B. D., IV, no. 320, p. 364; no. 321, p. 368.
[o] Obzor vnyeshney torgovli Rossiy, (1897), Introduction, p. 46; (1901), Introduction, p. 58; (1907), Introduction, p. 1; (1908), Introduction, pp. 3, 9, and table 19, p. 9.
[p] Ibid., (1907), Introduction, p. 3; (1908), Introduction, p. 1.

nations with which its growth had been most rapid and important; but in the year of the convention its proportion of the Russian total was only 2.8 percent, although Persia had risen from ninth to eighth place among the countries in the size of their commercial interchange with Russia.[q]

In some way Curzon unearthed figures for 1889 which showed that British trade with Persia was in excess of the Russian by fifty percent; but if his statistics were accurate then, the British advantage rapidly receded in the face of steady Russian gains, until by 1897 it had definitely disappeared.[r] Until 1902 Russia imported more goods from Persia than were exported, but in the following ten years of steady growth the balance was tilted to the other side, although the products taken by Russia were declared to constitute 69.8 percent of all the trade sent out from Persia.[s] The commodities exported from Russia to Persia were classified into 286 separate items, with subdivisions, but they are combined more comprehensively into four general groups. The most important group of Russian exports consisted of foodstuffs, closely followed, and in occasional years exceeded, by manufactures. Far in third place came the export of raw materials and half-finished products in a relatively stable amount in the years before the convention. Last of the groupings in worth, often fluctuating wildly, but tending to increase considerably after 1905, was the export of livestock. Russian imports from Persia fell into 218 separate items, which can also be compressed within the same four general groups as were the

[q] *Ibid.*, (1905), Introduction, p. 2; (1907), Introduction, p. 4, and table 10, p. 4.

[r] "La révolution persane et l'accord anglo-russe," *Revue des deux mondes*, 5e période, XLIV (1908), p. 653. For 1897 Russian exports to Persia were worth 16,036,032 rubles, and imports from Persia 18,649,667 rubles. (*Obzor vnyeshney torgovli Rossiy*, [1897], table II, pp. 2-3.) For the same year British exports to Persia amounted to £442,656, and the goods imported directly from Persia to £197,778. *Annual Statement*, (1899), table 31, p. 883.

[s] A. M. F. Rouire, *Anglo-russkoye sopernichestvo v Azii v XIX vyekye*, [Anglo-Russian Rivalry in Asia in the XIX Century], edited with notes by F. Rothstein, (Moscow, 1924), footnote 1, p. 144. There is an earlier, unrevised French edition, *La rivalité anglo-russe au XIXe siècle en Asie*, (Paris, 1908), which is used except when the reference is to the added material in the Russian edition. See also, *Obzor vnyeshney torgovli Rossiy*, (1907), Introduction, table 11, p. 5.

exports.[t] In the importations from Persia foodstuffs led the others, often being closely followed by raw materials and partly finished goods. In both of these categories, the Russian imports slightly exceeded the exports to Persia. The manufactures taken by Russia from the Persian trade occupied a poor third place. In last place again was the importation of livestock, of which Russia took more than it sent in a trade which was also increasing. Russian trade with Persia did mount into profitable sums, and the virtual monopoly enjoyed in the northern districts was jealously guarded and solicitously cultivated.

The British trade with Persia was rather less in money value, and was confined even more to the south of the country than was that of Russia in the north. In its own region, however, it possessed a predominance little less monopolistic. British trade has been described as constituting ninety percent of the total which used the Persian Gulf, and the commercial department of the foreign office claimed that of a trade of about £2,700,000 with Persia in 1903, two-thirds of this belonged to the United Kingdom, and the other one-third was Indian.[u] In 1889 Curzon's claim for the empire's trade with Persia put the total at nearly £3,100,000, and not quite ten years later Sir H. M. Durand, British minister to Persia, estimated it to be £3,500,000, from which figure it was ex-

[t] Detailed statistics can be found in the tables of the annual volumes of the *Obzor vnyeshney torgovli Rossiy*, and summaries by groups in table II. The total annual value of Russian exports to Persia between 1898 and 1907 printed in the following list is abstracted from the volume for 1907, table V, p. 90; and the imports from Persia, from table VIII, p. 450.

Year	Exports to Persia Value in rubles	Imports from Persia Value in rubles
1898	17,034,413	21,551,137
1899	17,859,000	21,696,374
1900	20,648,970	20,413,061
1901	23,486,446	25,481,931
1902	24,015,189	23,486,410
1903	27,386,305	26,480,435
1904	27,285,992	23,865,908
1905	26,059,806	22,311,555
1906	31,756,349	24,503,105
1907	28,263,675	25,313,910

[u] B. D., IV, no. 321, p. 366. The Belgian customs figures for 1901-1902 place the British-Persian trade for that period at over £2,430,000 (59,000,000 francs). The collection of the Persian customs had been placed in the hands of Belgian officials. *Revue des deux mondes*, 5e période, XLIV, 653.

pected to increase further. This prospect was not realized, but instead a diminution set in, until by 1905 exceptions were taken to new British expenditures in Persia to keep up with Russia "as not warranted by the volume of trade." [v] Although the official statistics compiled by the British customs house department do not approach the figures just mentioned, they do furnish an insight into the nature of the commerce Great Britain engaged in with Persia.[w] Always the largest in quantity and in value of the British exports were cotton goods. Occasionally the export of arms and ammunition would rise to considerable heights. The export of cuprous and ferrous metals at times touched encouraging figures, only to subside to consistently low levels. Some coal, coke and other fuel products left a noticeable trace, but a year's total could never have seriously affected the British mining industry. Nor was there much greater regularity among the supplies Britain purchased from Persia. Always the bulkiest commodity was sheep and lamb's wool, but this was declining with the years, while the importation of gum arabic, and allied gums, often amounted to more in value. There was a continual, although widely fluctuating demand for opium and other drugs, and an ever diminishing use for sea shells. British trade had not

[v] B. D., IV, no. 321, pp. 366, 368. Revue des deux mondes, 5e période, XLIV, 653.
[w] The total value of British exports to and imports from Persia between 1898 and 1907 given in the following list is taken from the yearly volumes of the Annual Statement.

Year	Exports to Persia Value in pounds	Imports from Persia Value in pounds	
1898	338,017	193,291	
1899	368,165	148,027	
1900	410,190	180,279	
1901	583,225	200,124	
1902	384,179	210,585	
1903	443,217	175,625	
1904	455,400	278,622	
1905	488,179	151,098	*451,390
1906	491,975	226,673	*482,011
1907	698,010	390,555	*626,009

* In the Annual Statement for 1909 a new basis for classifying imports was adopted. The previous method showed only the imports consigned direct from Persia; the new method includes these, and in addition the imports received from Persia through other countries. The figures preceded by the asterisk were compiled by the new method. No change was made in the calculation of the exports to Persia. Annual Statement, (1909), I, Introduction, p. vi; II, table 11, p. 208.

the volume or the value of Russian trade with Persia, and was more lacking in stability.[x] Russian trade was more generously helped out by bounties; but the importance of British commerce was more often magnified as an argument for support of the British political sphere in the south, and as a justification for threatening warnings to preserve it from possible inroads by other powers.[y]

[x] The text is based upon tables of statistics in the several volumes of the *Annual Statement*. Unlike the Russian *Obzor vnyeshney torgovli Rossiy*, the British counterpart is not as neatly arranged, and the table numbers, and their location, frequently vary. The statistics appear generally in volume II for each year. Evidence that British trade was still paramount in southern Persia in 1907, but meeting with increased Russian competition, is presented in Rouire, pp. 240-241.

[y] To illustrate Russian and British trade with Persia, the figures for the last full year before the convention (1906) are listed below. The Russian figures are from the *Obzor vnyeshney torgovli Rossiy*, (1906), table II, pp. 6-7; the British are from the *Annual Statement*, (1908), II, table 8, pp. 228-229; (1909), II, table 11, p. 208. At par of exchange, one pound sterling equalled 9.457 rubles.

	European Frontiers	Asiatic Frontiers
A. Exports from Russia to Persia, over		
1. Foodstuffs,	1,213 r.	16,657,550 r.
2. Raw and half-finished materials,	1,430	1,680,818
3. Livestock,	....	357,733
4. Manufactures,	113,334	12,944,271
Totals,	115,977 r.	31,640,372 r.
B. Imports to Russia from Persia, over		
1. Foodstuffs,	10,919 r.	13,074,230 r.
2. Raw and half-finished materials,	69,235	9,795,035
3. Livestock,	....	501,598
4. Manufactures,	1,318	1,050,770
Totals,	81,472 r.	24,421,633 r.

	In pounds sterling
C. Exports from Great Britain to Persia,	
1. Arms and ammunition,	1,240
2. Coal, coke and fuel products,	2,403
3. Cotton goods,	419,035
4. Metals, mostly cuprous and ferrous,	1,945
5. All else (particularly woolen goods),	53,979
Total exports from the United Kingdom,	478,602
Foreign and colonial merchandise exported,	13,373
Total of all exports,	491,975

	In pounds sterling
D. Imports to Great Britain from Persia,	
1. Opium and other drugs,	34,750
2. Gums, Arabic and others,	89,609
3. Shells,	1,789
4. Wool and its manufactures,	53,139
5. All else,	47,386
Total imports direct from Persia,	226,673
Imports received through other countries,	255,338
Total of all imports,	482,011

The actual strength of the Russian position in Persia, and
the suspicion that Russia intended to improve upon it in the
south and the east, caused Lord Curzon, in 1899, to consider
in detail the alternative policies by which the future of the
British ascendancy in the south could be safeguarded. After
nine months of investigation, the new viceroy of India crowned
his labors with the presentation of three wordy alternatives.
He labelled the first as a policy for the regeneration of Persia
by the common action of Great Britain and Russia. Together
they should insist upon reforms in the administration and
financial systems and, by lending the requisite funds, develop
the resources of the country, "in fact to convert the Persian
government by combined philanthropy from a moribund into
a solvent institution." There was no use considering such
friendly coöperation, because no one could then picture any
helpful disposition on the part of Russia. In the second place,
there was the old "eye for an eye" policy, the taking of corresponding measures for the protection of British interests in
the south in retaliation for Russian encroachments in the
north. If there were not sufficient elasticity in the execution
of this policy, it might force Great Britain to take burdensome
countermeasures at times inconvenient for doing so. Therefore it seemed advisable before adopting such a method to
probe whether or not there might be a chance "to conclude an
agreement with Russia for the joint patronage and development of Persia . . . in distinct and clearly defined compartments
by the two great powers, in other words for a recognition of
British and Russian spheres of interest in the dominions of the
shah." [z] This idea to divide Persia into spheres was by no
means new, for in 1888 and in 1891 it had appealed to an
earlier British minister to Persia, Sir H. Drummond Wolff,
and Curzon himself had come up as early as 1892 with a
proposal for lines demarcating British and Russian spheres. [a]

[z] *B. D.*, IV, no. 319, pp. 359-360.
[a] Highly gifted in composing literary definitions, Curzon has best explained
the intricate nature of a sphere of influence. "A sphere of influence," he said
in his Romanes lecture on "Frontiers" at Oxford in 1907, "is a less developed
form than a protectorate, but it is more developed than a sphere of interest.
It implies a stage at which no exterior power but one may assert itself in the

Now he recurred to this plan and reviewed an earlier proposal by Sir H. M. Durand for a line to run from Khanikin, on the Turkish frontier, through the Persian towns of Kermanshah, Hamadan, Isfahan, Yezd and Kerman until it reached Seistan in eastern Persia, the district which Great Britain was already determined to control exclusively. This line was declared to be indicative of the northern limit of British paramount influence, of which it was, indeed, a generous measure. It would have been fairer to recognize it as a reasonably accurate description of Russian expansion southwards. In 1899 Curzon believed that this line, with the more northerly town of Kashan substituted for Isfahan, was worthy of serious consideration as a feasible scheme for ending the Persian rivalry to the advantage of both parties. This appeared to be possible because, in the previous April, Russia had agreed to a delimitation of railroad spheres in China.[b] Although the viceroy realized that such a partition of Persia might hasten the breakdown of the shah's kingdom and lead to rival British and Russian protectorates in the south and the north, and "while not sanguine as to the prospects of success," he reached this mild opinion:

The experiment of an understanding with Russia as to future spheres of interest in that country is worthy of being made, in the interests both of Persia itself, and still more of harmony between the two great powers, upon whose relations the peace of Asia may be said to depend.[c]

The British government digested these remarks until July 1900 before making an answer, in which it realistically admitted that Russian influence was supreme in northern Persia, besides the fact that Russia also had such a favorable general position that it "dominates and threatens almost the whole

---

territory so described, but in which the degree of responsibility assumed by the latter may vary greatly with the needs or temptations of the case. The native government is as a rule left undisturbed; indeed its unabated sovereignty is sometimes specifically reaffirmed; but commercial exploitation and political influence are regarded as the peculiar right of the interested power." Fraser, p. 129.

[b] B. D., IV, no. 319, pp. 360-361. See above, chapter I.

[c] B. D., IV, no. 319, pp. 361-362. Before 1903 Curzon's opinion had regained its customary acerbity, and he considered the very thought of an Anglo-Russian agreement as "a sentimental hallucination." Ronaldshay, II, 308.

of Persia." London agreed that there was much to recommend an understanding with Russia by which each nation's sphere of influence should be defined and set apart. There was, however, not a sign that any such agreement could be had, so that no advantage would come from offering proposals. Quite the contrary was liable to happen if any overtures were disclosed to Russia, because it was suspected that "the shah would be informed of the proposal in such a manner as possibly to convey to his mind the idea that the partition of his territories between Great Britain and Russia was the immediate object of the present policy of Great Britain." [d] The home government could offer no better suggestion to the government of India than to keep its powder dry for any eventuality, and to proceed with its consideration of new military preparations for defending Indian interests in Persia. Serious warnings had been delivered to the decadent shah, who alone of his line showed no aptitude for ruling. He was told that grave issues would be involved if he ever lost sight "of the legitimate interests of Great Britain and India in the ports of the Gulf and in southern Persia." If Russia were granted concessions, then also must equivalent awards be made to Great Britain. [e] As Britain could not coöperate with Russia to make Persia over into a going concern, and as the Russians were not disposed to agree to share the spoils, the policy of matching gain with gain was alone left, strangely reminiscent of the old "threat and scuttle" from earlier years of the century. [f]

Russian policy towards Persia was perfectly well under-

[d] *B. D.*, IV, no. 320, p. 364. In 1905 Lansdowne was still complaining: "The conflict might become less acute if we could establish some working arrangement with her, but the Russian government have hitherto always objected to anything in the nature of a division of spheres of influence or interest." *Ibid.*, no. 321, p. 368.

[e] *Ibid.*, no. 320, pp. 364-365.

[f] This situation was still unchanged in 1902. Lansdowne carefully described British policy: "If . . . in the face of our warnings, the Persian government should elect to encourage the advance of Russian political influence and intervention [in southern Persia and Seistan], His Majesty's government . . . would regard themselves as justified in taking such measures as might appear to them best calculated to protect the interests so endangered, even though in the adoption of such measures it might no longer be possible to make the integrity and independence of Persia their first object as hitherto." *Ibid.*, no. 321 (a), p. 370.

stood, and its unloveliness lost nothing as the British described it. Even as with the Turkish empire, everything was done to keep Persia weak and in a state of decay, while everything was opposed that could reform or revitalize the government. Russian political and commercial domination was furthered by whatever means were useful. Always in the background was the vision of military intervention, if any excuse, such as internal disorders or political collapse, should be presented. By loans to a spendthrift shah, by control over customs revenue as security for advances to an increasingly impoverished government, whose porous capacity for more was never satisfied, Russian political interference at Teheran became almost unbeatable.[g] The time had not yet arrived for a safe, final dissolution of the Persian state. Spring Rice wittily portrayed the Russian feelings as "like a lady's doctor, they don't want the patient either to die or to recover." [h] With their position so favorable for more profit in the near future, there was no willingness on the part of Russians before 1906 to share Persia by agreement with Great Britain when all, or a large part, of the country would fall into their hands as naturally as a well-ripened apple drops from the branch. Many Englishmen freely granted, however distasteful it may have been, that the Russian inheritance would be a rich one, and that little could be done to change the will. Sometimes it was admitted that it would be foolish for Russia to agree to limit its aspirations; and on the few occasions that a British suggestion to agree over Persia was ventured, its rejection caused no surprise.[i] The Russian position often appeared so strong as to dominate the country, and a liberal portion of the northern region could be annexed probably at will, with Great Britain unable to offer any effective resistance.[j]

The British government pictured its policy towards Persia in kindlier terminology, and there may have been some war-

[g] *Ibid.*, no. 319, p. 359; no. 321, p. 367; no. 321 (b), p. 372; no. 322, pp. 375-376.
[h] Gwynn, I, 289.
[i] *B. D.*, IV, no. 321, p. 368; no. 321 (b), p. 372. *Kriegsschuldfrage*, VI, 651-652. Gwynn, I, 285. Ronaldshay, II, 99.
[j] *B. D.*, IV, no. 320, p. 364.

rant for leniency. In its own estimation, it seemed that the
Persian government should be well aware that British policy
for a hundred years had been devoted to friendliness for the
shah's kingdom. All through this long period Great Britain
had cherished no designs either upon the sovereignty of the
shah or against the maintenance of the territorial integrity
of his state. Consequently British policy, which wished to see
the *status quo* preserved, had constantly been opposed to the
undermining purposes of Russia. Great Britain had stead-
fastly endeavored to encourage the continued national existence of Persia with the hope of finding in it a buffer state
strong enough to prevent the direct contact of other great
military powers directly on the Indian frontier. Now, therefore, Great Britain had regularly sought "to infuse some
vitality" into the Persian government to steel it against Russian aggression, and to "encourage the development of British
commerce and enterprize in south and central Persia, both for
that purpose and as a desirable object in itself." [k]

British policy was hardly so altruistic. In so far as the
maintenance of the territorial integrity and national existence
of Persia served at the same time as a check upon the rival
ambitions of Russia, as well as left opportunity open for the
growth of British interests, some aid was furnished Persia.
The encouragement of British commerce and enterprise, that
part of the policy which was an object desirable in itself, which
had been persistently pursued in the south for fully a century,
had at last established that commercial preëminence which the
government was determined to maintain.[1] The Persian government knew that what support it would receive from Great
Britain was dependent upon the continued security of the
latter's interests in the south. If for any reason these should
be molested, then British policy would not hesitate "to consider what alternative course our interests might demand now
that the object to which our efforts had hitherto been directed
was no longer attainable." [m] The conclusions adopted on 22

[k] *Ibid.*, no. 321, pp. 366-367; no. 321 (a), p. 369. Grey, I, 148-149.
[1] *B. D.*, IV, no. 321 (a), p. 369.
[m] *Ibid.*, no. 321, p. 367; no. 321 (a), pp. 369, 370; no. 322, p. 376. See also
Grey, I, 148.

March 1905 by the Committee of Imperial Defence, during the Russo-Japanese war, furnished some indication of British policy towards Persia. No mention appeared of any intention to maintain anything more than the *status quo* in Persia, and the existing British claims along the shores of the Persian Gulf, because of commercial and strategic reasons. On the same grounds, British influence should be increased at Teheran in order better to control important railroad concessions.[n] How eagerly British policy came to favor a division of Persia into spheres of influence is revealed in the efforts of Lansdowne and Grey to reach an agreement of this kind with Russia as circumstances after 1903 forced Russia to share with others. When the opportunity finally came to feather the nest in southern Persia more snugly in collusion with Russia, British policy departed without a murmur "from the experience of 100 years, that Great Britain has no designs upon the sovereignty of the shah or the independence of his state."[o]

The disposition of Russia grew more agreeable to sharing Persia with Great Britain as defeats piled up in the war with Japan. After the revolutionary troubles broke out in Russia, sharing was an unavoidable necessity. At Teheran Sir Arthur Hardinge doubted whether the former proud attitude and high-handed actions could be successfully upheld in the presence of the renewed determination of Great Britain not to let Russia have its own way in Persia entirely unquestioned.[p] Then, too, the recent commercial activity and interest which Germany was taking in places where previously they had never been, alarmed the Russian government fully as much as they did the British. Russia was in no circumstances to oppose extensions of both British and German influence at the same time. Having no place of its own, Germany was a comparatively fresh interloper into the green fields of both Great Britain and Russia, who gave no indication of setting any limit to its commercial and financial inroads.[q] If Russia should

[n] *B. D.*, IV, no. 321, p. 371.
[o] *Ibid.*, no. 321 (a), p. 369.
[p] *Ibid.*, no. 321 (b), p. 373; no. 322, p. 376. See also *D. D. F.*, V, no. 447, p. 534.
[q] "German interests," as Curzon again aptly phrased his rebuke, "have a

be forced to bargain with Germany over Persia, every concession would be a net loss. In an agreement with Great
Britain, although the renunciation of further expansion would
be temporarily unavoidable, the Russian domination in the
north would be recognized unimpaired.[r] The Russian government had listened with patience and some approval to Lansdowne's overtures late in 1903, but had at that time declined
to consider any division of Persia into spheres, or to surrender any pretensions in the south, because there was "no
reason why their commercial development should be limited to
the northern half." [s] With the change in the Russian position
by the autumn of 1905, and in the face of continued German
intrusion, the prospect of a general reconciliation with Great
Britain had come to be more desirable, and such technical
difficulties as the delimitation of spheres of influence in Persia
were described, too optimistically, as things easily adjusted.[t]

This inclination for an Anglo-Russian settlement was
strengthened by the signs of an approaching political crisis in
the kingdom of the shah. All through 1905 there was an
increasing number of popular demonstrations and disturbances in Persia against the spineless government, turning into
the beginnings of a national revival on the part of the Persian
people. Demands were made for a constitutional and representative régime, with a government strong enough to stop
the former practice of selling out to the foreigners. The
shah's own length of life became a matter of speculation, and
the grant of some reforms appeared to be inevitable. A few
years earlier such an internal plight would have pleased the
Russian government, and any disorders would have furnished the occasion for military intervention with a subsequent
increase in the Russian control over the kingdom. Yet with
the Russian government distracted by efforts to overcome a

---

tendency to grow with some rapidity, and by steps which are not always
acceptable to their neighbors." *Ibid.*, no. 319, p. 357.

[r] *Ibid.*, no. 321 (b), p. 373.

[s] *Ibid.*, no. 181 (b), p. 185; no. 182, p. 187.

[t] *Ibid.*, no. 202, p. 216. For a good appreciation that the solution of the
Persian question was the key to Anglo-Russian agreement, see *D. D. F.*, III, no.
410, pp. 548-550.

revolution at home, the first indication of similar troubles in Persia stirred up no welcome anticipations. Now it seemed prudent instead, while there was time, for the Russian government to reflect upon "the best methods for dealing with the crisis when it actually arrives," and to coöperate with Great Britain in determining the shares of any legacy.[u]

Lansdowne's attempts during October 1905 to open discussions with the Russians for a general understanding had to be abandoned. The Russians, after some original hesitancy, reacted in a friendly enough manner, but soon had to explain that it would be hopeless to institute any discussions as long as the government was perplexed by the numerous problems arising out of the internal disturbances of the revolutionary movement. Early in 1906 Hardinge explained to Lamsdorff that the British government did not intend to act in Persia in a way that would harm Russian interests, and only expected in return an attitude of reciprocity, which Lamsdorff gladly undertook to assume. He observed that there was no need to fear that Russia would pursue a policy of adventure anywhere, nor did he think that subordinate officials would act in Persia, as sometimes they had, without having previously consulted with him.[v] Before any new proposals were made Grey had replaced Lansdowne at the foreign office. In his first conversation with Benckendorff he assured the ambassador that the Liberal government understood how unavoidable the postponement had been, and that it would be British policy not to do anything that would injure the chances for reaching a settlement at some future date.[w] So far as Persia

[u] *B. D.*, IV, Editors' Note, p. 356; no. 321 (b), pp. 372, 373; no. 322, pp. 375, 377. Neither the Russian nor the British government interfered seriously with the early stages of the Persian revolution, which was practically without influence upon the negotiations for the Persian arrangement. In fact neither wished for any extensive changes in the existing *status quo* which might upset the course of those negotiations. On 5 August 1906 the shah promised to summon a national assembly, called the Mejlis, and he opened its first session on 7 October. It drew up a constitution which the shah signed on 1 January 1907. He promptly died a week afterwards, the most ignoble representative of his dynasty. His eldest son became the next shah. The Persian internal situation was effervescent during 1907, but the Anglo-Russian convention was safely signed long before revolutionary disorders broke out again seriously in 1909. This time Russia, particularly, took a hand in the troubles.

[v] *B. D.*, IV, Appendix III, p. 623.

[w] *Ibid.*, no. 204, p. 218. Izvolsky, *Correspondance diplomatique*, I, 294.

was directly concerned, there was to be no attempt to take advantage of Russia's plight to make alterations in the *status quo* for the improvement of the British position; but Grey did tell the Persian minister that the sentiments of the Liberal cabinet were not less favorable to the shah's government than those entertained by their immediate predecessors.[x]

The improvement in the relations of the two countries was taken "as a recognition of the necessity of a strong Russia as a counterpoise in the European system" by Great Britain. Also in Persia, Anglo-Russian coöperation was made possible by the steadily sickening condition of the government. In its customary desperate financial predicament the Persian government had recourse to an old, established habit, and approached Russia for a loan. It is uncertain whether the conditions imposed were so onerous that even the Persian government refused to accept them, or whether the application was declined by Lamsdorff, who felt that it was simply throwing money away.[y] The Persians, in any event, turned to the British government with the request for an advance of some £800,000, which was refused on 23 January 1906, and denied a second time on 2 February, although the Persian government had intimated its willingness to place the entire control of the money in English hands.[z] The British government then advised Russia of its refusal to sanction a Persian loan, but expressed a desire to discuss a joint advance if the Russians thought it worth while.[a] Neither government showed much interest in the question before May, when the rumor of a Persian approach to Germany for a loan in return for concessions caused Grey to ponder whether a joint loan would not be a good, temporary expedient to frustrate German intrusion, and "simply to preserve things as they were till we could settle the whole question."[b] More than a month later Izvolsky, who had taken Lamsdorff's place, declared that

[x] *B. D.*, IV, no. 323, p. 377.
[y] *Ibid.*, no. 464, p. 508; Appendix III, p. 623.
[z] *Ibid.*, no. 324, p. 378; no. 325, p. 378.
[a] *Ibid.*, no. 326, enclosure, p. 379. *D. D. F.*, VIII, no. 378, pp. 497-498.
[b] *B. D.*, IV, no. 329, p. 382; no. 330, p. 383. See also Izvolsky, *Correspondance diplomatique*, I, 298-299.

Russia was unwilling to lend money to Persia, because neither the government nor private banks had any funds to spare.[c]

The rise of a revolutionary, nationalist movement in Persia came at an embarrassing time for Russia. To protect as much of the Russian position as he could, Izvolsky had proposed to Grey that some sort of *modus vivendi* in Persia should be arranged with which to meet any internal disorders. By 13 August 1906 Grey let Izvolsky know that Great Britain did not intend to interfere in the course of Persian affairs, and that Spring Rice, soon to set out for Teheran as the British minister, was to keep in close touch with his Russian colleague, the crafty and expert Hartwig, who was immediately instructed to coöperate with the British in all steps conducive to calming the situation in Persia.[d] Izvolsky was ready to go along in common with Great Britain in Persia, especially because of the difficulty of finding money for a loan, made worse by the suspicion that Germany might grant an advance in return for concessions. Both Izvolsky and Nicolson agreed that this would be most disadvantageous for the large interests which their governments had in Persia, and that friendly collaboration on temporary, local questions should not prejudice the grander attempt to negotiate for a general arrangement by which future relations would be regulated.[e]

It was not easy to get the discussions for a grand Persian settlement under way. From the beginning it had been the British plan that Izvolsky must first disclose the Russian views upon Persia. No inkling of the Russian conditions had come out, but the British were eager to discover whether they would be acceptable, or whether counter-suggestions would have to be made. Nicolson exercised much patience and did not try to force the matter, because this might be fatal if it

[c] *B. D.*, IV, no. 331, p. 384.
[d] *Ibid.*, no. 332, p. 384; no. 333, p. 384; no. 334, p. 385. Izvolsky, *Correspondance diplomatique*, I, 363.
[e] *B. D.*, IV, no. 330, p. 383; no. 336, pp. 386-387. In the previous June, Izvolsky had declared in a meeting of the Russian Finance Committee that it was the government's policy to come to an understanding with Great Britain in Persia, and that this must not be upset by other schemes. *Krasny Arkhiv*, IV, 113.

aroused Russian suspicions.[f] The delay was not entirely unwelcome in London as the government of India had formulated thoroughly impossible demands, over which nothing like
an agreement had yet been reached despite pressure and warning that there was no time to lose.[g] On 7 September when
Nicolson was authorized to inaugurate the Afghan negotiations, he was likewise requested to remind Izvolsky that he
could be sure that his proposals on Persia would be readily
received, without it being necessary to hold them up until after
the discussion on Afghanistan. Nevertheless when Nicolson
talked about Persian affairs and hinted that he would like to
know the Russian desires, Izvolsky simply looked at him
blankly and denied that he possessed any views.[h] A few days
later he expressed his personal opinion that he saw nothing
objectionable in Nicolson's proposal that the British region
in Persia should lie to the south of a line from Birjand to
Bandar Abbas. He reacted with great cordiality to the idea
of spheres of influence, which seemed to him the only method
of solving the Persian question and should be delimited as
soon as possible, though not in association with a financial
advance or loan to Persia.[i]

While Izvolsky had limited himself to unspecific expressions
of his own unofficial opinions, Nicolson believed that at last he
was showing some real interest. Nicolson did understand that
Izvolsky had serious obstacles to hurdle in the Russian government, especially the viewpoint of the Russian general staff,
which stood closer in spirit to the tsar than did the minister
of foreign affairs. Among his colleagues only the minister of
finance held that the British line was perfectly acceptable. To

[f] B. D., IV, no. 224, minutes, p. 240; no. 227, pp. 241-242; no. 339, p. 388.
Nicolson, p. 219.
[g] B. D., IV, no. 226, p. 241; no. 339, p. 388. The opposition of the government of India to a Persian agreement persisted, and Grey drew a distinction
between this and the equally determined objections of the military element in
Russia. "But our country not being in a state of revolution and our government
being properly organized we can overrule the opposition on our side: M. Izvolsky cannot tackle the opposition on his; hence the difficulty of the situation."
Ibid., no. 353, minute, p. 400.
[h] Ibid., no. 341, p. 389; no. 228, p. 242. The interdependence of the Persian
and Afghan solutions was recognized from the time of the first conversations.
Izvolsky, Correspondance diplomatique, I, 368.
[i] B. D., IV, no. 347, p. 392; no. 348, p. 393. Nicolson, p. 242.

anything definite, of course, the approval of Nicholas II would have to be won. With the emperor off on a yachting cruise, nothing could be done until he had returned and had had time in which to make his decision.[j] Yet this was encouragement enough for Grey to think out rather carefully what was to be British policy with regard to spheres in Persia. Towards the end of September he laid his plans before King Edward. In return for a British sphere in the south and east of Persia, including Seistan, Grey would concede a Russian sphere in the north and west. These two spheres were to be separated by a third which contained the desert and mountainous wasteland in the center, already euphoniously termed the whole of the rest of Persia, wherein common interests and general enterprize should have free play.[k] On 29 September when Nicolson asked Izvolsky to recognize the British sphere as a condition for coöperation in a joint loan to Persia, and as the starting point for a general settlement, his proposal galvanized Izvolsky to instant and effective objection. Nicolson therefore warned the foreign office that to rush him on this question would imperil the ultimate success of the entire negotiations. Nicolson's advice was heeded in London: no further attempt was made to force Izvolsky into the whole Persian question, and the special problem of a loan to the Persian government was henceforth considered as a separate transaction.[l]

Both governments admonished their ministers in Persia to coöperate, and to impress upon the consular representatives in remoter places that a truce in the old, traditional rivalry should be put into effect for the duration of the negotiations. Hartwig was all friendliness and cordiality to his British con-

[j] B. D., IV, no. 229, pp. 242-243; no. 348, p. 393; no. 349, pp. 393-394.
[k] Ibid., no. 347, minute, p. 393; no. 350, p. 395; no. 367, p. 409. Both Izvolsky and Kokovtsov, the Russian minister of finance, independently of Grey, thought that there should be middle ground between the two spheres of influence. This is the origin of what came to be the "neutral zone" of the Persian arrangement in the convention. Ibid., no. 349, p. 394.
[l] Ibid., no. 228, p. 242; no. 352, pp. 397-398. Nicolson, p. 242. Izvolsky, Correspondance diplomatique, I, 377. Grey was no longer in a hurry to draw out the Russian proposals on Persia. He believed that enough of the British standpoint had been revealed to convince the Russian government that a fair agreement was practicable. B. D., IV, no. 357, p. 401. Nicolson, p. 242.

frère, and assured him that he favored an agreement with Great Britain because of European considerations, although it seemed that he had trouble in controlling the actions of his subordinates, which made the policy of conciliation occasionally imperfect.[m] Spring Rice, too recently arrived to have any opinion on the general situation, nevertheless began early to oppose an understanding with Russia because of local, Persian circumstances. He discovered that the natives expected Great Britain to be perennially opposed to Russia, and he hoped that no territorial proposal in the nature of spheres of influence would ever be made. This would be the surest way to convince the most reluctant Persian that British policy had changed and no longer strove to uphold the integrity and independence of the country. People would then believe:

We were striving to buy off the hostility of Russia by surrendering to her exclusive control over the greater part of Persia, on condition that we were permitted to hold as our exclusive possession that small remaining portion which we considered necessary for the defence of our Indian possessions.[n]

This was precisely what was being determined upon in London; but Spring Rice believed increasingly in his own, contrary opinion, so that the course of events only strengthened his natural pessimism and called forth his strident protests.[o] Spring Rice's misery existed because, unlike Hartwig, he did not see that the European implications of an agreement were worth more than the good opinion of Persians in reward for support against Russia.

Two questions, subsidiary to the real negotiations, filled up most of the last quarter of 1906. The joint loan to Persia

---

[m] B. D., IV, no. 354, p. 400; no. 359, p. 403. G. P., XXV, part I, no. 8518, p. 23; no. 8516, p. 20. Izvolsky, Correspondance diplomatique, I, 407.

[n] B. D., IV, no. 360, pp. 403-404; no. 361, pp. 404-405.

[o] In a private letter of 21 December to Grey he pointed out that already the rumors of the efforts for an Anglo-Russian understanding had disillusioned liberal Persians, who no longer counted on British support. This realization alone was sufficient to restore Russian prestige almost to what it had been before the evil years since the Far Eastern war. "Altogether whether successful or not," he summed up, "the negotiations between England and Russia have been of enormous value to the latter. We have voluntarily surrendered our position here, in exchange for a promise. I hope that the Russian gov[ernmen]t may realize this: it is certainly true." Ibid., no. 377, pp. 420-421.

was still unsettled and bothersome, for the Persian government was in dire need of money. Grey did not want to lend any more to an already insolvent régime, while the Russian financial predicament made it practically impossible for Izvolsky to obtain money for the loan even if he had wished to sanction it. Certainly Grey, and probably Izvolsky, preferred to defer a loan unless it would help a new shah to make a fresh start.[p] Fear of an appeal to Germany, the danger that it might be accepted, caused them to instruct their ministers in Persia to investigate what amount seemed immediately required, and what steps could be taken to prevent its being squandered. Izvolsky begged the British not to attach serious conditions to their participation, because promptness appeared to be essential to forestall the possible intervention of third parties.[q] His procedure would be, first, to allow the Persian government a temporary postponement of the repayment of sums owed to Russian and British banks. Then, Great Britain should be content with a lien on the customs of the Persian Gulf and in southern Persia as security for its share of a loan. Lastly, the British government should make its share of the advance at once, because the Russian government was hardly able to participate so quickly.[r] When the fear of interference on the part of outside powers subsequently diminished, the Persian loan question was promptly allowed to lag again.[s]

In October 1906 the shah of Persia had opened the popular assembly of the people, which introduced a new difficulty into any joint loan. The Mejlis reflected popular opinion, and it had refused to sanction the government's request for a foreign loan. The Persian prime minister, nevertheless, was prepared to sign the contract for a loan, but Izvolsky and Nicolson agreed that this should be put off until it could be determined whether or not the consent of the assembly was really needed.[t] By the middle of December Grey and Izvolsky had concluded that any possible loan would have to be made pub-

[p] *Ibid.*, no. 336, pp. 386-387; no. 337, p. 387; no. 357, p. 401.
[q] *Ibid.*, no. 340, p. 389; no. 344, p. 391.
[r] *Ibid.*, no. 228, p. 242; no. 348, p. 393.
[s] *Ibid.*, no. 351, p. 396; no. 368, p. 411.
[t] *Ibid.*, no. 358, p. 402; no. 372, p. 416.

licly, and the Persian government would have to assume responsibility for it. As the fear of a German loan had disappeared, it seemed desirable to wait a little longer until the popular party and the Persian government had had an opportunity to compose their differences.[u] Only if the Persian government made a formal demand for the money should it be granted; but at the end of the year the outlook for tranquillity within Persia was so bad that Hartwig and Spring Rice, for an instant, recommended withdrawal of the joint offer. Suddenly, on 3 January 1907, the ministers reversed their opinion, but the entire question lapsed until after the convention was signed.[v]

The second question stood in close relationship to the general understanding respecting Persia. On 30 August 1906 the British foreign office received the first intimation that Persia was about to transfer control over the telegraph line between Meshed and Nasratabad, in Seistan, to the Russian government. A couple of days later the Persians admitted that the arrangements had been made some time ago, but denied that this transfer heralded other concessions to Russia. This announcement was received with considerable dissatisfaction in London, not only because of the material gain that Russia would obtain, but also because it marked a break in the maintenance of the *status quo* in Persia which Great Britain and Russia had lately tried to keep.[w] Part of this telegraph line was within the district of Seistan, from which Great Britain was determined to exclude Russian influence. Grey promptly instructed Nicolson to explain the objections to this transfer and to tell Izvolsky that some counter-concession would be demanded unless an adjustment was reached.[x] Meanwhile the

[u] *Ibid.*, no. 375, p. 418; no. 376, and enclosures, pp. 419-420.

[v] *Ibid.*, no. 379, p. 422; no. 380, p. 422. By the end of January 1907 Spring Rice reported that the Mejlis had control of all financial matters and that the government could not contract for a loan without its approval. (*Ibid.*, no. 383, pp. 424-425.) In February, Grey was prepared to authorize a joint loan if Izvolsky concurred, which he did; but no action was taken. (*Ibid.*, no. 386, and enclosure, p. 427.) Only on 9 October did Persia reopen the question of a loan; but neither Russia nor Great Britain were inclined to be accommodating. *Ibid.*, no. 464, pp. 508-509; no. 538, pp. 597-599.

[w] *Ibid.*, no. 335, and minutes, pp. 385-386; note 1, p. 385; no. 339, p. 388. Izvolsky, *Correspondance diplomatique*, I, 363-364.

[x] *B. D.*, IV, no. 339, p. 388; no. 342, p. 390. The Meshed-Seistan line closely

government of India had telegraphed a suggestion which Grey sent on to Nicolson. According to this proposal, the Persian government should be advised to place the whole of the telegraph line from Teheran to Meshed into Russian control, and that part which extended from Meshed into Seistan into British hands.[y]

Nicolson's communication was the first Izvolsky had heard of the whole matter. Upon investigation he discovered that Hartwig had made the arrangement on his own initiative, (the British foreign office had suspected that it was his job), but as it was simply held to be a minor technical interchange Izvolsky had not been bothered about it. He insisted that it was all a complete surprize to him, about which he would immediately obtain more information, although he promised that he would not countenance any disturbance of the *status quo* in Persia. His professions of ignorance were so unfeigned, that Nicolson was sure Izvolsky was telling the truth. [z] Yet at the end of September Nicolson had to bring up the subject again, because Izvolsky had never recurred to it. Nicolson emphasized the seriousness of the matter, which could become unpleasant if not quickly settled. He pressed for the acceptance of the proposed compromise before discussing any other Persian plans. Izvolsky twisted and squirmed, grasping for all sorts of arguments to postpone a decision, including his favorite way of stalling for time — promising to study Nicolson's proposal. He feared that such an agreement would make a great "noise," as it would prematurely reveal the nature of Anglo-Russian negotiations, so that third parties could make trouble. Nicolson laid bare these excuses, but he could not budge Izvolsky from his determination to go slow.[a]

paralleled the Persian-Afghan frontier and, with Russian control over the instruments at Nasratabad, British communication with India, which was an important part of the traffic on the line, would be inconvenienced, possibly endangered.

[y] *Ibid.*, no. 342, footnote 2, p. 390.

[z] *Ibid.*, no. 343, p. 390; no. 335, Grey's minute, p. 386. Izvolsky, *Correspondance diplomatique*, I, 365-366. In London, Benckendorff assured Hardinge that Izvolsky would be strongly opposed to the step, and also suspected this to be one of Hartwig's proceedings. *B. D.*, IV, no. 339, p. 388.

[a] *Ibid.*, no. 353, pp. 399-400. This was a serious disappointment to London.

Soon after" Izvolsky returned from Berlin in October 1906, Grey thought some progress should be made in the conversations on a Persian agreement, as proof that his visit did not mean that he had weakened in the face of German obstruction.[b] Izvolsky was still favorable to a settlement and was now reassured that Germany would not try to prevent an Anglo-Russian reconciliation. Izvolsky did, nevertheless, explain to Nicolson that he would require considerable time to put through his policy against a formidable opposition within the Russian government. The general staff was not disposed to abandon the Seistan district entirely to British influence, because its strategic value was important when held by Russia, but a menace to the Russian position in central Asia if controlled by Great Britain.[c] Izvolsky also spoke of a great mass of public opinion in Russia which remained unconverted to a policy of friendship with the traditional great enemy. An agreement would eventually come, although it was clear that Izvolsky would proceed with hesitation and deliberate caution. Nicolson tried to encourage him not to give undue weight to the opinions of the military party, who saw only one side of the question, and pointed out that public opinion in general was in favor of an agreement with several important journals, including the conservative *Novoye Vremya*, actually "singing

Grey remarked that if Izvolsky would only put this seizure right, he would have no fault to find otherwise with his attitude. (*Ibid.*, no. 352, minutes, p. 399.) It could well be that Izvolsky, finding himself by luck actually in possession of a concession of evident worth to Great Britain, meant to keep it in order to surrender it later in the negotiations at a good price.

[b] *Ibid.*, no. 235, pp. 249-250; no. 366, p. 407.

[c] Izvolsky, *Correspondance diplomatique*, I, 378. The British military attaché called upon General Palitzin, chief of the Russian general staff, to ascertain the views of the military party towards a Persian agreement. The general admitted that friendly relations with Great Britain were desired, but a division of Persia into spheres of influence was opposed as impractical. Palitzin did not volunteer any objections on strategical grounds. Both Grey and Hardinge minuted that, if Russia refused to admit the British sphere, it could only mean that the military "have aggressive intentions against India for which they want Seistan as a base." (*B. D.*, IV, no. 367, enclosure, pp. 410-411, minute, p. 411.) This was going too far; Seistan was also of defensive value to Russia against British aggression from India through Afghanistan. Actual aggression from either direction was quite visionary, yet both sides professed to fear it. A little later Grey qualified his statement by recognizing that Russians sometimes "put pressure upon us by making us think that they intend to attack" India. (*Ibid.*, no. 370, p. 414.) He also knew that the Russians were afraid of possible British military moves in Central Asia. Grey, I, 155.

paeans in praise" of the idea. Nicolson also recommended to his foreign office that something ought to be done to stimulate Izvolsky and to help him overcome indisputable opposition. British policy had insisted that the Persian proposals must emanate from Russia, but none had come. Now Nicolson suggested that this method should be reversed. He should be sent a draft that could be used for a preamble to an agreement, wherein were described the lines behind which Great Britain and Russia had special interests, and where no interference on the part of other powers could be tolerated. Of course the actual Russian line would have to be left blank, but this would be an inducement for Izvolsky to make good the omission. Nicolson believed that, if he could present some moderate proposals, Izvolsky would see that a fair agreement could be made, which could help him beat down the objections of the military members and convince the tsar that Russia would benefit by a settlement.[d]

Nicolson's suggestion was eventually accepted by Grey, who had a sketch draft of some Persian proposals ready to send by 17 November. These were not put into strictly treaty form, but were in the nature of an *aide-mémoire*, part of which Hardinge had modelled after the 1899 agreement on Chinese railroad spheres "so as to introduce terms already familiar to Russia." It was worth revealing this much to get something started, but not to push discussions too rapidly lest Russia should become suspicious of British motives.[e] The British draft contained a preamble which explained that both Russia and Great Britain were pledged to respect the integrity and independence of Persia, and in addition desired to maintain good order, peaceful development, and equal opportunities for the commerce and industry of all nations throughout the Persian empire. Great Britain and Russia had decided to make an agreement because each had special interests, based upon geographical and economic reasons, in seeing peace and order prevail within certain provinces of Persia. These provinces were

[d] *Ibid.*, no. 367, pp. 408-410; see also no. 236, pp. 250-251.
[e] *Ibid.*, no. 370, pp. 413-415. Grey, I, 156-158.

contiguous with, or in proximity to, the Russian frontier on the one hand and the frontiers of Afghanistan and Baluchistan on the other; and each of the two governments, being impressed with the detrimental effects of local friction on their relations with Persia and with one another, is anxious to avoid all ground for interference with the special interests of each in the Persian provinces [which were included within boundary lines expressed in the following two articles].

In the first draft article Great Britain offered to engage "not to seek or maintain for her own account, or on behalf of British subjects, any concessions of a political or commercial nature . . . and not to obstruct, directly or indirectly, applications for such concessions . . . supported by the Russian gov[ernmen]t" within a line which was left unmentioned, because Russia had never precisely defined it. The second draft article imposed identical obligations upon the Russian government within a British region, for which a definite line was expressed, running from a point on the Afghan frontier through the towns of Gazik, Birjand and Kerman, to Bandar Abbas on the Persian Gulf. This took in Seistan, because that part of the frontier of Afghanistan and all of Baluchistan in common with Persia were included by this description.[f]

This outline draft agreement on Persia, Nicolson left with Izvolsky on 3 December. He explained that it was offered to show that the British and Russian interests in Persia could be reduced to writing in a fashion that would make them secure, while no anxiety would be caused to Persia, or any restriction placed upon the legitimate commercial opportunities of other powers. Izvolsky read the paper, but he insisted that others might still regard it as a division of Persia into spheres of interest, to which they might object. Nicolson did not see how this could be true, so he left the draft confidentially in Izvolsky's possession for careful study.[g]

This communication first effectively opened up the whole

[f] *B. D.*, IV, no. 371, enclosure, pp. 415-416. In this draft the British line was bent out enough to take in the town of Kerman, and the phrase "sphere of influence" was carefully avoided in accordance with previous decisions by Grey. (*Ibid.*, no. 366, p. 407.) Izvolsky likewise did not desire to use the obnoxious phrase, and no Russian objection was made against Kerman remaining in the British region.

[g] *Ibid.*, no. 373, p. 417.

Persian question in the negotiations, and marked the last step in advance during 1906, as Izvolsky never got around to discuss details until into the next year. In fact 1907 began with misgivings for Nicolson, who thought that Izvolsky appeared less eager for an agreement, although towards the end of January he regained heart when Izvolsky announced that a Russian interdepartmental committee was soon to consider what Russian policy should be towards a broad understanding with Great Britain. The proposal that the more ardent Benckendorff should be present at the conversations while he remained in the Russian capital pleased Nicolson, who thought this would hasten Izvolsky along, as well as moderate opposition in military and court circles where Benckendorff mingled.[h] At the ministerial council meeting of 1/14 February Izvolsky persuaded the members to agree in principle that Russian policy should be directed towards reaching an agreement with Great Britain over Persia based upon spheres of influence, with the British proposal of their own line, including Seistan, likewise in principle accepted.[i] On the 18th Izvolsky advised Nicolson of the success he had won after much trouble, and two days later he handed over a draft convention which was a summary of the views held by the Russian government. The Russian version started off with a preamble which was practically identical with that of the British draft of the previous November. In the first article there appeared the first definition of the line for the Russian sphere, which was to start from the Turkish border near the town of Kasr-i-Shirin, pass through the towns of Isfahan, Yezd and Kakh, and to stop at the Afghan frontier opposite Kuhsan. The line for the British sphere as expressed in the second article simply repeated the British tracing. Izvolsky closed the Russian draft with a new paragraph, clearly incomplete because it presented only the Russian side, which provided that the revenues of the Persian customs, except those of Farsistan and the Persian Gulf, guaranteeing the amortization and the interest of loans con-

---

[h] *Ibid.*, no. 244, pp. 265-266; no. 248, pp. 269-270; no. 467, p. 522. Nicolson, p. 243.
[i] *B. D.*, IV, no. 253, p. 275; no. 388, p. 428. See above, pp. 150-152.

cluded by Persia with Russia, should be devoted to the same objects as in the past. The formulation of the British counterpart was evidently left to be done by the British themselves.[j]

Before Izvolsky gave over this draft he had explained that the question of the transfer of the Teheran-Meshed and Meshed-Nasratabad telegraph lines could best be settled by a separate arrangement outside the convention. He also believed that the existing concessions held by Great Britain and Russia should be maintained irrespective of whose sphere they should finally fall within.[k] The possible surrender of Seistan to British control occasioned weighty remarks by Izvolsky, because an abandonment of this strategic district would make necessary a careful examination of the position in which Russia would be left. The Russian general staff anxiously foresaw that the whole strategic *status quo* would be altered if in the future Great Britain should connect Seistan by rail to India either through Afghanistan or, further south, Baluchistan. The military men also plagued themselves with the vision that British relations with Afghanistan might become far more intimate, with the country developed and the Amir's wild army reorganized under British leadership. This would put Russia in a weaker military position than it formerly occupied, and in recent years the military party had been truly uneasy over a British invasion into the Russian possessions in central Asia.[l] Izvolsky asked if the British proposals regarding Afghanistan were ready for communication, because the Afghan and Persian questions were interrelated, and one could not be settled independently of the other. Nicolson did his diplomatic best to convince Izvolsky that the fears of the military party were exaggerated. He divined from Izvolsky's indirect remarks that the maintenance of the political *status quo* in Afghanistan was desired. Nicolson offered some reassur-

---

[j] *B. D.*, IV, no. 389, pp. 431-432.

[k] *Ibid.*, no. 388, pp. 428-429. The British foreign office was willing to arrange for the transfer of the telegraph lines in a separate transaction provided it would be signed at the same time as the Persian settlement. It was glad to agree to the maintenance of existing concessions because, on the whole, it was to British advantage to do so. *Ibid.*, no. 393, p. 436.

[l] *Ibid.*, no. 388, p. 429; no. 470, p. 524. Grey, I, 155.

ance in his admission that probably some agreement could be attained; but he told Izvolsky that he "was not yet in a position to communicate our proposals" on Afghanistan, although on 7 September 1906 Grey had authorized him to open discussions on the basis of instructions then on the way.[m]

The Russian draft impressed the foreign office as forming a satisfactory basis for discussion, and the prospect of agreement sufficiently good to warrant the communication of the Afghan instructions to Izvolsky, which Nicolson already had in his possession.[n] Certain amendments were made to the Persian proposals upon their receipt in London, but these were generally logical and fair. The line for the Russian sphere was modified so that it should terminate opposite Zulfikar rather than Kuhsan, as thereby it would be brought to the northernmost extremity of the Persian frontier with Afghanistan. There could be no question of yielding on this point, because it had become a British charge to settle all frontier disputes between these two countries by virtue of a treaty with Persia of 1857, and because of British control over the external relations of Afghanistan. To complete the British portion of Izvolsky's fragmentary paragraph it was proposed to add:

It is equally understood that the revenues of the Persian customs of Farsistan and the Persian Gulf as well as those of the Caspian fisheries and of the Posts and Telegraphs, shall be devoted, as in the past, to the service of the loans concluded by the gov[ernmen]t of the shah with the Imperial Bank of Persia.[o]

The Russian draft suggested other new matter for inclusion in a Persian agreement. The several sources of Persian

<hr/>

[m] B. D., IV, no. 341, p. 389; no. 388, pp. 429-430. Nicolson was encouraged by this long interview because he believed that the Russian government was "sincerely desirous of arriving at an arrangement with us," while Izvolsky was sure "sensible progress" had been made, so that he earnestly trusted to reach a satisfactory conclusion to the negotiations before long. Nicolson strongly recommended that the prevailing favorable conditions should not be allowed to disappear. He thought that most of the existing Russian nervousness would be cured if the British government could give assurances that no radical alteration in relations with Afghanistan would come in the future. Ibid., no. 388, pp. 430-431.
[n] Ibid., no. 390, p. 433; no. 472, pp. 525-526.
[o] Ibid., no. 389, minutes, pp. 432-433; no. 393, pp. 435-436.

income hypothecated for the repayment of monies borrowed from both Great Britain and Russia were to be devoted to their original purposes after the Persian convention was made. By that time some of the customs pledged to Russia would lie within the British region, while some assigned to Great Britain would come from the Russian sphere. The customs of Seistan, for example, were supposed to go to Russia, those of the Caspian fisheries to Great Britain; but each came from territory that would be under the influence of the opposite power. Now since the presence of Russian controllers of the customs in Seistan, in the event of a default in the interest payments, would be objectionable to Great Britain, and since it presumably did not matter who collected the customs so long as they were collected, the foreign office had material for a new article to submit for Izvolsky's approval. If ever there should be a default in the payments from pledged revenues, and therefore a possibility of the appointment of customs controllers within either sphere,

Great Britain would be prepared to undertake the collection and remission to Russia of the due proportion of customs revenues which may be affected to Russian loans in the British zone, if the Imperial government would agree to a similar arrangement as regards the revenues in the Russian zone which may be pledged to British loans.[p]

In one respect British diplomacy resorted to subterfuge. Hardinge became inspired on 26 February "to demand that the town of Teheran, as the seat of gov[ernmen]t and as the residence of the foreign legations should be regarded as a natural 'enclave.' On this point we could, if necessary, make a graceful concession later." [q] Grey took up the suggestion, and instructed Nicolson to tell Izvolsky that the British government "had originally intended" to demand that Teheran should be "a neutral enclave" within the Russian sphere. The British government was now ready to make a "most important concession" by waiving this demand, provided Russia would not oppose, without a previous agreement, the grant of concessions to British subjects, or to those of third powers, in

[p] *Ibid.*, no. 389, minutes, p. 433; no. 393, p. 436; no. 395, enclosure, p. 440.
[q] *Ibid.*, no. 389, minutes, p. 433.

what was formerly spoken of as the whole of the rest of Persia, but was now more shortly characterized as the neutral zone. The British reason for this request was entirely legitimate, because it would be manifestly unfair that the increased Russian prestige at Teheran "should be used on the spot there to our detriment in the neutral zone, which is governed like the rest of Persia from Teheran." [r] There is no reason to believe that Izvolsky would have refused this logical request had it been asked directly, and British diplomacy would have avoided an unworthy ruse.

These British amendments were given to Izvolsky in an *aide-mémoire* on 10 March, which Nicolson rounded out with a verbal exposition of the British reasons. Izvolsky accepted everything without precise comment for careful study, and Nicolson believed that he would work for the approval of most of the British changes. His only immediate objection came after Nicolson had explained the original British intention regarding the disposal of Teheran, or the engagement otherwise desired from Russia. After some purely diplomatic sparring, Izvolsky let Nicolson see that he would be willing to accept the condition that Russia would not oppose British efforts for concessions in the neutral zone, if such an engagement was reciprocal and no special mention made of third powers. He explained to Nicolson that he planned to have his reply to the British amendments ready in a short time, although he admitted that the military authorities were investigating the proposal that the Russian line should stop near Zulfikar, but he seemed not to expect any trouble about the alteration.[s] In these later conversations every major point had been raised that finally found its way into the arrangement. Before that was signed there had been many drafts and replies exchanged which prolonged the negotiations, but the resolution of the difficulties, if taken separately, appears clearly through the tangled course.

[r] *Ibid.*, no. 393, pp. 435-436.
[s] *Ibid.*, no. 395, and enclosure, pp. 437-440; no. 396, p. 441; no. 397, p. 441. Nicolson referred Izvolsky's solution respecting British concessions in the neutral zone to London, and on 13 March was able to advise Izvolsky that the British government was ready to accept it, and Izvolsky appeared satisfied.

The heart of any agreement over Persia was in the spheres of influence into which the country should be divided, their extent, and the degree of immunity that Great Britain and Russia should enjoy from any interference within their own preserves.[t] The British were interested primarily in securing India from Russian invasion, however remote, wherefore the insistence upon the inclusion of Seistan within their sphere.[u] The Russian government made no serious attempt to prevent the loss of this strategic district, possibly because British determination to have it had been so clearly indicated that any opposition was seen to be futile. For the rest of the British sphere it was enough to draw a line which took in that southern part of Persia within which British initiative was indisputably supreme, and which included the Persian side of the entrance to the Gulf, with all the shore line along the Indian ocean. By this arrangement the fancied dangers of a fortified port established by some other power were materially lessened; British naval supremacy would do the rest.[v] The first formulation of the line for this British sphere remained unchanged, indeed unquestioned, throughout the negotiations. Occasionally it was said that Great Britain desired to make its sphere "as small as possible." This casual statement fooled nobody; the British line was drawn to comprise everything that was essential, everything to which a defensible claim could be made.[w] It was not quite the same with the Russian sphere line. Izvolsky was cautious and delayed formulating his demands. When he did announce the Russian claim, it also reflected ade-

[t] Nicolson and Izvolsky frequently expressed the desire to avoid letting the phrase "sphere of influence" appear in the treaty, and circumlocutions were always found in British and Russian drafts. (*Ibid.*, no. 398, p. 442; no. 411, p. 455, where Nicolson wrote: "It was desirable to avoid employing those terms which might give rise to misapprehension." See also no. 418, p. 469; no. 420, p. 469.) Of course in their private conversations they freely used this concise and appropriate designation.

[u] *Ibid.*, no. 253, p. 275; no. 388, p. 429.

[v] "As regards the Persian Gulf, even admitting that the approach to those waters is not definitely barred, and in present circumstances this could hardly be achieved, we have for the defence of our interests in those regions our naval preponderance with which no power can compete." *Ibid.*, no. 429, p. 480; no. 448, enclosure 1, p. 496.

[w] *Ibid.*, no. 393, p. 435. Nicolson, p. 242. *C. H. B. F. P.*, III, 364. Sir Percy Sykes, *A History of Persia*, (London, 1921), II, 412.

quately the region of predominance in northern Persia, but it encountered British objections in two particulars: in the belated attempt to have Teheran formed into a neutral enclave, which never had a chance of acceptance, and in the insistence that none of the Russian sphere should parallel the Afghan border.[x] The Russians did not willingly accede to this exclusion, so that considerable pressure had to be put upon them before the British got their way. What was left of Persia outside of these two regions became the neutral zone, the poorest of the land, open to the general scramble of all comers. Only British and Russian policy toward each other in this left-over remained to be defined.[y]

When Nicolson explained to Izvolsky on 10 March the reasons why Great Britain insisted that the line for the Russian sphere must terminate in Persia at the intersection of the Russian and Afghan frontiers, the latter revealed that he had not drawn the Russian line, so that he would need to examine the proposed alteration carefully.[z] In his *pro-memoriâ* of 2 April, Izvolsky gave a guarded admission that he could meet the wishes of the British government, and would give a definite reply after he had received explanations on some of the other questions being discussed.[a] Izvolsky found it hard to give up everything, and he proposed a slight, but significant change in the modifications of the text of the convention which he submitted on 5 June. Instead of having the Russian line run directly from Kakh to the northeastern corner of Persia, as the British thought had been accepted in principle, under the guise of defining the line in a precise manner through intermediate points Izvolsky introduced a distinct bend to the south and east, approaching very close to the Afghan border, to include the town of Karez. The advantage sought would be the inclusion within the Russian sphere of a sanitation post, which protected Russian territory from the entrance of epidemics.[b] This healthy reason was not approved in London. It let Rus-

[x] *B. D.*, IV, no. 389, minutes, p. 433; no. 395, pp. 437-438.
[y] *Ibid.*, no. 395, pp. 438-439.
[z] *Ibid.*, no. 393, p. 435; no. 395, p. 437.
[a] *Ibid.*, no. 404, enclosure 2, p. 446. Nicolson, p. 251.
[b] *B. D.*, IV, no. 416, enclosure 1, p. 462.

sia reach Afghanistan from a new direction, something which "could not fail to excite hostile criticism in this country and create an atmosphere unfavorable to the agreement which it is to the general interest to avoid." [c] These objections in behalf of the general interest Nicolson mentioned to Izvolsky at the same time that he proposed the wording of the limits of the Russian sphere which was destined to find its way into the final arrangement.[d] Still Izvolsky found it hard to surrender, so in his memorandum of 8 July he described another line between Kakh and the corner which "fully complied with the desired conditions," yet also ran nearer the Afghan border, although less close than his preceding tracing.[e] Once more Nicolson employed the "necessary and obvious arguments" against the suggested meandering, until Izvolsky finally gave up, and the Russian line was drawn in the manner which kept that sphere from touching Afghanistan.[f] No attempt was made to alter the early description of the British line; the whole of the rest of Persia fell neatly into place between the Russian and British spheres, so that the geographical bands of the three zones that were thenceforth to mosaic Persia were finally settled.

It was of more importance, as Curzon's literary skill cleverly expressed the point in 1899, to arrive at an understanding "for the separate patronage and development of [Persia] in distinct and clearly defined compartments," other words for what benefits Great Britain and Russia were to enjoy within their spheres.[g] The first British proposal of 17 November 1906 had been in the nature of a self-denying ordinance, in that each contracting party was neither to seek nor to maintain for itself or for its subjects any concessions of a political or commercial nature within the sphere of the other, nor to obstruct in any manner applications for concessions supported by the other in its own region.[h] When Izvolsky got around to

[c] *Ibid.*, no. 425, p. 473.
[d] *Ibid.*, no. 429, enclosure, pp. 478-481.
[e] *Ibid.*, no. 447, enclosure, p. 495; see also no. 274, pp. 294-295.
[f] *Ibid.*, no. 449, p. 497.
[g] *Ibid.*, no. 319, p. 360.
[h] *Ibid.*, no. 371, enclosure, pp. 415-416.

answer this draft in February 1907 he said that the Russian government believed that it would be better to specify what these concessions were to be. In his draft convention of the 20th, concessions for railroads, banks, telegraphs, roads, transport and insurance were particularized. He also slipped in a further engagement that one party should not intercede in behalf of subjects of a third power for concessions in the zone of the other. This evidently escaped Nicolson's attention for six days, but when he discovered it he believed that it was worth retaining, "as it would exclude the possibility of the Russian government hereafter favoring the introduction of foreign enterprize into the British zone." [i] The British government quicky acknowledged on 18 March that it wished this reference to third powers retained.[j] In all the subsequent drafts these provisions descriptive of the advantages Russia and Great Britain were to have in their separate compartments were not disturbed. With regard to concessions in the neutral zone Izvolsky was willing not to oppose any grants sought by British subjects, without a previous arrangement with Great Britain, always provided a reciprocal engagement was given as regards grants to Russian subjects. He persisted in his desire not to accord specifically the same privileges to subjects of other powers. He preferred to retain the freedom of objecting to such concessions which might prove injurious to Russian commercial interests without needing to reach a prior agreement with Great Britain, in which a conflict of opinion could develop. Therefore this reference, he insisted, ought to be left out of the agreement.[k] Nicolson drafted a wording which covered these views. After minor changes by the British foreign office and Izvolsky, it became the third article of the arrangement respecting Persia.[l]

[i] *Ibid.*, no. 388, p. 428; no. 389, enclosure, p. 432; no. 398, p. 442; no. 400, p. 443.
[j] *Ibid.*, no. 401, p. 443.
[k] *Ibid.*, no. 395, pp. 438-439; no. 404, enclosure 2, p. 447. Nicolson advised that Izvolsky be permitted to have his way, and the British government at once concurred. *Ibid.*, no. 396, and note 1, p. 441.
[l] *Ibid.*, no. 398, p. 442; no. 406, p. 448; no. 411, enclosure, pp. 455, 456; no. 414, p. 460; no. 416, enclosure 2, p. 464; no. 425, p. 473; no. 456, enclosure, p. 503.

Certain concessions, however, that each already possessed would lie in the zone of the other when the convention should come into force. Both Izvolsky and Nicolson desired that these, which had to do with banks, telegraph lines, and visions of railroad routes, should be preserved. A slight reluctance to agree developed at the end of May when the British government desired to renew a telegraph contract with Persia for an additional term of twenty years from its termination in 1925. Two of the lines involved were situated in provinces due to fall within the Russian sphere. Izvolsky asserted that the proposed renewal would disturb the existing *status quo* in Persia which, at the start of the negotiations, each power had promised to respect; but the details of the matter he avoided discussing.[m] On 21 June Grey declared that the British government believed that the maintenance of existing concessions implied the right of their renewal, if Persian consent could again be won. To make it more palatable to Izvolsky, Grey offered to surrender British rights over the line between Teheran and Khanikin if no objection were raised against the prolongation of the others, chief among which was the line running from Teheran into southern Persia over Isfahan. After Nicolson explained this bargain, Izvolsky appeared willing to accept it.[n] Just before the agreement was concluded, in an *aide-mémoire* of 24 August, the Russian government accepted the British rights to the Teheran-Khanikin line, in return promising to raise no objections to the prolongation of the remaining British concessions.[o] In the final text, room was found to tack on to the end of the third article a sentence that all the concessions actually existing within the British and Russian spheres were to be retained as held.[p]

A similar problem had to be settled with regard to the Persian revenues put up as security for loans obtained from Russian and British sources. Not all of these revenues would be within the sphere of that power to which they were hypoth-

[m] *Ibid.*, no. 415, pp. 460-461, and note 1, p. 460.
[n] *Ibid.*, no. 426, pp. 473-474; no. 436, and minute, p. 485.
[o] *Ibid.*, no. 453, enclosure, p. 500.
[p] *Ibid.*, no. 456, enclosure, p. 503.

ecated. Izvolsky had early demanded that all such income accruing to Russia should be earmarked for the same purposes as in the past, and the British foreign office promptly formulated their counterpart. Nicolson thought there could be no objection to this, and Izvolsky let the matter rest without comment for several weeks. In his proposed amendments of 5 June he added that the sources of income should be similarly treated for such loans as might be concluded "up to the date of signature of the present arrangement." [q] These slight changes were acceptable to the British foreign office, and the reservation to each power of the revenues from whatever part of Persia put up as guarantees for the repayment of loans eventually formed the fourth article of the agreement. [r]

Suppose, however, that there should be a default in the payments from these sources, for Persia was not a good risk. The last thing the British wished to see, but the first that Izvolsky might request, was the presence of Russian controllers of customs collecting the revenues in the British zone. The British foreign office offered to collect and to remit the customs or pledged revenues due Russia from within the British sphere, in return for like service rendered by Russia. Izvolsky did not reject this proposal, but wanted to have certain details cleared up first. The Russian government, he pointed out, had the right specified in the loan contracts that it could step in and control the collection of pledged revenues in the event of any irregularity in the payments by Persia. Moreover, he would need to know in precise detail the nature of the British rights in Persia, in order to obtain a just appreciation of the obligations Russia would assume. [s] Nicolson explained the nature of British rights to take action in Persia when he handed over a draft of the proposed Persian agreement on 22 April. A long article composed by Grey and satisfactory to the India office covered the entire question. [t] A month later, on 23 May, Izvolsky submitted a counterdraft

[q] *Ibid.*, no. 395, p. 439; no. 404, p. 446; no. 416, enclosure 1, p. 462.
[r] *Ibid.*, no. 425, p. 473; no. 456, enclosure, p. 503.
[s] *Ibid.*, no. 398, pp. 442-443; no. 404, enclosure 2, p. 446. Nicolson, p. 251.
[t] *B. D.*, IV, no. 406, p. 448; no. 411, enclosure, pp. 455, 456.

which formed an adequate basis for verbal alterations by Grey and Nicolson to obtain accuracy, and to exclude every possibility that Russia could exercise that "right of control over such of the sources of revenue affected to the service of the Russian loans in Persia as lie within the British sphere" which Izvolsky had revealed that Russia had stipulated in its loan contracts.[u] This amended article received Russian and British approval during June, and dropped out of the discussions to become the fifth and wordiest of the articles in the arrangement respecting Persia. By it Russia and Great Britain agreed to enter into a friendly exchange of ideas to determine the means of control to be used by them in the event of irregularities occurring in the amortization or the payment of interest of the Persian loans, and that the measures adopted must "avoid all interference which would not be in conformity with the principles governing the present arrangement." [v]

As early as 22 April the rapprochement over these details had been so encouraging that Nicolson remarked to Izvolsky, "we were now practically very near the termination of the convention respecting Persia;" a most mistaken impression, but one with which Izvolsky had agreed.[w] That there were evident signs of progress had not escaped the Persian government. So unusual was the new tendency of Great Britain and Russia to coöperate in Persia that the shah's minister in London had asked Grey as early as March 1906 "whether the British and Russian governments had an understanding between each other." Grey had then denied that any agreement existed, but when the minister pressed his suspicions to the point of asking if there were intentions of making one, Grey threw sand in his eyes by replying that "it was impossible to say anything about intentions." [x] The minister was still inquisitive in October and repeated his earlier questions. Grey vaguely admitted that there were some inevitable discussions going on with Russia "owing to the present state of Persia . . .

[u] *Ibid.*, no. 413, enclosure 2, p. 459; no. 417, p. 466; no. 422, p. 472; no. 424, p. 472.
[v] *Ibid.*, no. 420, p. 469; no. 425, p. 473; no. 456, enclosure, pp. 503-504.
[w] *Ibid.*, no. 411, p. 455.
[x] *Ibid.*, no. 327, p. 380.

but we had not discussed anything which in any way would prejudice the independence or the integrity of Persia." [y] Only a week later the new Persian minister of foreign affairs had wind of the negotiations, and turned to Spring Rice for reassurance, which Sir Cecil gave as well as he could. This wise Persian had clear insight into the danger that threatened his country:

For years, [he recalled], England had been the natural and necessary friend of Persia. Was she going to abandon her ancient ally to her new friend? . . . It was feared that England, in order to arrive at a friendly arrangement with Russia, might consent to a general surrender of her interest in Persia, or what would be even worse, would negotiate a partition of the empire, into so-called spheres of interest, which was a convenient term for a veiled protectorate. Was England contemplating a Persian agreement with Russia on the model of the Morocco agreement with France? [z]

Shrewd as he was, and threatening as he did to find salvation in the bosom of Europe, his country, torn by internal political strife, was helpless in the arms of destiny. All Spring Rice could do for the rest of the year was to report the decline of British prestige, as the popular party in Persia gained the conviction that Great Britain was selling out to Russia. [a]

In order not to disturb the course of the Persian negotiations, Russia and Great Britain had agreed not to take any action that would change their relative positions within the country, and the ministers at Teheran were repeatedly told to work in concert with each other. [b] The revolutionary movement in the country produced much turmoil, and at the beginning of March 1907 Izvolsky was uneasy over the situation, to the point that he admitted his intention to consult with the military authorities what measures might possibly be taken.

[y] Ibid., no. 355, p. 400.
[z] Ibid., no. 358, p. 402.
[a] Ibid., no. 360, p. 404; no. 377, pp. 420-421.
[b] Ibid., no. 385, p. 426; no. 386, p. 427. Spring Rice complained that the Russian government was doubtless willing to remain neutral in Persia, but its local agents seemed eager to help the shah overcome the reform party. He thought Sir Arthur Hardinge's words applied as well in 1907 as when they were written two years before: "At London and St. Petersburg the European, here in Asia the Tartar, head of the Russian double eagle is most plainly visible." Ibid., no. 321 (b), p. 373; no. 381, p. 422; no. 412, p. 457.

He did not plan to do anything before previous consultation with Great Britain, but he thought both governments ought to agree upon some common action for the protection of their interests, if ever the necessity for joint intervention should arise. It might also be well if a joint warning were given to the Persian government of what would happen if the disorders got out of control.[c] The British government, on the other hand, was more alarmed at the viewpoint of the Russian government than apprehensive of actual danger in Persia. While not wishing to offend popular feeling in Persia by any ill-advised interference, the British foreign office favored continued coöperation with Russia in order to reassure Izvolsky's doubts or to keep Russian policy moderate.[d] On 25 March Izvolsky sketched for Nicolson the measures Russia proposed to adopt, but only if circumstances in Persia imperatively called for some action. In reply Nicolson gave his personal opinion of what steps his country might take, although carefully showing that the Persian situation did not impress him as immediately alarming.[e] As the discussions on the Persian agreement developed, as outbreaks in Persia did not occur, and doubtless in part as a result of British serenity, nothing ever came of the proposal for joint preparations. Nevertheless the strange sight of Great Britain forsaking the opportunity to aid the popular movement for coöperation with Russia to maintain a tottering shah, caused British prestige to swoon in Persia. This made Spring Rice bitter, and occasioned his impassioned fulmination against an agreement with Russia in an uninvited and undesired despatch of 11 April.[f] Two months later the reply written "in pained reproof" told him that the old policy "of attempting to support Persia against Russian advances" was no longer as advantageous as a "peaceful solution of this problem" with Russia.[g]

[c] *Ibid.*, no. 391, p. 434; no. 392, p. 435.
[d] *Ibid.*, no. 394, pp. 436-437.
[e] *Ibid.*, no. 403, and enclosure, pp. 444-445; no. 407, and enclosure, p. 449.
[f] *Ibid.*, no. 409, pp. 450-453. See above, pp. 164-165.
[g] *B. D.*, IV, no. 421, p. 471. Nicolson, p. 252. Grey minuted to another complaint from Spring Rice: "It [an agreement with Russia] may annoy Persia who has lived on the enmity between us and Russia, but we cannot keep up a quarrel with Russia in order to curry favor with the Persians." *B. D.*, IV, no. 412, minute, p. 458.

The prospect of a peaceful solution of the Persian question was nearly lost because of a British attempt to "insert a reference to the special interest of Great Britain in the maintenance of the *status quo* in the Persian Gulf" into the otherwise innocuous preamble.[h] This idea came originally to Sir Charles Hardinge, to which Grey gave his approval on 3 May. Some mention of this interest was deemed desirable for the eventuality that the Bagdad railroad might reach a terminus on the Persian littoral of the Gulf within the neutral zone, in order to facilitate British opposition to the concession of a port if no arrangement for participation in the railroad had been reached with Germany. This statement was desired for two other important reasons: first, because "it would give satisfaction here as insuring the neutrality of Russia in any question involving other powers in the Persian Gulf," and also because "we want some reference or admission in the text for shop-window purposes, and to disarm hostile criticism on the part of the extremists and conservatives in the h[ouse] of commons."[1] Izvolsky unwittingly furnished the opportunity for putting in the reference to the Persian Gulf when he proposed some verbal amendments to the preamble, and Grey instructed Nicolson to request its acceptance by Izvolsky because of the considerable importance attached to it in London.[j] Nicolson communicated the addition to Izvolsky on 24 June, and urged its acceptance because the proposition to which the Russian government was asked to subscribe was "incontrovertible," while this reference to the Gulf would insure public approval of the agreement as a whole in England.[k]

Nothing but disappointment came from the British attempt. Izvolsky would have nothing to do with it, and based his objections on irrefutable arguments. To start with he declared that Russia did not deny that "Great Britain had special and predominant interests in the Gulf," but he did recall that "during all our discussions regarding the Persian convention

[h] *Ibid.*, no. 417, p. 465.
[i] *Ibid.*, Editors' Note, minutes, p. 458; no. 428, minutes, p. 477.
[j] *Ibid.*, Editors' Note, p. 464; no. 425, p. 473.
[k] *Ibid.*, no. 428, p. 475; no. 429, pp. 477-478.

both governments had strictly limited themselves to treating of matters which concerned themselves alone, and which neither directly nor indirectly affected the interests of other powers." The Persian Gulf was not one of these matters. Its waters were by no means entirely within the boundaries of Persia. As to the claim of British predominance, which Nicolson had described as an undoubted and incontrovertible fact, Izvolsky questioned its being universally accepted, and suspected that neither Turkey nor Germany would agree to the British contention in full. He denied the assertion that this new addition was a vital necessity, because "he did not understand why if the matter were of such importance . . . it had not been brought forward earlier." His greatest reliance was placed upon the dissatisfaction such a statement would arouse in Germany, which had its eyes turned in that very direction, and on the impossibility for Russia to subscribe to anything that would impair relations with that alert, powerful neighbor.[1] Izvolsky, who deeply regretted the introduction of a fresh and controversial subject into negotiations which he was suddenly eager to conclude by 15 July, was positive that the risks of further delay could imperil the success of the entire arrangement. Nicolson, who "of course, argued with him, but did not share his opinion," was sure that "the more he reflects upon it the greater will be his objections to it." [m]

For the second time during the conversations Izvolsky had reared up and stood his ground. Nicolson was thoroughly impressed with his serious demeanor and his arguments. The criticism of the tardiness in bringing up so important a subject was unassailable. The anxiety of Izvolsky to hasten the agreements to a conclusion was noteworthy, and Nicolson suspected that "Berlin is causing uneasiness, and I understand opposition here is active in certain quarters." [n] The net result was that

---

[1] This argument convinced Nicolson. "It is perfectly clear to me," he wrote in his despatch of 24 June to Grey, "that M. Izvolsky will not run the risk of impairing in the slightest degree the good relations between Russia and Germany, especially at a time when Russia has not yet emerged from her internal difficulties or repaired the losses which she has suffered in a disastrous campaign." *Ibid.*, no. 429, p. 479.

[m] *Ibid.*, no. 428, p. 476; no. 429, pp. 478-479.

[n] *Ibid.*, no. 428, p. 476.

Nicolson pressingly recommended that "we should be conciliatory on minor details, and even on a question of public
sentiment, and lose no time in finally concluding negotiations
which have lasted for so many months."[o] He believed that
everything really essential had already been gained, even
more than was anticipated, which made a good defence against
criticisms. With skill, and almost with eloquence, he advised:

It would be most regrettable if an opportunity which may never recur
should be lost, and if, owing to insistence on points which are not of
vital importance, the hopes of a durable arrangement were to be disappointed. It seems to me that by the conventions, even as they at present
stand, we have secured all the guarantees which are necessary to the
safety of our Indian frontiers; and that we have removed to a reasonable
distance the danger of Russian aggression.[p]

In London, Hardinge and Grey agreed that "it was unfortunate that the insertion of the clause in the preamble relating
to the maintenance of the 'status quo' in the Persian Gulf was
an afterthought on our part," but they still wanted to have
Izvolsky accept it in order to insure "the neutrality of Russia
in any question involving other powers in the Persian Gulf."[q]
Nicolson was to point out that there was no requirement
placed on Russia to guarantee the British position, nor an
obligation to act against the interests other powers might
have. It would be acceptable if Izvolsky himself discovered
words which would promise Russian neutrality without affecting its relations to third parties. If, after all, no mention of
the Gulf appeared in the preamble, there would be no escape
from making a declaration in parliament in the same fashion
as Lansdowne had done in 1903; but this was not to be mentioned until it was hopeless to expect Izvolsky's consent to a

[o] *Ibid.*, no. 429, p. 480. The importance attributed to carrying the approval
of public sentiment for the acts of a parliamentary government, and the use
made of this as an argument for effect, are so often overemphasized that Nicolson's realism, in private, is worth noting. He was willing to leave public opinion on one side. This was not lost upon either Hardinge or Grey, who "would
draw special attention to what [Nicolson] says . . . as to the inconstancy of
public opinion as a factor and the solid advantages to be obtained from an
agreement." *Ibid.*, minutes, p. 481.
[p] *Ibid.*, no. 429, p. 480.
[q] *Ibid.*, no. 428, minutes, pp. 476-477.

statement in the preamble.[r] Meanwhile Izvolsky had given
Nicolson a memorandum on 28 June in which he repeated his
objections and begged that the British proposal would be
dropped. He also repeated the admission that the Russian
government did not deny at all the existence of British interests in the Gulf, and would be willing to examine the question
in discussions on some later occasion.[s] Nicolson still thought
that it would be impossible to persuade Izvolsky, recommended again that the clause be omitted, but suggested that
note could be taken of Izvolsky's recognition of British interests.[t]

Nicolson considered the position carefully and wavered
between making a graceful concession at once, or trying again
to overcome Izvolsky's unwillingness. He finally made a for-
lorn attempt, but when Izvolsky remained unmoved, Nicolson
gave up the quest. He told the foreign minister that some
unilateral pronouncement would doubtless be made by the
British government, to which Izvolsky interposed no objection,
merely asking to be given the general sense in writing, and
appeared to be greatly relieved.[u] One more British proposal,
however, crossed with the report of Izvolsky's refusal, and
Nicolson risked upsetting the harrassed minister a third time,
but again the latter replied that he found this suggestion also
inacceptable. Nicolson put every bit of pressure in his power
to bear upon the British foreign office to dissuade it from
hounding Izvolsky with any more proposals or variations, and
his plain warning that "a persistence in our request will have
the effect of blocking for some time the progress of our
negotiations, and unless we withdraw our proposal, of finally
leading to a deadlock" at last succeeded.[v] Grey thanked

[r] *Ibid.*, no. 430, p. 482.
[s] *Ibid.*, no. 431, pp. 482-483; no. 437, enclosure, pp. 486-487. Trubetzkoy, pp. 96-97.
[t] *B. D.*, IV, no. 432, p. 483.
[u] *Ibid.*, no. 433, p. 484; no. 435, p. 485; no. 439, pp. 488-489. Nicolson, p. 253.
[v] *B. D.*, IV, no. 434, p. 484; no. 438, p. 487; no. 440, pp. 489-490; no. 442, p. 491; no. 443, pp. 491-492. So eager had the British government been to have its way that Nicolson was advised that the French ambassador might be in-structed to intercede with Izvolsky. Nicolson sat down hard upon this prospect. He reminded the foreign office that at the outset an agreement, upon British insistence, had been made not to reveal details of the negotiations to third

Nicolson for his endeavors and abandoned the attempt. Instead note was formally taken of the Russian recognition of Britain's special interests in the Persian Gulf, while the terms of the public declaration would be communicated as soon as they had been devised.[w]

The substance and the manner of making a Persian Gulf pronouncement required careful attention from the Liberal cabinet. Lansdowne's declaration of 1903 would obviously serve as a model, for its words were strong, even if in substance they did not amount to much. The Liberals preferred to compose something with more weight, in which "some phrases more in accordance with usual diplomatic language" would be used.[x] The government of India was consulted, and regretted that

it should not have been possible to retain any mention in the preamble of [the] convention of British interests in [the] maintenance of [the] *status quo* in [the] Persian Gulf, as this would have removed most of the doubts which they have felt as to [the] advantages of the convention.

Of course some statement must now be made "in the most definite terms," and overt measures must thereafter be taken whenever an occasion was offered "to show that there is every intention to act up to [the] declaration."[y] The resourceful Nicolson suggested that, as the conclusion of the negotiations could hardly be reached before parliament rose for the summer, the declaration could be made in a covering despatch to the convention and published with it, which satisfied Grey.[z] A draft declaration was sent to Nicolson and he eventually gave a copy of it to Izvolsky, who found it acceptable after rectifying the rendering of the Russian recognition that it did not dispute British special interests in the Persian Gulf.[a] The

powers. There was no indication that Izvolsky had done so, (there is that Great Britain did so to Japan and France), but if he learned of this British request of France, he might feel at liberty to consult with Germany. The French ambassador did not make any representations to Izvolsky. *Ibid.*, no. 434, p. 484; no. 440, p. 489.
[w] *Ibid.*, no. 444, pp. 492-493.
[x] *Ibid.*, no. 444, minutes, p. 493.
[y] *Ibid.*, no. 448, enclosures 1 and 2, pp. 495-496.
[z] *Ibid.*, no. 445, p. 494; no. 446, p. 494.
[a] *Ibid.*, Editors' Note, p. 497; no. 451, and enclosure, p. 498.

revised declaration was sent to Nicolson on 29 August and was published with the text of the convention. Sir Francis Bertie, the British ambassador at Paris, described it as a sort of "avis au lecteur," so that "nobody can in future plead ignorance of our attitude in regard to the Persian Gulf." [b]

The remaining verbal substitutions in the preamble were easily settled, until the sole important problem left was the transfer of telegraph control over the lines between Teheran and Meshed, and from Meshed to Nasratabad. While the Persian agreement remained a matter of uncertain outcome, Izvolsky was slow about discussing the transfer; but when the rest of the questions proved capable of settlement, this point was also efficiently arranged. A start had been made when Izvolsky proposed to seek an adjustment outside of the Persian arrangement itself, which appealed to Nicolson and the British foreign office, provided it should be completed at the same time. Nicolson sent a draft annex covering the transfer to London for approval, and soon thereafter reported that Izvolsky was also examining methods for effecting an exchange. Izvolsky studied Nicolson's draft with his customary care, but there was no indication that any serious difficulty would arise. [c] In June, British insistence upon the transfer was repeated along with an offer to carry on these negotiations with Benckendorff in London, but Izvolsky never took up with this suggestion. A few days later Nicolson announced that the British government was ready to give up the portion of the line between Meshed and Seistan which lay within the Russian sphere in Persia, in return for a friendly attitude towards the request for the prolongation of some British telegraph concessions in other parts of the country. [d] Izvolsky seemed willing to enter into this bargain, but it was not until near the end of the Persian negotiations in general that he definitely accepted the British proposals, and was prepared to sign a separate ar-

[b] *Ibid.*, Editors' Note, p. 497; no. 455, pp. 501-502; no. 462, p. 507.
[c] *Ibid.*, no. 397, enclosure, pp. 441-442; no. 405, p. 447; no. 411, p. 455.
[d] *Ibid.*, no. 423, p. 472; no. 426, p. 474; no. 430, p. 482. The India office had no objection to a junction of the British part of the Meshed-Seistan line in the neutral zone provided a suitable spot was found. The place most favored was Turbat-i-Haidari. *Ibid.*, Editors' Note, minutes, p. 485.

rangement along with the Persian agreement regulating the exchange of most of the Meshed-Nasratabad line for all of the Teheran-Meshed line as controlled by Great Britain.[e] This special arrangement was not to be published simultaneously with the convention, and only in September did the two governments first instruct their ministers at Teheran to apply for Persian approval of the exchanges to insure their accomplishment.[f]

This concluded the negotiations for the settlement of the Persian question between Great Britain and Russia. These had limped frequently with painful caution, but the arrangement in which they culminated formed the largest and weightiest part of the convention of 1907.[g] The conventional diplomatic preamble recited a mutual engagement on behalf of Great Britain and Russia to respect the integrity and independence of Persia, a sincere desire for the preservation of order throughout the empire and for its peaceful development (although no obligation was assumed to insure this), while equal advantages for the trade and industry of all other nations should be permanently established. Because each of the contracting parties had a special interest, founded upon geographical and economic reasons, in the actual maintenance of peace and order in certain Persian provinces adjoining or in proximity to the frontiers of Russia, or of Afghanistan and Baluchistan, wherein they also desired to avoid all cause of conflict between their own interests, Great Britain and Russia proceeded to divide Persia, in the three following articles, into a British and Russian sphere of influence and a neutral zone which, however, they carefully avoided calling by such truthfully descriptive names.[h] The first article described the

[e] *Ibid.*, no. 436, p. 485; no. 453, p. 500; no. 454, p. 501.
[f] *Ibid.*, no. 460, p. 506; no. 461, pp. 506-507.
[g] The French original text of the arrangement respecting Persia is in *B. D.*, IV, no. 456, enclosure, pp. 502-504, and Appendix I, pp. 618-619. An English translation of the convention of 1907 is in *B. F. S. P.*, C (London, 1911), pp. 555-560.
[h] All through the negotiations Grey covered this over in his reassurances to Persia. The Persian minister came to him on 21 June and told him of the anxiety in Persia over a division of the land into spheres of influence. Grey's answer is remarkable: "I told him this was not a correct impression. It would be more correct to say that the agreement at which we desired to arrive was one by which we should not push our influence in those parts of Persia which

Russian sphere as lying beyond a line starting from Kasr-i-Shirin, passing through and including Isfahan, Yezd and Kakh, and ending at a point within Persia at the intersection of the Russian and Afghan frontier. In this region Great Britain engaged not to seek either for itself, or to support in favor of British subjects or those of third powers, any concessions of a political or commercial nature whatever, among which those for railways, banks, telegraphs, roads, transport and insurance were especially mentioned. Great Britain completed the engagement by a promise not to oppose, directly or indirectly, any demands for such concessions pressed by the Russian government. Russia, in return, assumed an identical obligation in favor of Great Britain in the second article, and the British sphere was delimited as that part of Persia which was behind a line going from the Afghan frontier by way of, and including, Gazik, Birjand and Kerman, until Bandar Abbas was reached. The third article really constituted a neutral zone out of all the rest of Persia, in the great deserts of which the trade and industry of all powers could freely compete. Both Great Britain and Russia promised not to oppose the grant of concessions to each other in this region without a previous arrangement. Tucked in at the end of the article was the reference to the continuation of all existing concessions as actually held in the parts of Persia described in the first and second articles.[1]

The concluding two articles of the Persian arrangement regulated in careful detail the question of the customs and other revenues pledged as guarantees for the amortization and the payments of interest on loans contracted by the shah's

---

bordered on the frontiers" of Russia and adjacent parts of the British empire. The reply received upon an almost contemporaneous inquiry directed to Izvolsky was not satisfactory to the Persian government. Whether Izvolsky's failure to please by his explanations proceeded only from greater honesty or less skill cannot be determined. See *B. D.*, IV, no. 427, p. 474, and minutes, p. 475.

[1] One of the most famous of the cartoons to appear in the London *Punch* (2 October 1907) vigorously depicted the intent of these three articles. The cartoon was entitled: "The Harmless Necessary Cat." A fine Persian feline appears in the center, with an alert, but startled glance, flanked by a British Lion and a Russian Bear. The following colloquy is subjoined: "British Lion (to Russian Bear): 'Look here! *You* can play with his head, and *I* can play with his tail, and we can *both* stroke the small of his back.' Persian Cat: 'I don't remember having been consulted about this.' "

government with the Banque d'Escompte et des Prêts de Perse, a Russian institution, and the Imperial Bank of Persia, the British counterpart, both primarily official establishments. The fourth article specified that the revenues of all the Persian customs, except those from Farsistan and the Persian Gulf, were to be devoted to the same purposes as in the past, namely, as guarantees for the amortization and the interest payments of all the Russian loans concluded by Persia up to the date of the signature of the arrangement. The revenues from the customs of Farsistan and the Persian Gulf, as well as those of the fisheries along the Persian shore of the Caspian sea, and from the Posts and Telegraphs, were to afford the same guarantees to British loans made up to the signature of the arrangement. The last article contemplated irregularities or defaults in the payments, and the ensuing necessity for Russia to establish control over sources of revenue pledged to the service of its loans, but coming from the region of the British sphere; or of analogous action on the part of Great Britain over sources of revenues which would lie within the Russian sphere. Now these two powers in such an eventuality promised to enter into a friendly exchange of views before taking any action, in order to determine in common accord the measures of control to be instituted, and to avoid all interference (in the region of the other) which would not be in conformity with the principles governing this entire Persian arrangement. These five articles, with the preamble, composed the whole of the arrangement proper; and there were no secret clauses.[1]

Outside the treaty, the contemporaneous transfer of Persian telegraph lines had not been perfected and was not published with it; but the British positive declaration of its special interests in the Persian Gulf, the result of actions in those waters for more than one hundred years, did appear. The declaration explained its separate existence because it had not been thought appropriate to mention the Persian Gulf, which was only partly within Persia, in a treaty which was

[1] B. D., IV, no. 457, p. 504.

concerned with regions of that empire which did touch the frontiers of Russia and Great Britain in Asia. No difficulties over this question were expected between these two governments in the future, for during the negotiations the Russian government had "explicitly stated that they do not deny the special interests of Great Britain in the Persian Gulf — a statement of which His Majesty's government have formally taken note." The declaration closed with the *avis au lecteur* to other powers, which was its main object:

> In order to make it quite clear that the present arrangement is not intended to affect the position in the Gulf, and does not imply any change of policy respecting it on the part of Great Britain, His Majesty's government think it desirable to draw attention to previous declarations of British policy, and to reaffirm generally previous statements as to British interests in the Persian Gulf and the importance of maintaining them.
>
> His Majesty's government will continue to direct all their efforts to the preservation of the *status quo* in the Gulf and the maintenance of British trade; in doing so, they have no desire to exclude the legitimate trade of any other power.[k]

In this fashion Great Britain and Russia tried to settle the rivalry of their conflicting interests in Persia, mostly by recognizing the position of things as it had come to be through the quarrels of the past, and intending to face the future in tuneful accord. Indications of renewed German activity in Persia fortified the desire of the British and Russian governments "to act in the closest possible coöperation."[1] The troubles between the shah and the new governmental institutions of Persia persisted, but there was no immediate sign of a Russian desire for military intervention, as there might have been a few years before. Izvolsky thought it best to await the course of events. It did not greatly matter what political order existed in Persia, so long as peace and quiet reigned.[m]

[k] *Ibid.*, no. 455, pp. 501-502.
[1] *Ibid.*, no. 464, p. 509. Nicolson wrote in this annual report for 1907: "The activity of the German legation at Teheran has greatly preoccupied the Russian minister for foreign affairs, as he fears that Germany may acquire a strong position in the capital and with the assembly, and contrive to secure a predominant influence. He regards this activity as one expression of the dissatisfaction of the German government with the conclusion of the Anglo-Russian convention, and as indicating a desire to cause both governments as much embarrassment as possible." See also Izvolsky, *Correspondance diplomatique*, I, 103-105.
[m] *B. D.*, IV, no. 463, p. 507.

CHAPTER SIX

THE CONVENTION RESPECTING AFGHANISTAN

O F ALL the lands of Asia, Tibet alone excepted, Afghanistan had least association with the civilized world. It was unique among the states of the continent in that it was entirely landlocked, but this was no handicap to a wild country whose inhabitants had scant use for the products, barring firearms, or customs of foreigners. The people of the country were rude, Mohammedans by religion, herders more than anything else by peaceful profession, but robbers and fighters in their happier exertions. Many of the hill tribesmen were crafty, unruly warriors, excellent shots, as the British soldiers particularly discovered during the Afghan wars of the nineteenth century. Afghanistan was a generally foreboding, unprofitable place. Yet before the end of the last century, to a couple of generations of British and Russian military men and foreign office officials, because of its geographical setting, Afghanistan was a name to conjure with: a prime cause of continual suspicion, although less of actual trouble, in the relations of these two imperialistic rivals in Asia.

On the eve of the negotiations for a general understanding, Great Britain was the paramount political power in Afghanistan. This position had been acquired as the result of nearly a century's successful imperialism, including three Afghan wars. Concern for the defence of India furnished the motive for all actions, because of itself Afghanistan offered small lure. Into the Punjab and the northwestern frontier districts of India, where British rule had come late and remained precarious, turbulent Afghan tribes, among which the Afridis, the Waziris and the Mohmands were distinguished, spasmodically swooped down from their hills to add to the confusion and instability.[a] Afghan Amirs had no real control over these

---

[a] As late as 1907 these uncontrollable tribes still made it "very difficult" for Great Britain "to undertake any engagements about Afghanistan." *B. D.*, IV, no. 256, p. 278.

peoples; many British punitive expeditions were sent to impress upon them the importance of staying at home, but never with lasting success. The need for supreme influence in Afghanistan became imperative in the last quarter of the nineteenth century as the Russian conquests in central Asia progressed. By 1885 there was a common Russian-Afghan frontier of several hundred miles, where a few years before there had been none at all. Signs were not lacking of increasing and questionable relations between Russian traders, military missions, and Afghan officials. One of these missions was a partial cause of the third Afghan war. Upon its successful, but hardly glorious conclusion, Great Britain obtained treaty warrant for its exclusively privileged relations. In return for the recognition of Abdurrahman Khan, in 1880, as Amir of the country, a subsidy of £80,000 a year, increased in 1893 to £120,000, and an engagement to aid him resist aggression by any foreign power, Great Britain acquired the right to control what foreign relations Afghanistan should have with the outside world.[b]

Russia, on the other hand, was without any special position, and knew it, for a long time. Beginning with the assurances of 1868, which were renewed nearly a dozen times before the end of the century, Russia had told Great Britain that it "recognized Afghanistan as entirely outside the sphere of Russian action." [c] Passing time changed this, and the Russian position in central Asia vastly improved until, while Great Britain was enmeshed in the Boer war, the previous, spontaneously given declarations were ruined by the insinuations in the memorandum communicated to the British foreign office on 6 February 1900. In this document, couched in bland and persuasive style, the Russian government once more declared that Afghanistan remained outside its sphere of action, but then proceeded to recount the sensible modifications which had lately intervened, in order to establish a foundation for more intimate relationships with Afghanistan. It was pointed out that, after the joint Anglo-Russian commission had delimited the north Af-

[b] *Ibid.*, no. 466 (a), note 1, p. 520.
[c] *Ibid.*, I, no. 376, p. 306; no. 377, enclosure, p. 310. Trubetzkoy, p. 103.

ghan boundary between 1885 and 1895, Russia was coterminous with Afghanistan for a great distance. Thanks also to the civilizing mission undertaken in central Asia by both Great Britain and Russia, the first fruits were being exhibited in the improved well-being of the natives. The completion of the Transcaspian railroad, along with the absorption of Bukhara within the Russian economic system, combined with all the other benefits, had resulted in "a remarkable progress in the frequency of commercial relations." Afghan merchants in considerable numbers did business in Russian territory, while Russians and natives of Bukhara crossed back into Afghanistan. In consequence a whole series of new questions was arising, but their convenient settlement was daily becoming more difficult because the Amir retained all authority in his own hands. The Russian government had no direct relations with Kabul, and to prolong such an entirely abnormal situation could only be detrimental to Anglo-Russian interests. The institution of a regular order in the intercourse with Afghanistan would certainly exercise a salutary effect upon the friendliness between Russia and Great Britain, but mere palliatives would only make things worse.

Therefore the Imperial government believes it to be its duty to bring to the attention of the cabinet at London that it regards the reëstablishment of direct relations as indispensable between Russia and Afghanistan on what concerns frontier affairs. These relations will not have any kind of political character.[d]

The cabinet at London did not quite know what to make of this memorandum which had been suddenly sprung upon it.[e] The Russians were advised that the communication would be sent to the government of India, but that there would be no discussion of the substance before an opinion had been returned by the viceroy. Salisbury temporized by instructing Sir Charles Scott, the ambassador of the day in St. Petersburg, to ask concerning large bodies of Russian troops which were

[d] *B. D.*, I, no. 376, pp. 306-307.
[e] *Ibid.*, IV, no. 465, p. 512. Mr. Parker wrote from the embassy in St. Petersburg that "we are confronted, owing to the ambiguous language employed, by the difficulty of understanding exactly what it is intended by its originators to be." *Ibid.*, I, no. 377, enclosure, p. 310.

reported quartered close to the Afghan frontier, which "seemed at variance with the very friendly tone of the memorandum." The foreign minister, Muravyev, explained that very few troops had been sent to the Afghan frontier, so that any rumors of large movements were solely from sources desirous of provoking alarmist impressions.[f] From another direction less solacing explanations complicated matters. On 21 February the Russian political agent at Bukhara, M. Ignatyev, addressed a letter to one of the Amir's trading agents, which the British government got hold of after the Amir had complained of this action at Simla. The Russian troop movements were explained away in this script as a test upon the capacity of the Transcaspian railway. That this had attracted uncommon attention was only because it "chanced" to come just when Great Britain "was suffering continual reverses, which still continue, in her war with the little state of the Transvaal." What proved more offensive to London than this reminder of current events was Ignatyev's sincere desire that his letter "might prove the first step towards the establishment of direct friendly relations between Russia and Afghanistan, and be productive in opening up Afghan territory to mutual trade."[g] This letter furnished more appropriate ground upon which to address a complaint to Muravyev against recent Russian actions because, while the Boer war was still of uncertain outcome, Salisbury preferred not to engage in "a discussion of the Russian proposal regarding direct relations with Afghanistan." Furthermore, there was some disposition to admit, on certain assumptions, that the British government "might entertain the consideration of the proposals."[h] The Russian position in Afghanistan indeed must have improved.

The reaction of the government of India to the memorandum of February 1900 of course was hostile. Before June several despatches were addressed to London in which its "insuperable objections" were set forth at some length. The long line of Russian disclaimers that Afghanistan was entirely

[f] *Ibid.*, I, no. 377, enclosure, p. 309; IV, no. 465, p. 512.
[g] *Ibid.*, I, no. 377, enclosure, p. 309; IV, no. 465, p. 513.
[h] *Ibid.*, I, no. 377, enclosure, p. 311; IV, no. 465, pp. 512, 513.

outside the sphere of Russian action was recalled. The bases
upon which the demand for direct relations was put were either
refuted or belittled. The number of frontier disputes that
could not be solved on the spot were few, and Ignatyev had
even admitted in his letter that no frontier disagreements had
arisen since the time that the boundary had been surveyed and
fixed.[i] No credence was given to the Russian charge that the
existing means of regulating commercial relations with Afghanistan through British good offices were inadequate, while
the assertion of a great growth in the trade was contradicted
without qualification.[j] The strongest objection to the proposed
direct relations was that they would become political in spite
of everything, for "it would . . . be impossible for any agent,
and especially a Russian, to divorce himself from a political
character and attributes." If a Russian envoy ever reached
Kabul, then the exclusive British control over Afghan foreign
policy would be menaced. Any condominium would produce
the worst possible effect in India, while the Amir would ascribe
such a concession to British weakness, possibly even welcoming
it. At London, however, there was a more moderate reaction
which believed that the Russian memorandum might be only
an invitation to permit direct Russian correspondence with
Afghanistan on local and commercial questions. If this assumption were right, it was something that the British government might consider at a more opportune moment.[k]

The material was on hand for a withering interchange of
more than three years, which resulted in a much clearer disclosure of British and Russian attitudes towards Afghanistan,
and the troubles that must be conciliated in any future settlement. Only at the end of November 1900 did Scott receive

[i] In September 1905 Hartwig assured Hardinge that "there was at this
moment in the ministry for foreign affairs a document prepared by General
Kuropatkin in 1899 in which it was stated that the actual frontier of Russia
and Afghanistan was ideal and should under no circumstances be modified."
Ibid., no. 192, p. 200.
[j] It was contended that the Amir "stifled [trade] on the Russian side even
more than on the Indian frontier." Irrespective of what the actions of the
Amir may have been, here the government of India was completely in error,
as the Russian-Afghan trade had been developing, and was to expand still
more rapidly in the coming years. *Obzor vnyeshney torgovli Rossiy*, (1907),
table V, p. 88; table VIII, p. 448.
[k] *B. D.*, I, no. 377, enclosure, pp. 310-311; IV, no. 465, p. 512.

274 THE ANGLO-RUSSIAN CONVENTION OF 1907

instructions to protest against the Ignatyev letter, because of its political connotations, and to insist that the proceeding should be investigated, besides demanding that a like incident should not occur again. Count Lamsdorff, for Muravyev had died in the meantime, was surprized two months later when Scott first had the opportunity to bring the letter to his notice. He agreed that the communication was "highly improper" and promised to make inquiries. In October 1901 Hardinge, then chargé d'affaires, again reverted to the letter, but Lamsdorff could tell him nothing because "he had for the moment forgotten the question." Next Lamsdorff attempted to justify Ignatyev's action as a proper one, although the latter was advised to clear up for the Amir the real purport of the proceeding; whereupon the incident was allowed to rest.[1]

The important question of Russian direct communication on local and commercial matters with Afghanistan also lay dormant until October 1901, probably because the Russians were content to rely on the impression created by their original memorandum, while Great Britain had no desire to stir up this dangerous situation during the dubious days in South Africa. Yet when the Russians raised the whole question anew, the India office quickly pointed out "the serious objections of allowing the matter to rest where it was." In January 1902 very full instructions were accordingly sent to Scott to guide him in handling this weighty subject.[m] The carefully considered British attitude was formally laid before Lamsdorff on 3 February. On this issue the British government declared:

They did not desire to contend that there was no force in the arguments in favor of direct communications between the frontier authorities on matters of local detail . . . but they held that, in view of their position as having charge of the foreign relations of Afghanistan, arrangements for this purpose could only be made with their consent, and proposals upon the subject would only be entertained by the Amir if brought forward and recommended by them. Before attempts were made to frame any such proposals, it seemed essential to have more precise explanations in regard to the method which the Russian government would desire

[1] After further fruitless exchanges in February 1902, it was dropped altogether. *Ibid.*, I, no. 377, enclosure, pp. 311-312; IV, no. 465, pp. 513-514.
[m] *Ibid.*, I, no. 377, enclosure, p. 311; IV, no. 465, p. 514.

to see adopted for the exchange of such communications, the limitations to be placed upon them, and the means of insuring that those limitations would be observed. They would be happy to consider and discuss any communication from the Russian government on this point.[n]

Lamsdorff doubtless perceived that any independent Russian action would be effectively circumscribed by this procedure, so he made no reference to the question for many months. The British did not lose sight of this evasiveness, and in November reminded him that, while willing to discuss the issue in the most friendly spirit, they would object to any change in the existing system without previous agreement. Still Lamsdorff kept silent, so that the British ambassador "considered the outlook as somewhat discouraging," because there was no sign of a desire on the part of Russia to avert a possibility of a conflict of interests by a frank discussion.[o]

A better start was made in 1903 when Benckendorff, who had just begun his long tenure as ambassador in London, inquired during one of his earliest interviews with Lansdowne "whether a solution might not be found by means of a 'negative' understanding, under which certain matters should be specifically excluded from local treatment" with Afghanistan. Lansdowne was encouraged and considered the idea worthy of attentive examination, but nothing materialized as Lamsdorff refrained from any definite commitments.[p] In his memorandum of 5 February 1903 the minister declared that no discussions were necessary because the Russian views had been sufficiently set forth three years before, while the details of the subject could only be settled as the result of experience. Rus-

[n] *Ibid.*, no. 465, p. 514. At this same period Lamsdorff told Scott that Russian public opinion was moderating against England, while the desire for an understanding "was especially strong in financial and commercial circles in Russia, and had a strong advocate in M. Witte." Lamsdorff himself "seemed to look forward with confidence to the ultimate realization of this desirable aim." This sentiment was rarely expressed in 1902. *Ibid.*, I, no. 338, p. 273.

[o] *Ibid.*, no. 377, enclosure, p. 312. *D. D. F.*, II, no. 453, pp. 555-556; no. 485, p. 608. A statement appeared in the *Novoye Vremya* for 19 December 1902 to the effect that Russia had made no request of Great Britain, but had merely intimated a decision to have direct relations with Afghanistan, concerning which no further explanations had been given. This statement came from the Russian foreign office, but Lamsdorff later said that "it lacked his personal official sanction." *B. D.*, I, no. 377, enclosure, p. 312.

[p] *Ibid.*, IV, no. 465, pp. 514-515. Newton, pp. 271-272.

sian relations with Afghanistan must be given an open, straightforward character, although not political, in which the possibility of sending agents into the country in the future was likely, even if their despatch was not yet contemplated.[q] Lamsdorff was now basing his position on the fact that Russia could not be forever bound by the terms of assurances voluntarily given under different circumstances. In the course of generations circumstances changed, and misunderstanding alone could come from an attempt to make old declarations of policy and intentions fit in new conditions.[r] The government of India deemed this a repudiation of the Russian engagements, although also "probably a piece of bravado" to cloak their actual failure to achieve the desired relations with the Amir. Lansdowne, however, explained to Benckendorff on 24 March that the British government might be content to allow the question to rest, provided there should be a full, previous consultation before Russia attempted any new departure which could upset the existing order of things. He promised that his government would deal with any proposals in a reasonable and conciliatory spirit, but that otherwise Russia was held to be "deeply committed" to the maintenance of the *status quo* in Afghanistan.[s]

For a while Benckendorff was without any further instructions, so general negotiations were suspended. The British government profitted by the delay to carry on a correspondence with the government of India. They agreed that any proposal to send Russian agents into Afghanistan would be dangerous, although non-political communications between local officials on minor frontier questions could be tolerated, if the Amir would consent to them. The Amir Habibullah had acted offishly to both Russia and Great Britain, even refusing the latter's annual subsidy and declining to visit in India during Curzon's viceroyalty. On 28 July 1903 Habibullah, in reply to a request for his views, gave the assurance

[q] *B. D.*, I, no. 377, enclosure, p. 313; IV, no. 465, p. 515.
[r] *Ibid.*, I, no. 377, enclosure, p. 313; II, no. 295, note *, p. 248; IV, no. 465, p. 516.
[s] *Ibid.*, I, no. 377, enclosure, p. 313; IV, no. 465, p. 515.

that he did not wish to confer with the Russian government, and actually protested against the actions of its officials. His lack of cordiality was believed to strengthen the British stand in the event of future conversations with Russia.[t]

The next troublesome incident came from an unexpected direction. In May friction arose between Russian and Afghan officials over some minor incidents, especially the destruction of a few boundary pillars near Herat. Russian officials from the governor of the Transcaspian region down to two Turkoman sowars, sent a stream of letters directly to the Afghan governor of Herat, who delayed answers pending the arrival of instructions from the Amir. A British proposal of 27 May proffered the services of an official from Seistan to investigate and settle the frontier incident with a Russian colleague of suitable rank. On 22 June Lansdowne protested against the literary efforts of local Russian officials as constituting a practice opposed by Great Britain. Both moves were met by dilatory tactics on the part of Lamsdorff, and British inquiries were repeated during July and August. Lamsdorff declared that the matter had been referred to the governor of Tashkent. At least once he gave the impression that everything had escaped his memory; yet all the while indications of Russian activity near Afghanistan multiplied. At last on 21 August, the Russian government sent a refusal of all British assistance in settling the boundary dispute, because there was "no reason to modify the views" proclaimed in the old memorandum of February 1900.[u] This position aroused both the governments in London and in India to action.

The Indian government proposed to proceed with the arrangement for the despatch of a British officer to the scene of the Afghan frontier dispute, which the British approved, and determined to make further representations to Russia.

[t] *Ibid.*, I, no. 377, enclosure, p. 314; IV, no. 465, p. 517.
[u] *Ibid.*, no. 465, pp. 517-518. On 7 November 1903 Benckendorff offered a logical and appeasing explanation. He admitted that the original boundary had been marked by a joint Anglo-Russian commission, but this incident "was not one in which a new boundary was to be demarcated. All that was necessary was that certain posts which had fallen down should be set up again, and for this purpose it had not seemed necessary to resort to combined action." Lansdowne was "unconvinced by this argument." *Ibid.*, II, no. 258, p. 223.

The whole attitude of the British government towards Russian activity was reviewed, and the restoration of the boundary pillars by joint supervision was insisted upon.ᵛ This long three years' sparring was terminated by a Russian note of 5 October, which was so "peremptory in tone, and almost discourteous in its terms" that it was "deeply resented" by the British government.ʷ The communication, in ambiguous words, based the refusal of the ministry for foreign affairs to consider the British proposals not only upon the clear exposition of the Russian views set forth in the memorandum of February 1900, but also on the necessity for direct relations with Afghanistan caused by the changes which had occurred in central Asia in recent years. The question of the restoration of the boundary posts did not affect the general order of things, so the ministry for foreign affairs reiterated its firm decision to follow the procedure indicated in previous communications, and therefore considered the question as definitely closed.ˣ The British government informed Lamsdorff that, if any frontier incidents arose out of Russian actions, the full responsibility and the consequences must rest upon the Russian government. A month later when Benckendorff came around to soothe the hurt feelings, Lansdowne told him that the Russian stand had been so decided that he "should have considered it inconsistent with [his] duty" to reopen the question.ʸ

Benckendorff came around because Russia was becoming dangerously involved in the Far East with Britain's yellow ally. The ambassador observed that Russia had now dropped the demand to send agents into Afghanistan. He sought to excuse the Russian note because Lamsdorff had been away at the time some official in the foreign office had drafted it.ᶻ Lansdowne expressed his pleasure that Lamsdorff wanted "a

ᵛ *Ibid.*, IV, no. 465, pp. 518-519.
ʷ *Ibid.*, no. 181 (b), p. 184; no. 182, pp. 186-187; no. 466, p. 519.
ˣ *Ibid.*, Appendix II, p. 621. Spring Rice summed up this whole correspondence in a single sentence: "Russia has notified her intention of sending, when she pleases, her agents into Afghanistan." *Ibid.*, no. 466, p. 519.
ʸ *Ibid.*, no. 466, p. 520; II, no. 258, p. 223.
ᶻ *Ibid.*, no. 258, p. 223. Benckendorff's statement may have been quite true. The note was written in the name of the ministry for foreign affairs.

change for the better" in Anglo-Russian relations, which led
to the attempt late in 1903 to reach an understanding on the
"various questions outstanding" between the two nations, but
which was nipped by the outbreak of the Japanese war.[a] Advantage was taken by Great Britain of the war to send the
Dane mission to Kabul, where the old agreements made with
Habibullah's father were renewed without alterations by the
new treaty of 21 March 1905. After this the Amir paid the
first visit of his reign to India.[b] The Russian government was
helpless to oppose British activity, and must have accounted
itself lucky to obtain Lansdowne's assurance that no attempt
would be made to annex or occupy any Afghan territory, as
well as his approval of Benckendorff's "appropriate description" of Afghanistan as a "buffer state." In those days Russia
had to walk with "utmost circumspection" and deprecated any
raising of the whole Afghan problem.[c]

Russia was still in none too strong condition to bargain
effectively over Afghanistan during the negotiations for the
convention of 1907, yet nevertheless had a position which
could not be ignored, with a future potentiality for doing evil,
if not good, that made agreement preferable to rivalry. Actual
intercourse was limited chiefly to commercial exchanges between Russian traders and central Asiatic natives with the
Afghans, all of the business passing over the common frontier.
Despite the unqualified, false assertion of the government of
India in 1900 that "there had been no growth of trade," in
each of the ten years before the convention, except the revolutionary ones of 1905 and 1906, the volume of Russian trade
with Afghanistan increased.[d] Between 1901 and 1913 the

[a] *Ibid.*, no. 258, p. 222; IV, no. 183, p. 188.
[b] *Ibid.*, no. 466 (a), note 1, p. 520. Ronaldshay, II, 344-348. Habberton, pp.
74-75.
[c] *B. D.*, IV, no. 466 (a), pp. 520-521; no. 466 (b), p. 521. The tsar also, in
April 1905, favored "maintaining Afghanistan as a buffer state, but that there
were some arrangements necessary in order to enable the neighboring people
to live in amity with each other." *Ibid.*, no. 266, p. 288.
[d] The following table is compiled from the statistics in the *Obzor vnyeshney
torgovli Rossiy*, (1907), table V, p. 88; table VIII, p. 448.

Year	Exports to Afghanistan Value in rubles	Imports from Afghanistan Value in rubles
1898	727,637	2,208,974
1899	981,836	1,594,606

volume multiplied threefold, growing by leaps and bounds
after the convention was signed.[e] Of course, this trade with
Afghanistan was only a drop in the bucket in the world total
that Russia had, for in the years before the convention it
amounted to merely three-tenths of one percent of the whole,
which placed Afghanistan nineteenth in the list of nations that
traded with Russia.[f] Undeniably some indeterminable portion
of this commerce was bounty-fed, against which Great Britain
loudly complained. In 1907 Poklevsky-Kozell, who was temporarily in the foreign office at St. Petersburg, explained that
bounties were given only in the instance of sugar and petro-
leum, and his statement was at least not contradicted, possibly
also not believed.[g] Russian exports were overwhelmingly manufactured products and articles of metal, while sugar took first
rank among the foodstuffs that the natives purchased. There
was a steady trickle of raw materials and half finished goods imported from Russia, and meager supplies of livestock, although
for the years after 1903 this was completely stopped. In all the
years before the convention Russia imported more from Afghanistan than it sent. This crude land had few manufactures
to export, so the Russian trade was top-heavy with importations
of raw materials, as caracul, cotton, and wool, and of things
partly fabricated. Considerable livestock was bought from

1900	898,664	2,116,070
1901	1,196,829	2,951,809
1902	1,902,564	2,384,126
1903	2,031,024	2,993,009
1904	2,584,306	2,665,422
1905	2,327,876	2,527,411
1906	1,892,853	2,184,013
1907	2,197,535	2,940,787

[e] Reisner, *Krasny Arkhiv*, X, 60-61. In 1912 Russian exports to Afghanistan
reached 6,464,050 rubles, and imports from Afghanistan reached 5,381,398
rubles. *Obzor vnyeshney torgovli Rossiy*, (1912), table II, pp. 6-7.

[f] *Ibid.*, (1905), Introduction, table 4, p. 2; (1907), Introduction, table 10, p. 4.

[g] Sugar that cost 20 kopecks well within the Russian empire, after being
shipped into Afghanistan was sold in Herat for between 17 and 18 kopecks.
B. D., IV, no. 474, p. 528; see also no. 472, p. 526; no. 478, p. 534. Reisner,
Krasny Arkhiv, X, 61. It is amusing to note that Poklevsky, who was acting
for Izvolsky, asked Nicolson "what facilities were accorded to British Indian
traders in Afghanistan." Nicolson answered: "I really did not know, and that
I had telegraphed recently to enquire." No reply is reproduced. *B. D.*, IV,
no. 474, p. 528.

the Afghan herders, and some foodstuffs were taken.[h] All told, therefore, there was some decent justification for the contention that Russia's relation to Afghanistan had altered with time, and valid foundation for the demand that direct relations over frontier questions and matters of trade should be established.

The British interest in Afghanistan was only to a small extent economic, and the trade directly with Great Britain was always insignificant. Independent figures begin just before the convention when, of the total imports from Afghanistan, the amount of £3,108 was retained in the United Kingdom in 1905, but only to a value of £309 during 1906. In the year of the convention itself £281 worth of goods from Afghanistan was kept, but the first figures for British exports in that year were far higher than they were to be again before the world war. In 1907 Afghanistan was a British customer to the value of £76,575, all but £15 of which was spent for arms, ammunition and military stores, although the British government hoped the Afghans would never get much of these dangerous products.[i] The trade with India was certainly larger, sometimes being worth nearly half a million pounds sterling, but there is no reason to expect that much would be exchanged

[h] The text is based upon tables of statistics in the several volumes of the *Obzor vnyeshney torgovli Rossiy.* See also Reisner, *Krasny Arkhiv,* X, 60-61. To illustrate Russian trade with Afghanistan the figures for 1906 and 1907 are reproduced from the *Obzor vnyeshney torgovli Rossiy,* (1906) and (1907), table II, pp. 6-7.

A. Exports from Russia to Afghanistan:

		1906	1907
1.	Foodstuffs,	71,096 r.	120,922 r.
2.	Raw and half finished materials,	83,465	35,889
3.	Livestock,	....	....
4.	Manufactures,	1,738,292	2,040,724
	Totals,	1,892,853 r.	2,197,535 r.

B. Imports to Russia from Afghanistan:

		1906	1907
1.	Foodstuffs,	229,013 r.	366,904 r.
2.	Raw and half finished materials,	1,471,636	2,079,821
3.	Livestock,	452,543	465,631
4.	Manufactures,	30,821	28,431
	Totals,	2,184,013 r.	2,940,787 r.

[i] *Annual Statement,* (1909), II, table 11, p. 208; (1912), II, table 10, p. 272. All figures are rudimentary, and British imports are never itemized. No statistics appear until 1909.

between an impoverished country and one that was hopelessly backward. Real British interest in Afghanistan centered in the defence of India, in the broadest application of the expression. In a minor way this included the means of keeping the vexatious hill tribes confined inside the Afghan frontier. This annoyance had been partially checked before 1907, because previous punitive expeditions had exercised some salutary effect, while the creation of the Northwest Frontier Provinces and Kitchener's military rearrangements had produced a strong administration and an alert protection. The major British concern was to retain the control of Afghan external relations in order to keep all other powers, particularly Russia, from meddling inside Afghanistan, and consequently from sneaking closer to India.

This position, however, was also being changed by the circumstances of time. Russia had come much closer as a result of the assimilation of huge territories in central Asia, until it peeked directly into India over the Pamirs, as well as through the side door of Afghanistan. This new position had become so strong that the British government recognized that it "ensured to her a safe stepping stone for a fresh move." [j] The Russian notification of 1900 that direct relations on non-political subjects with Afghan officials were to be instituted, raised the whole question. The British were prepared to permit this intercourse, but with the distinct reservation that Russia would continue to hold Afghanistan as outside the sphere of its action, and that British control of Afghan foreign relations should be unmodified.[k] It was in connection with Afghanistan that the British military leaders most of all feared the danger of Russian action from the Turkestan steppes, with the dead ends of newly constructed railroads lying close to the threatened frontier. This alarm persisted despite the

---

[j] B. D., IV, no. 320, p. 363. "As [Russia] has advanced her influence has increased." (Ibid., p. 364.) Lately the progress of German influence in the Mohammedan east, the growth of Moslem military capability, and the occasional appearance of German agents in Kabul added to the British uneasiness. If this should incite an Afghan outburst against foreign tutelage, possibly a new Anglo-Afghan war could not be avoided. Reisner, Krasny Arkhiv, X, 59.
[k] B. D., IV, no. 181 (b), p. 185; no. 182, p. 186; no. 199, p. 213; no. 466 (a), p. 521.

absence of any overt act year after year, and the presence of tremendous natural barriers. So deeply had this become ingrained in the British imagination that it took more to remove it than Benckendorff's assurances of 1905 that an invasion of India was "only to be found in the most shallow brains of the military classes," or General Palitzin's admission in 1907 that "this of course was nonsense, and in fact, the idea of an invasion of India was a mere phantasy that had never been seriously entertained by responsible Russians."[1] Mere phantasy it may have been, but for years Russia had used military movements near the Afghan frontier as a means of exerting pressure upon Great Britain in the event of disagreements anywhere in the world.[m] Strangely enough, from about this same time, the Russians began to fear British aggression in central Asia, especially because British officers might reorganize and control the Amir's army and build him strategic railroads.[n] Russian and British positions in Afghanistan were more in a state of fluctuation and uncertainty on the eve of the convention of 1907 than anywhere else in Asia. It is no wonder that the attempts to get what each wanted, and what the other hated to concede, made this part the most disputatious of the whole reconciliation.

The conversations on Afghanistan were the last to be taken up, although Grey had authorized them on 7 September 1906.[o] Meanwhile Nicolson had sat upon his instructions during the winter's disappointments. When he heard that a council of ministers was to examine the question of an understanding with Great Britain, in February 1907, he was in favor of divulging the proposals on Afghanistan because of their moderate and conciliatory nature, in order to strengthen the position of those Russian officials in sympathy with the policy of agreement. The Russians, indeed, had wanted to

[1] *Ibid.*, no. 192, p. 200; no. 476, enclosure, p. 530. See also no. 243, p. 263.
[m] Izvolsky confessed that this was true; and sections of the Russian press regretted that this Damocles' sword, which had for so long been effective against Great Britain, should be shattered by the renewal of the Anglo-Japanese alliance in 1905. *Ibid.*, no. 172 (b), p. 179; no. 195, pp. 206-207. Reisner, *Krasny Arkhiv*, X, 56. Fraser, pp. 140-141.
[n] B. D., IV, no. 253, p. 275; no. 256, p. 278. Habberton, p. 68.
[o] B. D., IV, no. 341, p. 389.

know them because the Afghan question stood in close connection with the Persian; but Grey was unwilling to disclose
these essential demands before Russia had indicated the nature
of its stand respecting Persia.[p] The Russian draft on Persia
of 20 February made the prospect of eventual agreement sufficiently good to warrant the communication of the British
views on Afghanistan. On the 23rd Nicolson handed over a
draft paper for Izvolsky to consider, which was identical with
the instructions that had been sent from London the previous
September.[q] In advance of the discussions Nicolson seems to
have sincerely believed that it would not be difficult to win
Russian approval, except for the suppression of bounties to
their trade. He anticipated that the Russians, because of their
anxiety over British future actions, would press for some
admission that Great Britain would not attempt to improve
its position in Afghanistan further than existing treaties permitted. There might be some trouble in meeting this wish, but
Nicolson advised that the continuous course of the negotiations should not be interrupted.[r]

When he gave the paper containing the British views to
Izvolsky, Nicolson specially commented on the topics. He
reminded Izvolsky that on several occasions in the past the
Russian government had given assurance that Afghanistan
was outside its sphere of influence. The British government
was aware that some inconvenience existed in the absence of
direct communication between Russian and Afghan officials
over questions of a local and non-political nature, but this
question would be considered in making an agreement. Since
the Amir would have to give his consent to any arrangements, it would be necessary for the British to know in
detail what these would be, in order to approach the Amir
who was under British guidance in all his foreign relations. The essential substance of this formed the first two
points of the British views in the paper. The third item was

---

[p] *Ibid.*, no. 467, p. 522; no. 468, p. 523; no. 469, p. 523; no. 471, note 1, p.
525. Izvolsky, *Correspondance diplomatique*, I, 368.
[q] *B. D.*, IV, no. 390, p. 433; no. 472, enclosure and minute, p. 526.
[r] *Ibid.*, no. 470, p. 524; see also no. 388, pp. 430-431.

a requirement that Russia must send no agents into Afghanistan, whereupon Izvolsky asked exactly what was meant by "agents." Nicolson explained that the term comprised officials, officers, agents of all categories, and the like. A sore spot was touched in the fourth place when the British demanded that the "bounties in subsidies" given to Russian trade with Afghanistan be discontinued. Lastly, in some measure of recompense for discontinued bounties, Russian traders were to be accorded the same facilities in Afghanistan as were enjoyed by British and Indian traders, if the Amir consented. Again in reply to a request for the meaning of the expression "bounties in subsidies," Nicolson said that this dealt with "bounties in the shape of subsidies." Izvolsky made no further comment, but promised to supply the Russian views after he had studied those he had just received.[s]

Nearly a month passed without an indication of a Russian reply. When 20 March came, Nicolson told Izvolsky that he hoped soon to have the Russian proposals, but was filled with misgivings when Izvolsky was not ready, because "in respect to Afghanistan the matter was not in his hands, but was being studied by others." From these indications he telegraphed to London his fear that the Russian proposals would prove unacceptable, while the foreign office determined to "be stiff about Afghanistan."[t] It was clear enough upon what grounds the difficulty could be expected. Izvolsky revealed that there might be a proposal to permit commercial agents in Afghanistan, and that some security would be wanted against the possibility of British officers organizing the Amir's army, or assisting him in the construction of strategic railroads, which could transform that country "from a 'buffer state' into an *avant-garde* of the Indian empire."[u] A few days later Poklevsky asked Nicolson directly how far the British government would be able to reassure the Russian government on this point, but Nicolson had no authority to promise more

[s] *Ibid.*, no. 472, and enclosure, pp. 525-526.
[t] *Ibid.*, no. 473, and minute, p. 527; no. 474, and note 1, p. 528.
[u] *Ibid.*, no. 473, p. 527.

than that any suggestions would be well considered.[v] Thus all of March and April passed with no Russian proposals: the general staff was examining the question; Izvolsky was discussing the subject of bounties with the minister of commerce; an interdepartmental committee was to consider the Afghan negotiations on 14/27 April, and then proposals could probably be expected a few days later.[w] Nicolson regretted the delay because the main points respecting Tibet and Persia appeared settled. Furthermore the conversations had attracted the attention of the press, which printed the misinformation that was "oozing out," so that the quicker all matters could be concluded the better it would be.[x] At last, on 6 May, Izvolsky told Nicolson that he was sincerely doing his best to push matters along. He had secured the assent of all the interested ministers to the essential proposals, which would probably be in accord with the British views. No attempt was being made to delay the agreement, but the full concurrence of the other departments was necessary to arrange anything durable, so he feared that a little more time would be required. Although Nicolson confessed his disappointment, he had to be content to wait.[y] Only on 15 May were the Russian views on Afghanistan transmitted.

That May afternoon Izvolsky handed over with fulsome comment a draft convention which embodied the entire Russian position on Afghanistan. He read it over with Nicolson and referred to his "really hard fight" to overcome the conflicting views in the government. Its broad principles, he now trusted, corresponded fairly accurately with the British views,

[v] *Ibid.*, no. 474, p. 528. Grey noted: "We should I imagine be able to give the assurance suggested by M. Poklevsky." (*Ibid.*, minutes, p. 529.) The British military attaché deduced from his farewell visits to General Palitzin, chief of the general staff, and to General Polivanov, assistant to the minister for war, that "Russia is really anxious to guarantee herself from any hostile action on the part of Afghanistan, goaded on by ourselves, and from any insidious advances that we may make under cover of Afghanistan whether for purposes of offence or of defence." (*Ibid.*, no. 476, enclosure, pp. 530-532.) Grey was also "convinced that the apprehension of the Russians that we might adopt an aggressive policy against them in central Asia is a real one on their part." *Ibid.*, minute, p. 532.
[w] *Ibid.*, no. 474, p. 528; no. 475, p. 529; no. 476, p. 529.
[x] *Ibid.*, no. 473, p. 527; no. 474, pp. 528-529.
[y] *Ibid.*, no. 477, p. 533.

particularly in the second article where Russia formally recognized that Afghanistan was outside its sphere of influence, and engaged to use British intermediation for all political relations. Nicolson replied that he "was sure this would be fully recognized at home." [z] This Russian draft started off with a preamble which explained the desire for an Afghan agreement in order to assure the perfect security of the frontiers with each power, and to maintain there a solid and lasting peace.[a] With only minor changes this preamble found its way into the final convention. The first article expressed a wish very dear to the Russians, namely, that Afghanistan should form a buffer state between the possessions of the two contracting parties. After the second article, already noticed, had accorded an important principle in favor of Great Britain, the third veered sharply back to the Russian side. The engagement was proposed that Great Britain should neither annex nor occupy any part of Afghanistan or its dependencies, (an expression which mightily puzzled the British),[b] nor interfere in the internal affairs of the country. Further, the British government was to undertake not to exercise its influence in Afghanistan except in a pacific interest, neither itself to take, nor to encourage Afghanistan to take, any military measures which could be considered a menace to the Russian frontier. The fourth article contained an engagement on the part of Russia to send no agents into Afghanistan qualified, however, by the explanation that if the development of Russian commerce in the future should demonstrate the advantage of commercial agents in the country, the Russian government would enter into an exchange of views with Great Britain. Yet the following article expressed a balancing provision for the establishment of direct relations for the settlement of non-political, local questions between the

[z] Nicolson pointed out to the foreign office: "It should be borne in mind that the Russian government have made a great departure from the attitude that they had hitherto maintained in formally acknowledging that Russia must treat with the Amir only through the intermediary of His Majesty's government and in engaging not to despatch agents into Afghanistan." *Ibid.*, no. 478, pp. 534-535.
[a] The text of the Russian draft convention is printed in the first column in *ibid.*, no. 483, pp. 541-544. Nicolson's comments are in no. 478, pp. 534-535.
[b] *Ibid.*, no. 481, pp. 537-538.

Russian and Afghan authorities of the frontier provinces specially designated for that purpose. Touching indirectly on the subject of bounties, the Russian government alternately explained and promised that it had not used in the past and would not use in the future special favors in the Russian trade with Afghanistan, except such as were or would be generally applied to all Russian exports to whatever country. The Russian draft wound up with a still more complex seventh article designed to insure equal facilities to Russian trade and merchants in Afghanistan. In all matters of duties, internal taxes, and other relations, the Russians were to stand on the same footing and enjoy the same privileges as British and Indian traders did, or should at any future time. It was understood that a uniform customs tariff should be established along the whole Afghan frontier; but how this was to be accomplished inside an internally independent sovereignty the Russian draft left entirely to the imagination.

Much of this draft was acceptable to London, yet after careful consideration and consultation with the India office such changes were made that the British counterdraft turned out to be a very different document.[c] Grey emphasized to Benckendorff that he was favorably impressed with the Russian draft, but that there would eventually be some alterations to make.[d] The British government accepted the preamble without question because it was inoffensive, as well as the second article which renewed the Russian pledge that Afghanistan was outside of its influence; but to all the rest there were many observations and changes made.[e] The Russian desire to see Afghanistan remain a buffer state was understood, and there was no intention to go back on Lansdowne's approval of it as an appropriate description. Neither Hardinge nor Grey, however, knew exactly what the term implied, so this whole

[c] The government of India was particularly rabid in its views over Afghanistan, so most of the consultation with Indian authorities took place with the India office. "Recently we have left the gov[ernmen]t of India entirely out of our account, and questions which have arisen have been treated directly between us [the foreign office] and the India office." *Ibid.*, no. 274, p. 294.

[d] *Ibid.*, no. 480, p. 536.

[e] *Ibid.*, no. 481, p. 537.

article was to be deleted from the British reply, although some reference to Afghanistan's geographical situation "as an intervening state between British and Russian territory" might be alluded to, perhaps in the preamble, if Russia insisted upon any reference.[f] The engagement suggested in the Russian third article, that Great Britain should neither annex nor occupy Afghan territory, was held to be dangerous, because it was more than could be promised. There was also no intention to repudiate the assurance given in 1905 by Lansdowne that Great Britain had no expectation "of appropriating Afghan territory or of interfering in the internal affairs of the country." The difficulty hung upon the one word "occupy" of the Russian proposal.[g] Grey had told Benckendorff early in April 1907 that Afghanistan was looked upon as a source of danger to British security in India, especially if its military potency should improve. This had been held in mind a few years before when military reforms were being carried out in India, while British opinion attached considerable importance to Afghanistan remaining isolated and inaccessible.[h] It also appeared that Izvolsky's first proposals had caused King Edward heartaches, and that he was insisting that British hands should not be tied in relations with the Amir.[i] Consequently the British intended to qualify that part of the engagement not to "occupy" any Afghan territory, simply because if an unfriendly Amir should break his treaty agreements with Great Britain, or incite some of his wild tribesmen to raid in British preserves, another expedition to Kabul might become a temporary necessity. There would, on the other hand, be no objection to engage not to "annex" any portion of Afghanistan.[j] So far as concerned that part of the fourth article

[f] *Ibid.*, no. 478, minutes, p. 535; no. 479, p. 536; no. 481, p. 537; no. 484, p. 545.

[g] *Ibid.*, no. 466 (a), p. 521; no. 478, minutes, p. 535; no. 480, p. 537.

[h] Reisner, *Krasny Arkhiv*, X, 57. Benckendorff relayed this to Izvolsky in a despatch of 5 April 1907. No corresponding reference is in the *B. D.*

[i] Lee, II, 570.

[j] *B. D.*, IV, no. 481, pp. 537-538. The British therefore included in their counterdraft a sentence about the treaty signed by the Dane mission in Kabul in 1905. The Russians were asked to make the engagement bilateral by also promising not to annex or to occupy any part of Afghanistan. *Ibid.*, no. 484, p. 545.

which opened the way for the presence of Russian commercial agents in Afghanistan in the future, Izvolsky had explained that this additional clause was inserted to forestall objections, but that it was quite harmless, likely to remain inoperative in practice. If such a contingency ever should arise, the two governments had merely to exchange views, which did not even imply that Great Britain needed to consent to such agents being sent. Because of this declaration, the British foreign office made no objection, but simply reworded its draft to entail the necessity of agreement, rather than of an exchange of views, on the measures to be taken.[k]

The last three Russian draft articles dealing primarily with commercial matters were even less acceptable, mostly because they raised the question of the Amir's consent on internal affairs, for which Great Britain could assume no guarantee. To some of the proposals the British raised no objections, and would so inform the Amir, but the commercial stipulations as a whole would have to be phrased more vaguely.[l] Where Izvolsky had equivocated on the subject of bounties to Russian trade in his sixth article, this was rejected because it implied the right to favor that intercourse with the same old system which was considered to be one of bounties.[m] For the contents of the fifth and seventh articles, that there should be direct communication between Russian and Afghan officials on local, non-political questions along the frontier; that Russians should be accorded all trading facilities enjoyed by British and Indian traders in Afghanistan at any time, and that a universal customs tariff should apply at all frontiers, these were all of such a positive character that they would tie the Amir's hands. He must himself consent to be bound, and since he was independent in internal affairs, Great Britain could not compel his sanction. Izvolsky understood this, but since Russia promised by the convention to have no direct relations with the Amir, Great Britain must be the one to arrange these details. A passive

k *Ibid.*, no. 478, p. 534; no. 481, p. 538; Editors' Note, p. 541.
l *Ibid.*, no. 478, minutes, p. 535.
m *Ibid.*, no. 481, p. 538. No substitute provisions, however, were inserted in the British counterdraft, from which the Russian article was dropped.

attitude on the part of the latter would not satisfy Russia; something positive would have to be done to the benefit of Russia. Nicolson granted the force of these observations and promised that the British government would try to discover a satisfactory phraseology.[n] The foreign and India offices recognized the advisability of doing something effective, so that Russia would not otherwise endeavor to obtain the objects it desired in its own way, because "we can hardly with reason claim to have sole control of the foreign relations of Afghanistan if we fail to put before the Amir, and to endeavor to obtain his consent to, arrangements which have been agreed upon between the British and Russian gov[ernmen]ts."[o] This was not easy to acccomplish because a wording was required which would convince Russia that Great Britain was not evading its responsibilities, yet which would consider the susceptibilities of the Amir. Any wording must avoid definitely committing this jealous oriental, so that there would be no need "to obtain his acceptance of the provisions of this instrument before proceeding to its signature, a formality the accomplishment of which would entail a very considerable delay." Every consideration was shown for him, so far as concerned his internal administration, by making the Russian proposals dependent upon his eventual consent.[p] When satisfactory wordings were found to overcome all these difficulties, the British counterdraft was delivered to Izvolsky on 17 June 1907.

In the British text the whole form of the convention was recast, so that it really represented a fresh start.[q] The preamble remained essentially the same, while the first article repeated the Russian recognition of Afghanistan as outside its sphere of influence, with all political relations to be conducted through the intermediation of Great Britain. The further undertaking not to send any agents into the country was now included here. The long, verbose second article contained an innovation where, to match the Tibetan arrangement, refer-

[n] *Ibid.*, no. 478, pp. 534-535.
[o] *Ibid.*, Editors' Note, p. 541.
[p] *Ibid.*, no. 481, p. 538; Editors' Note, p. 541.
[q] *Ibid.*, no. 484, and enclosure, pp. 545-546. The text of the British counterdraft is printed in the second column in *ibid.*, no. 483, pp. 541-544.

ence was made to the British position in Afghanistan by virtue
of its treaty relations. Then followed the engagement not to
alter the *status quo* in Afghanistan, and the reassurance to
Russia that Great Britain would take no measures in that
country, nor encourage it to take any, that could threaten the
Russian frontier in central Asia. At the end of the article the
British project included a similar renunciation on the part of
Russia in order to make the undertaking bilateral.[r] The
British third article was to permit "Russian and Afghan
authorities on the frontier specially designated for the purpose" to have direct relations with each other in settling non-
political local questions "when the consent of the Amir shall
have been obtained by H[is] M[ajesty's] gov[ernmen]t and
communicated to the Russian gov[ernmen]t by them." "Due
regard being had to the Amir's sovereign powers" conditioned
the fourth and last article of the British counterdraft, wherein
both contracting parties affirmed "their adherence to the principle of equality of commercial opportunity," so that any
facilities which had been, or might thereafter be obtained by
British and British-Indian traders should also be enjoyed by
the Russians. If the future progress of commercial relations
established the need of commercial agents in Afghanistan, then
the two governments were to agree on the measures to be
taken.[s]

This was undoubtedly a formidable, clearly reasoned document, essentially fair, yet containing much that would cause
the Russian government to reflect upon, particularly in the

[r] This article read: "The British government having recorded in the treaty
signed at Kabul on the 21st March, 1905, that they recognize the agreement
and the engagements concluded with the late Amir Abdur Rahman, and that
they have no desire to interfere in the internal government of his territories,
Great Britain engages not to annex or to occupy in contravention of that treaty
any portion of Afghanistan or to interfere in the internal administration of the
country, provided that the Amir fulfils the engagements already contracted
towards His Majesty's government under the abovementioned treaty. Great
Britain further undertakes to exercise her influence in Afghanistan only in a
pacific sense towards Russia, and will not herself take in Afghanistan, or
encourage Afghanistan to take, any measures threatening the Russian frontier.
On the other hand, the Russian government undertake not to annex or to occupy
any part of Afghanistan, or to take any measures involving interference with
the internal government of the territories of the Amir." *Ibid.*, no. 483, pp.
542-543.
   [s] *Ibid.*, pp. 543-544.

second article. Nicolson therefore tried to reassure Izvolsky by recommending it highly, with trust and belief that "the desiderata of the Russian government had been met." He also stressed "the earnest desire" of the British "that no time should now be lost in terminating all our conventions." Because this project had been altered most by changes in arrangement and drafting, Nicolson professed to see no reason for long delays. Izvolsky promised to do his best, but there were others to consult, which probably meant the dreaded general staff along with the ministers of commerce and finance. This made Izvolsky's observations "distinctly not encouraging as to the period which would elapse" before a reply would come. It was most disconcerting to have him "not deny that we had preserved the 'grandes lignes', but that the whole 'économie' of the project had been altered." [t] How greatly that "économie" had been disturbed, the next two months of intricate conversations fully revealed.

Of course some things were quickly settled and pushed out of the way. Other points gave rise to doubts which postponed the progress of the negotiations. After two weeks had passed without any reply to the British counterdraft, nor with one in sight for another week or ten days, Nicolson told Izvolsky of his inability to "understand what difficulties could exist in the way of accepting our proposals." [u] Izvolsky explained that no objections were found against the elimination of articles, nor the rearrangement of others, nor the mention of the treaty obligations of the Amir to Great Britain. What really was wrong Nicolson practically had to worm out of Izvolsky, when three subjects turned out to be troubling the Russian government. The least important appeared on the surface to be a quibble of words concerned with the direct relations of Russian and Afghan officials at the frontier. The Russian expression for these officials ran in terms of "the authorities of the frontier provinces," which the British rendered simply as the "authorities on the frontier." Of more importance, however, was the Russian complaint over the references to the Amir.

[t] *Ibid.*, no. 484, pp. 545-546.
[u] *Ibid.*, no. 486, p. 547.

On this score Izvolsky distinguished that the British counter-draft

had made all the engagements by which Russia might benefit, such as the frontier relations and trade, dependent on the consent of the Amir, while all the obligations which Russia took upon herself were to become operative immediately the convention was signed.

The third difficulty was to prove the most perverse, and had to do with the British attempt to make a bilateral engagement out of the obligation neither to annex nor to occupy any portion of Afghanistan. Izvolsky properly pointed out that this had been made an unconditional one upon Russia, at the same time that the British made theirs dependent upon whether or not the Amir lived up to his treaty promises.[v] Izvolsky supported his contention with logical and weighty arguments, sometimes becoming "a little excited," yet "always courteous and friendly."[w] Nicolson saw much of the justification for Izvolsky's stand, and realized that the minister himself was not causing the trouble, but was being harrassed by the Russian general staff. What dissatisfied Nicolson most was the thinly concealed "desire to place Russia on exactly the same footing as ourselves in respect to Afghanistan." Yet this equality was precisely what Great Britain intended to prevent, if there should be a convention at all.[x]

In the discussions during the first half of July the reasons became clearer why Russia wanted the direct relations with Afghanistan carried on through "the authorities of the frontier provinces." These officials, Izvolsky asserted, were the proper ones to whom to entrust the "discharge of the duties foreshadowed," whereas mere "authorities on the frontier" would be subalterns, not competent for these tasks. To Nicol-

[v] *Ibid.*, no. 486, pp. 547-548; see also no. 485, p. 547. Here Izvolsky mumbled something "as to the desirability of holding over certain points to be arranged subject to the signing of the conventions." Nicolson thought there might be something in this. Nothing more was done with it.

[w] *Ibid.*, no. 486, p. 549; no. 490, p. 552.

[x] *Ibid.*, no. 486, p. 548; no. 487, p. 549; no. 490, p. 552. Lee, II, 570. Izvolsky once remarked that Great Britain "apparently wished to restrict relations between Russian and Afghan officials within very narrow limits," to which Nicolson quickly rejoined that "certainly we did so intend." *B. D.*, IV, no. 487, p. 549.

son's way of thinking the foreshadowed duties related to such trifling matters as horse thievery and sheep stealing, while Izvolsky was sure that the questions to be settled would be of wider scope.[y] It was this that the British intended to prevent, although even the wording "authorities on the frontier" was bad enough, because it opened the door "to intervention by Russian officials in the affairs of Afghanistan and we have to rely upon the good faith of Russian authorities to see that the provision is not improperly used." While it was understood in London that the Russian description was a proper one for their authorities, since Benckendorff and Lansdowne had talked about them in 1905 as "frontier officials" the British wording remained entirely consistent, so that Nicolson was advised to express the hope that it would be accepted to avoid any further argument.[z] Izvolsky also insisted upon his objections against making all the benefits that Russia might obtain rest upon the consent of the Amir. If he did not consent, every Russian advantage was destroyed, which was a very one-sided, strange and inconvenient bargain. The British attitude, correctly enough, was founded on the inability to bind the Amir to any obligations in his internal affairs, wherein he retained his independence of thought and action, which Great Britain desired and intended to preserve. The British promised that pressure would be put upon him to obtain that consent, and Russia should now rely upon British good faith to secure the stipulated benefits.[a] This was too intangible to satisfy Izvolsky, who came up with the idea that he would have to propose an additional article which would make the convention valid only after the consent of the Amir had been extracted; for by this method Russian gains would not remain illusory.[b]

Where Nicolson expected to encounter the greatest difficulty was with the bilateral engagement neither to annex nor to occupy Afghanistan, for here the Russian and British posi-

[y] *Ibid.*, no. 486, p. 548; no. 487, p. 549.
[z] *Ibid.*, no. 487, minute, p. 550; no. 489, p. 551.
[a] *Ibid.*, no. 486, p. 548; no. 488, p. 550; no. 489, p. 551.
[b] *Ibid.*, no. 490, p. 552; no. 491, enclosure, p. 553. This suggestion by Izvolsky became the fifth article of the final treaty.

tions were sharply separated. Izvolsky was entirely unwilling
to have this obligation binding upon Russia so long as Great
Britain would only assume it conditionally upon the Amir
living up to his treaty promises. Because Great Britain alone
assumed to be judge in the matter, and could therefore proceed at any moment to occupy or even annex the country, this
would change the existing situation there, as well as throughout central Asia. Consequently Izvolsky saw the necessity for
a "saving clause," that the Russian engagement held good
while no change occurred in the actual state of things in
Afghanistan.[c] Yet both Hardinge and Grey found such a
proposal "quite inadmissible." [d] Russia could no more be
allowed to avoid an unconditional undertaking than Great
Britain could assume one. A pledge not to occupy or annex
Afghanistan by Great Britain would free the Amir from his
chief fear and incentive to keep his treaty obligations, while
it would in turn rob the British of the best means of exerting
pressure upon him, even in the event of a dispute between him
and Russia. No "intolerable provocation" was expected from
the Amir, and no contingency was anticipated that would require a forceful intervention in Afghanistan. Once again
Izvolsky "must trust us not to make use of force except in
last resort;" but Izvolsky insisted on some sort of saving
clause.[e] Each side held its ground tenaciously until Nicolson
conceded that in his conversations with Izvolsky "we practically went over old ground and made no headway." [f] By 14
July Izvolsky agreed that it would be better for Nicolson to
"run over to London" to consult with the foreign office. Six
days later Izvolsky gave Nicolson his full views in a memorandum, which Nicolson sent on ahead of his own arrival.[g]

Nearly a month passed before Nicolson returned to St.
Petersburg and communicated the British answer to Izvolsky.
While home Nicolson had consulted with those members of
the government more directly interested in the negotiations,

[c] *Ibid.*, no. 487, p. 549; no. 490, p. 552; no. 491, enclosure, p. 553.
[d] *Ibid.*, no. 487, minute, p. 550.
[e] *Ibid.*, no. 488, p. 550; no. 489, p. 551; no. 490, p. 552.
[f] *Ibid.*, no. 490, p. 552.
[g] *Ibid.*, no. 490, note 1, p. 551; no. 491, enclosure, pp. 553-554.

296 THE ANGLO-RUSSIAN CONVENTION OF 1907

and they had unmistakably profitted from his presence, because
the proposals drawn up after the consultations reflected a
laudable moderation of the stiff British attitude.[h] Nicolson
read the memorandum, which contained all that was possible
for his government to grant towards meeting the wishes of
Russia, to Izvolsky on 12 August. Here, on a minor point,
for giving up the ambiguous expression of "buffer state" in
reference to Afghanistan, and modelling after similar words
in the Anglo-French declaration of 1904 relating to Egypt
and Morocco, the British government was willing to declare
that it had "no intention of altering the political status of
Afghanistan." With regard to the direct relations between
frontier officials, the British excellently explained that the
main purpose was to secure the special designation of a limited
number of Russian and Afghan officials residing either
on the frontier or in the frontier provinces to be duly
authorized to enter into direct relations. A small number
would insure two desirable advantages: the Amir would
be less upset by the new situation, while other difficulties would not be created by the interchange of letters between
any unauthorized persons. The British government proved
entirely conciliatory over the necessity of the Amir's consent
in order to win the benefits of the treaty due Russia. It would
lose no time, once the convention was signed, in acquainting
the Amir with what was desired of him. Izvolsky's suggested
additional article, providing that the convention would not
come into force before Russia was informed that the Amir
had consented, was accepted. Even toward the Russian
objections to subscribing to an unconditional undertaking not
to occupy or annex any part of Afghanistan, the British position softened. Considering that this contingency was met
adequately by the Russian declaration that Afghanistan lay
outside its sphere of influence, it was suggested that this engagement on the part of Russia could be left out of the con-

[h] *Ibid.*, no. 493, p. 556. Grey, I, 159-160. Hardinge and Grey feared that
"this Afghan convention is . . . likely to give trouble and may require some
straight talking." *B. D.*, IV, no. 487, minute, p. 550; see also no. 274, pp. 294-
295.

vention.[1] If this apparent concession proved insufficient, Nicolson had an "alternative solution" to propose. This envisaged the retention of the British conditional and the Russian unconditional obligations in the second article, which was then to be supplemented by this sentence: "Should any change occur in the political status of Afghanistan, the two governments will enter into a friendly interchange of views on the subject."[j]

Nicolson hoped that these generous proposals would permit the winding up of the negotiations in "a very few days," for there now seemed to be no obstacles in the way. Indeed Izvolsky did remark that "certainly a great step had been made towards an agreement," and that Nicolson "could rely with confidence on his doing his utmost to push matters on." He would require a little time for his habitually careful study, while the tsar, at the moment engaged with the military manoeuvers, would require a little longer still.[k] After his careful study, in an informal talk Izvolsky explained why the deletion of the Russian engagement not to annex or to occupy Afghanistan did not remove Russian objections. Russia was thoroughly tied down already by its recognition that Afghanistan was outside its sphere of influence, but Great Britain still could, under certain conditions, take measures there that would change the entire situation. Izvolsky accordingly remarked that "contractual obligations taken in regard to an object cannot remain in full force if a change occurs in the object." He had a realistic reason for demanding a more equitable solution, for:

At present Russia was quite free to do as she liked with regard to Afghanistan: of course it would be an unfriendly act but it would not be a violation of any obligations. After [the] signature of [the] convention her position would be quite different and she would be closely bound.

To even things up he had two solutions to offer: either to insert an additional article to provide that the two govern-

---

[i] *Ibid.,* no. 492, enclosure, pp. 554-556.
[j] *Ibid.,* no. 492, p. 554.
[k] *Ibid.,* no. 493, p. 556. Nicolson reported that Izvolsky's "first impressions were distinctly favorable." Grey later wrote that "Izvolsky would not have it at first." Grey, I, 160.

ments would exchange views if the situation in Afghanistan was altered, or for him to send a despatch to Benckendorff, to be published with the convention, "saying that if the political situation were changed Russia was freed from her obligations."[1]

Nicolson made it perfectly clear that the latter solution "would never do," but gave no indication that he had been authorized to make a concession in keeping with the former.[m] Izvolsky hastened to complete a new Afghan draft treaty, which he presented to Nicolson on 19 August, a day sooner than he had planned. This draft was almost a complete summary of the existing state of the negotiations, the only important innovation in which was the introduction of a new article, the sixth, to provide for any future change in the position of Afghanistan and the Russian obligations in that event. In Izvolsky's wording it read:

If any modification whatever occurs in the political status of Afghanistan, the high contracting parties will enter into a friendly interchange of views with the object of insuring the maintenance of the equilibrium in central Asia.

This differed in some respects from the British formulation which Nicolson had in reserve, but had not yet disclosed. Izvolsky explained that his reference to central Asia was to avoid any impression that "Russia wished to interfere with the relations between Great Britain and Afghanistan."[n] Nicolson tried hard to prevent the insertion of the article, but Izvolsky declared that without it Russia could not sign the convention. The British government, for its part, would not

---

[1] *B. D.,* IV, no. 494. p. 557. Nicolson explained what Izvolsky "was driving at" in holding out for a friendly exchange of views, if Great Britain ever altered the political status of Afghanistan, in a later despatch. "Russia could not possibly view with indifference the establishment of the forces of Great Britain or of British administration in close propinquity to the Russian frontier or in occupation of strategical positions in Afghanistan." *Ibid.,* no. 504, p. 563.

[m] Because Izvolsky had spoken privately, and would officially explain in three days' time, Nicolson used the interval to perfect a few details with the foreign office, because Izvolsky would then desire to lose no more time in prolonged discussions or in references home. *Ibid.,* no. 494, p. 557; no. 493, p. 558.

[n] *Ibid.,* no. 497, p. 559; no. 498, pp. 559-560; no. 499, p. 560. There is definite indication that Nicolson had talked over this formula with Izvolsky before he went to London in July. *Ibid.,* no. 494, and note 1, p. 557.

accept Izvolsky's wording; it was so ambiguous that it could admit of unforeseen demands and complications, while the word "whatever" simply could not be used. Nicolson was instructed to ask Izvolsky to use the British formula for the additional article.[o]

In his correspondence with the foreign office in London, Nicolson agreed that it was essential that nothing should be done to weaken the special position of Great Britain in Afghanistan. Izvolsky's recent remark that Russia was restrained from taking any action, whether diplomatic or otherwise, by the engagements assumed in the first article of the British June counterdraft, impressed Nicolson. He therefore suggested that British prestige might actually be enhanced by permitting Russia not to take the unconditional obligation, which would indicate that there was no fear of the possibility that Russia might wish to intervene in Afghanistan. Since the British government had already recognized the truth of Izvolsky's remark, Nicolson thought it would be safe to give up the unconditional engagement on the part of Russia, while the British qualified engagement could be retained, with the formula for consultation inserted in a separate article.[p] To this solution Grey would not agree, and Nicolson was authorized to propose that both the British and the Russian engagements should be totally suppressed; or, if the formula were to be retained, then also both engagements must be expressed in the second article; or, to leave out the Russian engagement and also the formula for the separate article.[q] Nicolson at once called upon Izvolsky to submit these proposals, who received them with "very evident pleasure." He personally leaned toward the suppression of both obligations, but promised an official reply after he had consulted the tsar.[r]

Izvolsky was with the emperor on the evening of 22 August, and late that night wrote Nicolson a letter to tell him how happy he was to recommend the acceptance of the British

[o] *Ibid.*, no. 497, p. 559; no. 502, p. 561.
[p] *Ibid.*, no. 496, p. 558; no. 500, p. 561.
[q] *Ibid.*, no. 496, p. 558; no. 501, p. 561; no. 508, pp. 566, 567.
[r] *Ibid.*, no. 505, pp. 563-564; no. 508, pp. 566, 567.

offer to his colleagues, but that his definite answer must wait until after a council of ministers, to be held on the evening of the 24th, had approved. On the 23rd Nicolson found Izvolsky "quite sanguine" as to the outcome, while on the next day, as they collated the French texts to be sent to London, his only anxiety was whether British approval would come in time to sign the convention on the last day of the month. That evening the council was held, but strong opposition suddenly developed. Izvolsky argued until "he was hoarse," yet when the council broke up around two of the morning, he was in the minority, the chairman, P. A. Stolypin, and one military member alone on his side. The emperor's approval had been given with the reservation that the ministers must unanimously accept the whole convention. There was nothing for Izvolsky to do except to summon Nicolson "very early on Sunday morning the 25th" to explain, much perturbed, how the ministers had muddied the waters.[s] That afternoon Nicolson had a telegram on the way to London, breaking the bad news with the laconic sentence: "An unexpected and serious hitch has occurred."[t] The trouble had come on two counts. Of lesser seriousness was the objection raised by the minister of commerce that the words "equality of commercial treatment" in the article on trade relations did not necessarily imply equality of customs duties. To cover this failure a note from Nicolson to Izvolsky was wanted which would clear up this doubt. The real difficulty lay in the other demand of the majority, that Great Britain should assume the qualified obligation neither to annex nor to occupy any portion of Afghanistan, while Russia took no engagement, yet with the formula to hold friendly conversations in the event of any change occurring in the political position of the country retained in a separate article.[u]

Izvolsky recounted how he had been set upon in the council for having yielded too much, and that he was surprised at the tenacity with which the opposition had been maintained. He attributed the opposition to dislike of his foreign policy

[s] *Ibid.*, no. 508, pp. 566-567.
[t] *Ibid.*, no. 506, p. 564. Nicolson, p. 254.
[u] *B. D.*, IV, no. 506, p. 564.

in general, but particularly to the recent agreements with Japan. The animosity was "largely directed against him personally and . . . not in reality concerned with the merits of the case." To overcome the critical situation in the most satisfactory way, he urged that the British government should accede to the wishes of the majority of the council. Otherwise Izvolsky must wait upon the tsar, lay before him the divergence of opinion, and take the emperor's pleasure. The emperor's pleasure might be the acceptance of the views of the minority, which would insure signature; yet this would leave the majority dissatisfied, and liable to hinder the smooth execution of the convention. Should Nicholas go along with the majority, then not only would the entire convention be sacrificed, but Izvolsky would inevitably have to relinquish his portfolio. Nicolson promised to refer everything to his government, but offered no hope of its favorable decision. He did Izvolsky the personal justice of reporting that "it is not necessary to argue with him, as he is of our opinion." [v]

On 27 August Nicolson returned with an *aide-mémoire* which recited that the British government was "much disappointed that an unexpected difficulty has arisen when the negotiations were apparently on the eve of being happily concluded." While eager to meet the views of the Russian government, nevertheless it would be impossible to go further than the alternatives already proposed. The explanatory note on the equality of tariff duties was refused "not only because it is superfluous, but also because it might imply an obligation on the Amir to draw up a complete tariff." Then, for the first time in the course of the negotiations, Grey pointed out for Izvolsky's benefit that something more than an Asiatic settlement would be lost, if the reconciliation between the two nations fell through. No doubt this was well perceived, even if not previously mentioned by Izvolsky, but Grey first delicately phrased this best of all possible gains that must have lurked concealed in the consciousness of many minds:

His Majesty's government sincerely trust that the Imperial Russian

[v] *Ibid.*, no. 506, pp. 564-565; no. 508, pp. 567-568. Nicolson, p. 254.

government will appreciate that larger issues are indirectly at stake than those directly involved in these agreements, for it has throughout been the expectation and the belief of His Majesty's government that an agreement as to their respective interests in Asia, if executed in a friendly manner, would so influence the disposition of public opinion in Great Britain as to make friendly relations possible on questions which may arise elsewhere in the future. Without such an agreement this expectation must be disappointed.[w]

This was the final exhortation for an agreement with Russia, and the British trust in the appreciation of the larger issues by the Russian government was well-founded.

The first reaction of Izvolsky to the British reply was one of deep dismay, for he thought it was the end of things. He cordially agreed with the reasoning upon the additional advantages possible to be derived elsewhere, but he regretted that the answer had not accepted the solution of the majority of the council on the engagements respecting Afghanistan. It would have helped if he could have received a private, explanatory note to show to the minister of commerce, interpreting the phrase "equality of commercial treatment" to include uniform duties, as that would indicate to his colleagues that "he had not failed all along the line." Nicolson argued a long time on this point, and told him that a statement in the British memorandum recognized that his objection was satisfied by the very term "equality of treatment." Izvolsky still thought it could be otherwise, nor did he agree that the unsigned memorandum was the equal of an explanatory note. Nicolson succeeded in cheering him up enough that he promised to do his best to win the consent of the council to one of the British alternatives which had been proposed.[x] On the morning of the 28th Izvolsky was in better spirits, and employés of his office were busily occupied preparing the documents for signature. A final decision would be made that afternoon by the council of ministers which, if favorable, would allow the signature to take place on Saturday the 31st. Once more he came back to the commercial question, because

[w] B. D., IV, no. 507, p. 565; no. 510, enclosure, p. 571.
[x] Ibid., no. 509, pp. 568-569; no. 510, pp. 569-570.

the minister of commerce was not satisfied. If Nicolson could write a note, neither for publication nor for inclusion in the convention, which should state that Great Britain interpreted the expression of "equality of treatment" as including equal duties, he would render a great service. Nicolson himself was not opposed, and recommended that the foreign office gratify Izvolsky's harmless wish.[y]

Everything turned out happily on the night of the 28th after the council had been held, because after a long discussion it approved the Afghan convention. The alternative which it accepted suppressed the Russian unconditional promise neither to occupy nor to annex any part of Afghanistan, excluded the additional article by which Great Britain agreed to enter into an exchange of views if any change was caused in the political status, and retained only the British conditional engagement. The texts were submitted for the tsar's approval on the 29th, so that the signatures could be affixed on the 31st.[z] Izvolsky received partial compensation when Nicolson gave him the explanatory note which he had requested to satisfy the objection raised against the commercial equality provision, which once Nicolson said was "ridiculous" and the British government "superfluous," but which Bompard, Nicolson's French colleague, "who is an expert in such matters," thought deserved some addition to imply the inclusion of equal customs duties.[a] At last Nicolson could write to Grey that "the negotiations

[y] *Ibid.*, no. 510, p. 570.

[z] *Ibid.*, no. 511, p. 572; no. 512, p. 573. Nicolson was "rather surprised" that the council of ministers chose not to retain the formula by which Great Britain agreed to enter into an exchange of views with Russia should there be any change in the political position of Afghanistan. It is difficult to see why Nicolson was surprised, because one of Izvolsky's solutions of 17 August, which Nicolson promptly declined, had provided that if there were any alteration, then "Russia was freed from her obligations." (*Ibid.*, no. 494, p. 557; see above, pp. 298-299.) The Russian government must have preferred to take its chances in future incidents; and on 21 May 1908 Izvolsky remarked to the British chargé, Mr. O'Beirne, that "the Russian government entertained the hope that Great Britain would not find it necessary to take such action in Afghanistan as would alter the *status quo* and oblige the Imperial government to reopen the question." (*B. D.*, IV, no. 515, p. 575.) Undoubtedly this Russian way would act as a more effective deterrent to any British inclination to improve their position in Afghanistan than a promise given to discuss changes with Russia — after they had been made.

[a] *Ibid.*, no. 508, p. 568; no. 510, and enclosure, pp. 570, 571.

are now concluded," while Izvolsky, with his mind turned
towards a vacation, wrote Nicolson that he expected definitely
to leave St. Petersburg on Sunday, to be in Karlsbad on 8
September.[b]

This much mauled convention was concluded, its preamble
stated, "in order to assure the perfect security" of the British
and Russian frontiers in central Asia and to maintain a solid
and lasting peace there.[c] To help attain this, a now swollen
first article began with the declaration that Great Britain did
not intend to change the political status of Afghanistan. Moreover, Great Britain promised not to use its influence except in
a pacific sense, and of itself would not take in Afghanistan,
nor encourage Afghanistan to take, any measures which would
menace Russia. In return the Russian government now formally recognized that Afghanistan was beyond the sphere of
Russian influence, and engaged to make use of British intermediation in all of its political relations with that country.
Russia finally promised not to send any agents into Afghanistan. The long disputed second article contained the reference
to the Kabul treaty of 21 March 1905, wherein had been
recorded the British recognition of the agreements and engagements entered into with the deceased Amir Abdurrahman.
Great Britain disclaimed any desire to interfere in the internal
administration of the country, and would not annex or occupy
any portion of Afghanistan in contravention of that treaty, if
the Amir fulfilled his engagements already contracted by him
·in the same treaty towards Great Britain. The third article
permitted specially designated Russian and Afghan authorities
on the frontier or in the frontier provinces to set up direct
relations with each other to settle local questions, not political
in character. Commercial aspects were compressed within the
fourth article. Here Great Britain and Russia affirmed that
the principle of equality of commercial opportunity applied to

[b] *Ibid.*, no. 511, p. 572; also the facsimile of Izvolsky's private letter to
Nicolson.

[c] The French original text of the convention respecting Afghanistan is in
B. D., IV, no. 483, third column, pp. 541-544, and Appendix I, p. 619. An English translation of the convention of 1907 is in *B. F. S. P.*, C (London, 1911),
pp. 555-560.

Afghanistan. They agreed that every facility which had already been, or should in the future be acquired by British or British Indian trade or traders would be equally accorded to Russian trade or traders. If the growth of Russian commerce demonstrated the necessity for commercial agents, then both governments would agree on what measures to take, regard being had for the sovereign rights of the Amir. The fifth and last article expressed the Russian demand that the stipulations of the convention did not come into force until the Russian government had been notified by the British government that the Amir had consented to them.

Because of this article, the Afghan convention had a peculiar sequel. The official publication of the entire convention was delayed until the Amir should receive the Afghan text through a messenger of the government of India. In this manner the correct wording would be the first to reach him, and he would not receive prior, misleading descriptions from interested parties. Morley declared that the Amir was sixteen days away from Simla, and the convention was only telegraphed from London on 6 September.[d] Habibullah was on a tour of his domain when he was reached, but in his written reply of the 29th he advised that he could not deal with a subject of this importance until he returned to his capital. This attitude was deemed reasonable, and there seemed to be no doubt that he would eventually consent, although Morley had suspected that "he may be *slow.*" Only on 25 November did Habibullah reach Kabul, and the year closed without notice of his decision.[e] The Amir had never been cordial in his relations with the British since his reign had begun in 1901. He had a mind of his own or, as the displeased British preferred to believe, a stubbornness of disposition, with the result that from the start he refused to sanction the treaty. He protested decidedly against some of the provisions, but he had also to have regard for his personal welfare and his position on the throne if he should accept the convention; and these were serious matters

[d] *B. D.*, IV, no. 513, pp. 573-574; Editors' Note, p. 579; no. 524, p. 584; no. 526, p. 587.
[e] *Ibid.*, no. 526, p. 587; no. 549, p. 614. *C. H. B. F. P.*, III, 361.

in Afghan politics.[f] Near the end of 1908 "a very lengthy and rambling" letter came from him, which left open the possibility of further discussions, as well as made them necessary. Nicolson was no longer hopeful because the Afghans, "like other semi-civilized Orientals, were slow in their procedure and singularly difficult to convince."[g] Habibullah never was convinced.

Two British punitive expeditions in February and May 1908, to suppress frontier raids by wild Afghan tribes, and the Amir's recalcitrancy, made a pretty kettle of fish. Izvolsky referred seriously to the existing situation, but gave comforting reassurance when he said that "Russia meant absolutely to observe the spirit of the convention."[h] Unregenerate to the end, the government of India held the opinion that Russia had foreseen the possibility of a disagreement with the Amir, and had caused provisions to be inserted in the convention to provoke this result. Nicolson was sure that this view was false, that Russia more likely had never suspected that Great Britain would not obtain the Amir's consent. He also excellently described the embarrassing position in which a half-civilized Oriental Amir had placed Great Britain:

Moreover we should have to publicly admit that although we decline to permit Russia to have any direct relations with the Amir, we are ourselves incapable of exercising any effective influence over that potentate in matters of external policy affecting his country. Russia would, in that case, have some justification in asserting that we were useless as intermediaries, and that it would be more to her advantage to treat direct with the Amir should the occasion for doing so ever arise. If the Afghan convention has to go by the board . . . I should imagine that our prestige would suffer seriously throughout the middle and far East. . . . The consequences would be more serious, and would flow over a wide field.[i]

The convention did not have to go by the board because, in November 1908, the British government was "especially gratified with the willingness of M. Izvolsky to act upon the as-

[f] Reisner, *Krasny Arkhiv*, X, 61-62.
[g] *B. D.*, IV, no. 517, p. 577.
[h] *Ibid.*, no. 514, and note 1, p. 574; no. 515, p. 575.
[i] *Ibid.*, no. 516, pp. 575-576.

sumption that the convention concerning Afghanistan was in
force, although the consent of the Amir had not yet been
received." Not long afterwards the two governments arranged for the convention to be in force without the Amir's
consent being necessary, although during the period of the
negotiations this was a prime requisite.[j] Whether this arrangement was the result of the new spirit infused into Anglo-
Russian relations by the rapprochement of 1907, or only the
concession by Russia of something no longer of value in the
face of British impotency in Afghanistan, worried nobody right
away: the sequel had had its happy ending.

[j] *Ibid.*, no. 517, p. 576; Editors' Note, p. 577.

CHAPTER SEVEN

THE RECEPTION OF THE CONVENTION

S UCH a remarkable achievement as the conclusion of an Anglo-Russian convention could not be long concealed. From time to time during the negotiations, especially in the last half year, rumors of their existence appeared in the public prints of Europe. Occasionally a shrewd summary of the probable terms of agreement was published, but more often the versions were marked by their misinformation. This could lead to undesirable comments, and Izvolsky in particular wished to escape such annoyance, since he was sensitive to press criticisms, by the disclosure of the official text at the earliest possible moment. The British were in less of a hurry. Nicolson preferred that there should be no announcement in advance of official publication, and proposed that no detailed notice should be released until the government of India had placed a copy into the hands of the Amir of Afghanistan. Izvolsky agreed, and the British government saw no objection to the announcement of the fact of signature in the Sunday papers on 1 September, although Izvolsky was admonished not to allow the outlines of the agreement to leak out, even by means of an indiscretion.[a] It was not easy to keep Izvolsky in line. He soon complained that he must give something to the Russian press, which was "clamoring for information" and "abusing him for his silence."[b] The Russian acting minister for foreign affairs, M. Gubastov, informed Nicolson that he understood that Izvolsky might let the influential journal, *Novoye Vremya*, have an outline of the convention around the middle of September. Nicolson tried to forestall any premature revelation, but he had little hope that secrecy would last more than a few days longer.[c] The break came on 6/19

---

[a] *B. D.*, IV, no. 511, p. 572; no. 513, pp. 573-574. *G. P.*, XXV, part I, no. 8534, p. 40. This was the real reason for the delay in publication, not in order to withhold it until after parliament had risen. Grey, I, 160-161.

[b] *B. D.*, IV, no. 523, p. 584.

[c] *Ibid.*, no. 521, p. 581.

September when the newspaper *Ryech* appeared with a substantially accurate summary. No harm resulted because the ratifications of the convention were exchanged in St. Petersburg on the 23rd, and publication followed on the 26th.[d] The convention was thus loosed upon a suspecting public.

Diplomatic courtesy required, or made desirable, that prior, confidential notification be given to some great powers, and to a few others upon whom the news should be broken gently. Izvolsky suggested before leaving for his vacation that Great Britain and Russia should jointly address an explanatory, reassuring communication to the Persian government, besides making some notification of the Tibetan arrangement to China. For the rest, he proposed that each contracting party should be at liberty to offer confidential announcements to those whom it should select. It was not a Russian custom to offer such information to the Porte, but it was desired to give a general idea of the convention to France.[e] The British foreign office was sympathetic to the scheme, and also desired to favor a few nations. It entirely approved making simultaneous communications to Persia and China; insisted on being first with the Amir. It desired particularly to inform France and Japan, although the Japanese ambassador in London practically knew the substance of the convention already from conversations with Grey. These indications should be verbal and strictly confidential, and the powers in general should not be made acquainted with the text until shortly before its publication. Nicolson privately warned Gubastov that "it would be wise to say nothing at Washington as it was most difficult to prevent leakages there."[f] The British foreign office sent a telegram on 5 September directing that verbal explanations be given Japan, and others to France and to the Amir on the following day. Spring Rice and Hartwig presented a joint

---

[d] *Ibid.*, no. 317, note 1, p. 354; no. 456, note 2, p. 504; no. 536, p. 596. *G. P.*, XXV, part I, no. 8536, pp. 42-43. The German chargé in St. Petersburg reported that the indiscretion in the *Ryech* was committed by a Reuter correspondent, Bryanchaninov, and that it was greatly regretted by the Russian government and by Nicolson.

[e] *B. D.*, IV, no. 519, p. 579; no. 525, p. 586.

[f] *Ibid.*, no. 519, p. 579; no. 525, and enclosure, pp. 586-587.

note dated the 11th to the Persian government, while the two ministers at Peking transmitted the arrangement respecting Tibet on the 25th. The official text of the convention was distributed among the great powers on 24 September.[g]

While these necessary details were being arranged, the chief artificers of the settlement scurried away in quest of rest and pleasures. Izvolsky got away ahead of everybody, going first to Karlsbad. Arrangements were made for him to have the honor of lunching, on 5 September, with King Edward at Marienbad, "where the cure, as usual, agreed wonderfully" with him.[h] Before the luncheon, Izvolsky had a conversation with Sir Edward Goschen, the British ambassador at Vienna who was in attendance upon the king. Izvolsky remarked to Goschen that "he had sometimes been almost in despair" of overcoming the opposition to the convention at home, while it had taken "all the patience at his command to withstand the continual 'hammering' to which he had been subjected from Berlin." He then paid gracious tribute to Nicolson, who had always understood conditions, and he asserted that "a wiser choice of negotiator could not possibly have been made."[i] Izvolsky suspected that his troubles with the convention were not finished. At home he would have to meet violent criticism from the military party, who were "to a man against him," besides from the large number of reactionaries. He was afraid of Germany, because it was becoming active in Persia where it seemed anxious to be on a footing "totally out of proportion" to its real interests. Yet the convention was worth this trouble because, while its terms dealt with distant countries, "to him the chief significance . . . was peace in the Far East, and time for the political and military regeneration of the empire." He hoped that "it would make its effect felt also nearer home."[j] Izvolsky then was kindly received by King Edward at luncheon, while at the conclusion of the private audience afterwards

[g] Ibid., no. 317, note 1, p. 354; Editors' Note, p. 579; no. 529, enclosure, p. 589; no. 536, and note 1, p. 596.
[h] Ibid., no. 523, p. 584.
[i] Ibid., p. 582. Nicolson, p. 233. See also Izvolsky, p. 294.
[j] B. D., IV, no. 523, p. 583; V, no. 379, p. 443.

he was presented with the Grand Cross of the Victorian Order.[k] To a man of Izvolsky's inclinations, his vacation was already a success.

No one received more genuine plaudits for his good work than did Nicolson. Hardinge expressed cordial appreciation of his friendly coöperation, because the realization of an agreement with Russia had been his "dream for the last four years."[1] Morley wrote from Lake Leman that the country owed Nicolson "a great debt." He understood that the carrying out of the convention would encounter trouble in Russia, but he conceded that "I shall have to keep a very vigilant eye in my diocese."[m] Grey likewise assured Nicolson that everything he had done was a success, and wished that he "could be multiplied at will so as to be available at once in every place where there were difficulties."[n] Nicolson himself had already thanked Grey for his kind support, invaluable guidance and advice, as well as for "the considerate manner in which you have always acted towards me."[o] Into this feast of harmony a sour note was later injected from Teheran by Spring Rice. He sent his congratulations to Grey upon the signature along with hopes for the enjoyment of a well deserved rest. He then ventured to set forth his views again, until his letter read like his official despatches. He warned Grey that his difficulties were only beginning in Persia, because Great Britain had bartered its prestige to become an accomplice of Russia for a consideration.[p]

The reaction to the news of an Anglo-Russian convention by certain governments was eagerly awaited. The French gov-

[k] *Ibid.*, IV, p. 584. Shortly afterwards, in a letter to Nicolson, the king wrote: "I was much pleased with my conversation with M. Izvolsky at Marienbad . . . and to renew my acquaintance with him. He is undoubtedly a very able man and I believe honest and straightforward." *Ibid.*, no. 535, p. 596.

[1] *Ibid.*, no. 520, p. 580.

[m] *Ibid.*, no. 526, p. 587. Nicolson, p. 256.

[n] *B. D.*, IV, no. 537, p. 596. Nicolson, p. 255. King Edward wrote that Nicolson's skill had resulted in "a great triumph for British diplomacy" and placed him "in the front rank of our diplomatists." (*B. D.*, IV, no. 520, p. 580; no. 535, pp. 595-596.) The tsar expressed his pleasure to Nicolson, and "looked forward also to the establishment of thoroughly friendly feelings." *Ibid.*, no. 545, pp. 606-607.

[o] *Ibid.*, no. 288, p. 304.

[p] *Ibid.*, no. 532, pp. 593-594.

ernment, ally of Russia, friend of Great Britain, interested
and encouraging onlooker throughout the period of the negotiations, gave little public display of its pleasure. When Clemenceau, then premier, was shown a summary of the terms,
he thought it was "very satisfactory," because the settlement
of these Asiatic questions cleared the ground for coming
discussions on the Bagdad railway, along with the important
question of the Persian Gulf. Cambon, the French ambassador
in London, assured Grey that Great Britain "had got much
the best of the agreement." [q] The Austro-Hungarian government showed no great concern for the details of the agreement, because its attention was fully absorbed by internal problems, and by the negotiations with Hungary on imperial questions. Both Izvolsky and Goschen had agreed that the general
impression was favorable, particularly at the removal of causes
of friction in many parts of the world, along with the additional guarantee for the preservation of the general peace. It
seemed desirable to keep relations between Austria and Russia
calm by avoiding subjects upon which they did not agree.[r]

Great Britain and Russia were especially solicitous that the
Persian government should justly appreciate the benefits which
would accrue to it from the provisions of the arrangement. A
note was drawn up for joint communication which summarized
the friendly solution achieved for the purpose of avoiding
conflicts of interest or future misunderstandings, in order not
to "place the Persian government in an embarrassing situation
in any respect whatever." The two governments emphasized
that they "have not for a moment lost sight of the fundamental
principle of absolute respect of the integrity and independence
of Persia," and left it to that government to "convince itself
that the agreement . . . can but contribute in the most efficacious
manner to the security, the prosperity, and the internal devel-

[q] *Ibid.*, no. 527, p. 587; no. 537, p. 596. The French press was chary in its
comments upon the convention, the details of which it discussed casually. Nevertheless there was no doubt of the appreciation of the agreement which had
brought its ally and its friend together. A. Maurice Low, "Russia and England
Agree," *Forum* (New York), XXXIX (1908), 340. See also *Paul Cambon*, p.
241; Bompard, p. 278.
[r] *B. D.*, IV, no. 541, p. 601; no. 548, pp. 611-612.

opment of Persia." [s] With only minor alterations Spring Rice
and Hartwig presented this explanatory memorandum to the
foreign minister under date of 11 September, but it came too
late to act as a cure for Persian suspicions.[t] It can hardly be
said that Spring Rice was a happy choice for his post, for he
was completely out of sympathy with the policy of a Persian
agreement with Russia, nor was he in good health.[u] The
British foreign office had failed to give him timely warning
of the signature of the convention, with the result that for
three days he denied the existence of any agreement after the
papers had published the news, and then he said that "in any
case there could be no question of a division of Persia, or of
intervention." [v] The formal notification reached him on 4
September, but the Persian government had already analyzed
the rumored agreement. The comments which Spring Rice
heard were hostile, especially to Great Britain, "who was
regarded as having sold Persia to Russia and as having betrayed the cause of Persian independence." Because of the
internal disorders and the impotence of the government,
Spring Rice concluded that energetic measures were needed to
curb the growing excitement.[w]

A veritable campaign was put on by the British to make the
arrangement palatable to the Persians. On 4 September, on
his own initiative, Spring Rice sent an explanatory letter to the
minister for foreign affairs in which the assurances already
given by Russia and Great Britain were renewed. He took
measures to make this statement publicly known.[x] He called
upon "a gentleman connected with the political societies" to
convince him of the purity of British motives, and the inno-

---

[s] *Ibid.*, no. 521, enclosure, p. 581. See also no. 518, p. 578; no. 524, pp. 584-
585; no. 525, enclosure, p. 586.

[t] *Ibid.*, no. 529, and enclosure, pp. 588-590.

[u] *Ibid.*, no. 532, pp. 593-594. Sykes, II, 414. The foreign office intended to
have Spring Rice come home for medical care. Gwynn, II, 103.

[v] *B. D.*, IV, no. 530, p. 590. Shuster, p. xxiv. Spring Rice called attention
to this failure to inform him with typical asperity. To Sir Valentine Chirol
he wrote: "They have thrown a stone into the windows here, and left me to
face the policeman. . . . This was, I suppose, a sign that Persian public opinion
was not to be considered." Gwynn, II, 103.

[w] *B. D.*, IV, no. 530, p. 591.

[x] *Ibid.*, p. 590; Editors' Note, p. 590.

cence of the Persian arrangement. He dilated upon the provisions that promised respect for the independence and integrity of Persia, besides the principle of the open door for commerce:

I pointed out that the agreement was but one of many, all couched in similar terms, and all aiming at the maintenance of the *status quo* in Asia, and the final conclusion of the policy of aggression which had so long been pursued by the European nations, with such deplorable results both to themselves and to the Asiatic peoples.[y]

Nicolson himself passed off the most disingenuous description upon the Mushir ul Mulk, Persian minister in St. Petersburg, who called on the 24th to inquire for the terms of the agreement:

He would see [Nicolson believed] that the arrangement was eminently favorable to Persia, and how baseless were the reports that Russia and Great Britain had contemplated a partition of Persia. The two powers had merely agreed not to annoy each other in certain regions, and the rights and prerogatives of the Persian government were fully recognized and remained unaffected and undisturbed. It was not correct to speak of "spheres of influence," as by that expression it might appear as if the two powers wished to restrict the liberty of action of the Persian government in certain regions, and to exercise influence therein themselves. Nothing of this was meant by the arrangement; . . . To this surely the Persian government could not object, and indeed they should be gratified at the restraint which each power had imposed upon itself, and above all on their having solemnly recognized the integrity and the independence of Persia.[z]

The Mushir ul Mulk also dissembled when he said that "the arrangement appeared to him thoroughly satisfactory," but Nicolson believed himself "well aware that Persians are adepts in concealing their real sentiments." Even in diplomacy Nicolson had used most deceitful language, yet Grey agreed that his words had been "most judicious and right and should be entirely approved."[a]

[y] *Ibid.*, no. 530, p. 591.
[z] *Ibid.*, no. 538, p. 598.
[a] *Ibid.*, no. 538, and minute, pp. 598-599. The Persian chargé told his German colleague: "Other states may regard the new Anglo-Russian policy as practical and necessary, but Persia stands only to lose by it; it will pay the costs." *G. P.*, XXV, part I, no. 8535, p. 42.

The Persians, however, turned out to be "other semi-civilized Orientals . . . singularly difficult to convince." The country was again in political turmoil, and the popular leaders, already imbued with a deep distrust of Russia, found what confidence they had hitherto had in the sympathy of a liberal England rudely undermined. It was quickly perceived that "England had definitely withdrawn her opposition to Russian aggression in return for a share of the spoil." Because Persia appeared to have no means of resistence, the future seemed hopeless.[b] Spring Rice had often warned his government that an agreement with Russia would be considered a betrayal of Persia, in consequence of which British prestige would tumble. All through September 1907 Spring Rice was busy writing despatches to show that what he had predicted had come true. Other sources bore out his charges.[c] The violent attitude of the Persian politicians and press was directed largely against Great Britain, while Russia was seldom mentioned. Great Britain fell from grace; but Russia for many years had been accorded no grace. Great Britain was no longer looked upon as a protector, and a strong feeling of indignation was rising against it in Persia, "far stronger in fact than against Russia, who is not accused of disguising her policy or of ever having pretended to friendship for the Persian people, or a desire for Persian prosperity and independence." [d] Spring Rice did what he could to explain the British views and preserve British prestige. From many persons he learned that opposition to the arrangement in Persia would be lessened, if Great Britain and Russia would join with Persia in inviting other powers to adhere to the clause respecting the independence and integrity of the country. Such action would prove that the clause was not a mere blind, but would be regarded as a "pledge of good

[b] B. D., IV, no. 530, p. 591.

[c] Sykes, II, 414. Shuster, p. xxiv. A letter addressed to Professor Browne, author of The Persian Revolution, was read in the house of commons on 17 February 1908. It said in part: "The action of England has alienated from her the good opinion and sympathy of all Persians. . . . Its immediate effect in Persia is, however, the complete destruction of the friendship which the Persians have entertained for the English." Parliamentary Debates, 4th series, CLXXXIV, 548.

[d] B. D., IV, no. 531, pp. 592-593; no. 532, p. 594.

faith and proof that we mean [the] principles in question to be part of public law and not subject to the will of two powers." Hartwig was also supposed to be in favor of this proposal.[e] Of course the British government would have nothing to do with this suggestion, not only because it would give an excuse to other powers, Germany first of all, to meddle in Persian affairs, but also on the higher ground that a request from Persia for the endorsements of others was "neither courteous nor necessary," it being "a slur on our good faith." The Russian government thought likewise.[f] It was all Persia could do to survive the internal incidents of the following years, but with the outbreak of the world war Persian hostility to both tormentors, especially towards Great Britain, was perfectly clear and understandable.[g]

Above all else the attitude of Germany was watched. No attempt had ever been made to conceal the fact of the negotiations from the German government. British diplomats, but especially Izvolsky, endeavored to lull German suspicions with frequent assurances that any Anglo-Russian agreement would scrupulously respect all German interests, and that no question in which Germany was involved would be settled without its proper participation. Those promises, it is only just to indicate, were perfectly kept. Although neither contracting party disclosed any details, from many sources, particularly from London, the German foreign office received quite exact knowledge of the probable terms of the agreement. It would consist of several "protocoles de désintéressement," but there would be absolutely no political alliance.[h] In the first of three model reports sent during September by the chargé d'affaires von Miquel from St. Petersburg, he shrewdly summarized how most of the driving force for the reconciliation came from the British. Russia had hung back, and to a degree had been compelled to go along because of its

<hr/>

[e] *Ibid.*, no. 528, p. 588; no. 529, p. 589; no. 530, p. 592. The Russian foreign office "had heard nothing from Monsieur de Hartwig on the subject." *Ibid.*, no. 534, p. 595.
[f] *Ibid.*, no. 533, p. 594; no. 534, and enclosure, p. 595.
[g] Gwynn, II, 103. Sykes, II, 414.
[h] *G. P.*, XXV, part I, no. 8532, pp. 36-37; no. 8533, pp. 37-40.

weakness. Miquel suspected that the greater British interest
in the negotiations betokened a desire for more freedom of
action in its entire foreign policy, but that the settlement
would hardly be transformed into an entente cordiale.[i]
His despatch of the 25th contained a summary of the
convention with his first comments. Where the treaty concerned Asia, contrary to earlier rumors, very few innovations
existed, while the establishment of the lines for British and
Russian interests in Persia was alone of fundamental importance. What impressed him most was that "the meaning of the
Anglo-Russian agreement lay not so much in Asia, but much
more in Europe, where its consequences could be made noticeable for a long time." It would be British influence that
would rise in Europe; what Russia won was time for reorganization, undisturbed by any other power.[j]

After two days' further reflection, Miquel completed his
analysis of the convention. He believed that the negotiations
had been so skilfully conducted that no nation, including his
own, could take offence at any of the provisions. Yet Germany
was the nation most affected by the agreement, which some
quarters believed Great Britain had made, less because of
danger in Asia, but rather because of "the growth of a threatening power in Europe." No one could reproach Great Britain
for its policy, and could only marvel at its success. The full
realization of the result, Miquel described with poignant
regret:

As cleverly as the wording of the treaty may be composed, the impression is unescapable that the powers have set up a syndicate with which
we shall have to reckon. This compulsion towards close association is a
compliment, even if a troublesome one, to the German army, the German navy, our commerce, and the talent of the German people in particular for development.[k]

In the face of all the assurances of the peaceful nature of
the agreement, which Bülow already in April 1907 had pub-

[i] *Ibid.*, no. 8535, pp. 41-42; no. 8537, pp. 45-46.
[j] *Ibid.*, no. 8536, pp. 43-45. The kaiser entirely agreed, and believed that
Great Britain "will become still more unpleasant to us in Europe than before."
Ibid., marginal notes 5 and 6, p. 45.
[k] *Ibid.*, no. 8537, pp. 46-47.

licly declared was awaited without disquietude, the immediate reaction of the German government had to be moderate or non-committal.[1] As soon as word of the signature
was known, Bülow prepared, on 1 September, his recommendation for the attitude of the press. If the convention
corresponded to the earlier indications, as he anticipated it
would, he admonished that "it is essential that the agreement
shall be reviewed quietly and factually." [m] Therefore it was
possible to say, two weeks after the text had become public property, that "the attitude of the Imperial government . . .
is perfectly correct in tone;" but there were other ways of
determining that the reception of the convention by Germany
was "not very favorable." [n] The German press derived vicari-
ous delight from the spotty reception accorded by Russian,
English and French newspapers to the convention, and instituted a campaign to assure its readers, by means of selected
quotations, that public opinion in those countries did not think
well of the business.[o]

Something of course must be mentioned of the manner in
which public opinion took up with this latest novelty. Public
opinion in England was a many-faceted phenomenon, not the
unity implied by the expression, while to speak of a public
opinion in Russia, even by 1907, is premature. Throughout
the negotiations the public of neither country was kept abreast
of their course, while the rumors and misinformation that did
appear were always deplored. That is not to say that either
side was indifferent to making the terms of the convention as
pleasing as possible to the most powerful, critical element in
public opinion. From time to time Nicolson buttressed some
demand with the additional plea of the good effect its acceptance would have upon British public opinion, but Izvolsky
would not be moved by this consideration. Less often he referred to it on his own account, but he more frequently, and
accurately, alluded to the attitude of this powerful group in

[1] *Ibid.*, no. 8531, footnote **, p. 35. *B. D.*, IV, no. 269, p. 291.
[m] *G. P.*, XXV, part I, no. 8534, Bülow's marginal note, p. 40.
[n] *B. D.*, IV, no. 540, minute, p. 600; no. 542, pp. 601-602. Izvolsky, *Correspondance diplomatique*, I, 231.
[o] *B. D.*, IV, no. 542, p. 602.

the government, or of that influential section at the court. The British Liberal ministers themselves never worried unduly on the score of public opinion, because they felt confident that they had a sufficient number of followers in their parliamentary majority to approve anything within reason that they should present. The estimation held of the public print was sufficiently revealed by Hardinge's words to Tschirschky on the occasion of the king's visit to the kaiser at Cronberg on 16 August 1906: "Considering that the bulk of the press in England was more or less associated with the views of the opposition it would be absurd to attach undue importance to its opinions." [p] Izvolsky's extreme sensitiveness to criticism by the press may have affected his vanity, but seldom his policy. The "serious hitch" immediately before the conclusion of the convention came from the unfriendly groups in the government, not from public opinion in Russia. This much may be said with perfect confidence: not one provision contained in the convention of 1907 found its way in primarily because public opinion would have insisted upon it; not one provision was kept out of the convention simply because public opinion would not have stomached it.

The newspaper and periodical press did, indeed, generously notice the appearance of the convention. Its terms were summarized with more or less accuracy, and commented upon too often without proper appreciation. Because of this, as well as because of the little influence wielded, to devote much detail to the printed reception would be of small value. In Russia, Izvolsky was prepared for "an avalanche of criticism" from the military and the reactionary minded. He would receive every support from the liberal party in Russia to which "he belonged in spirit," but it was clearly neither powerful nor very influential. [q] After the convention did appear, the "tone" of the press turned out to be "a most agreeable surprise," with the articles in the papers he had feared most not going beyond the limits "of legitimate criticism." This

[p] Ibid., III, no. 425, p. 367; IV, no. 258, p. 281; no. 429, minutes, p. 481.
[q] Ibid., no. 523, p. 583.

was true in part because, as Izvolsky slyly added, "of course I had prepared the way a little." [r] Press views varied all the way from the recognition by the *Novoye Vremya* that "Russia lost every possibility of threatening India" to the fanciful statement in the *Slovo* that the treaty would "secure Russia from any danger she may have feared from the ambition of Germany." [s] The improvement in the comments of the Russian press after the publication of the convention went beyond what "could ever have been expected in so short a time," which was directly attributable to the friendly way Great Britain and Russia coöperated in the Persian internal crisis during the final months of 1907.[t] Some individuals whose opinions carried weight, opposed the arrangement at the time and afterwards. From Paris, Prince Kochubey, "a bitter Anglophobe," accused Izvolsky of pursuing a timid policy, because of little confidence in the military power of Russia, as well as out of servility to a tsar "imbued with Anglophile sentiments." The signature of the convention "endorsed the renunciation of Russia's natural ambitions in Asia." [u] Muravyev, the Russian ambassador in Rome, found the division of Persia into spheres contrary to Russian traditional policy, highly unprofitable for Russia, and completely useless.[v] Count Witte, always ready to disparage anything not his own work, ponderously characterized the convention as a change in policy from a flirtation with Germany to a flirtation with Great Britain. His final judgment was that the convention by itself was of no especial importance: its significance would grow out of future relationships, as Russia was the ally and Great Britain the friend of France.[w] Later day communist opinion has looked upon the convention of 1907 and also found it wanting, less because it was a piece of hateful, nationalistic imperialism, but more because it "tied Russia hand and foot, giving it nothing in

---

[r] *Ibid.*, no. 541, p. 601; no. 546, p. 608.
[s] See London *Times*, 17 March 1908, p. 15. Low, *Forum*, XXXIX, 340.
[t] *B. D.*, IV, no. 464, p. 510; no. 547, p. 609.
[u] *Ibid.*, no. 542, p. 602.
[v] Wroblewski, *Kriegsschuldfrage*, V, 1224-1225.
[w] Witte, *Vospominaniya*, II, 405-406; see English edition, p. 432. See also Onslow, *Slavonic Review*, VII, 549.

return," neither in the struggle with Germany, nor for the strengthening of its influence in Persia or in central Asia.[x]

The public greeting given the convention in England was not wholly cordial. Izvolsky noticed that despite "one or two discordant notes," the disposition of the press had been generally favorable.[y] In his own final judgment Grey was quite satisfied, although compelled to concede, even while not agreeing, that "people here do not think that the convention, as an isolated bargain, is a good one; but they will be pleased if it leads to a generally friendly attitude of Russia towards us." [z] The convention was criticized by the conservatives, among whom Curzon was prominent, and by the more radically minded who disapproved of the callous indifference shown to Persia and fumed at the implied condonation of tsarism by the signature of any agreement with Russia.[a] The important *Manchester Guardian* damned with faint praise:

The Anglo-Russian convention seems to us to merit neither strong praise nor strong blame. Things in Persia, Afghanistan, and Tibet were drifting in certain directions. The convention in each case takes note of the drift, formalizes it, and, as it were, legalizes it. Such agreements are often worth making, but they seldom give sufficient cause for having the bells rung, or for tearing out hair either, and so it is with this one.[b]

The periodicals were filled with their share of special articles, among which a good one was a rarity. The judgment pronounced on the convention by the political writer Calchas for the *Fortnightly Review* was eminently fair. He appreciated that the guarantee of the safety of the British dominion in India was a result that "would have beggared the most vivid imagination of a few years ago;" that the partition of Persia had been effected for all practical purposes, and that the tsar was very nearly the suzerain of the shah.[c] The famous *Specta-*

[x] Rouire, Introduction by F. Rothstein, (Russian edition), p. 5. See also Reisner, *Krasny Arkhiv*, X, 57-66.

[y] *B. D.*, IV, no. 544, p. 604.

[z] *Ibid.*, no. 550, p. 616. Grey, I, 155.

[a] Lee, II, 572. Onslow, *Slavonic Review*, VII, 549. "The Anglo-Russian Convention," *Spectator*, XCIX (1907), 420.

[b] Low, *Forum*, XXXIX, 340.

[c] Calchas, "The Anglo-Russian Agreement," *Fortnightly Review*, LXXXVIII (1907), 546-548. The writer in the *Spectator* said of Persia: "Of course, it is

tor floundered badly in its belief that the Anglo-Russian convention dealt with Asia alone:

If it has any effect upon the equilibrium of Europe, it will be an effect wholly unpremeditated. Such results, of course, are conceivable; . . . but, on the whole, we do not think that the convention will have any directly recognizable influence upon what we call the balance of power in Europe.[d]

The Viennese newspapers passed favorable notice upon the signature of the convention as an event of great political significance, calculated to furnish additional security for the general peace. Its terms did not particularly interest the press which made few references to them, but this "remarkable reticence" seemed properly ascribable, as in the case of the government, to the absorbing interest taken in the internal politics of the empire.[e] From Budapest there came an article from the pen of Professor Arminius Vambéry. The result of the negotiations, which had been conducted in a "huckstering spirit," gave him no delight. He was certain that Russia would become mightier and more daring in its policies, penetrating further into southern Persia, where the outlet into warm waters still beckoned. It would be a long day before "the whale and the elephant will walk in brotherly love and affection over Asia." The convention was a mistake for Great Britain because its interests were harmed, so that "in the form it came out, it would have been much better not to come out at all." [f]

The guidance and direction that the German press had

---

sad that Persia should decline. . . . She was already mortgaged and controlled. . . . All that has happened now is that the doctors have told her the truth." *Spectator*, XCIX, 420.

[d] *Ibid*. See also *Living Age*, CCLV (1907), 315-316. The anonymous writer of an ill-tempered contribution to *Blackwood's Magazine* expressed his belief that "there is not the smallest foundation for the supposition that the cause of permanent peace has gained one iota by the arrangement." "Britain and Russia in the Middle East," *Blackwood's Magazine*, CLXXXIII (1908), 153.

[e] *B. D.*, IV, no. 522, p. 582; no. 541, p. 601.

[f] A. Vambéry, "The Anglo-Russian Convention," *Nineteenth Century and After*, LXII (1907), 895-896, 903. Curzon found the dismal views of this article much to his liking, subsequently declaiming similar thoughts, and using the expression "huckstering spirit" in the debate in the house of lords without reference to Vambéry, or his article. For this unacknowledged borrowing he was twitted and embarrassed in the course of the debate.

received was quite faithfully observed. Izvolsky had been uneasy over the possible German reaction, but was neither surprized nor irritated when the newspapers spoke about the agreement, with a few hostile exceptions, in "bitter-sweet language." [g] Sir Frank Lascelles reported from Berlin that the document had "on the whole been very favorably received," yet he gave such press summaries that at the end Hardinge and Grey perceived that the opposite was more nearly true. Lascelles did point out that most of the press found satisfaction in so far as the terms had cut across no German interests. The papers also plainly saw that all of the existing causes of friction between Russia and Great Britain in central Asia had been settled. More especially in the organs of the commercial world, the dissatisfaction was less successfully hidden. Some chagrin was exhibited because two powers had composed their differences without the participation, and possibly at the expense, of Germany. What happened in Afghanistan or Tibet was of no concern, but if Persia had actually been divided into commercial spheres, then German legitimate trade expansion would be menaced. In that event Germany could probably do nothing for a time, and such a solution would hardly promote the peace of the world, which was persistently proclaimed to be the aim of British policy. [h] In one of the best periodical articles to appear in any country, Professor Hans Delbrück succinctly declared:

For the time being it is again England which in its convention with Russia concerning relations in Asia can point anew to a brilliant success. . . . What the English have conceded are truly trifles, what they have won is for them of the very highest worth, so far as treaties in general mean anything. . . . How could Russia enter into such a treaty? Merely on account of foreign relations it is, indeed, hardly to be ex-

[g] B. D., IV, no. 523, p. 583; no. 541, p. 601. Izvolsky told Nicolson that the German reception "had been far better than he had anticipated." He was not deluded by that, for he continued: "It is however, impossible to deny that the convention is by no means welcome to Germany and we must both expect to see her cause us trouble . . . not only in Persia . . . but everywhere." Ibid., no. 546, p. 608.

[h] Ibid., no. 540, pp. 599-600. The British minister at Munich, Mr. Fairfax Cartwright, was more positive in his conclusion that "the Anglo-Russian agreement does not meet with the approval of the leaders of German public opinion." Ibid., no. 542, pp. 601-602.

plained. Perhaps the key is to be sought in the financial policy of Russia . . . and persons in St. Petersburg hope, by means of the most extreme concessions, to tie themselves up with the English market.[i]

The publication of the convention came shortly after parliament had risen, which left plenty of time to prepare replies to whatever criticism could be anticipated during the debates on its acceptance.[j] The opposition won a resounding addition in the return of Lord Curzon to public life for the occasion. Since his resignation from the viceroyalty of India after his unsuccessful quarrel with Kitchener, he had been out of favor with both political parties. Even with Lansdowne's effective assistance, Curzon barely defeated his opponent in an election in order to be returned to the house of lords as a representative Irish peer.[k] Curzon could be counted upon for wordy opposition to the agreement with Russia. Already on 25 September, a day before the public release of the text, his disillusionment was total. He wrote to a kindred spirit, Earl Percy, whom Nicolson had described as "an effective critic," to reveal his distress at the understanding:

The Russian convention is in my view deplorable. It gives up all that we have been fighting for for years, and it gives it up with a wholesale abandon that is truly cynical in its recklessness. Ah, me, it makes one despair of public life. The efforts of a century sacrificed and nothing or next to nothing in return. When parliament meets there ought to be, but I suppose will not be, a demonstration in force.[l]

After parliament reassembled the question was discussed, but in the debates of the lords it was treated as something "outside the sphere of party politics," while in the house of commons, instead of being greeted by a demonstration in force, only "a thin house" turned out.[m] The house of lords took up the subject first on 6 February 1908, at which time Curzon

[i] D[elbrück], *Preussische Jahrbücher*, CXXX (1907), 197. Dillon thought, in his own article, that Russia entered into the agreement more because of a "yearning" for "peace, order and happiness." For one of Dillon's capabilities and sources of information his contribution is disappointingly lean. E. J. Dillon, "The Anglo-Russian Agreement and Germany," *Contemporary Review*, XCII (1907), 700.
[j] Grey, I, 160-161. B. D., IV, no. 549, pp. 612-616.
[k] Newton, p. 365.
[l] Ronaldshay, III, 38. Nicolson, p. 251.
[m] London *Times*, 18 February 1908, p. 9.

sallied forth on his maiden speech. This was a "shrill denunciation" in which he waylaid the noble lords for an hour and a quarter with "the condensed result of the studies and travels of more than twenty years," all of which was by then, his biographer mourns, "of purely academic interest." [n]

The Anglo-Russian convention of 1907, Curzon vouchsafed to those who heard him, sacrificed everything and was occasionally humiliating: "the conception was right, but its execution was faulty." He could find nothing good to say about it. In Persia the convention surrendered everything of value to Russia. Not enough attention, said he, had been given to the lines demarcating the spheres: the Russian region was abnormally large, the British zone too small and poor. "There is no gap whatever between them except such as was created by the great sand deserts which stretch across the heart of Persia." Nothing was gained in Afghanistan, not even the Amir's consent. The Tibetan clauses were an "absolute surrender," while to consult with Russia about the evacuation of the Chumbi valley was degrading.[o] He quoted from a speech delivered by Grey at Berwick during the recess, wherein the foreign secretary had claimed that "we have safeguarded the Indian frontier without foregoing commercial prospects in any part of Persia where we had any," in order to impute great ignorance to the speaker.[p]

In his presentation of the government's case the undersecretary for foreign affairs, Lord Fitzmaurice, replied *seriatim* to Curzon's criticisms; accused him of cavilling; of spending "a great deal of learning and verbal refinement" upon insignificant points; and drew the distinction that he thought he was "engaged in answering, not the front bench opposite, but the noble lord himself." [q] He defended the zone conceded to Russia in Persia as bounded by "a line which recognizes existing facts, and not a line which creates any particular right

[n] *C. H. B. F. P.*, III, 362. *Parliamentary Debates*, 4th series, CLXXXIII, 1023. Ronaldshay, III, 44.
[o] *Parliamentary Debates*, 4th series, CLXXXIII, 999-1024.
[p] *Ibid.*, p. 1007.
[q] *Ibid.*, pp. 1035, 1037, 1039.

or disability which does not at present prevail." Furthermore, it was a pleasure to disclose that the Imperial Bank of Persia had informed the foreign office of its approval of the treaty.[r] The accusation of losses sustained by the British in Tibet, Fitzmaurice met by reminding Curzon that the records enabled him to detect "a certain note of difference between the view of Tibet taken by the noble lord and that taken by his colleagues" in the incidents of a few years ago. Neither was it "the desire of the British government in India, any more than it was that of Russia, to take up an adventurous policy in Tibet."[s] After Lord Lamington had followed with a few ineffectual remarks, considering the lateness of the hour, (it was seven-forty in the evening), the remainder of the debate was put over until the following Monday, 10 February.[t]

At the appointed time that knowing veteran, Lord Sanderson, resumed with a weighty defence of the convention. He dwelt on the positive and permanent engagements respecting Persia and Afghanistan obtained from Russia in place of the hitherto "rather fluid assurances" given only in correspondence or conversations. He showed how the Russian government had freely supported its position by treasury aid, while the British government balked at incurring pecuniary liability, without which little could be done. The Persian Gulf was properly omitted from the convention:

The special interests of Great Britain in the Gulf are matters of fact, but they are not very easy to define, the less so because they seem to me to be always expanding, and definition might be found to operate by way of limitation.[u]

Lord Reay soon followed with another uncommonly good defence. He was convinced that trade relations with Persia were secure, while the respective British and Russian spheres simply accorded with the existing facts.[v] He saw nothing

[r] *Ibid.*, pp. 1032, 1035.
[s] *Ibid.*, pp. 1039, 1042.
[t] *Ibid.*, pp. 1043-1047.
[u] *Ibid.*, pp. 1307, 1309.
[v] "There is no concession made and no advantage gained which is not already, to a certain extent, at all events, possessed by Russia, and the line of demarcation of our sphere gives us what is most essential to our interests." *Ibid.*, p. 1318.

alarming about the local settlement of border disputes between
Russia and Afghanistan; nor was there anything undignified
in the evacuation of the Chumbi valley. That action reaffirmed
an earlier pledge, and the conditions which had been imposed
had been fulfilled.[w] Moreover, Lord Reay called attention to
the wider benefits that could result from the reconciliation:

There is no doubt that the tension which existed in our relations with
Russia in regard to Asia had a reflex action of a most detrimental character on international relations in Europe. I think, therefore, that we
have every reason to approve of this treaty which initiates a new era in
the conduct of our foreign relations, not only in Asia, but also elsewhere.[x]

The convention of 1907 corresponded so well with the objects
which Lansdowne had striven for in approaching Russia between 1903 and 1905 that it was difficult for him to find anything seriously to complain about. As a matter of fact his
remarks were so reasonable that Grey called them "a summing
up in favor of the convention."[y] A few objections, mostly
for form's sake, he raised but did not answer. He was utterly
wrong, however, when he asked his hearers not to forget that
"it was Russia that sought this agreement, for until lately we
know that she kept us at arm's length." [z]

The debate had proceeded with lordly placidity until near
its close, but some animation came while the Earl of Crewe,
Lord President of the Council, summed up for the government. He defended the convention with vigor, reminding
Lansdowne that Russian trade was becoming supreme in the
neutral zone where it likely could not be stopped, while even

---

[w] *Ibid.*, pp. 1320-1323. In the house of commons, on 17 February 1908, Morley likewise declared that this was true. (*Ibid.*, CLXXXIV, 560.) It is probable
that the defenders of the convention were here in error. "The trade-marts
were not effectively opened — our agent reported, indeed, that they were
effectively closed — but . . . the Chumbi valley . . . was evacuated." (Younghusband, p. 433.) There was no increase of trade with Tibet. Fraser, p. 146.

[x] *Parliamentary Debates*, 4th series, CLXXXIII, 1323.

[y] *B. D.*, IV, no. 550, p. 616.

[z] *Parliamentary Debates*, 4th series, CLXXXIII, 1334. Lansdowne feared,
for instance, that Russian competition in the neutral zone would be disadvantageous to Great Britain. Doubtless it would be, but the opportunity was
equal. Then, in return for equal commercial treatment in Afghanistan for
Russia, there was no corresponding provision in favor of Great Britain in the
Asiatic regions of Russian predominance. Yet there was no British rivalry at
all in Bukhara, Turkestan, or Transcaspia. *Ibid.*, pp. 1326, 1331.

in the south of Persia, Russia exercised some influence. Oftentimes Crewe took especial pains to refute remarks made earlier
by Curzon. In Persia the latter had "somewhat underrated"
Russian influence, which led him to go "beyond what was
justified by the facts of the case." Much was now different
than it had been "when he was travelling in those parts of the
world." It was impossible to delimit a smaller sphere for
Russia, the line for which did include Yezd, "over which the
noble lord shed a tear." [a] During the entire debate no other
speaker had come to Curzon's aid in sharing his sourest notes.
Curzon grew nettled, and interrupted Crewe, between whom
there ensued some jockeying.[b] By the time Curzon made his
closing speech his attitude was short and snapping. Once again
he called upon his intimate travel acquaintance with the old
Persia to sustain his convictions, and he deplored the whole
bargain. In his haughtiest manner he finally found it unnecessary to say anything more, because no substantial remarks had
been offered against the criticisms he had propounded! [c] Even
so, the lords did not throw out the convention, but the debates
upon it had "served to signalize Lord Curzon's return to
public life." [d]

The house of commons got around to its consideration of
the convention a week later, and accepted it after one lengthy
debate on 17 February 1908. Here the opening attack came
from Curzon's correspondent, Earl Percy, whose opposition
to an agreement with Russia which, he declared, never kept
a treaty, had been known to the foreign office since May 1907.[e]
Like Curzon, his remarks were bitterly critical, but more
general in their substance, and professed to see nothing in the

[a] *Ibid.*, pp. 1336-1338, 1339.

[b] *Ibid.*, pp. 1338-1339.

[c] *Ibid.*, pp. 1344-1353. During the debates Curzon had passed off some quotations on the Persian settlement, which had appeared in the *Novoye Vremya* of
13/26 September 1907, as "impartial" and from a "safe source of information."
His informant had been Mr. Lucien Wolf, who had culled the quotations from
bad translations in the pro-German *St. Petersburger Zeitung*. A series of letters
on this question in the London *Times* was concluded on 17 March 1908 by
one from the London correspondent of the *Novoye Vremya* who scathingly
denounced this carelessness in British statesmen.

[d] Ronaldshay, III, 44.

[e] *B. D.*, IV, no. 270, p. 292; no. 271, pp. 292-293.

convention upon which to congratulate Great Britain.[f] Nevertheless the two critics had found so much fault that Grey had
believed "it was absolutely necessary to put the case for the
convention strongly." [g] His own speech was a spirited defence,
the high spot on the question in the commons. He explained
to the members that in making the agreement with Russia
strategical considerations had been paramount. In this respect
the inclusion of Seistan within the British sphere was the most
important single factor, so the British line had been arranged
with that in view.[h] In truth, as was brought out in the debate,
this fancy for Seistan was simply a change in fashion. Once
upon a time the possession of Quetta was a strategic necessity;
then in the last quarter of the nineteenth century, the forward
march of danger to India was envisaged as coming through
Turkestan, while by 1907 the easiest way to attack India was
through Seistan. This was secured in the convention of 1907,
but whether that fact guaranteed the immunity of India from
Russian aggression was questionable. About the sole, sound
criticism in the speech by Lord Ronaldshay, then Curzon's
echo in the commons, later his voluminous biographer, exposed
this doubt. He failed to see

> how we had secured any immunity which we did not possess before.
> Seistan, if war was ever to come, was as much at the mercy of Russia
> today as before the treaty was concluded, and that the position of Seistan
> would ever become a greater menace to us than it was at present was
> sufficiently doubtful in view of the physical features of the country.[i]

In answer to the constant objections that Russia had been
too favorably treated in Persia, Grey found most effective
replies in delineating the rapid progress of the Russian advance

---

[f] *Parliamentary Debates*, 4th series, CLXXXIV, 469-480.

[g] *B. D.*, IV, no. 550, p. 616.

[h] *Parliamentary Debates*, 4th series, CLXXXIV, 481-482. On 7 March 1907
Grey had told Benckendorff: "The direct object of a settlement between Russia
and ourselves was to secure the Indian frontier; but there was also an indirect
object, viz: to be on good terms with Russia, . . ." (*B. D.*, IV, no. 256, p. 279.)
Grey believed the security of India was assured by the convention. "There were
no more nerves or apprehensions about that." Grey, I, 154, 160.

[i] *Parliamentary Debates*, 4th series, CLXXXIV, 503. This was privately
recognized in the foreign office. Hardinge wrote that if Russia "wished to
attack Afghanistan the Russian forces could easily invade the country in travers-
ing our zone long before we could do anything to prevent them, even if any
other steps were possible." *B. D.*, IV, Editors' Note, minutes, p. 458.

during the last twenty years, facts which Curzon had forgotten, who had used "sheer rhetoric" when he charged that
British diplomacy had thrown away the gains made in the
course of a century. Grey admitted that Russian trade in
Persia exceeded British, that it was increasingly competing
in the south, and was assisted by the government, with the
ever present shadow of military force in the background. He
passed off the omission of any reference to the Persian Gulf,
(something heartily desired during the negotiations), as advantageous because, if the Bagdad railway should finally be
built, then the western shore of the Gulf would be the more
important, about which Russia had nothing to say at all. He
pronounced his firm belief that "in this agreement we have
given up nothing that was not gone before. All that we have
sacrificed in Persia are some possibilities — exceedingly remote — of trading. In Tibet and Afghanistan we have sacrificed nothing at all." [j]

A long, but hardly inspired debate followed, in which many
members from the rank and file of the house, besides more
notable figures, chipped in their opinions. Mr. Balfour, as
leader of the opposition, was in good form, being skeptical of
an arrangement which he thought had conceded too much
unnecessarily. Many members, who had at some time in their
lives set foot upon Persian soil, emulated Curzon and mentioned their travels, as if to give forceful authority to their
words. One witty member, Mr. Ellis Griffith, effectively
stopped such ostentation by the remark:

To have visited the country seemed to him no great qualification for
making a relevant speech. . . . Therefore he would not state one way
or the other whether he had been there or not. . . . It was more important
to have read the convention than to have been to Persia.[k]

Others took especial delight in taunting, at a safe distance,
Curzon on some of his vulnerable observations. Sir H. Norman entered heavily into the defence, and roundly declared
that he was sure that Grey's stigmatization of Curzon's speech

[j] *Parliamentary Debates*, 4th series, CLXXXIV, 481-489, 496.
[k] *Ibid.*, p. 523.

as "mere rhetoric" was "a reproof with which every student of foreign affairs would surely concur."[1] Mr. Evelyn Cecil became statistical, and distressed, to discover that Russia got 272,800 square miles "of the best portion of Persia," while Great Britain obtained 141,100 square miles, "including much that was desert," which left all of 217,180 square miles in the neutral zone.[m] Mr. Rees was more philosophical: northern Persia was already "past praying for," while in recent years Russian peaceful penetration into the south had "considerably strengthened" its position.[n] In the commons, even as in the lords, objection was frequently raised against the use of British influence to secure equality of commercial treatment for Russia in Afghanistan. This appeared to be a provision not matched by any corresponding obligation on the part of Russia to secure the same privileges for British trade in those regions of central Asia under Russian domination. Grey clarified this question in his concluding speech shortly before the close of the debate:

We are engaged to use our influence with the Amir to secure that any facilities given to British traders are to be given to Russian traders. The reciprocal obligation would have been that Russia was to use her influence with the Amir to secure for us that facilities which are given to Russian traders shall be given to British traders. That would be putting them on an equal footing with us. But we look to ourselves with the Amir. It is our business to secure from the Amir any concessions which he gives to Russian trade; it is not Russia's business to secure them for us.[o]

The convention of 1907 was actually mentioned in the Russian imperial duma on the occasion of Izvolsky's first appearance before that body on 27 February / 11 March 1908. He gave a general outline of the purposes of his foreign policy, and referred to the convention as an illustration. He explained his great concern to do all that he could "for the maintenance of the general peace." He advised the duma with great unctuousness of his optimism that he could succeed

[1] *Ibid.*, p. 513.
[m] *Ibid.*, p. 527.
[n] *Ibid.*, p. 533.
[o] *Ibid.*, p. 557.

in his task. His supply of optimism was of a perfectly healthy variety because, as he said amidst applause and shouts of "bravo," it was rooted "in an unshakable belief in the strength, the intelligence and the patriotism of the Russian people." It was this confidence which sustained him, or any other Russian foreign minister, in the difficult problems confronting the nation, and made it possible to achieve results.[p] To aid the cause of peace an agreement had been reached with Japan in the summer of 1907. Likewise with Great Britain, the ally of Japan, an agreement had been signed which had for its subject "several special questions relating to central Asia." It constituted an "indubitable pledge for the maintenance of the general peace and the durability of our new relations with Japan."[q] This was the sum total of Izvolsky's remarks on the convention before the representatives of the Russian people. Professor Paul N. Milyukov, leader of the Constitutional Democratic party, welcomed Izvolsky upon his début, and expressed satisfaction that Russian policy would follow peaceful channels. He did, however, discern a shade of optimism that was none too well-founded. It was a source of contentment to know that conciliatory tendencies were paramount in relations with Japan, with no thought of pursuing a policy of revenge. It was equally pleasant to know that the rapprochement with Great Britain removed at last in an important degree the danger of a collision of interests in Tibet, Afghanistan and Persia.[r] No further remarks on the convention of 1907 figured in the debates of the duma.

Out of this welter of variable opinion, who really did win most profit from the convention? With surprizing unanimity most English, and western European writers have insisted

[p] *Stenografichesky otchet: Gosudarstvennaya duma*, third convocation, first session, (1908), pp. 118-119. The duma had no voice in Russian foreign affairs. In illustration of its powerlessness, on 4/17 April 1908, the secretary of the duma read a complaint which charged, *inter alia*, that the ministry of foreign affairs, and foreign policy, remained outside the control of the duma more than anything else; that foreign policy was never submitted in advance, but was carried on behind the scenes; and that it ignored the "interests of the broad, popular masses." *Ibid.*, pp. 1825-1826.
[q] *Ibid.*, p. 118.
[r] *Ibid.*, pp. 119-122.

that Russia gained most of the advantage. If this were true, it would require some neat explanation how it was that a nation, in an inferior international position because of the recent, humiliating military defeat by Japan, with a government still distracted by internal unrest and changes in its political structure, had come out on top of a long negotiation in which it had been the passive participant. It would hardly have been tactful for English writers openly to claim a diplomatic triumph; while what little comment was subsequently expressed by Russians had small circulation, besides being in a language seldom understood in the rest of the world. The general unfamiliarity with the subjects settled in the agreement contributed to the difficulty of properly appraising the results, so that later commentators have been content to follow the early lead, and to assume that Russia profitted more than Great Britain. It is, however, fairer to hold that, on the whole, the convention was nearly an equal bargain; but whatever distinct advantages were contained in it came to the credit of Great Britain, the stronger and the consciously active party in the negotiations.

The Tibetan arrangement was harshly judged by the sponsors of the Lhasa expedition, who bemoaned the surrender of its results, which could only permit China to strengthen its former, shadowy suzerainty.[8] Even here, the concessions obtained by Great Britain through the Lhasa agreement of 1904 and the Chinese treaty of 1906, were now formally recognized by Russia. This gave the British a definite economic and commercial advantage, for whatever it was worth. In political affairs both parties agreed to approach Tibet only through the intermediary of the Chinese suzerain power, but what few direct relations were permitted, were excepted in favor of Great Britain. The sole advantage gained by Russia was the permission of personal access to the Dalai Lama, and all the lesser lamas, for the empire's Buddhist subjects. This

[8] *C. H. B. F. P.*, III, 365. *Annual Register*, (1907), 387. Fraser, p. 132. The convention "practically undid all the results of Lord Curzon's mission." (*Round Table*, II, 415.) For a more moderate judgment, poorly expressed, see Perceval Landon, "The Anglo-Russian Agreement: Relative Loss and Gain," *Fortnightly Review*, LXXXVIII (1907), 727.

relationship, however, had been going on for so long that it could not have been prevented, but these pilgrimages were now regularized until they were much less likely to develop political complexions. Russia was saddled with so many disabilities that all its ambitions for conquest in Tibet, if any had actually been contemplated, were effectively circumscribed. Great Britain, on the other hand, had obtained "formal Russian consent to the maintenance of a preferential position . . . in Tibet over all other foreign countries in regard to frontier and commercial matters," along with a general position for imperialistic advances in the future better than any possessed in the past.[t]

If Great Britain had not obtained adequate recognition in the convention of 1907 for its privileged position in Afghanistan, no treaty would have been concluded at all. Nothing was gained that was wholly new. It was of prime importance that Russia was bound by assurances on three points, now given in writing in the form of a definite treaty engagement, hitherto only admitted verbally and not considered binding for all future time. These points included the declarations that Afghanistan was outside the sphere of Russian influence; that all political relations with the Amir would be conducted through Great Britain, which controlled his foreign affairs; and that no Russian agents would be sent into the country. Afghanistan thereby became acknowledged as a British protectorate in fact. No comparable concession in return was granted Russia. The most valuable recompense to Russia came in commercial relations, when Great Britain promised to argue with the Amir in behalf of equal opportunities and facilities for Russian trade in Afghanistan. This could hardly be avoided if Great Britain was to have sole influence with the Amir, and was an obligation willingly assumed in order to keep Russia from attempting to interfere in behalf of a growing trade. The provision that Russian commercial agents in Afghanistan might become necessary was mere window-

[t] *B. D.*, IV, no. 549, pp. 614-616. *C. H. B. F. P.*, III, 365. Witte, *Vospominaniya*, II, 410. "Peace in Asia," *Independent*, LXIII (New York, 1907), 827-828.

dressing, which could be made real only if Great Britain agreed; but Izvolsky had already conceded that this need not be granted, if ever the question were raised. The other possible advantage for Russia came in the permission of direct relations of a non-political character between Russian and Afghan authorities at the frontier. This had been admitted by Lansdowne in his negotiations in 1903. It was also a concession of something that had actually been going on for many years; nor was it worth much to Russia because, by other limitations in the convention, no subjects of major importance could be effectively, or legally, broached. Afghanistan remained a buffer state between territories of the Russian and British empires in Asia, in which Russia could have no diplomatic influence where Great Britain had all that there was, although promising not to use it in any way hostile to Russia.[u]

The Persian clauses of the convention of 1907 were the weightiest, and it is precisely here that later commentators have generously awarded Russia the lion's share. This has been so because the Russian zone was far larger and richer than the British and included the capital city. This is undeniable, but superficial. Russian penetration had thoroughly covered all of Persia contained in the limits of this zone, and had been rapidly expanding into the regions beyond. Russian political influence at Teheran was proverbial, with no other power able to compete successfully against it. The concession of the Russian sphere in northern Persia could not have been avoided, but had it not been delimited Russia might well have won more. It was in this sphere where other nations, more particularly Germany, had lately shown signs of activity, which Russia must face alone, and perhaps have to yield favors.[v]

[u] B. D., IV, no. 549, pp. 613-614. Annual Register, (1907), p. 377. Trubetzkoy, p. 103. Witte, Vospominaniya, II, 410. Dillon, Contemporary Review, XCII, 694.

[v] Annual Register, (1907), p. 376. Rouire, pp. 271-272. Wroblewski, Kriegsschuldfrage, V, 1228. Dillon, Contemporary Review, XCII, 697. Angus Hamilton, "The Anglo-Russian Agreement: the Question of Persia," Fortnightly Review, LXXXVIII (1907), 740. Witte declared that it should have been Russian policy gradually to make northern Persia into a province of the Russian empire. Witte, Vospominaniya, II, 407-408.

The British sphere in the south was not the equal in size of the Russian, nor was the British ascendancy within it as supreme. After a century's predominance "British trade and enterprize have so far failed to obtain any permanent results" beyond a few concessions, still guaranteed by the convention. Yet Russia had completely recognized the British position, "and no payment in money has been made for it."[w] The commercial value of the zone was not, in 1907, its main attraction, although it was the region of the known oilfields, the full richness of which only subsequently became apparent. The Russians knew that their trade stood small chance of profitable growth in the region served by the water-borne traffic in the Persian Gulf.[x]

The British sphere in southern Persia had been virtually settled before any other question was touched, and this settlement had been determined by military and strategic details. What was wanted, and won, was to secure that part of Persia from future Russian penetration upon which the military security of India was assumed to depend. The line for the British zone, with its inclusion of southeastern Persia adjacent to Afghanistan and Baluchistan, with the addition of the valuable district of Seistan, conferred the desired military security for India.[y] It had been determined by what the government of India and Lord Kitchener had said was adequate and defensible. Kitchener had expressed the wish that "we should limit our responsibilities to the semi-desert areas of Persian Baluchistan, Kain, Seistan and Kerman," while generally acting "on the supposition that Persia was valueless." Rarely has a wish been so perfectly fulfilled; Persia became a better, and a farther removed barrier for India than Afghanistan ever had been.[z] Whether the military security of India against Russian invasion had been materially improved is doubtful; what was

[w] B. D., IV, no. 549, p. 613.
[x] Wroblewski, Kriegsschuldfrage, V, 1228. Trubetzkoy, p. 101.
[y] Dillon asserts that the British government declined to accept all that the Russian government offered to concede in Persia. He admitted that "that sounds incredible, but it is true." There is no other evidence to suggest that it was true. Dillon, footnote 1, p. 351.
[z] Nicolson, pp. 241-242. C. H. B. F. P., III, 364. Sykes, II, 412. Korff, p. 47. Rouire, pp. 280-281. Popov, Krasny Arkhiv, XIX, 63.

important, however, was that Britishers thought so.[a] Precisely in this partition of Persia into spheres where Russia supposedly won the most, it was actually another British gain. Grey himself understood this:

The gain was equal — on paper. In practice we gave up nothing. We did not want to pursue a forward policy in Persia; nor could a British advance in Persia have been the same menace to Russia that a Russian advance in Persia might be to India. It is no wonder that the Russian foreign minister had some difficulty in getting military authorities in Russia to give up something of real potential value to them, while we gave up what was of little or no practical value to us.[b]

To be confirmed in the possession of something less than was actually controlled, while conceding rather more than the situation warranted, can not be claimed as a large reward for Russia.

In the region of the Persian Gulf, Russia emerged from the negotiations without a shred of advantage. The subsidized line of steamers from Odessa into those waters had never paid their way; Russian trade to southern Persia had only been profitable when it had come overland from the north. The real interest had been for a warm water port as a way of escape the year round from ice-bound coasts, or from exits blocked, because controlled, by other powers. Since 1903 it had been intimated that Russia would require a port on the Gulf, and both Lansdowne and Grey had shown a willingness to consider such a demand sympathetically. It was one of the wonders of the final negotiation that Russia never brought up the subject. A port on the Persian Gulf could have satisfied no Russian need, except vanity. Instead, Russia placidly abandoned the whole of that region into British hands, and allowed Bandar Abbas, which commanded the strait of Ormuz and

---

[a] Spring Rice knew that "no scheme of defence of which we are capable would be enough to secure [India's] safety. . . . England won't cease to exist if India is lost, and it is certainly not a question of life and death for us." (Gwynn, II, 91-92.) In his speech before the Committee of Imperial Defence on 26 May 1911 Grey declaimed: "With regard to the defence of the Indian frontier, that has been immensely simplified by the Anglo-Russian agreement. . . ." Also: "What a relief that has been for the last four or five years!" The Earl of Crewe amened: "That is quite true." B. D., VI, Appendix V, p. 789.
[b] Grey, I, 154-155.

the entrance to the Gulf itself on the eastern side, to fall within the British sphere.[c] In a separate note Russia admitted British special interests in the Gulf. After Grey had delivered his public declaration, the British hold over the Gulf was technically more secure than ever before. For the rest, the superiority of British naval force would suffice. Yet in return for this surrender, the convention showed no recompense for Russia.

The general view that Russia got the better bargain simply is not true. The French ambassador at London had realized this at once; the British foreign office could list the advantages gained; and Grey summed up everything in a single sentence:

I do not agree . . . that, even as an isolated bargain, the convention is a bad one, because anyone behind the scenes knows that what we have gained strategically is real, while the apparent sacrifices we have made commercially are not real.[d]

A like opinion was held by Baron Taube, then a legal adviser in the foreign office in St. Petersburg. After Izvolsky handed him the treaty text to read, he exclaimed:

I can indeed find in this document what you wish to give England, but not what it gives us! You renounce Afghanistan, you renounce the Persian Gulf in the southern zone — which could perhaps someday assure us the outlet to the open sea which we vainly seek in the direction of Constantinople — and you receive nothing in return except the north of Persia, where we already are actually masters.[e]

If Russia got compensation for what it surrendered, it must be sought outside the convention. Izvolsky, for one, thought he had this adequate return because, as he replied to Taube: "I receive the political support of Great Britain in Europe. . . . And who knows whether events will not make it necessary for us to bring the historical problem of the straits question again upon the carpet. . . ."[f] If this represented the offset which

[c] Trubetzkoy, pp. 104-105. Rouire, pp. 269-270. Grey wrote afterwards: "I did not expect her [Russia] to bother about the Persian Gulf, but I thought it probable that at the first opportunity she would talk to us about the Straits in the Near East." Grey, I, 155.

[d] B. D., IV, no. 537, p. 597; no. 549, pp. 612-616; no. 550, p. 616. Grey, I, 155.

[e] Taube, p. 128.

[f] Ibid., p. 128; footnote 2, p. 164.

Izvolsky was delighted to have won, he had not a particle of warrant for his satisfaction,[g] but a year passed before bitter disillusionment made him a wiser man. While the convention was being negotiated the British foreign office had admitted that it was prepared to abandon its longstanding attitude, and would favorably consider proposals for a change in the régime at the straits to the advantage of Russia at some suitable time; but no engagement to do so was ever given. Undoubtedly Izvolsky attached too great an importance to this merely platonic encouragement, which led him rashly headlong in 1908 into the terrible mistakes which curdled his whole career. In London, after the Austrian annexation of Bosnia and Herzegovina and the independence of Bulgaria had been proclaimed, to save himself from a complete fiasco Izvolsky did raise the question of a new solution for the Straits problem to be accomplished with British assistance.[h] His frantic pleas were "carefully considered" after which Grey gave Izvolsky a memorandum, on 14 October, wherein the British government acknowledged that "the opening of the Straits is fair and reasonable, and in principle they will not oppose it." This was, however, qualified by the observation that "the consent of Turkey would be a necessary preliminary to any proposal," but then "if the proposal made was that the Straits should be open on terms of perfect equality to all, . . . no exception could be taken."[i] Izvolsky accepted the British memorandum, "although it did not give all he had hoped for," and once again nothing definite had been promised him.[j] Miserably

[g] During a conversation in Paris in August 1929 Baron Taube described to the writer how supremely confident Izvolsky had been, in private, that he had obtained such a valuable concession from Great Britain. Sazonov was equally elated in 1915. Taube warned each minister at the time that there was still a long way to go before their optimism was justified.

[h] *B. D.*, V, no. 379, pp. 442-443. For the details of the Bosnia-Herzegovina crisis see Bernadotte E. Schmitt, *The Annexation of Bosnia, 1908-1909*, (Cambridge, 1937).

[i] *B. D.*, V, no. 377, p. 441. Grey, I, 158-159. Nicolson, p. 282. *Livre noir*, II, 458. In a private letter on the following day Grey assured Izvolsky: "At a favorable time I should be ready to support this view at Constantinople; for the moment, however, Turkey, who is beset by sudden troubles, has asked that no pressure should be applied to her to do now reluctantly what she might do willingly later on." *B. D.*, V, no. 387, p. 452.

[j] *Ibid.*, no. 394, p. 456. "Grey certainly played his cards with skill. He both evaded a Russian proposal which, in the form presented, was unsatisfactory,

wrong as Izvolsky had been, correct as the British refusal to help him was, British good faith on a revised attitude towards Russian aspirations at the Straits was also badly tainted.[k] Clearly the Straits question formed no recompense to Russia for the concessions made in the written agreement.

The convention of 1907 settled Asiatic rivalries exclusively, yet had its greatest importance in Europe — which it never mentioned. Great Britain had striven to bring Russia back into European affairs from a Far Eastern excursion as an additional source of strength against a growing, aggressive German ascendancy. The settlement of Anglo-Russian conflicts in Asia was first necessary before any benefits could accrue to the new friendship elsewhere in the world.[l] In its European aspect this convention removed the last traces of British isolation, and brought needed support against the possible hegemony of Germany in Europe. For Russia it has been assumed that it guaranteed security in the years required for recuperation and rehabilitation from war and revolution. An alliance with Great Britain could have afforded Russia military security in Europe only to a small extent. Help for the rebuilding came in the opening up of the London money market to assist France in supplying Russia with the funds needed in the process. At the time of its making, the Anglo-Russian convention was concluded in a spirit of defence of endangered national well-being: it was truly a reconciliation, not an entente.[m] German

and strengthened his own position with Turkey; ..." Schmitt, *The Annexation of Bosnia*, p. 54.

[k] For an array of remarks by British diplomats opposing Grey's views and policy on the Straits question through 1915 see Taube, footnote 1, p. 366. Nicolson later insinuated that Izvolsky did not know precisely what he wanted. (Nicolson, pp. 265, 273.) Izvolsky clearly wanted to gain the right for Russian warships to pass in and out of the Straits freely, without the same right being accorded to foreign ships. Baron Taube is much closer to the truth when he charges that Izvolsky had not thought out whether it was to the best interests of Russia to have this change occur. Taube, pp. 164-165. See also Izvolsky's own later exposition: Hélène Iswolsky, "Les papiers d'Iswolsky. Correspondance inédite (1906)," *La revue de France*, XIV (1934), 430-431.

[l] *G. P.*, XXV, part I, no. 8536, pp. 44-45; no. 8537, p. 46. *B. D.*, III, no. 299, p. 267; IV, no. 507, p. 565; no. 510, p. 571; no. 544, and minutes, p. 605. The British foreign office anticipated that "the removal of all causes of discord in Asia will no doubt contribute to more harmonious relations between the two powers in Europe." *Ibid.*, no. 549, p. 616.

[m] In a descriptive leaflet for the fourth volume of the *British Documents* its title, "The Anglo-Russian Rapprochement," is justly defended as being selected

policy and expansion had done much to bring the two old
enemies together, but the change from burning hatred to
ardent love was not at once accomplished. At its inception the
Anglo-Russian rapprochement had the strength of an infant;
it was concluded in fear of Germany, not as an instrument
of aggression deliberately forged against Germany. As late
as July 1908 Nicolson characterized the need of a friendly
Russia and France for the good of British international position, and how precariously balanced those relationships yet
remained:

If we wish, and I presume that we do wish, in the interest of peace, to
avert the possibility of any power assuming a position from which she
could dictate to others, a close understanding with France and Russia is,
I submit, an object for the attainment of which every effort should be
made. We have secured an undertaking with France. That with Russia
is in its very early infancy, and will require, for reasons which I need
not explain, careful nurture and treatment. Any serious check to this
infant growth may kill it before it has advanced in years, and its disappearance would doubtless eventually react on our relations with
France.[n]

Almost a year after its conclusion, therefore, the Anglo-Russian convention had cut no teeth. A gifted and conciliatory
German foreign policy could probably have kept it toothless
forever.

Several factors would have assisted Germany had the effort
been made. The relations between the tsar and the kaiser had
regained much of the cordiality that had been lost in the Björkö
disaster. Their affectionate correspondence continued; their
personal meetings had been resumed. In the years after 1905
the tsar was busy retaining as much of his power as he could.
If ever the kaiser's verbal solicitude for the principle of monarchical solidarity had been supported by tangible acts, they
could have reaped their handsome rewards from a threatened
throne. For his own part Izvolsky regarded the new conven-

"in order to mark a shade of difference between it and the somewhat closer
agreement known as the Anglo-French *Entente*." The most recent German work
ignores this distinction in its title and in its treatment. See Ludwig Poltz,
Die Anglo-Russische Entente 1903-1907, Winsen (Luhe), 1932.
    [n] B. D., IV, no. 516, p. 576.

tion "as a purely negative insurance and one which should not be allowed to affect his relations with the Central Powers." [o] In August 1907 it was still commonly believed that he leaned towards Germany, and that he desired to become Russian ambassador in Berlin, where he could be counted upon to promote "a closer understanding between his country and Germany." [p] After the convention was signed, the British foreign office expected him to do what favors he could to placate the strong western neighbor, to have "very intimate relations with Berlin, and a desire to follow advice and guidance from that capital." More than he could have known, Nicolson was right when he wrote that "it would be of great interest to follow the developments of Russian diplomacy in the near future." [q] Before and after the Reval meeting of King Edward and the tsar on 9 and 10 June 1908, Izvolsky continued to assure Germany that he wished for "the most cordial relations," while no new political combination or any widening of an old one was contemplated. [r] Izvolsky went out of his way to be agreeable to Germany in minor questions concerning the Baltic and North seas, the Åland islands, and German-Russian relations in Persia. Only after his merciless defeat in the Bosnian crisis did Izvolsky cease to cultivate German friendship. [s]

Most important of all, the Anglo-Russian convention itself was an unstable solution, by no means the firm foundation for future action that the German government believed from the beginning that it was. The British, however, knew that it was still a weak reed, not the result of a natural development. Nicolson was sure that if it had remained limited to an Asiatic settlement "it would unquestionably have led to a permanent estrangement between England and Russia." [t] This totally escaped German comprehension, so that the easiest way by which Great Britain and Russia could be kept apart was

[o] Nicolson, p. 260.
[p] B. D., VI, no. 23, p. 41, and King Edward's minute, p. 42.
[q] Ibid., IV, no. 544, pp. 604-605, and Grey's minute, p. 606; no. 548, p. 611.
[r] G. P., XXV, part II, no. 8799, p. 441; no. 8802, pp. 445-448; no. 8810, pp. 458-461. Siebert, no. 553, p. 483.
[s] For details see Taube, pp. 113-158. G. P., XXV, part I, pp. 101-175.
[t] Nicolson, pp. 261-262.

ignored. It was a serious flaw in the convention that it settled Anglo-Russian difficulties in Asia largely on the basis of existing positions, without regard for future possibilities. When Russia began to recover, its dissatisfaction with the limitations placed upon further expansion in central Asia increased, — another indication that Great Britain had gotten the best of the bargain. In a few years all was turmoil again, but one reason why the old rivalry was not resumed was because Great Britain tried to keep Russia in line in Europe. In Persia, particularly, the Russians took a high hand, while Great Britain remonstrated, acquiesced, and went along. Grey has admitted that "Persia tried my patience more than any other subject. I once told Benckendorff that if Russia made things too difficult the policy of friendly agreement with her might become impossible." [u] That threat never worried the Russians, who knew how badly their support was needed to prevent German domination in Europe.[v] Before 1914 both the Persian and Afghan settlements had become so unsatisfactory that new partitions, with additional profits for Russia, were being considered; while Tibet by 1912 had been effectively split into an Outer and Inner region, with Great Britain in control of the former. Under the influence of the world war, the secret treaty signed at St. Petersburg in 1915 promised full gratification for Russian traditional demands at Constantinople, in return for which another negotiation assigned most of the neutral zone of Persia to Great Britain, save for a few small bits to Russia. Early in 1917 a partition of Afghanistan, whereby Russia was to gain at least a commercial sphere in the north, was nearly ready for acceptance.[w] German policy

---

[u] Grey, I, 162. Onslow, *Slavonic Review*, VII, 551.

[v] Sazonov, the successor of Izvolsky as Russian foreign minister, wrote to Poklevsky-Kozell in Teheran on 25 September / 8 October 1910: "We may rest assured that the English, engaged in the pursuit of political aims of vital importance in Europe, may, in case of necessity, be prepared to sacrifice certain interests in Asia in order to keep a convention alive which is of such importance to them. This is a circumstance which we can, of course, exploit for ourselves, as, for instance, in Persian affairs." Siebert, no. 116, p. 99.

[w] For details see Siebert, pp. 49-141. Reisner, *Krasny Arkhiv*, X, 64-66. *Kriegsschuldfrage*, V, 880-881. Rouire, note by F. Rothstein, (Russian edition), pp. 167-168. None, of course, of these contemplated sharings of the spoils of war ever materialized.

before the war had been of such a nature that it had failed
to take any advantage of the tendencies of the Anglo-Russian
rapprochement to crumble; on the contrary, it did more to
keep Great Britain and Russia together, in spite of the disin-
tegration of the Asiatic provisions of the convention of 1907,
than any other factor.

German policy had been neither gifted nor conciliatory.
The sight of other powers replacing their rivalries by agreements made possible by mutual sacrifices furnished an example
which might have suggested German emulation, but did not.
German policy was what Great Britain and Russia had expected it would be. Izvolsky had warned Nicolson in November 1907 that both nations must be prepared to see Germany
assume "an active policy" which would cause trouble "not only
in Persia . . . but everywhere." [x] It was first experienced in
Persia where, despite disclaimers, Izvolsky thought the German government "to be too busy . . . and . . . anxious to gain
a footing totally out of proportion to their actual interests."
German presence was becoming an annoyance in Teheran,
where Izvolsky feared it could develop a strong position, able
to threaten Russian political predominance.[y] Early in the
negotiations he had realized that he must buy off German
hostility for fear of a repetition of the Morocco crisis, and
he had begun to discuss an arrangement by which Germany
should leave Russia alone in its northern Persian zone, in
return for the surrender of Russian objections to plans for
construction of the Bagdad railway. After the convention was
signed, it was still felt that "some solatium" would have to be
tendered Germany as a peace offering.[z] The Germans blamed
Izvolsky for proceeding more slowly thereafter, as if he no
longer desired an agreement. Izvolsky probably was not
eager, for by then it was generally accepted that "in any
understanding with Germany the latter power would gain
all the advantages," while its diplomacy and policy were no

[x] B. D., IV, no. 546, p. 608.
[y] Ibid., no. 523, p. 583; no. 544, p. 605; no. 548, p. 610.
[z] Ibid., no. 388, p. 430; no. 548, p. 610. Siebert, no. 549, p. 478. Izvolsky,
Correspondance diplomatique, I, 103-105. For details of these negotiations see
G. P., XXV, part I, pp. 103-173.

longer trusted, so that "friendship with Germany soon lapses into vassalage." [a] German tactics had been persistently asser- tive in Persia in a rapid attempt to acquire trade and political influence. Izvolsky protested against this intrusive activity, but seldom had any lasting success, which produced a stronger desire "to act in the closest possible coöperation" with Great Britain.[b] In the reaction after the Russian government had felt itself left in the lurch by the British in the Bosnian crisis, by the Potsdam treaty of 1911, the kaiser obtained profitable terms for German commercial competition in northern Persia, and the withdrawal of Russian opposition to the Bagdad rail- way. Germany undertook to respect the political position of Russia in its Persian sphere, and to renounce the acquisition of railroad concessions within it.[c] This agreement, however, instituted no change in German foreign policy, which continued to be grasping and dictatorial. The Potsdam treaty caused no permanent rift in Anglo-Russian relations; so the British foreign office lived through what was only a bad fainting spell.

German apologetics have steadily ignored the nature of German policy, and have concentrated upon the doctrine of the deliberate encirclement of the empire, in attempting to establish the innocence of Germany for the outbreak of war in 1914. With this vital omission, the idea of encirclement is admirably suited to its purpose. There is no escape from the fact that Great Britain, France, and Russia composed a triplice in opposition to German activity, or that geographically they formed a loose ring around the German border. The doctrine was initially enunciated before the Anglo-Russian convention was signed, in which the rôle of instigator and prime mover was assigned to King Edward VII. Although the British king possessed no such power, nor wielded so great an influence, he is accused of plotting to keep Russia and Germany apart, be-

    [a] B. D., IV, no. 544, p. 604; no. 548, p. 610. Conrad Bornhak, Die Kriegs- schuld! Deutschlands Weltpolitik 1890-1914, (Berlin, 1929), p. 414.
    [b] G. P., XXV, part I, pp. 147-173; part II, no. 8802, p. 447. B. D., IV, no. 464, p. 509.
    [c] Edward M. Earle, Turkey, the Great Powers, and the Bagdad Railway, (New York, 1923), pp. 239-242. Witte, Vospominaniya, II, 409; see English edition, p. 434. Dennis, p. 31.

sides building up the ring that hemmed Germany in, frustrating the proper aspirations and the natural expansion of that vigorous, young empire.[d] When the convention was signed, Miquel declared that it was due to the diplomatic skill of his chief, Ambassador von Schoen, that "it was not to be regarded as an advance of the British anti-German encirclement policy," although the kaiser noted his opposite opinion.[e] In this finespun theory the meeting between King Edward and Nicholas at Reval is a pivotal point, because it supposedly crowned the work of the convention and vitalized it against Germany. It was not so important a royal visit as many of those customarily exchanged between the kaiser and the tsar. The Reval meeting was outstanding primarily because it was the first time since he had ascended the throne that King Edward had visited Nicholas. From both sides the German government was fulsomely, and honestly, assured that nothing had been planned to the detriment of Germany.[f] Much of the mystery associated with the meeting has been induced by the insinuations and speculations of the encirclement propagandists. Emperor William's own conviction was definite: "Consequently financial reform of the empire! Many indirect taxes; strong fleet; strong army! Powder dry!"[g] It was precisely the attitude epitomized here that dominated German policy to 1914, and that insured the drawing together of a ring of nations increasingly more determined to keep the bull from breaking through. Yet the first great, open expression of this attitude, in the

[d] Stieve, p. 13. Bülow, *Denkwürdigkeiten*, II, 29-30. E. Reventlow, *Deutschlands auswärtige Politik, 1888-1914*, (Berlin, 11th edition, 1918), pp. 313-314. Hermann Kantorowicz, *Der Geist der englischen Politik und der Gespenst der Einkreisung Deutschlands*, (Berlin, 1929), is the fullest discussion of the subject. It is an exoneration of Great Britain from the charge of deliberate encirclement of Germany, and an incisive dissection of the propaganda manufactured to sustain this delusion in vigor.

[e] *G. P.*, XXV, part I, no. 8538, p. 48.

[f] *Ibid.*, part II, pp. 441-494. Bülow, *Denkwürdigkeiten*, II, 326-327. Witte, *Vospominaniya*, II, 432.

[g] *G. P.*, XXV, part II, no. 8807, kaiser's final note, p. 454. On 8 January 1909 he wrote the tsar that rumors of German uneasiness about the convention of 1907 and the visit at Reval were "all nonsense!" The cause for German concern was quite different. "It is the patent fact that for the last two years Russian policy has been gradually drawing away from us more and more, evolving always closer toward a combination of powers unfriendly to us." (*Kaiser's Letters*, pp. 223-224.) It is still characteristic of such German complaints that the question "why?" is never asked.

Bosnia-Herzegovina crisis, resulted in a resounding German victory, after which Bülow pronounced the fear of encirclement "a diplomatic illusion devoid of political actuality." [h] Indeed it seemed so, and much less was heard of the complaint of encirclement before 1914. Since then, frantic attempts have been made to infuse the idea with new life, so that it could perform its white-washing labors, but the verbal adornment of language remains its sole achievement.

Simply because the Anglo-French entente of 1904 and the Anglo-Russian convention of 1907 formed two new groupings which, with the older Franco-Russian alliance, laid the foundation for the triple entente, peaceful relations between these powers and Germany were not necessarily impossible. Izvolsky had been anxious to keep on the best possible terms with Germany despite the convention with Great Britain, if for no other reason than that he could not afford to do otherwise.[i] France originally desired negative advantages from the new arrangements, hoping they would be strong enough to prevent either an intolerable check upon its national ambition, or a bloody collision forced by Germany.[j] Grey stuck to his early opinion that there could be friendly Anglo-German relations, provided they did not involve forsaking France and Russia, although he had to put the proviso with increasing seriousness in 1911 in his speech before the Committee on Imperial Defence:

We must make it a cardinal condition in all our negotiations with Germany that if we come to any understanding with Germany of a public kind which puts us on good relations with Germany it must be an understanding which must not put us back into the old bad relations with France and Russia. . . . It must also be clear that, side by side with that, it will become equally apparent that there is no chance of a disturbance of the peace between Germany and France or Germany and Russia.[k]

Before war came, all three entente powers either had made, or were negotiating to make, colonial agreements with Germany

[h] Lee, II, 732.
[i] B. D., IV, no. 544, p. 604; no. 548, pp. 610-611. Nicolson, p. 260.
[j] Livre noir, I, 16.
[k] B. D., VI, Appendix V, p. 783.

which contained important concessions to the expansive ambitions of the vigorous, young empire belatedly seeking its place in the sun. Peace, and good relations, could have existed. The Anglo-Russian convention, born out of fear into weakness, for the better defence of long established interests against unwelcome, persistent German intrusion, survived its inherent unnaturalness under the blows of German attempts to destroy it. The more German policy took occasion to test its strength in successive international crises, the firmer it found the strange association to be holding together. The future of the convention, the determination of Great Britain and Russia to oppose further advances by Germany, was not plotted at Reval, but arose out of the humiliation of the Bosnian trial prepared for them.[1] The same menacing German attitude that made the Anglo-French entente truly cordial only after the first Morocco crisis, transformed the thin Anglo-Russian rapprochement into a second entente, never quite cordial, but effective enough for all that. Unchanging German policy which by its arrogance and assertiveness brought those ententes into being, also kept them alive. They grew stronger year by year, better able and perfectly willing to preserve their cherished national interests from molestation; but actively aggressive against Germany, or desirous of war, they never were.[m] Even in 1929 an intelligent, well-mannered German audience became restive when the sympathetic Dr. George P. Gooch, in a quiet, almost plaintively pleading voice, read to it his reasoned judgment:

Neither Lansdowne nor Grey ever thought to plan or to support the encirclement of Germany. An undertaking of this nature would have bordered upon insanity. It was, however, possible that we would become involved in the quarrels of our new friends, not one of which was con-

[1] "It was the violent attitude adopted by Austria and Germany in the Bosnian crisis which transformed what was a negative arrangement applicable only to Asia into a positive understanding applicable mainly to Europe." Nicolson, p. 261.
[m] G. P. Gooch, "Die Entstehung der Triple Entente," *Berliner Monatshefte*, VII (1929), 597-599. (This is the printed summary of two lectures read in German by Dr. Gooch in the English seminar building at the University of Berlin on 21 and 22 February 1929, which the writer attended.) See also *Livre noir*, I, 8, 12.

tent with the *status quo*. It was also possible that the policy of the Central Powers could drive us to a closer friendship with France or Russia than we wished for, and that the entente could be finally transformed into something which was not unlike an alliance.[n]

That transformation came to the Anglo-Russian convention most of all because it was more profitable for the two old enemies to bury their own hatreds to face unitedly the greater dangers that German policy and tactics presented. In less than a decade from the time the German foreign office had believed that Great Britain and Russia could never agree, the convention of 1907 was a reality. In less than another decade that feeble association had grown to sufficient intimacy so that the two contracting parties started out partners in the greatest of wars. At a time so early that his words were guesses, on 24 February 1908, right after parliament had accepted this Anglo-Russian convention, but with amazing accuracy, Sir Edward Grey divined the future career that it could have:

I am quite pleased, from the point of view of general policy, that events are bringing Russia and us together. But a combination of Britain, Russia, and France in the Concert must for the present be a weak one. France has her hands full in Morocco, and is naturally reluctant to run the risk of even diplomatic friction in connection with any other matter which might re-act [*sic*] unfavorably on her in Morocco. Russia is weak after the war, and her internal affairs are anything but secure.

Ten years hence, a combination of Britain, Russia, and France may be able to dominate Near Eastern policy; and within that time events will probably make it more and more clear that it is to the interest of Russia and us to work together; but we must go slowly.[o]

<hr>

[n] Gooch, *Berliner Monatshefte*, VII, 596. Among the notes made by the writer at that time, an indication supports memory that the audience broke out at this point with scattered muffled, negative gutterals, interspersed with a few louder cries. Others made the amusing German sibilant sound for the restoration of quiet that often is more disturbing than the disturbance. The chairman partly rose, and extended a restraining hand. The commotion ceased, to be followed by a slightly nervous, but good-natured mirth. The lecturer continued with merely the slightest break in his pace, but a sensitive point had been touched.

[o] *B. D.*, IV, no. 550, pp. 616-617.

BIBLIOGRAPHY

SOURCES

GEORGE PEABODY GOOCH and HAROLD TEMPERLEY, editors, *British Documents on the Origins of the War*. London, 1927-. Volumes I-VI.

JOHANNES LEPSIUS, ALBRECHT MENDELSSOHN BARTHOLDY and FRIEDRICH THIMME, editors, *Die Grosse Politik der europäischen Kabinette 1871-1914. Sammlung der diplomatischen Akten des Auswärtigen Amtes*. Berlin, 1922-1927. Volumes XIV-XXV.

FRANCE, MINISTÈRE DES AFFAIRES ÉTRANGÈRES, COMMISSION DE PUBLICATION DES DOCUMENTS RELATIFS AUX ORIGINES DE LA GUERRE DE 1914, *Documents diplomatiques français (1871-1914)*. 2e série *(1901-1911)*. Paris, 1930-. Volumes I-VIII.

British and Foreign State Papers. Volumes XC, XCI, XCVIII, C.

Obzor vnyeshney torgovli Rossiy po Yevropeyskoy i Aziatskoy granitsam, [Survey of the Foreign Trade of Russia over the European and Asiatic Frontiers], A Work of the Statistical Division of the Department of Customs House Duties. St. Petersburg, 1897-1914. Volumes for 1895-1912.

Annual Statement of the Trade of the United Kingdom with Foreign Countries and British Possessions, Compiled at the Customs House from Documents Collected by that Department. London, 1896-1913. Volumes for 1895-1912.

HANSARD, *Parliamentary Debates*, 4th series. Volumes CXX, CXXI, CLXXXIII, CLXXXIV.

Stenograficheskv otchet: Gosudarstvennaya Duma, [Stenographic Report: Imperial Duma]. 27 February / 11 March 1908; 4/17 April 1908. Third convocation, First session.

HÉLÈNE ISWOLSKI, editor, (with introduction and notes by GEORGES CHKLAVER), *Au service de la Russie. Alexandre Iswolsky. Correspondance diplomatique, 1906-1911*. Volume I. Paris, 1937.

HÉLÈNE ISWOLSKY, "Les papiers d'Iswolsky. Correspondance inédite (1906)," *La revue de France*, XIV (1934), 36-54, 265-281, 422-439.

BARON ALEXANDER MEYENDORFF, editor, *Correspondance diplomatique de M. de Staal (1884-1900)*. Two volumes. Paris, 1929.

ISAAC DON LEVINE, (edited by N. F. GRANT), *The Kaiser's Letters to the Tsar*. London, [1920].

BENNO DE SIEBERT, (edited by GEORGE ABEL SCHREINER), *Entente*

Diplomacy and the World. Matrix of the History of Europe, 1909-14. New York and London, 1921.

BENNO DE SIEBERT, editor, *Graf Benckendorffs diplomatischer Schriftwechsel. Neue stark vermehrte Auflage der diplomatischen Aktenstücke zur Geschichte der Ententepolitik der Vorkriegsjahre.* Volume I. Berlin and Leipzig, 1928.

RENÉ MARCHAND, editor, *Un livre noir. Diplomatie d'avant-guerre d'après les documents des archives russes, novembre 1910-juillet 1914.* Two volumes. Paris, 1922-1923.

"Der in Björkoe abgeschlossene russisch-deutsche Vertrag vom Jahre 1905," *Kriegsschuldfrage,* II (1924), 454-501. Translated from the original documents in *Krasny Arkhiv,* [Red Archive], V (1924), 5-49.

"Die zaristische Diplomatie über Russlands Aufgaben im Orient im Jahre 1900," *Kriegsschuldfrage,* VI (1928), 638-670. Translated from the original documents in *Krasny Arkhiv,* XVIII (1926), 3-29.

"Unprinted Documents. Russo-British Relations during the Eastern Crisis: VI. The Russo-Turkish War," *Slavonic Review,* V (1927), 424.

MEMOIRS AND BIOGRAPHIES

MAURICE BOMPARD, *Mon ambassade en Russie, 1903-1908.* Paris, 1937.

BERNHARD, FÜRST VON BÜLOW, (edited by FRANZ VON STOCKHAMMERN), *Denkwürdigkeiten.* Four volumes. Berlin, 1930.

LADY GWENDOLEN CECIL, *Life of Robert, Marquis of Salisbury.* Volume IV, *1887-1892.* London, 1932.

UN DIPLOMATE, *Paul Cambon, ambassadeur de France, 1843-1924.* Paris, 1937.

AGNES FRY, editor, *A Memoir of the Right Honourable Sir Edward Fry, G. C. B., 1827-1918.* Oxford, [1921].

VISCOUNT GREY OF FALLODON, *Twenty-Five Years, 1892-1916.* Two volumes. New York, 1925.

H. H. FISHER, editor, *Out of My Past: the Memoirs of Count Kokovtsov.* Stanford University, California, 1935.

J. L. GARVIN, *The Life of Joseph Chamberlain.* Volume III, *Empire and World Policy, 1895-1900.* London, 1934.

STEPHEN GWYNN, editor, *The Letters and Friendships of Sir Cecil Spring Rice. A Record.* Two volumes. Boston and New York, 1929.

BERNHARD HULDERMANN, *Albert Ballin.* Berlin, 1922.

ALEXANDER IZVOLSKY, (translated by CHARLES LOUIS SEEGER), *Recollections of a Foreign Minister. (Memoirs of Alexander Iswolsky.)* Garden City, N. Y., 1921.

SIR SIDNEY LEE, *King Edward VII. A Biography.* Two volumes. London and New York, 1925-1927.

JOHN, VISCOUNT MORLEY, *Recollections.* Two volumes. New York, 1917.

LORD NEWTON, *Lord Lansdowne. A Biography.* London, 1929.

HAROLD NICOLSON, *Sir Arthur Nicolson, Bart. First Lord Carnock. A Study in the Old Diplomacy.* London, 2nd edition, 1930.

MAURICE PALÉOLOGUE, *An Ambassador's Memoirs.* Three volumes. New York, 6th edition, n. d.

ANDREW M. POOLEY, editor, *The Secret Memoirs of Count Tadasu Hayashi.* London, 1915.

EARL OF RONALDSHAY, *The Life of Lord Curzon.* Three volumes. London and New York, 1928.

ALEXANDER A. SAVINSKY, *Recollections of a Russian Diplomat.* London, 1927.

J. A. SPENDER, *The Life of the Right Honourable Sir Henry Campbell-Bannerman, G. C. B.* Two volumes. London, 1923.

BARON MICHAEL A. TAUBE, *Der grossen Katastrophe entgegen. Die russische Politik der Vorkriegszeit und das Ende des Zarenreiches (1904-1917). Erinnerungen.* Berlin and Leipzig, 1929. Superior to the French edition *La politique russe d'avant-guerre et la fin de l'empire des tsars.* Paris, 1928.

COUNT SERGEY YULEVICH WITTE, *Vospominaniya,* [Memoirs]. Three volumes. Berlin, 1922-1923. The English edition by ABRAHAM YARMOLINSKY, *The Memoirs of Count Witte,* Garden City, N. Y., 1921, is inadequate.

REFERENCE BOOKS

Annual Register. London.

EUGENE N. ANDERSON, *The First Moroccan Crisis 1904-1906.* Chicago, 1930.

CONRAD BORNHAK, *Die Kriegsschuld! Deutschlands Weltpolitik 1890-1914.* Berlin, 1929.

ERICH BRANDENBURG, *Vom Bismarck zum Weltkriege.* Berlin, 2nd edition, 1925.

EDWARD G. BROWNE, *The Persian Revolution, 1905-1909.* Cambridge, 1910.

BERNHARD, FÜRST VON BÜLOW, *Deutsche Politik.* Berlin, 1916. Translated by M. A. LEWENZ, *Imperial Germany.* New York, 1917.

ARCHIBALD ROSS COLQUHOUN, *Russia against India; the Struggle for Asia.* New York, 1901.

GEORGE NATHANIEL CURZON, *Persia and the Persian Question.* Two volumes. London, 1892.

TARAKNATH DAS, *British Expansion in Tibet.* Calcutta, n. d.

TYLER DENNETT, *Roosevelt and the Russo-Japanese War*. New York, 1925.

ALFRED L. P. DENNIS, *The Anglo-Japanese Alliance*. Berkeley, California, 1923.

EMILE JOSEPH DILLON, *The Eclipse of Russia*. New York, 1918.

EDWARD MEAD EARLE, *Turkey, the Great Powers, and the Bagdad Railway*. New York, 1923.

SIDNEY BRADSHAW FAY, *The Origins of the World War*. Two volumes. New York, 1929.

EUGEN FISCHER, *Holsteins grosses Nein. Die deutsch-englisch Bündnisverhandlungen von 1898-1901*. Berlin, 1925.

LOVAT FRASER, *India under Curzon and After*. London, 3rd edition, 1911.

MORRISON BEALL GIFFEN, *Fashoda: the Incident and Its Diplomatic Setting*. Chicago, 1930.

GEORGE PEABODY GOOCH, *History of Modern Europe, 1878-1919*. New York, 1923.

IRENE GRÜNING, *Die russische öffentliche Meinung und ihre Stellung zu den Grossmächte 1878-1894*. Berlin, 1928.

WILLIAM HABBERTON, *Anglo-Russian Relations concerning Afghanistan, 1837-1907*. Urbana, Illinois, 1937.

OTTO HAMMANN, *Der neue Kurs*. Berlin, 1918.

OTTO HAMMANN, *Deutsche Weltpolitik 1890-1912*. Berlin, 1925.

H. E. H. JERNINGHAM, *Russia's Warnings*. London, 2nd edition, 1885.

HERMANN KANTOROWICZ, *Der Geist der englischen Politik und der Gespenst der Einkreisung Deutschlands*. Berlin, 1929.

BARON SERGEY A. KORFF, *Russia's Foreign Relations during the Last Half Century*. New York, 1922.

IVAN YAKOVLEVICH KOROSTOVETZ, *Pre-War Diplomacy. The Russo-Japanese Problem*. London, 1920.

ALEXIS KRAUSSE, *Russia in Asia*. New York, 1899.

WILLIAM L. LANGER, *The Diplomacy of Imperialism 1890-1902*. Two volumes. New York, 1935.

LUDWIG POLTZ, *Die Anglo-Russische Entente 1903-1907*. Winsen (Luhe), 1932.

ANDREW M. POOLEY, *Japan's Foreign Policies*. London, 1920.

J. -P. REINACH, *Le traité de Bjoerkoë (1905). Un essai d'alliance de l'Allemagne, la Russie et la France*. Paris, 1935.

ALPHONSE M. F. ROUIRE, *La rivalité anglo-russe au XIXᵉ siècle en Asie*. Paris, 1908. Edited, with annotations, by F. ROTHSTEIN, *Anglo-russkoye sopernichestvo v Azii v XIX vyekye*. Moscow, 1924.

BERNADOTTE E. SCHMITT, *The Annexation of Bosnia, 1908-1909*. Cambridge, 1937.

BIBLIOGRAPHY 355

BERNADOTTE E. SCHMITT, *England and Germany, 1740-1914.* Princeton, 1916.
W. MORGAN SHUSTER, *The Strangling of Persia.* New York, 1912.
F. A. SKRINE, *The Expansion of Russia 1801-1899.* Cambridge, 1905.
FRIEDRICH STIEVE, *Iswolski und der Weltkrieg.* Berlin, 1925. Translated by E. W. DICKES, *Isvolsky and the World War.* New York, 1926.
SIR PERCY SYKES, *A History of Persia.* Two volumes. London, 2nd edition, 1921.
ANDRÉ TARDIEU, *France and the Alliances.* New York, 1908.
PRINCE G. TRUBETZKOY, *Russland als Grossmacht.* Stuttgart and Berlin, 1917.
A. W. WARD and G. P. GOOCH, editors, *The Cambridge History of British Foreign Policy.* Volume III, *1866-1919.* Baltimore, 1923.
COLONEL FRANCIS YOUNGHUSBAND, *India and Tibet.* London, 1910.

ARTICLES IN PERIODICALS

Times (London).
New York Times.
"Britain and Russia in the Middle East," *Blackwood's Magazine,* CLXXXIII (1908), 152-162.
"Dnevnik A. A. Polovtseva," [Diary of A. A. Polovtsev], *Krasny Arkhiv,* IV (1923), 63-128.
"La révolution persane et l'accord anglo-russe," *Revue des deux mondes,* 5ᵉ période, XLIV (1908), 622-659.
"Peace in Asia," *Independent,* LXIII (1907), 827-828.
"The Anglo-Russian Agreement," *Living Age,* CCLV (1907), 323-334.
"The Anglo-Russian Agreement," *Spectator,* XCIX (1907), 420-421.
"The Durbar and After," *Round Table,* II (1912), 395-421.
"The Marquis of Salisbury," *Quarterly Review,* CXCVI (1902), 647-676.
MAURICE BOMPARD, "Le traité de Bjoerkoe," *Revue de Paris,* XXV (1918), 423-448.
CALCHAS, "The Anglo-Russian Agreement," *Fortnightly Review,* LXXXVIII (1907), 535-550.
CALCHAS, "Why Not a Treaty with Russia?" *Fortnightly Review,* LXXIV (1900), 677-686.
A. RUSTUM BEY DE BILINSKI, "Great Britain and Russia," *Nineteenth Century,* L (1901), 723-736.
HANS DELBRÜCK, "England und Russland," *Preussische Jahrbücher,* CXXX (1907), 197.
EMILE JOSEPH DILLON, "The Anglo-Russian Agreement and Germany," *Contemporary Review,* XCII (1907), 690-700.

C. Eliot, "The Buddhism of Tibet," *Quarterly Review*, CCIII (1905), 192-220.

J. W. Gambier, "A Plea for Peace — an Anglo-Russian Alliance," *Fortnightly Review*, LXXIV (1900), 998-1008.

George Peabody Gooch, "Die Entstehung der Triple Entente," *Berliner Monatshefte*, VII (1929), 594-599.

Luella J. Hall, "Germany, America, and China, 1907-8," *Journal of Modern History*, I (1929), 219-235.

Angus Hamilton, "The Anglo-Russian Agreement: the Question of Persia," *Fortnightly Review*, LXXXVIII (1907), 734-743.

K. K. Kawakami, "Prince Ito's Confidential Papers," *Foreign Affairs* (New York), XI (1933), 490-500.

William L. Langer, "Die Entstehung des russisch-japanischen Kriegs," *Europäische Gespräche*, IV (1926), 279-322.

A. Maurice Low, "Russia and England Agree," *Forum* (New York), XXXIX (1908), 339-342.

Count Max Montgelas, "Russland und Europa 1904-1914," *Berliner Monatshefte*, VIII (1930), 237-247.

C. Nabokov, "Why Russian Statesmanship Failed," *Contemporary Review*, CLXXXIII (1923), 178-187.

Earl of Onslow, "Lord Carnock," *Slavonic Review*, VII (1929), 540-553.

A. Popov, "Angliyskaya politika v Indii i russko-indiyskiye otnosheniya v 1897-1905 g.g.," [British Policy in India and Russian-Indian Relations in 1897-1905], *Krasny Arkhiv*, XIX (1926), 53-63.

A. Popov, "Anglo-russkoye soglasheniye o razdele Kitaya (1899 g.)," [The Anglo-Russian Agreement on the Partition of China in 1899], *Krasny Arkhiv*, XXV (1927), 111-134.

I. Reisner, "Anglo-russkaya konventsiya 1907 goda i razdel Afganistana," [The Anglo-Russian Convention of 1907 and the Partition of Afghanistan], *Krasny Arkhiv*, X (1925), 54-67.

Alexander A. Savinsky, "Guillaume II. et la Russie. Ses dépêches à Nicolas II, 1903-1905," *Revue des deux mondes*, 7ᵉ période, XII (1922), 765-802.

Theodor Schiemann, "Russisch-englische Beziehungen unter Kaiser Nikolaus I," *Zeitschrift für osteuropäische Geschichte*, III (1913), 490-492.

Arminius Vambéry, "The Anglo-Russian Convention," *Nineteenth Century*, LXII (1907), 895-904.

Arnold White, "Anglo-Russian Relations," *Fortnightly Review*, LXXXII (1904), 960-968.

Victor Augustin Wroblewski, "Murawjews Denkschrift aus dem Jahre 1900 und die englisch-russische Konvention von 1907," *Kriegsschuldfrage*, V (1927), 1221-1228.

INDEX

Abaza, A. M., Russian admiral: 44, 59.

Abdurrahman Khan, Amir of Afghanistan: 270, 271, 272, 273, 279, 305.

Aehrenthal, Alois, Baron, Austro-Hungarian ambassador in St. Petersburg: 119, 138.

Afghanistan: Russian declarations of disinterest in, 7, 41, 165, 270, 276; improvement of Russian position, 270-271, 272, 276, 278, 279, 282-283; extent of trade with Russia, 271, 272, 273, 279-281; British influence in, 7, 154, 156, 174, 246, 269-270, 273, 274-275, 282, 291, 292, 308; extent of trade with Great Britain, 281-282; boundary uncertainties and delimitations, 8-9, 10, 166, 270-271, 277-278; Russian memorandum of 6 February 1900, 41-42, 270-271, 273, 277, 282; Dane mission, 70-71, 85, 279, 289; a "buffer state," 71, 151, 246, 279, 285; appearance of German agents, 282; *convention of 1907 respecting:* British demands prepared, 132; authorization to open discussions, 133, 141, 154, 247, 283; slow progress during 1906, 141, 283; Russian councils of ministers, 165-166, 283, 301-302, 303-304; difficulties in solving problems, 167-168, 252, 285, 286, 293, 295-304; maintenance of British position and control, 287, 289, 292, 296, 305; Russian renunciation of political relations, 284, 287, 288, 291, 297, 298, 300, 305; Afghanistan as a "buffer," 287, 288-289, 297, 305; attempts to prevent future alterations in British and Russian positions, 284, 285, 292, 294, 295-296, 297-298, 299-300, 301, 304, 305; limitations upon presence of Russian agents, 285, 287, 290, 291, 292, 305; restriction of bounties to Russian trade, 284, 285, 288, 290; equality of facilities for Russian trade, 285, 287, 288, 290-291, 292, 301-302, 303-304, 305-306; Russian frontier officials and relations, 284, 287-288, 290, 292, 293, 294-295, 297, 305; Amir's consent to convention, 284, 290, 291, 292, 293-294, 295, 297, 306, (consent refused) 306-307, (convention considered valid) 307-308; the last "hitch," 301-304, 320; final text of Afghan convention, 305-306; estimate of the convention, 335-336; proposals for revision, 344.

Afridis, an Afghan tribe: 269, 282.

Åland islands: 343.

Alexander III, Emperor of Russia: 11, 12.

Alexeyev, E. I., Russian admiral: 44, 53, 59.

Algeciras conference: 97, 109, 110, 115, 124.

Alvensleben, F. J., Count von, German ambassador in St. Petersburg: 56, 69, 82.

Ampthill, Baron, acting viceroy of India: 70, 191.

Anglo-French entente (1904): 348, 349.

Anglo-Japanese alliance: 47-48, 185, (negotiations and terms, 1902) 48-50, (reception by Russia and France) 50-52, (renewal in 1905) 92-93.

Anglo-Russian agreement over China (28 April 1899): 18-20, 21, 22-25, 28-30, (terms) 31, (Chinese objections) 31-32, 243.

Anglo-Russian convention (31 August 1907): *course of the negotiations:* British liberal government sought agreement with Russia, 108, 125-126, 192; increased Anglo-Russian cooperation, 114-115, 123, 234; Izvolsky ready to negotiate, 121; press rumors about negotiations, 121-122, 155, 161, 286, 309; Nicolson opened discussions, 127-128; mode of procedure, 129; first British views on Tibet, 128-129, 192-193; Russian reply, 194-195, 201-202; Izvolsky's delays, 129-130, 133-134, 141, 146, 235-236, 241, 250, 285, 286, 293, 298; incidents offending Russia, 130-132; Izvolsky's need to know German attitude, 135, (Berlin visit, October 1906, and reassurances) 136-137, 139, 242; Persia to be divided into zones, 143, 236; British demands over Persia upset Izvolsky, 143-144, 237, 241; first British sketch of Persian settlement, 145, 146, 243-244; delay caused by Russian-Japanese negotiations, 146, 148; Nicolson's discouragement, 147-149, 203, 245; meetings of Russian council of ministers, 150-153, 165-166, 175, 245, 283, 301-302, 303-304; Russian draft proposals for Persian settlement, 154, 245-246, 284; British outlines respecting Afghanistan (all parts of convention broached by 23 February 1907), 155, 284-285; Russian inquiries for concessions at Straits, 156-160; increased pace of negotiations, 161; inquisitiveness of foreign powers, 162-164, 256-257; failure of British demands concerning Persian Gulf, 166-167, 259-264; difficulties over Afghan solution, 167-168, 172, 174, 252, 285, 286, 293, 295-304; French and Russian treaties with Japan, 168-169; Russian assurances over Swinemünde meeting, 171-172; the "style" for the final document, 172-174; the last "hitch," 175, 301-304, 320; wider benefits of agreement beyond Asia, 175, 238, 302-303; conclusion of the negotiations, 176, 304-305; see also Afghanistan, Persia, and Tibet; reception of the convention: publication, 306, 309-310; notification to certain powers, 309-311, 314; attitude of France, 313, Austria-Hungary, 313, Persia, 313-317, Germany, 317-319; press and public opinion in England, 319-320, 322-323, Russia, 319-321, Austria-Hungary, 323, Germany, 319, 323-325, France, 313; house of lords debates, 325-329; house of commons debate, 329-332; duma debate, 332-333; European significance of convention, 311, 318, 323, 328, 339, 341-342, 350; opinion that Great Britain gained most advantage, 334-341, 344; early weakness and instability, 341-342, 343; subsequent strengthening, 346, 349-350.

Austria-Hungary: 313, 323, 340.

Bagdad railway: 52, 101, 122, 123-124, 137, 152-153, 158, 171, 218, 259, 313, 331, 345.
Balfour, A. J., British prime minister: 2, 16, 76, 331.
Baltic fleet, Russian: 71-72, 78, 80, 86.
Baluchistan: 244, 246, 265, 337.
Bandar Abbas: 141, 236, 244, 266, 338.
Batum: 215.
Benckendorff, Alexander, Count, Russian ambassador in London: 55, 56, 67, 71, 74, 77, 94, 102, 110, 120, 147, 149, 163, 193, 199, 206, 220, 241, 245, 264, 275, 283, 295; interview with

Lansdowne (7 November 1903), 57, 142, 218, 277-278; relations with Grey, 108, 156-158, 159-160, 205, 233, 288, 289, 330, 344; suggested Russia desired concessions at Straits, 112, 150, 156, 159-160.
Berlin, Congress of: 6.
Bertie, Sir F., British ambassador in Paris: 135, 264.
Bezobrazov, A. M., Russian adventurer: 44, 53, 59.
Bhutan: 178.
Birjand: 141, 236, 244, 266.
Bismarck, Otto, Prince von: 17.
Björkö: 97, 103, 105, 170; meeting of tsar and kaiser, 87-89; terms of treaty, 89-90; Bülow's disapproval, 90-91; opposition of Lamsdorff and Witte, 98-99; Russian rejection of the treaty, 99-100.
Black Sea squadron, Russian: 66, 67.
Blackwood's Magazine: 323.
Bloody Sunday: 85.
Boer war: 30, 35, 270, 272, 274; Muravyev's proposals for mediation, 36-39, 42, 105, 125.
Bompard, Maurice, French ambassador in St. Petersburg: 99, 100-101, 139, 148, 149, 150, 161-162, 262-263, 304; concern over Björkö rumors, 95, 100; over Swinemünde meeting, 171.
Bosnian crisis: 340, 343, 346, 348, 349.
Boxer rebellion: 44.
Browne, E. G., British writer on Persia: 212, 316.
Bukhara: 271, 272, 328.
Bülow, Bernhard, Count, later Prince von, German chancellor: 2, 47, 56, 62, 80, 85, 86-87, 96, 118, 171, 172; disapproval of Björkö treaty, 90-91; attitude towards Anglo-Russian negotiations, 102-103, 122, 138, 162-163, 318-319; relations with Izvolsky, 118, 123, 170-171, 242; declared "encirclement" an illusion, 348.
Buriats: 182, 194, 198-199, 203.

Calcutta convention between Great Britain and China (17 March 1890): 179, 187.
Cambon, Paul, French ambassador in London: 56, 58, 313, 339.
Campbell-Bannerman, Sir H., British prime minister: 114, 131-132.
Cartwright, Fairfax, British minister at Munich and Stuttgart: 155, 324.
Caspian fisheries customs revenues: 247, 248.
Cassini, A. P., Count, Russian am-

bassador at Madrid, representative at Algeciras conference: 110, 124.
Caucasus region: 215.
Cecil, Evelyn, M. P.: 332.
Ceuta: 39.
Chahbar: 216, 218.
Chamberlain, Joseph, British statesman: 3, 34, 46-47, 185.
China: loans by foreign powers, 17-18, 22-23, 24-25; territorial concessions, Kiaochow, 18, Port Arthur, 18, 23-24, 25-26, Weihaiwei, 26-27, to France, 27, not to Italy, 27; objections to Anglo-Russian agreement of 1899, 31-32; Russian occupation of Manchuria, 43-44; displeasure over French and Russian treaties with Japan (1907), 169; relations with Tibet, 178, 179, 181, 188-189, 191, 193, 196, 197, 200, 206, 209.
Chinese-British adhesion convention over Tibet (27 April 1906): 188-189, 192, 203, 207, 208, 209.
Chinese-British regulations (5 December 1893): 179, 180.
Chumbi valley: 147, 178, 188, 189, 191, 203-204, 210, 328.
Churchill, Lord Randolph, British politician: 11.
Clemenceau, Georges, French premier: 313.
Crete: 114.
Crewe, Earl of, Lord President of the Council: 328-329, 338.
Cronberg: 320.
Curzon of Kedleston, Baron, British politician, viceroy of India: 181, 182, 184, 186, 213, 222, 223, 226-227, 231-232, 327, 331; attitude towards Russia, 12-13, 181, 183, 216, 227; forward policy in central Asia, 52, 181, 190, 220; Persian Gulf promenade, 52, 218; sponsored Younghusband's Tibetan expedition, 58, 183, 185; despatch of 1899 regarding Persia, 214, 226-227, 252; British reply of 1900, 214, 227-228; criticized Anglo-Russian convention, 322, 323, 325, (house of lords debates) 326, 329.

Dalai Lama, ruler of Tibet: 68, 181, 182, 186, 194, 198-201, 202, 203, 209, 334.
Dane, L. W., foreign secretary to the government of India: 70-71, 85, 279, 289.
Delbrück, Hans, German professor and publicist: 324-325.
Delcassé, Théophile, French minister

of foreign affairs: 50, 51, 56, 60, 61, 77; fostered improved relations between France and Great Britain and Russia, 34, 35, 55, 57, 64, 83-84.
Dillon, E. J., British correspondent: 110, 127, 325, 337.
Dogger Bank: 78, 85; the incident, 72; British reaction, 73-75; arbitration arranged, 75-76; final award, 83-84.
Dorzhev, a Buriat Buddhist in Tibet: 182-183, 200.
Drummond Wolff, Sir Henry, British diplomat: 11-12, 226.
Dufferin and Ava, Marquess of, viceroy of India: 7, 10.
Duma, Russian: 116, 131-132, 149, 169, 332-333.
Durand, Sir H. M., British minister in Teheran: 223, 227.

Edward VII, King of Great Britain and Ireland: 67, 74, 95, 96, 131, 133, 136, 161, 172, 237, 289, 320, 346; meetings with Izvolsky at Copenhagen, 64-66, Marienbad, 311-312; messages to Nicholas II, 104, 109; rejected Witte's proposal to visit Russia, 112, 113; Reval meeting with tsar, 343, 347.
Egypt: 68, 158.
Encirclement of Germany: 125, 346-348.
Eulenburg, Philipp, Prince zu, former German diplomat: 97, 99.

Farsistan customs revenues: 245, 247, 267.
Fitzmaurice, Lord E., later Baron, British parliamentary under-secretary of foreign affairs: 159, 326-327.
Fortnightly Review: 322.
France: desired improved Anglo-Russian relations, 34, 35, (regretted Anglo-Japanese alliance) 50-51, 55, 76, 93-94, 168, 313; unwilling to join in continental alliance with Russia and Germany, 81-82, 87, 98, 99-100; agreement with Japan, 149, 168-169; relations with Russia, 55, 77, 121, 139, 146; attitude towards Anglo-Russian convention, 313, 348.
Franco-Japanese treaty (10 June 1907): 168-169.
Franco-Russian dual alliance: 55, 77, 147, 348.

Gazik: 244, 266.
Germany: declined agreement with Great Britain, 2, 29, 47; attitude

towards improved relations between Russia, Great Britain and France, 56, 102-103, 169; attitude towards Anglo-Russian reconciliation, 122, 134, 137-138, 155, 162-163, 171, 242, 260, 318; supplied coal to Baltic fleet, 78; agreement with Russia (12 December 1904), 82; relations with Russia, 1, 44, 64, 77, (proposals for continental alliance) 78-83, 84-85, 87-91, (failure of Björkö treaty) 98-100, 152-153, 169, 242, 260, 343, 345, (Potsdam treaty, 11 August 1911) 346; claim of encirclement, 125, 346-348; failure to counteract Anglo-Russian convention, 342-348, 349.

Giers, N. K. de, Russian minister of foreign affairs: 8, 12.

Goluchowski, Agenor, Count, Austro-Hungarian minister for foreign affairs: 35, 39.

Gooch, G. P., British historian: 349-350.

Goschen, Sir Edward, British ambassador in Vienna: 311, 313.

Great Britain: rivalry with Russia, 3-8, 52, 63-64, 71, 177, 181-182, 217, 218, 228, 242, 270-272; attitude towards reconciliation with Russia, 11-17, Salisbury's proposal of 1898, 18-20, Chinese agreement of 28 April 1899, 31, 227, more inclusive agreement wanted, 33, 228, "second attempt" of 1901, 45-46, Lansdowne's 1903 negotiations, 54-55, 57-59, 279, failure but hope for future revival, 62, 64, 85, resumption after Russo-Japanese war, 101-102, 104; culmination of efforts by British conservative government, 104-106; objection to Russian occupation of Manchuria, 44-45; readiness to form alliance with Japan, 47, treaty of 1902, 48-50, renewal in 1905, 92-93; aware of Japanese hostility to Russia, 48, 54, 60-61; liberal government sought agreement with Russia, 108, 125-126, 132-133, 150, 192, 204, 233; relations with China, 26-27, 179, 188-189, 206; relations with France, 55, 84, 100-101, 125, 168; relations with Germany, 2-3, 15, 29, 46-47, 101-102, 115, 124, 125-126, 158, 234, 317, 348-349; continued to foster relations with Russia after the convention, 341, 342, 344, 348, 350.

Grey, Sir Edward, British secretary of state for foreign affairs: 73, 113, 116, 161, 165, 202, 213, 242, 244, 256, 286, 296, 297, 298, 310, 312, 328; became foreign minister, 107-108; favored reconciliation with Russia, 46, 107-108, 114, 115, 149, 192, 231; attitude towards Germany, 115, 163, 171-172, 234, 239, 348; directed negotiation of convention, 116, 124, 127, 132-133, 142-143, 145, 155, 167, 173, 196, 237, 240, 248, 255, 259, 263, 283, 300; Persian Gulf declaration, 167, 267-268, 339; relations with Benckendorff, 108, 156-158, 159-160, 205, 233, 288, 289, 330, 344; relations with Izvolsky, 123, 139, 235, 240, 242, 340; foresaw more than local significance of the convention, 302-303, 350; defended the convention, 315, 322, (in commons debate) 330-331, 332; opinion that Great Britain profitted most from convention, 338, 339.

Griffith, Ellis, M. P.: 331

Gubastov, Russian acting minister of foreign affairs: 309, 310.

Gyangtse: 67, 187.

Habibullah Khan, Amir of Afghanistan: 70, 276-277, 279, 306-307.

Hamadan: 227.

Hamilton, Lord G. F., British secretary of state for India: 183-184.

Hardinge, Sir Arthur, British minister in Teheran: 213, 231, 257.

Hardinge, Sir Charles, British ambassador in St. Petersburg, then permanent under-secretary of the British foreign office: 58, 64, 67, 69, 94, 95, 100, 108, 109, 111, 119, 124, 145, 150, 153, 189, 200, 241, 242, 243, 248, 259, 273, 274, 296, 297, 312, 320, 330; audiences with Nicholas II, 76, 102, 104, 109; recommended "a friendly advance" to Russia, 101; resumption of negotiations with Lamsdorff, 103-104, 106, 233.

Hartwig, N. H., Russian minister in Teheran: 235, 237-238, 240, 241, 273, 310, 314, 317.

Hassan Khan, Mirza (Mushir-ul-Mulk), Persian special envoy to London and St. Petersburg: 256-257, 265-266, 315.

Hatzfeldt, Paul, Count von, German ambassador in London: 1-2.

Hayashi, Tadasu, Baron, later Viscount, Japanese ambassador in London: 47-50, 92-93.

Herat: 280.

Holstein, Friedrich von, counsellor in

German foreign office: 78, 79, 88, 162; belief that British, French, and Russian rivalries could not be solved, 1, 3, 56, 350.

Ignatyev, Russian political agent in Bukhara: 272-273, 274.

India: 186, 215, 220, 223, 246, 281; British fear of Russian aggression against, 7, 14, 42, 64, 93, 101, 142, 153, 215, 220, 242, 250, 261, 269, 282, 330, 337; relations with Persia, 216, 219, 228.

India, government of: 271, 272, 276, 277, 279; excessive demands annoyed home government, 69-70, 142-143, 183-184, 186, 189, 236, 272-273; informed that British policy contemplated agreement with Russia, 108, 133, 184, 205, 236; consulted during Anglo-Russian negotiations, 196, 197, 203, 208, 263, 288, 307; ignored during final stages, 172, 255, 288.

Inter-Parliamentary Union, London meeting: 131-132.

Isfahan: 227, 245, 266.

Ito, H., Marquis, later Prince, Japanese statesman: 49, 50.

Izvolsky, A. P., Russian minister of foreign affairs: 92, 99, 131, 136, 138, 142, 148, 149, 163, 172, 192, 234, 244, 250, 266, 268, 307-308, 309, 336; meetings with Edward VII at Copenhagen, 64-66, Marienbad, 311-312; appointed foreign minister, 117; character, 117-119, 130, 320; policy, 120-121, 235; pinnacle of his career, 176; attitude towards Germany, 121, 122-123, 135, (Berlin visit, October 1906) 136-137, (in council of ministers) 152-153, 162, 169, 170-171, 311, 317, 324, 343, (negotiations over Persia) 345-346, 348; favored agreement with Japan, 120, 146, 148-149, 169, 333; in Russian council of ministers, 150-153, 165, 175, 245, 301-302, 303-304; relations with Bülow, 122-123, 170-171, 242; relations with Grey, 123, 176, 235, 240, 340; relations with Nicolson, 127, 139-140, 141, 143, 146, 158-159, 166-167, 168, 173, 176, 193, 194-195, 197, 202-204, 206-209, 236, 237, 241-242, 244, 245-247, 249, 251-252, 253, 254-256, 258, 259-260, 262-264, 284-287, 291, 293-296, 297-304, 319, 324; slowness in conduct of Anglo-Russian negotiations, 129-130, 133-134, 146, 199, 207, 235-236, 241, 250, 285, 286, 293, 298;

ensured good press reception of convention, 321; remarks on convention in duma, 332-333; anticipated German unpleasantness after convention, 324, 345; opinion of the convention, 339-340, 343.

Japan: relations with Great Britain, 26-27, 310; proposed understanding, 47; alliance of 1902, 48-50; renewal in 1905, 92-93; relations with Russia, 20, 45, 48, 54, 121, 136; negotiations before Russo-Japanese war, 59-61; course of the war, 62-63, 84-85, 86-87; peace of Portsmouth, 91-92; negotiations for supplementary agreement with Russia, 146, 148-149; treaty of 30 July 1907, 168-169, 170; treaty with France (10 June 1907), 168-169.

Kakh: 245, 251, 252, 266.

Karez: 251.

Kashan: 227.

Kasr-i-Shirin: 245, 266.

Kerman: 227, 244, 266, 337.

Kermanshah: 227.

Khanikin: 227.

Khedivial decree: 68.

Kiaochow: 18, 20.

Kinsky, Prince, former Austro-Hungarian diplomat: 155.

Kitchener of Khartum, Viscount, British commander in chief of army in India: 151, 282, 325, 337.

Kochubey, Prince V., a Russian Anglophobe: 321.

Kokovtzov, V. N., Count, Russian finance minister: 152, 165, 236, 237, 293.

Komura, M., Baron, Japanese minister of foreign affairs: 53.

Korea: 42-43; Japanese designs against, 49-50, 59, 62, 93.

Kronstadt: 130-131.

Kuhsan: 245, 247.

Lamington, Lord: 327.

Lamsdorff, V. N., Count, Russian minister of foreign affairs: 22, 23, 43, 55, 56, 73, 80, 107, 109-110, 114, 138, 233, 234, 274-275, 277, 278; inability to control Far Eastern policy, 44, 53, 59; feared war with Japan, 45, 60-61, 278; sought French and British mediation, 61-62; regretted Anglo-Japanese alliance, 50-51; his counter-declaration, 51-52; resented 1905 renewal, 94; protested against Lhasa convention, 69, 189; disclaimed designs on Tibet, 184, 191, 198-199; opposed to alliance with Germany, 79, 82, 84, 88, (Björkö treaty) 98-100; willing to discuss an understanding with Great Britain, 57, 103-104, 116, 142, 275; resignation, 116-117.

Lansdowne, Marquess of, British secretary of state for foreign affairs: 67, 69, 70, 71, 74, 75, 87, 142, 179, 228, 277, 278, 295, 325, 336, 338; "second attempt" for Chinese agreement with Russia, 46-47; negotiated alliance with Japan (1902), 47-50, renewal (1905), 92-93; failed to moderate Japan's attitude towards Russia, 61; Persian Gulf warning (1903), 53, 167, 218, 261, 263; opposed further penetration of Tibet, 184, 186, 189-190; sought a general agreement with Russia, 54-55, 56, 57-58; failure on outbreak of Russo-Japanese war, 59; hope for future revival, 62, 233; resumption of negotiations, 101, 104, 185, 218, 220-221, 231, 275-276; culmination of his efforts, 105-106; comments on Anglo-Russian convention, 328.

Lascelles, Sir F., British ambassador in Berlin: 137, 324.

Lee, Sir Sidney, British writer: 36-37, 39.

Lhasa convention between Great Britain and Tibet (7 September 1904): terms, 68-69, 187-188; Russian protests, 68-69, 189-190; British embarrassment, 69-70, 189-190; convention modified, 70, 190-191; reaffirmed in Anglo-Russian convention, 203, 204, 207, 208, 209, 334.

MacDonald, Sir Claude, British minister at Tokyo: 54.

Macedonia: 114.

Manchester Guardian: 322.

Manchuria: Russian occupation, 44; refusal to withdraw, 45; renewed conditions for evacuation, 46, 52, 53; Japanese demands on Russia, 59-60, 62.

Mejlis, Persian parliament: 233, 239, 240.

Mensdorff, Albert, Count von, Austro-Hungarian ambassador in London: 103, 119.

Meshed: 220.

Meshed-Nasratabad telegraph line: 240-242, 246, 264-265.

Metternich, Paul, Count von Wolff-, German ambassador in London: 76, 102, 107, 108, 124, 155, 161.

Milyukov, P. N., Russian politician: 333.

Miquel, Hans von, first secretary of German embassy in St. Petersburg: reports on Anglo-Russian convention, 317-318, 347.

Mohammed Ali, Shah of Persia: 233, 268.

Mohammed Ali Khan, Mirza, Persian minister of foreign affairs: 257.

Mohmands, an Afghan tribe: 269, 282.

Mongolia: 182, 198; Anglo-Russian discussions over a frontier formula, 200.

Monson, Sir Edmund, British ambassador in Paris: 34.

Morier, Sir Robert, British ambassador in St. Petersburg: 214.

Morley, John, later Viscount, British secretary of state for India: 108, 133, 306, 312, 328.

Moroccan question: 86, 88, 96, 97, 109, 112, 135, 349.

Motono, Itschiro, Baron, Japanese ambassador in Paris: 60.

Muravyev, Michael, Count, Russian minister of foreign affairs: 18, 25, 43, 272, 274; attitude towards Great Britain, 2, 17, (favored Chinese agreement, 1898) 21, 30, (Boer war mediation project) 34-39, (memorandum of 1900 on possible profits for Russia) 39-43, 216.

Muravyev, N. V., Russian ambassador in Rome: 120, 321.

Muzaffur-ud-Din, Shah of Persia: 214, 228, 229, 233, 239.

Nelidov, A. I., Russian ambassador in Paris: 77, 78, 98, 99-100, 120.

Nepal: 178.

Nicholas II, Emperor of Russia: 16, 17, 36, 44, 75, 80, 91, 102, 113, 131, 161, 166, 183, 198, 279, 300, 312; relations with William II, 20, 77-78, 81-82, (Björkö meeting) 87-89, 99, 100, 129, (Swinemünde meeting) 170-171, 342; attitude towards Great Britain, 21, 24, 77, 79, 88, 89, 109; Reval meeting with Edward VII, 343, 347; attitude towards negotiation of Anglo-Russian convention, 128, 129, 149, 155, 194, 301, 302, 312.

Nicholas Nicholayevich, Russian Grand Duke: 99.

Nicolson, Sir Arthur, British ambassador in St. Petersburg: 7, 109, 132, 148, 155, 192, 248, 250, 268, 280, 307, 309, 315; British representative at Algeciras conference, 109, 110, 124; attitude towards Russia, 125-126, 147, 283; audience with Nicholas II, 128; advice to Grey during negotiations with Russia, 140, 144, 145, 154, 162, 195, 237, 243, 247, 253, 260, 261, 262, 263, 284, 300, 304, (trip to London, July-August 1907) 168, 296; relations with Izvolsky, 127, 137-138, 139-140, 141, 143, 146, 158-159, 166-167, 168, 175, 176, 193, 194-195, 197, 199, 202-204, 206-209, 236, 241-242, 244, 245-247, 249, 251-252, 254-256, 258, 259-260, 262-264, 284-287, 291, 293-296, 297-304, 319, 324; praised for his work, 311, 312; saw necessity of fostering good relations with Russia after the convention, 342, 343.

Norman, Sir H., M. P.: 331-332.

Northwest Frontier Province of India: 269, 282.

Novoye Vremya: 275, 309, 321, 329.

O'Conor, Sir Nicholas, British ambassador in St. Petersburg, later in Constantinople: 18, 19, 23, 24, 28, 163.

October manifesto, Russian: 116.

Osten-Sacken, N., Count von der, Russian ambassador in Berlin: 36, 38, 78, 99, 100, 117, 118.

Palitzin, General, chief of the Russian general staff: 242, 283, 286.

Pamirs: 10, 282.

Parker, Alwyn, third secretary of British embassy in St. Petersburg: 271.

Penjdeh incident: 9-10.

Percy, H. A. G., Earl, M. P.: 325, 329-330.

Persia: Russian ascendancy, 7, 33, 140, 212-216, 221, 226, 229, 250-251, 316, (renewal of interference after 1907) 344; extent of trade with Russia, 212, 213, 215, 218, 221-223, 225; British penetration in southern part, 52-53, 141, 214, 215-219, 230-231, 250; extent of trade with Great Britain, 216-217, 218, 219, 223-225; German commercial penetration, 134, 135, 136-137, 141, 144, 152-153, 217, 231, 234-235, 239, 268, 311, 336, 345-346; foreign loans and negotiations, 114, 133-134, 141, 143-144, 147-148, 219; 229, 234-235, 237, 239-240; revolutionary disorders, 232-233, 234,

235, 256, 257-258, 268, 314, 316; suggestions for British and Russian spheres, 141, 142-143, 145, 152, 226-227, 231, 232, 236; Anglo-Russian coöperation in Persia, 237, 240, 257, 268; British policy sacrificed Persia for agreement with Russia, 114, 164, 231, 235, 238, 257, 258, 312, 314, 316; attitude towards Anglo-Russian convention, 164, 256, 313-317; *arrangement of 1907 respecting*: Izvolsky unprepared to discuss, 141, 236; agreement to define spheres, 141, 236; difficulty of Persian solution, 142, 244; avoidance of use of term "sphere of influence," 144, 244, 250; first British sketch of Persian settlement, 145-146, 243-244; meeting of Russian council of ministers, 150-152, 245; Russian draft proposals, 245-246; British attempt to make Teheran an enclave, 248-249, 251; British demand for Seistan, 244, 245, 246, 250, 252; disposition of telegraph lines, 254, 264-265, 267; special interests of British in Persian Gulf, 166-167, 259-264, (Grey's declaration) 267-268, 339; respect for integrity and independence of Persia promised, 243, 265; the Russian zone, 237, 244, 245, 247, 250-252, 265-266; the British zone, 237, 244, 245, 250, 252, 266; the neutral zone, 237, 251, 252, 266; maintenance of Russian and British existing concessions, 244, 246, 252-254, 266; equality of opportunity as accorded foreign commerce, 243, 244, 248-249, 251, 253, 265, 266; pledged Persian revenues and customs, 219, 229, 239, 245-246, 247, 248, 254-256, 266-267; final text of the arrangement, 265-268; estimate of the arrangement, 336-339; proposed alterations after 1907, 344.

Persian Gulf: 52, 58, 112, 142, 215-216, 217, 219, 223, 245, 250, 267, 313, 331, 337, 338-339; Salisbury's warning (1899), 217; Lansdowne's warning (1903), 53, 167, 218, 261, 263; British demands during negotiation of convention, 166-167, 259-264; Grey's declaration (1907), 263-264, 267-268, 339.

Poklevsky-Kozell, S. A., first secretary of Russian embassy in London: 96, 158, 280, 285, 286, 344.

Polivanov, General A. A., assistant in the Russian ministry of war: 286.

Port Arthur: 18, 23-24, 25-26, 61-62, 84, 120.
Portsmouth, England: 161.
Portsmouth, peace of (5 September 1905): 91-92, 146, 170, 176.
Punch (London): 266.
Punjab: 269.

Quetta: 330.

Radolin, H., Prince von, German ambassador in Paris: 2, 95.
Reay, Lord: 327-328.
Rees, J. D., M. P.: 332.
Reval: 343, 347, 349.
Revelstoke, Baron, British financier: 101.
Ronaldshay, Earl of, M. P.: 330.
Roosevelt, Theodore, President of the United States: 84, 86-87.
Rouvier, Maurice, French premier: 88, 96, 100.
Rozhdestvensky, Z. P., Russian admiral: 72, 73, 75, 83, 86.
Russia: advance in central Asia, 6, 42, 165, 178, 182, 270, 282-283; feared British aggression, 7-8, 71, 151, 174, 242, 246, 283, 286, 299; tone of press towards Great Britain, 17, 57, 94, 127, 242-243, 275, 283, 320-321; dissatisfied with Anglo-Russian agreement of 1899, 32, 105; consideration of possible profits during Boer war, 39-43; displeasure at Anglo-Japanese alliance (1902), 50-52, and at renewal (1905), 94; apathy during Russo-Japanese war, 62, 63, 64, 85, 86; need for foreign loans, 99, 111-112, 341; supported France at Algeciras, 109, 115; effects of 1905 revolution on foreign policy, 85, 86, 108, 110, 112, 115, 120, 127, 136, 231-233, 260; willingness to discuss agreement with Great Britain, 108, 110, 115, 127, 134, 235; relations with China, 18, 31-32, 42-43, 169, 206; relations with Japan, 20, 48, 50, 59-62, 87, 121, 136, 146, 168-169; relations with Germany, 44, 64, 77-83, 87-91, 98-100, 121, 134-137, 144, 152-153, 166, 169, 170-171, 231-232, 260, 343, 345, 346.
Russian communist criticism of convention: 321-322.
Russian military and court groups, opposition to Anglo-Russian agreement: 134, 147, 149, 167, 175, 201, 236, 242, 245, 286, 293, 311, 320.
Russian Volunteer fleet: 66.

Russo-German commercial treaty of 1904: 78.
Russo-Japanese treaty (30 July 1907): 168, 170, 176, 302, 333.
Russo-Japanese war: negotiations before outbreak, 59-61; Lamsdorff's efforts for peace, 60-61; Japanese attack on Port Arthur, 61; course of the war, 62-63, 84-85, 86-87; peace, 87, 91-92, 176.
Ryech: 310.

Salisbury, Marquess of, British prime minister and secretary of state for foreign affairs: 15, 33, 125, 271; uncertainty of isolation as a policy, 45-46, 105; Persian Gulf warning (1899), 217; attitude towards Russia, 12, 16, 272, (proposals of 1898) 18-20, 105.
Sanderson, Sir T. H., later Lord, British under-secretary of state for foreign affairs: 327.
Sazonov, S. D., Russian chargé d'affaires in London: 69, 340, 344.
Schoen, Wilhelm von, German ambassador in St. Petersburg, later foreign secretary: 118, 122, 123, 135, 137, 170, 347.
Scott, Sir Charles, British ambassador in St. Petersburg: 28, 31, 64, 271, 273-274, 275.
Seistan, province of Persia: 134, 140, 145, 151, 152, 154, 215, 217, 220-221, 227, 240, 242, 245, 246, 248, 250, 277, 330, 337.
Shimonoseki, peace of (1895): 182.
Shuster, Morgan, American adviser to Persian government: 212.
Sikkim: 178, 179, 180, 187, 190.
Slovo: 321.
Spectator: 323.
Spring Rice, Sir Cecil, British chargé d'affaires in St. Petersburg, later minister in Teheran: 109, 112, 113, 116, 148, 185, 213, 217, 229, 240, 257, 278, 310, 314-315, 338; opposed to Anglo-Russian convention, 164-165, 238, 258, 312, 316-317.
Staal, E. E., Baron de, Russian ambassador in London: 8, 11-12, 46, 108.
Stolypin, P. A., Russian chairman of the council of ministers: 301.
Straits, question of the: Muravyev's project (1900), 39-40; Russian desire for concessions in agreement with Great Britain, 112-113, 150, 156-160, 165; Izvolsky's attitude towards, 120, 140, 159, 160, 339-341;

British attitude towards concessions to Russia, 140-141, 146, 156-160, 339, 340-341; Turkish interest in, 163, 340; secret treaty of St. Petersburg (1915), 344.

Stumm, Wilhelm von, German chargé d'affaires in London: 127.

Swinemünde: 170-171, 172.

Tashi Lama, Tibetan religious potentate: 198, 201.

Taube, M. A., Baron, legal adviser in Russian foreign office: 72, 83, 84, 99, 339, 340, 341.

Teheran: 248-249, 251.

Teheran-Meshed telegraph line: 246, 264-265.

Tibet: position of and relations with Russia, 59, 178, 180, 182-183, 191; position of and relations with Great Britain, 178-181, 185, 187-189, 191, 192, (British control over Outer Tibet) 344; insignificance of Tibetan trade, 180, 187, 328; Younghusband expedition, 58-59, 67-70, 185-191; *arrangement of 1907 respecting*: British preliminary proposals, 127, 128-129, 192-193; Izvolsky's reply, 193-195; geographical proximity of British possessions to Tibet, 190, 193, 194, 201, 206, 208, 209; the limits of Tibet, 195-197; problem of the Dalai Lama, 197-201, 209-210; definition of British special position, 193, 194, 202, 203, 204, 206-209; conditions for evacuation of of Chumbi valley, 203-204, 210; limitations upon political and religious missions, 193, 194, 201, 202-203, 209-210; limitations upon Russian scientific parties, 194-195, 197, 205-206, 210; renunciation of concessions and assignments of Tibetan revenues, 193, 210; final text of the arrangement, 209-211; estimate of the arrangement, 334-335.

Times (London): 69, 329.

Tschirschky, Heinrich von, German foreign secretary: 89, 155, 320.

Tsushima: 86.

Turbat-i-Haidari: 264.

Turkey: 101, 114, 163, 260, 340.

United States: 169, 310.

Vambéry, Arminius, Hungarian writer on central Asia: 323.

Wallace, Sir D. M., British publicist: 126, 127.

Waziris, an Afghan tribe: 269, 282.

Weihaiwei: 26-27.

Wilhelmshöhe: 172.

William II, German Emperor, King of Prussia: 34, 37, 38, 40, 63, 65, 72, 108, 118, 134, 137, 172, 318, 320; Rominten meeting with Witte, 96-98; relations with Nicholas II, 20, 77-78, 80, 81-82, 86, (Björkö meeting) 87-89, 95, 99, 129, 130, (Swinemünde meeting) 170-171, 342, 347; characterization of German policy (1908), 347.

Witte, S. Yu., Count, Russian statesman: 18, 20, 26, 28-29, 33, 59, 77-78, 81, 117, 127, 149; negotiated Portsmouth treaty, 91-92; on return journey visited Paris, 95-96, Berlin, 96, with kaiser at Rominten, 96-98; aided in denunciation of Björkö treaty, 99-100; proposal for Edward VII to come to Russia to conclude an agreement, 110-112, 113, 116; criticized Anglo-Russian convention, 321, 336.

Wolf, Lucien, newspaper correspondent: 329.

Yatung: 179.

Yezd: 227, 245, 266, 329.

Younghusband, Colonel Francis, British agent: 85, 185, 186, 188, 191; expedition into Tibet, 58, 59, 67-70, 185-191.

Zinovyev, I. A., Russian ambassador in Constantinople: 165.

Zulfikar: 166, 247, 249.